Business Cultures in Europe

Business Cultures in Europe

Collin Randlesome
and
William Brierley
Kevin Bruton
Colin Gordon
Peter King

Heinemann Professional Publishing

Heinemann Professional Publishing Ltd
Halley Court, Jordan Hill, Oxford OX2 8EJ

OXFORD LONDON MELBOURNE AUCKLAND SINGAPORE
IBADAN NAIROBI GABORONE KINGSTON

First published 1990

British Library Cataloguing in Publication Data
Randlesome, Collin
    Business cultures in Europe.
    1. Business enterprise. Europe
    I. Title
    338.6094

ISBN 0 434 91728 1

Typeset by Hope Services (Abingdon) Ltd
Printed and bound in Great Britain
by Billings, Worcester

Contents

Contributors

Collin Randlesome is a Senior Lecturer in European Management at the Cranfield School of Management. He has been based at Cranfield since 1972 after holding academic posts at the universities of Erlangen and Basle. He contributed a major section on West Germany to the influential report, *The Making of Managers*, which was later expanded into a book in 1988. In addition, he has worked on an audio visual German language teaching project aimed at business executives and is the author of articles on aspects of management in Germany.

William Brierley is a Senior Lecturer in Italian and European studies at Portsmouth Polytechnic. He has also lectured on the European Community since 1978, and his special fields of interest include left-wing political culture, the peace movement and trade unions in Italy. He is currently developing computer applications to the teaching of business Italian.

Kevin Bruton was appointed to a new Chair in Spanish at the University of Stirling in 1990, after previously holding lecturing posts at the University of Salford, Heriot Watt University and Middlesex Polytechnic. He has considerable marketing management experience in industry, and has published widely on modern Spanish poetry, on politics and business culture in Spain and on language teaching methodology. He has held many appointments and sits on the National Council of the International Higher Education Standing Conference.

Colin Gordon is a Senior Lecturer at the CRanfield School of Management where he has been Director of the MA in European Management Programme for the last five years. He contributed the section on France to *The Making of Managers* and is currently writing the sections on doing business in France for a major audio visual French language teaching project (BBC) aimed at business executives. He spends much of his time develping courses in French business schools and companies and lecturing widely on both French and general European business issues.

Peter King (Professor Emeritus) recently retired as Professor of Modern Dutch Studies at Hull University, where he was based from 1976–88 following twenty-four years as a lecturer in Dutch at Cambridge University. He is the author or co-author of a number of publications concerning Dutch language and culture, including *Dawn Poetry in the Low Countries* (1971), *Multatuli* (1972) and *The Netherlands* (1988).

Preface

If a country's 'culture' can be defined as 'the state of intellectual development among a people', then 'business culture' might be held to be 'the state of commercial development in a country'. But the concept of business culture surely embraces this and much more: it also takes in the attitudes, values and norms which underpin commercial activities and help to shape the behaviour of companies in a given country. These companies, in their turn, develop their own individual 'corporate cultures' which, put simply, manifest 'the way we do things round here'.

Implicit in the definition of a country's business culture provided above is the fact that there is no such thing as a single, homogeneous European business culture. Europe contains as many business cultures as it does countries. Although the similarities between the business cultures in Europe are legion, so are the differences.

What are the determinants of the business cultures of European countries? What are the factors affecting the similarities and differences between countries? It is self-evident that the relationship between business and government, the shape and orientation of the economy, the financial institutions, and the trade unions all exert a profound effect on the business cultures of all European countries. But is, for example, the attitude of business to green issues equally significant for the business cultures everywhere in Europe? Is, say, the practice of élitism sufficiently widespread to count as a determinant of business cultures in all European countries? The answer in both cases is 'no'. In contrast, the response of the business community to the completion of the European Community's (EC's) single market by the end of 1992 is highly significant, since it demonstrates the way in which business hopes to come to terms with the free movement of goods, services, capital and labour and all that such implies for the future.

In other words, the business culture in a particular country grows partly out of what could be called the 'current business environment' of that country. Yet business culture is a much broader concept because alongside the impulses which are derived from the present business environment figure the historical experiences of the business community, such as the periods of hyperinflation in Germany in 1923 and again after the Second World War. Of equal significance for the business culture are the future hopes and aspirations, not only of business but also of society at large in a given country. How long, for example, should people work in any one week in the 1990s and beyond?

This book attempts to portray the six major business cultures in the EC as indicated by the size of gross domestic product (GDP) at current prices and exchange rates. Thus the countries included are, in order of GDP size and appearance in the book, West Germany, France, Italy, the United Kingdom, Spain and the Netherlands.

The individual chapters in the book concentrate on those determinants of business culture which are held to be significant for the country under review. Some determinants are common to all six countries; others are relevant for several of the six; others still for one or two only.

Each chapter focuses on the business culture of the country concerned in the late 1970s and throughout the 1980s up to the turn of the decade.

The authors have not hesitated to use foreign words and concepts in their chapters because such expressions contribute much to the depiction of the nuances in the business culture of any country. They have, however, been at pains to provide a translation of the term in the foreign language on its first appearance in the chapter.

A conscious attempt has been made to use the common statistical base provided by the Organization for Economic Cooperation and Development (OECD) wherever possible, and especially with regard to leading economic indicators such as growth rates and inflation, so that the reader can make meaningful comparisons between countries. Where common statistics are not available, reputable national sources have been used. Sources have been indicated for all tables.

At the end of each chapter a list of publications has been provided in the form of references and suggestions for further reading. Here only publications or standard works have been included which might stimulate the reader to delve deeper into special aspects of the business culture in the country under review. These lists should not be regarded as exhaustive.

The authors trust that an understanding of the six major business cultures in the EC will lead to a better appreciation of the structures and strategies of industries, markets, and consumer preferences in the countries covered. While it may not constitute the most important element of a practitioner's knowledge, much that is in the book could make that vital difference between actually gaining a contract or merely coming close.

Collin Randlesome
Cranfield School of Management

Acknowledgements

The authors would like to thank the *Financial Times* for permission to quote and refer to the newspaper. They are also grateful to Professor Charles Handy and Pitman Publishing for allowing them to use some of the material from *Making Managers*. Equally, they extend their thanks to the editors of the Price Waterhouse *Guides to Doing Business* in various countries for permission to quote from these works, especially in the sections of the chapters on business and the law. Similarly, the authors are grateful to *The Economist* for permission to quote and to the Economist Intelligence Unit for allowing them to refer to their annual *Country Profiles* and quarterly *Country Reports*, which are available for all the countries covered in the book. Finally, they thank Times Newspapers Limited for permission to use material which originally appeared in *The Sunday Times* and *The Times*.

Permission to reproduce tables and statistics has kindly been given by *Acquisitions Monthly*, the Bundesanstalt für Arbeit, BSL Business Strategies, the Central Bureau voor de Statistiek, NV SDU, Datastream International *Employment Gazette*, and the OECD, whose publications are available through HMSO.

1 The business culture in West Germany

Collin Randlesome

Introduction

Most West German companies are not in business to make profits which will subsequently be distributed to shareholders as dividends; they are in business to generate surpluses in order to stay in business.

This aspect of business culture goes a long way towards explaining much that puzzles the foreign observer. Above all, it reflects the conservatism and strength which are such outstanding features of the business culture in this country.

Conservatism and strength manifest themselves in:

- Over 40 per cent of GDP still being derived from manufacturing industry, including construction, in the third-largest economy of the OECD countries.
- DM 59 billion per annum, or approximately 2.8 per cent of GDP, being spent on research and development (R & D).
- Private commercial bank commitment to non-financial companies in the form of company rescues and the long-term holding of large amounts of equity.
- The training of some 1,800,000 apprentices per annum, a significant percentage of whom may not be given a permanent position by the company training them.

By any measure of performance, West German business has flourished in the past from adopting a conservative approach but has done so in what could be called conditions of continuous change. However, with shorter product life cycles, more volatile markets, and increased competition on a global scale – conditions of discontinuous change – concern is being expressed in certain quarters as to whether West German companies are best equipped to face the challenges of the 1990s and beyond.

Criticism has focused particularly on aspects of the business culture such as:

- A tendency of West German companies to be product-led rather than market-oriented.

- Manufacturing companies 'making nails with heads on', i.e. over-engineering their products.
- Risk-aversion by large companies, with their preference for straight-forward bank funding rather than complex share capital from financial markets.
- Publicity-shyness, especially by small and medium-sized firms which still cling to a legal status that allows them to remain extremely discreet even when they expand.
- Lack of an entrepreneurial spirit throughout West German business, one of the manifestations of which is that the country figures at the bottom of the European management buyout league, with only thirty-six recorded by the end of 1988.

The Federal government in Bonn and the governments in the individual Federal states, including West Berlin, have displayed an awareness of some of these criticisms of the country's business culture, and a number of policies have been introduced to change this culture. Equally, business in West Germany is subject to the changes imposed by the country's non-governmental institutions. Finally, the completion of the EC's single market and the accompanying welter of legislation are already influencing the ways in which West German business people think and act.

Business and government

The business culture in West Germany is affected inter alia by the attitudes and policies adopted by the Federal government in Bonn and by the governments of the individual Federal states. In general, the relationship between business and government in post-war Germany has been a function of the political tenets of the party in power and the economic circumstances prevailing at the time. However, the fact that not a single year goes by without important elections being held at Federal or state level contributes to compromises and even inconsistencies between policy making and implementation.

Federal government

The official policy which all post-war Federal governments claim to have espoused, to a greater or lesser degree, is that of the **soziale Marktwirtschaft** (social market economy). The policy was established by Ludwig Erhard, initially in his capacity as Allies-appointed Director of Economic Affairs and later as Minister of Economic Affairs in the first four Federal cabinets after the Second World War. Indeed, Konrad Adenauer, the first post-war Federal Chancellor, provided a significant definition of social market economy, which he called: 'A renunciation of planning and the direction of production, labour or sales, but within a comprehensive economic policy which also embraces social measures to ensure the welfare of the population as a whole, including provision for the needy.'

The Federal Chancellor for most of the 1980s has been Helmut Kohl. He came to power in Bonn in October 1982, in a centre-right coalition led by the Christian Democrats (CDU) and their Bavarian sister-party, the Christian Socialists (CSU), with the Free Democrats (FDP) as junior partners. His accession to government marked the end of a thirteen-year period dominated by the Social Democrats (SPD) in centre-left coalitions with the FDP.

The new government under Helmut Kohl promised the people of West Germany the **wirtschaftliche Wende** (economic turnaround). What the country and business needed, according to Chancellor Kohl, was less state intervention of the type which had become commonplace in the last thirteen years, and more market instead. From the very outset of his Chancellorship, he pledged to put the market back into the social market economy! In addition, he stated that West German business had to rediscover the spirit of entrepreneurship which had made possible the **Wirtschaftswunder** (economic miracle) of the 1950s and 1960s.

Indeed, the state of the economy facing Helmut Kohl's government at the end of 1982 was anything but miraculous, with the leading indicators showing:

- Economic growth at minus 1 per cent in real terms (only the third minus figure since 1950).
- Inflation above 5 per cent (a very high figure for West Germany).
- Current account in equilibrium.
- Unemployment at an annual average of 1.85 million per month, or 8.8 per cent of the working population.

In addition, investment was down by 5 per cent on the previous year and private consumption down by 2 per cent, both in real terms.

As the *1983–1984 OECD Economic Survey on West Germany* observed: '. . . the new Federal government faced the difficult task of pursuing its medium-term goal of reducing government expenditure and intervention in order to achieve a durable improvement of growth and investment conditions, while at the same time supporting activity in the short run, the economy being in deep recession. In shaping the budget for 1983, it relied mainly on the retrenchment measures already proposed by its predecessor. But it raised the cuts in social expenditure to a total of DM 12 billion and placed limits on wage and salary increases of civil servants. In addition,

. . . it proposed improved incentives for private investment which, however, were to be financed by tax increases.'

An upturn in business activity began early in 1983 after a recession which had lasted for approximately three years. This recovery was initially due to domestic demand but became increasingly sustained by external requirements for goods made in West Germany. The rise in consumer prices fell to about 3 per cent per annum; the current account stayed in surplus; and even unemployment began to fall slightly.

Despite the favourable economic developments in the course of 1983, the CDU party lost the state elections in Hesse that year. CDU delegates were criticized in their constituencies for the Federal government's rigorous cost-cutting policies; business people began to demand more positive policies to take advantage of the economic upswing; *Bild*, the daily newspaper with the largest circulation in West Germany, demanded in its largest banner headlines: 'Do something, please!'

Cuts in Federal government subsidies, a clampdown on excessive bureaucracy, and a total overhaul of the tax system had already been promised, but in the autumn of 1983 Helmut Kohl launched a further initiative. In what has become known as his Marshall Plan speech, he proclaimed to a meeting of the CDU/CSU parliamentary party the privatization of state holdings in certain companies. The sale of Federal assets was intended to reduce the Federal borrowing requirement and at the same time to release the venture capital with which to subsidize future-oriented technologies. Shortly afterwards, Federal Finance Minister Gerhard Stoltenberg announced the partial privatization of the Federal holding in Veba, a large conglomerate company. Veba was to be only the first of several companies to be privatized. Others mentioned at the time were Volkswagen, Lufthansa, the national carrier, and Schenker, the Bundesbahn's very profitable subsidiary specializing in freight forwarding.

The tone had been set and the policies put in place, but what were the results by the time of the next Federal elections in January 1987?

Despite four years of cyclical upswing, real growth had averaged only just over 2 per cent, and unemployment had risen to in excess of two million or almost 9 per cent of the workforce. However, the current account had shown healthy surpluses, and inflation had remained low, at an average of less than 2 per cent over the period.

But what of other Federal government policies? As *The Economist* commented on 7 May, 1988: 'In most other OECD countries, governments – conservative and socialist alike – have been deregulating, privatizing and cutting taxes.' They had been keeping the state out of business's decisions and letting markets, not governments, steer economic developments. In this respect, '. . . Helmut Kohl's government has done very little. Many of its subsidies to farmers, steelworkers, shipbuilders, coalminers and the rest have increased.' The cash subsidies alone were estimated to cost the taxpayer the equivalent of 2.2 per cent of GDP in 1988.

The price for all this profligacy in the public sector was that rates of business and personal taxation were still extremely high. Despite the promised 'tax reform of the century', pandering to special interest groups had delayed the much-needed legislation. In 1987, West German companies were confronted with a total tax of 70 per cent on retained earnings, double the rate in the United Kingdom. An unmarried West German with an annual income equivalent to $20,000 sacrificed 40 per cent of it in tax and social security contributions – between 10 and 20 per cent more than in any other of the five largest OECD economies. The marginal rate for a West German on a half-average income was 36 per cent, as against only 7 per cent in the United States of America. Reform of the taxation system was due for completion in 1990, but even then the top rate of income tax was likely to be 53 per cent and corporation tax 50 per cent – still some of the highest rates in any of the OECD countries.

Similarly, the Federal government's privatization programme was very much a stop-start affair up to 1987. A start was made in 1984 with the sale of part of the government's holding in Veba for DM 800 million, thus reducing ownership from 43.85 to 30 per cent. In March 1985, a concrete action plan for further sales of Federal-held assets in thirteen companies was tabled by the government. But a year later it was decided to proceed with the sale of part of its holdings in only five cases. In June 1986, VIAG, a chemicals, energy and aluminium company, offered 40 per cent of its shares to private shareholders and was partly privatized, thus raising DM 766 million. But the jewels remained in the crown: the Federal government retained 75 per cent of the Lufthansa shares and 20 per cent of Volkswagen.

As far as business interests are concerned, one of the most positive aspects of Helmut Kohl's Chancellorship up to 1987 was probably the redistribution of wealth which was achieved. Taking into consideration taxes, social security contributions and the rate of inflation, the incomes of employees actually fell in the period from 1982 to 1985 by DM 17.5 billion as calculated on the basis of 1985 figures. Over the same period, the incomes of entrepreneurs rose by DM 100 billion. In 1986, profits also rose much more steeply than wages. However, business failed to invest proportionately. Of the net increase in revenue enjoyed by business from 1982 to 1986, which amounted to DM 154 billion, only DM 22 billion was reinvested in capital goods and plant in West Germany. Outward investment flourished instead, especially towards the United States, and worries about **Industriestandort Deutschland** (West Germany as a location for industry) began to appear – themes to which future reference will be made (see pages 12–14).

Helmut Kohl enjoyed at least two strokes of good fortune in the period from October 1982 to the end of 1986. Only three months after he first came to power, the recession ended and business activity began to pick up again. Then, in 1985 oil prices decreased dramatically – an extremely favourable development for an economy such as West Germany's which is so dependent on imported sources of energy. He perhaps enjoyed a third piece of good fortune over the same period in that the SPD, the main opposition party, was in massive disarray.

Nevertheless, in the Federal elections held in January 1987, Helmut Kohl's CDU and its sister-party, the CSU, recorded their worst performance since 1949, winning only 44.3 per cent of second votes cast. Fortunately for Chancellor Kohl, the SPD, with 37 per cent of second votes also performed badly – their worst results since 1961. His coalition partners, the FDP, did well, with 9 per cent, while **Die Grünen** (The Greens) enjoyed their best Federal election results ever, polling 8.3 per cent.

Despite the disappointing results, the centre-right coalition returned to power with the slogan **Weiter so** (more of the same). The policies remain as before, but so do many of the problems:

- An economy which, despite an impressive surge towards the end of the decade, has tended to grow only slowly compared with other OECD countries.
- Unemployment at around two million.
- A state pensions scheme which is becoming increasingly hard to fund from current contributions on account of the rising dependency ratio.
- Disturbing demographic trends of an ageing and declining population, the influx of immigrants from Eastern Europe and East Germany notwithstanding.

In April 1989, Helmut Kohl reshuffled his cabinet, changing three of the top four posts, together with five others. Gerhard Stoltenberg was removed as Finance Minister and replaced with Theo Waigel of the CSU; Hans Klein, also of the more conservative CSU, became minister spokesman responsible for the projection of the Chancellor's personal image. But neither changes in personalities, let alone refurbished images, will solve West Germany's basic problems.

By the time of the Federal election, due in December 1990, the country will look back on too many years of economic underperformance. The problem is that growth of about 2 per cent is too poor a performance to solve the underlying economic difficulties but too good to engender the kind of crisis atmosphere of 1982, when major changes suddenly became possible. The OECD has suggested that West Germany could be trapped in a vicious circle where slow growth today leads to slow growth

Table 1.1　*West German growth rates (1979–89)*

Year	(%)
1979	4.0
1980	1.5
1981	0.0
1982	− 1.0
1983	1.9
1984	3.3
1985	1.9
1986	2.3
1987	1.8
1988	3.4
1989	3.3

Source: OECD

tomorrow. Average growth of just over 2 per cent depresses business confidence and discourages investment. If the low rate of investment persists, fiscal injections even of the modest variety envisaged in the tax reform could result in major inflationary impulses.

At the turn of the decade, it was generally agreed that West Germany's shortcomings lie not so much in the macroeconomic policies which have been pursued by Helmut Kohl's three governments but in their failure to overcome constraints on the supply side of the economy, such as the overregulation of services and labour-market rigidities – themes to which subsequent reference will be made (see pages 15 and 30).

State governments

West Germany's decentralized political organization means that individual Federal state governments have more power than in comparable nations. Although the official Federal government policy is non-intervention in business, one administrative level lower, in the ten Federal states and West Berlin, the country's politicians are enthusiastic interventionists on behalf of business interests in their particular domains.

The result is that often state policies clash openly with Federal policies. The sale of the Federal government's 20 per cent stake in Volkswagen was announced in 1983, and confirmed in 1985, but did not finally take place until March 1988. One of the reasons for the delay was because the company is the largest employer in Lower Saxony, and the CDU state government was reluctant to entrust the carmaker's fortunes to the whims of private shareholders. Indeed, the state of Lower Saxony still retains approximately 20 per cent of the Volkswagen shares.

Equally, Franz Josef Strauss, the late Minister President of Bavaria, objected most vigorously to the planned sale of the Federal government stake in Lufthansa. He suspected that a lower Federal stakeholding might result in the company changing its aircraft-purchasing policy from Airbus to Boeing. This would have affected the fortunes of Deutsche Airbus GmbH, which is located just outside Munich.

Perhaps, however, the leading proponent of state interventionism is the CDU Minister President of Baden-Württemberg, Lothar Späth. He has persuaded many high-technology businesses to settle in his state by establishing centres of excellence for research into biotechnology and information technology, such as those at the universities of Stuttgart and Ulm. In addition, he inevitably came to prominence in the Daimler-Benz series of takeovers (AEG, Dornier, MTU and MBB) since the car company has its headquarters in his state capital of Stuttgart. Minister President Späth was especially active during the Dornier takeover because the aerospace company is based at Friedrichshafen in the south of Baden-Württemberg. In the course of protracted negotiations, Lothar Späth smoothed the way for the Dornier family and Daimler-Benz to finalize the transaction, which duly occurred when the car company bought 66 per cent of the shares. The State of Baden-Württemberg itself secured 4 per cent.

In sharp contrast, SPD's Oskar Lafontaine is beset by low-technology problems in the Saarland, where the Arbed-Saarstahl steel company has made huge losses. The remedy which he has recommended for Arbed's problems is nationalization. This has been turned down by the centre-right coalition in Bonn, not only on grounds of cost but also because the proposal runs contrary to its own fledgling privatization policy. Increased Federal subsidies have thus proved necessary to keep Arbed in business – much to the chagrin of the Federal government, with its avowed preference for a hands-off approach in the relationship between government and business.

Business and the economy

The business culture in West Germany is dominated by considerations of manufacturing and the wealth-creation associated with it. Indeed, the **Wohlstandsgesellschaft** (affluent society) in present-day West Germany depends to a very large extent on the high-quality output of its manufacturing industries. High-value-added products, high technology and technical innovation are fundamental to maintaining this affluence, and almost all large companies devote a considerable amount of their resources to R & D, in many cases as much as 10 per cent of turnover. Manufacturing, including construction, accounts for some 42 per cent of GDP – significantly more than in any of the other large OECD economies.

West Germany is not only successful at **Technik** (the art and science of manufacturing useful artefacts), it is also most adept at selling these manufactured items abroad. Products made in West Germany enjoy a larger share of world trade than those of any other country. Nevertheless, the country's manufacturing industries are not without their problems; nor are they being supported by a dynamic services sector, on account of the supply-side rigidities already noted.

Manufacturing

Even by the late 1960s, manufacturing was by far the most important sector of the West German economy, the contribution of agriculture having diminished steadily since the war until by 1989 it was responsible for only some 1.5 per cent of GDP. The traditional smokestack industries were severely affected by the oil crises of 1973 and 1979, though many of them have since staged impressive recoveries. Before the first oil shock, the country had to import 55 per cent of its energy requirements, but nationwide conservation measures cut energy consumption by roughly 6 per cent from 1973 to 1983. West Germany is fortunate to possess large coal deposits, so it also shifted away from oil-fired power stations towards coal-fired and nuclear-ones, until The Greens came to prominence.

As *The Economist* of 26 November 1988 recalled, energy conservation policies could not fully protect the manufacturing sector of the economy from the two oil crises. In addition, the country's goods producers had to discard energy-intensive capital equipment and dismiss workers. Manufacturers of chemicals, pharmaceuticals, cars and aircraft all emerged from the oil-exacerbated downturn by installing more energy-efficient plant and reducing their workforces.

Consequently, manufacturing industry's investment in new machinery and plant increased as a proportion of GDP between 1974 and 1984. While GDP rose at an average rate of 2 per cent per annum, private industry's investment in new equipment increased by almost 3 per cent a year. As has already been noted, this level of private investment has not been sustained since 1984.

West Germany's major manufacturing industries are:

Iron and steel

In conjunction with coalmining, the iron and steel industry was one of the largest in the country until the mid-1970s. Thereafter, it suffered a sales crisis on account of oversupply on the world market. The receipt of public subsidies has since helped to promote the modernization of the industry, but its future will depend to a large extent on the world demand for special steels.

Mechanical engineering

Despite the predominance of small businesses, mechanical engineering is one of the largest sectors of manufacturing industry. In 1986 it employed a million people and turned over DM 165 billion.

Vehicle building

This is the largest single sector of manufacturing industry in the country in terms of turnover. In 1986 turnover amounted to DM 195 billion, with a workforce of 845,000. After Japan and the United States, West Germany is the third largest car-manufacturing country in the world. In 1986 4.3 million cars and 300,000 utility vehicles such as trucks and buses were made, as well as 66,000 motorcycles and 3.3 million bicycles.

Electrical engineering

With a turnover of just under DM 162 billion in 1986 and more than a million employees, the electrical engineering industry figures prominently in the group of major industries in terms of its importance to the national economy. Siemens is the flagship of this sector, Europe's largest and the world's fourth largest company in electrical and electronic products. In 1987, Siemens had 41,000 R & D staff and a research budget of DM 6.2 billion.

Precision instruments and optical goods

The structure of the precision engineering and optical goods industry, as of the watch and clockmaking sector, is accounted for by medium-sized companies. With some 130,000 employees, they constitute together one of the smaller sectors, but in international terms are among the largest in the world. These industries invest between 6 per cent and 10 per cent of turnover per annum in R & D in an attempt to safeguard competitiveness.

Chemicals

The chemical industry is the most important sector of the basic materials and production-goods area of West German industry. Of its workforce of 586,000 in 1986, almost one third were employed in the three largest chemical companies in the world – Hoechst, BASF and Bayer – which are also among the seven largest firms in the country. In addition, there are large numbers of medium-sized companies. In 1986, the West German chemical industry turned over DM 168 billion.

All of these industries have achieved success on account of the West German fascination with Technik and painstaking attention to the detail of the product – to such a degree in fact that manufacturing companies have been widely criticized for being product-oriented, even systems-oriented, rather than market-led. Yet these industries could not have been so successful for so many years with so many products without heeding the message of the markets. Nor has success been confined to the domestic market or even Europe.

The contribution of exports to output is greater for West Germany than for any other large OECD country. It rose from roughly 22 per cent of GDP in 1967 to 32 per cent of GDP in 1987. As could be expected from a predominantly manufacturing economy, manufactured goods constitute the major element – 77 per cent in 1987 – of the country's exports. Similarly, West Germany's proportion of world exports increased from 11 per cent in 1967 to 13 per cent in 1987. The country's record within the EC is even more impressive: it was responsible for 53 per cent of all intra-community exports in 1987, compared with 44 per cent in 1967.

It cannot be denied, however, that manufacturing industry in West Germany is experiencing its share of problems. While it is not possible to share the criticisms of one American commentator – that the country is only skilled at making last century's products, and could soon become the new Sick Man of Europe because it is deficient in information technology and biotechnology, the industries which, it is alleged, are about to dominate the next century – certain aspects of the manufacturing economy do give grounds for concern.

One problem which has come into sharper focus recently is that of the **Nord-Süd Gefälle** (north-south divide). During the time of the economic miracle, the states in the north and west were the boom areas, the base for the country's smokestack or heavy industries. The south was less economically developed. But even then, West Germany's north-south divide was small compared with Italy or the United Kingdom (see pages 126 and 168). As the *Financial Times* noted on 28 October 1987: 'Though it is true that the north contains the problem industries like steel and shipbuilding, while the south has a large share of the high-technology businesses, German industry is so regionally diversified that there is no shortage of examples to counter the cliché.' All the same, a glance at the state-by-state growth rate increases and unemployment statistics over a sufficiently large timescale, and working roughly from north to south, does reveal a disturbing trend (Table 1.2).

Table 1.2   *Regional growth and unemployment rates (1973 and 1988)*

	Growth rate (1973–88) (%)	Unemployment 1973 (%)	1988 (%)
Bremen	26	2.0	15
Hamburg	30	1.0	14
Schleswig-Holstein	44	2.0	10
Lower Saxony	38	2.0	12
North Rhine-Westphalia	30	1.0	11
West Berlin	31	1.0	11
Saarland	38	2.0	12
Rhineland-Palatinate	44	1.0	8
Hesse	50	1.0	7
Baden-Württemberg	48	1.0	5
Bavaria	60	2.0	6

Source: OECD/Bundesanstalt für Arbeit (Federal Labour Office)

The national average growth rate over the period 1973–88 was 42 per cent, and the national average unemployment rate 9 per cent.

The embryonic north-south divide has been promoted by the interventionist activities of politicians at the Federal state level in the south. As already noted, the policies of Lothar Späth in Baden-Württemberg and the late Franz Josef Strauss in Bavaria have attracted new sunrise, or high-technology, companies to the southern states. Their efforts were undoubtedly aided by the proximity of such celebrated holiday areas as the Black Forest and the Alps, since ever more West Germans are beginning to favour the **Freizeitgesellschaft** (leisure society) for the erstwhile **Leistungsgesellschaft** (high-performance society) – further themes to which reference will be made (see pages 38 and 47).

Far more disturbing than the north-south divide are the worries being expressed in certain quarters on the topic of **Industriestandort Deutschland** (Germany as a location for industry). Critics have concentrated on the surge of West German investments abroad, a dearth of inward investment, and the failure of West German companies to invest in their own country.

Over the period from 1985 to 1987, outward investment by West German companies totalled DM 51 billion, almost double the DM 27 billion recorded for the three preceding years. Taking 1986 as an example, the following major acquisitions were made:

- Hoechst bought Celanese for DM 5.7 billion.
- Bertelsmann, the publishing company, purchased Doubleday and RCA for DM 1.6 billion.
- Deutsche Bank took over the Banca d'America e d'Italia at a cost of DM 1.2 billion.
- Volkswagen paid DM 1.1 billion for Seat.
- Allianz, the insurance company, spent DM 1 billion on Cornhill.

The scale of these investments need not necessarily be interpreted as evidence of a deterioration in West Germany's attractiveness as an industrial site – it could also be regarded as proof of the country's stronger integration into the world economy. It might be held that it is only natural for companies to secure their export-built market shares abroad by investing on the spot. A company whose sales in another country reach a certain level may find it advantageous to invest there in order to move closer to the foreign market by shifting production facilities. This would reduce transport and distribution costs or avoid existing and impending protectionist legislation.

But West Germany itself has lost some of its appeal as a target for direct foreign investments from abroad. Though Goldstar, the Korean electronics company and Alps, another electronics firm but from Japan, set up in West Germany in 1988, total inward investment from 1978 to 1988 was only DM 28.5 billion. The reasons most frequently quoted for this lack of inward investment, and for the slowdown in investments in West Germany by domestic companies, are the high levels of corporate taxation, which have already been noted, and the burden of labour costs.

Only in Switzerland are overall labour costs higher than in West Germany. Though this is not so much due to increases in gross hourly rates as to the sustained rise and relative weight of indirect labour costs, it does have a deterrent effect on companies considering West Germany as a country in which to invest. In 1987, for example, the country's manufacturers had to provide an extra DM 83.10 for every DM 100 of salary.

However, wage costs around the world cannot be compared without taking into account the differences in productivity. During the 1980s, productivity growth in West Germany averaged 2.5 per cent per annum, compared with 4 per cent during the 1960s. It came down as the technical progress in the country's capital equipment lapsed. In the 1980s, unit labour costs increased in real terms, and profitability diminished as the rise in real wage costs was not fully matched by productivity improvements. The deceleration in investment growth is clearly linked with the decline in profitability, and West Germany remains a relatively high-cost economy.

A company's choice of business location is not influenced by rates of corporate taxation and real unit labour costs alone. The innovation potential of an economy, its degree of technological sophistication, and the know-how it produces are all determined to a large extent by the size of its R & D outlays. Here, West Germany occupies a top position internationally. Annual research spending totalled some DM 59 billion in 1988, of which some DM 14 billion was earmarked by the state or by institutions of higher learning for basic research.

Perhaps, however, West Germany's most important competitive advantage lies in its system of business education and vocational training, which is regarded as a model by many other industrialized countries, and as such deserves separate consideration later in the chapter (see pages 41–46).

Other factors working in favour of Industriestandort Deutschland are its position in the centre of Europe, and its modern infrastructure. Geographically, the country lies at the heart of the European Community, with ready access to a market of more than 320 million consumers. In addition, it also represents a gateway to the East, i.e. to the economies of the COMECON countries which are becoming increasingly attractive in the light of *glasnost* and *perestroika* and the momentous changes in Eastern Europe. Moreover, in many of the Eastern bloc countries, an area of erstwhile German economic influence, the German language has remained the *lingua franca* of business.

The all-embracing concept of the 'infrastructure' becomes clearer, in terms of its contribution to the smooth running of manufacturing industry, if one looks at the individual elements. Among other things, the West German infrastructure consists of a total of 173,000 kilometres of regional and national roads, including 8400 kilometres of motorways whose total length is due to be increased to more than 10,000 kilometres by the year 2000. Infrastructure also implies 30,000 kilometres of railway track, of which 11,000 have been electrified, together with a rolling stock consisting of some 10,000 locomotives, 14,000 passenger carriages and over 30,000 goods waggons. Part of the infrastructure is accounted for by 4400 kilometres of navigable waterways, 1400 kilometres of the total being made up of canals. The Rhine–Main–Danube Canal will soon provide a link between the North Sea and the Black Sea. Infrastructure includes 1,700 kilometres of pipeline through which 60 million tonnes of crude oil are pumped each year, and eleven international airports of which Frankfurt is one of the busiest in the world.

References to the infrastructure imply references to services, and current concern about Industriestandort Deutschland could linger in the minds of potential foreign investors and domestic businesses alike, unless substantial progress is forthcoming in this sector.

Services

The services sector in West Germany is much more regulated than manufacturing industry, and growth in the economy as a whole could be higher if regulations and red tape did not cramp entrepreneurial verve in services. Alfred Herrhausen, the late Chairman of the management board at the Deutsche Bank and regarded by many as the most powerful man in West German business until he was killed by a terrorist bomb in November 1989, stated in *The Wall Street Journal* of 6 July 1988: 'Deregulation and open markets are a must: they would promote competition and stimulate demand.'

Against this background, it is interesting to note that growth in private services has increasingly exceeded growth in manufacturing. At two percentage points, the differential over the period from 1979 to 1985 was larger than in most other OECD countries. At the same time, however, the rise in service employment was small by international comparison.

Growth in service employment has been held back by a whole series of market regulations. Of these, restrictive practices in insurance, road haulage, telecommunications and the guild-based crafts system, as well as limitations on shop-opening hours, are prime examples. Insufficient access to venture capital may also have prevented the creation of small firms, which are particularly important for the provision of services.

Typical of the restrictions in this sector of the economy are the regulations on the retail trade, the country's third largest 'industry' employing 2.4 million people in some 380,000 outlets. As the *Financial Times* of 28 October 1987, pointed out, ever since West Germany's **Ladenschlußgesetz** (Shop Opening Hours Act) became law in 1956, the country's retail establishments were obliged to follow a strict business routine. Shops could open any time after 7 a.m., though some only began business much later, but all had to close by 6.30 p.m. during the week and by 2 p.m. on all but one Saturday per month. However, the Act was full of loopholes. Petrol stations, for example, could remain open later as long as they did not sell any goods beyond motorists' immediate needs – a proviso which was subjected to the most liberal of interpretations by almost every petrol station in the land. Newspaper kiosks were also allowed to remain open at different hours. Yet there were even stranger exceptions with special rules for retailers in spa towns or shops in rural areas, which could sell certain items on Sundays.

In September 1989, the Federal government reformed the Act to let shops stay open until 9 p.m. on Thursday evening every week, but opposition built up to even this short weekly extension. The trade unions objected on social grounds. They argued that especially their women members would suffer through longer working hours and spend less free time with their families. Similarly, the opposition to the change included some of the largest retailers in the country. Wulf Ridder, spokesman for Kaufhof, did not believe that there was any pressing need to stay open longer. Other retailers pointed to the large number of shops outside city centres which close early even on the once-per-month Long Saturdays, when they could stay open longer if they wanted.

Progress in the liberalization of the whole services sector looks like being slow. The Federal government has set up a deregulation commission but it was not expected to report until mid-1990 at the earliest. Perhaps the country's main hope for deregulation lies with the completion of the European Community's single market, which will enforce liberalization on a grand scale, even in West Germany's almost sclerotic services sector.

Business and the law

West German society is ordered and orderly. The concept of the **Rechtsstaat** (rule of law) is constantly emphasized, and there are regulations and decrees governing most aspects of life in the country. Indeed, it has often been maintained that the West Germans assume that anything not specifically permitted by the law is **verboten** (forbidden)!

The business culture takes the law equally seriously. Business activities are carried out, in general, within a clearly-defined framework, the **Handelsgesetzbuch** (Commercial Code). In addition, West German companies employ large numbers of law graduates to make sure that neither they nor their business partners break any of the rules. While it is not true that 'business by litigation' is the order of the day in the country, West German firms can be characterized as litigious by persuasion, and legalistic in many of their dealings.

To give an impression of the legal framework within which the country's firms operate, and thus how law affects the business culture, it will suffice to describe in brief the most important corporate entities found in a business context. A more comprehensive account can be found in the Price Waterhouse *Guide to Doing Business in West Germany*, but the essential points are as follows:

1   **Aktiengesellschaft – AG (corporation)**
    This is the most advanced form of West German company and the only one whose shares can be traded on a stock exchange. There are

approximately 2000 AGs in the country. The AG is regulated by the **Aktiengesetz** (Corporations Act) of 1965. At least five founder shareholders must sign the statutes before a notary public. These persons then appoint the **Aufsichtsrat** (supervisory board) and the **Vorstand** (management board), which together file the formation documents with the trade register at the local court in the district where the company is to have its main seat. The minimum share capital for an AG is DM 100,000, of which at least 25 per cent must be paid in. All shares have a specified par value, the legal minimum of which is, in most cases, DM 50.

Basic to the concept of an AG is the transferability of its shares. Thus bearer shares predominate. Some AGs also issue registered shares with limitations on transferability. Others have inserted clauses in their company statutes to the effect that no single shareholder may at any time exercise more than a certain percentage of total voting rights. A typical example of this is one of the large West German banks whose statutes restrict such to 5 per cent. Others still have adjusted their statutes to ensure that non-voting shares are also issued. Provisions such as these limit the transferability of shares and make it virtually impossible for investors to buy up large quantities of an AG's shares on the stock market. They cannot in effect purchase a controlling interest and then take over the management of the company.

The management organs of an AG are the management board, the supervisory board and the Annual General Meeting (AGM) of shareholders. Although company statutes define the relationship between these three bodies to a certain extent, the Corporations Act and other legal provisions do set a general framework. The management board is responsible for the daily management of the company. The other two bodies have certain rights to information on management activities but have little power to restrict the management board in its dealings with third parties. The management board must consist of at least one member. If the total number of employees in the company exceeds 2000, one member of the management board must take prime responsibility for personnel matters. This **Arbeitsdirektor** (personnel manager) is required to devote himself full-time to employee matters, which means that all companies requiring a personnel manager need a management board of at least two.

The main responsibilities of the supervisory board are to monitor, guide and advise management on behalf of the shareholders. The supervisory board can consist of between three and twenty members, depending on share capital and the number of employees. In companies with fewer than 500 employees, all the members of the supervisory board are appointed by the shareholders. If the company employs between 500 and 2000 persons, one-third of the supervisory board members are appointed by employees. In larger companies, employee representation rises to one-half. This aspect of the business culture will be discussed more fully later in the chapter (see pages 36–37).

The responsibilities of the shareholders at the AGM are limited in scope. They decide by majority vote on: appointment of their representatives on the supervisory board; appropriation of profits; dismissal of members of the supervisory and management boards; appointment of auditors; changes in statutes; and liquidation of the company.

2 **Gesellschaft mit beschränkter Haftung – GmbH (private company)**
This form of corporate entity, which has a limited number of shareholders, is generally selected for family businesses and similar firms where the owners wish to exercise close personal control. The legal formalities, particularly at the formation stage, are less complex than for an AG. Moreover, prior to 1 January 1987, the GmbH was not subject to statutory audits. For all financial years beginning on or after this date, companies' audit requirements depend on size criteria only, and not on legal form.

Private limited companies are formed under the **GmbH-Gesetz** (Limited Liability Companies Act) of 1892 as amended. Many of the provisions regulating the actual operation of a GmbH are, however, based on other laws. The result is that most of the differences between a GmbH and an AG have effectively disappeared.

The formation of a GmbH is simpler than for an AG, but statutes must still be presented to a notary public. A GmbH may be formed by a single shareholder. The minimum share capital required is DM 50,000, of which one-quarter, but at least DM 25,000, must be paid up. A GmbH does not usually issue share certificates, but when it does these must be registered and cannot be made freely transferable.

The management bodies of a large GmbH and their duties are similar to those of an AG. The management board of the AG is, however, replaced by one or more directors, generally called **Geschäftsführer** (managing director(s)). But this is more a distinction in title than in function. A supervisory board is not usually required for a GmbH unless it regularly employs more than 2000 people, but if one is formed, its duties and functions are similar to those of the supervisory board in an AG.

3 **Offene Handelsgesellschaft – OHG (general partnership)**
The OHG is a partnership formed on the basis of a partnership agreement. The members may be natural persons or legal entities but they may not exclude themselves from the liabilities of the partnership. Profits or losses are ascribed to the partners as agreed.

4 **Kommanditgesellschaft – KG (limited partnership)**
This form of partnership is similar to an OHG except that the **Kommanditist** (limited partner(s)) can limit their liability in the partnership's debts to the amounts of their capital contributions. But at least one partner must assume unlimited liability, i.e. the **Komplementär** (general partner(s)). The management of the KG is the sole right and responsibility of the general partner(s). The limited partner(s) are excluded from the conduct of the company's affairs but may object to actions by the general partner(s) if these lie outside the firm's normal business activities.

In a KG, the general partner may be a limited liability company. If so, the legal designation is amended to **GmbH & Co KG.** This is quite a common device in order to obtain the benefits of a partnership but without incurring legal liability. Thus, the limited partners subscribe for the entire partnership capital and form a GmbH to hold the general partnership share as well as to exercise management control. The GmbH acts here at the direction of its own shareholders and its unlimited legal liability is effectively worthless to an unsatisfied creditor because its only asset is its stake in the partnership's capital. This can, however, be as low as zero.

5 **Gesellschaft des bürgerlichen Rechts – GbR (civil law partnership)**
In this entity, members agree to share in specified aspects of their own separate businesses. Law firms are a typical example where each partner shares in office costs but otherwise keeps his income as personal earnings.

6 **Einzelkaufmann (sole trader)**
In such a construction, an individual conducts business as a single owner. His or her liability for the settlement of debts is unlimited. The trade name must be registered, and a sole proprietor must use his or her full name but may add to it a description of the business.

No contribution on the law and the business culture in West Germany would be complete without mention of the **Prokurist.** He or she – it usually is he – is an employee of an AG or GmbH to whom the power of procuration has been granted by members of the management board in an

AG or managing director(s) in a GmbH. This means that he is legally
entitled to act for the company in business matters and to bind the firm
vis-à-vis third parties. On letters received from West German AGs or
GmbHs, two signatures will be found. The one at the bottom left usually
belongs to the Prokurist. Without his signature or that of a member of the
management board or one of the managing directors, the letter would not
be legally binding on the company.

Business and finance

Conservatism and overall strength, which are such outstanding features of
the whole of the business culture in West Germany, are nowhere more in
evidence than in the country's major financial institutions. This should not
imply, however, that the Bundesbank, the Big Three private commercial
banks and the financial markets are without their critics. Nor does it mean
that long-delayed reforms of the financial institutions can be postponed
much longer. In fact, all the country's financial services are currently under
scrutiny from one quarter or another, and radical changes can be
anticipated.

The Bundesbank

Even by the late 1950s, the West Germans had concluded that money was
far too important a commodity to be left to politicians! Established in
Frankfurt in 1957 by the **Bundesbank Act**, the country's central bank is:
'. . . required to support the general economic policy of the Federal
government. (But) in exercising the powers conferred on it by this Act it
shall be independent of instructions from the Federal government.' This
high degree of autonomy has been zealously guarded ever since.
Moreover, the Bundesbank has seldom shirked from imposing the policies
which it has deemed to be appropriate, even at the risk of incurring the
wrath of the political party or parties forming the Federal government at
the time.

The Act is also quite specific as to the central bank's duties: 'The
Deutsche Bundesbank shall regulate the volume of money in circulation
and of credit supplied to the economy, using the monetary powers
conferred on it by this Act, with the aim of safeguarding the currency. . .
Both the independence of the Bundesbank and the stated goal of
'safeguarding the currency' are a reflection of deep-seated West German
fears of inflation.

Twice in less than half a century, in 1923 and again after the Second

World War, the Germans suffered from periods of total inflation when, quite clearly, the currency had not been safeguarded. Memories of these bouts of hyperinflation are still etched on the popular consciousness. In the first, workers were being paid their wages twice a day, taking them home in wheelbarrows, then rushing out to spend their virtually worthless money before the prices in the shops rose even higher. In the second, the Reichsmark (RM) had been virtually ousted as the medium of exchange by the cigarette and the nylon stocking! This bout of hyperinflation was not terminated until the Currency Reform was introduced in 1948, when the Deutsche Mark (DM) replaced the RM.

Given these experiences, it is small wonder that the West Germans should want to leave monetary policy to the professionals, i.e. the central bankers, and then specifically charge them with the task of 'safeguarding the currency'. Moreover, the Deutsche Bundesbank's record in controlling inflation has been extremely good.

Table 1.3   *West German inflation (1969–89)*

Year	(%)	Year	(%)
1969	1.9	1980	5.1
1970	3.4	1981	6.3
1971	5.3	1982	5.6
1972	5.5	1983	3.7
1973	6.9	1984	2.8
1974	7.0	1985	2.6
1975	6.0	1986	− 0.3
1976	4.3	1987	0.3
1977	3.7	1988	1.4
1978	2.7	1989	3.0
1979	3.8		

Source: OECD

Over the period from 1969 to 1989, the rate of inflation in West Germany exceeded the average rate for all OECD countries in two years only, 1972 and 1973. In the other years, it has been significantly below the average (Table 1.3).

The Bundesbank's success in keeping inflation in check has found favour in a whole succession of OECD reports, which constantly praise the central bank's skill and pragmatism. Perhaps the most resounding testimony to its efforts is contained in the *1987-1988 OECD Economic Survey*, which states: 'The sensitivity of the average citizen to inflationary developments and the negative impact of inflation on the real side of the economy would seem to be much greater in West Germany than in most other OECD countries. Not surprisingly, therefore, price stability objectives have always figured at the top of the policy priorities of German monetary authorities, and the Bundesbank as the "inflation watchdog" has been constitutionally entrusted with a high degree of independence. Given both the strong commitment to the maintenance of price stability and the wherewithal to fight inflation effectively, the German price record has traditionally been better than generally elsewhere.'

But the Bundesbank has no grounds for complacency. In 1988, a Joint Finance and Economics Council was set up by the French and West German governments. The Council is composed of the economics and finance ministers and central bank presidents of the two countries. It meets four times a year to coordinate policy, and was established under a supplementary protocol to the Franco–German friendship treaty. As such its provisions would have prevailed over those of the 1957 Bundesbank Act which guarantee the West German central bank a degree of autonomy enjoyed by no other. After furious objections from the Bundesbank, and particularly its President, Karl Otto Pöhl, the Federal government inserted a memorandum in the treaty to the effect that the Joint Council is consultative and not decision-taking.

As *The Economist* observed on 13 February 1988, behind this anger lie significant differences between the Bundesbank and the French. The latter complain that the West German central bank does little to support their Franc in the European Monetary System (EMS). Indeed, the French have maintained for a long time that the EMS is in reality a DM-dominated zone in which all the other countries have to bow to the Bundesbank's severe monetary policies. Initially, this strict discipline was appreciated by the French, but with inflation apparently under control in France, it is being interpreted as an obstacle to growth.

The Bundesbank is apprehensive that the Joint Council will be usurped by the French to press their demands for a European Central Bank. Karl Otto Pöhl maintains that he would like a European Central Bank some time in the future, but only if it has as much freedom from political interference as the Bundesbank enjoys. He contends that West German inflation has been among the lowest in the world because the central bank has not been obliged to finance deficits incurred by the Federal govern-ment or to trim monetary policy to satisfy short-term political expedients. The establishment of a politically-dependent European Central Bank, he concludes, would promote inflation and jeopardize the limited progress which the EMS has realized to date.

The Big Three

Standard & Poor's, the US credit-rating agency, regularly awards AAA status to only fourteen banks in the world. The Deutsche Bank, the Dresdner Bank and the Commerzbank, West Germany's Big Three private commercial banks, are prominent members of the exclusive AAA Club. Even in a country which is vastly overbanked, with one branch per 1370 head of the population and one bank employee for every 100, the Big Three dominate because of their close links with big business.

The ties between the Big Three and large West German manufacturing companies were investigated in the 1970s by the Gessler Commission. It ascertained that the power of these banks lay in the combination of the proxy votes cast by banks on behalf of other shareholders at company AGMs; the tradition of the 'house bank' which keeps a firm linked to one principal lender; the sheer size of the banks' equity holdings; and the many seats on company supervisory boards to which these shareholldings give entitlement.

Concern lingers about the Big Three's influence on non-financial companies. Wolfgang, Kartte, President of the **Bundeskartellamt** (Federal Cartel Office), recently affirmed much of the criticism of the Gessler Commission. In 1986, the Deutsche Bank had a direct equity holding of 35 per cent in Phillip Holzmann (construction); over 25 per cent in Daimler-Benz (vehicles); over 25 per cent in Hapag-Lloyd (shipping); over 25 per cent in Karstadt (department store chain); 18 per cent in Horten (another department store chain); and 6 per cent in Allianz (insurance). In the same year, the Dresdner Bank owned direct stakes of 25 per cent or more in Hapag-Lloyd (shipping), Flender Werft (shipbuilding), Gold-Pfeil (leather), Dortmunder Union (brewing) and Heidelberg Zement (cement). Also in 1986, the Commerzbank held more than 25 per cent of Karstadt and further substantial direct stakes in Sachs (ball bearings) and Hannoversche Papierfabriken (paper).

In addition, the Big Three's indirect involvement is sometimes masked by holding companies. The Deutsche Bank had a 75 per cent share of a Frankfurt holding company which owned 25 per cent of Horten; another 25 per cent of the same holding company belonged to the Commerzbank. Similarly, the Commerzbank had a twice-removed interest in Daimler-Benz through its 25 per cent share in a Munich firm which owned 25 per cent of a holding company, which in its turn had 25 per cent of Daimler-Benz.

The large equity holdings by the Big Three entitle members of their management boards to sit on the supervisory boards of non-financial companies. In the 1960s, Hermann Abs, a former Chairman of the management board at the Deutsche Bank, sat on the supervisory boards of over thirty firms! A law has since been introduced to restrict to ten the number of supervisory board seats which can be held simultaneously by any one natural person. Nevertheless, in the mid-1980s members of the management board of the Deutsche Bank had seats on the supervisory boards of BASF and Bayer (chemicals); Siemens, BBC, SEL, and AEG-Telefunken (electricals); Volkswagen and Daimler-Benz (vehicles); Thyssen, Klöckner, Rheinmetall and Arbed Saarstahl (steel); Karstadt, Kaufhof and Horten (department store chains); Bertelsmann and Gruner + Jahr (publishing); and many more.

At first glance, it would appear that there is a clear case of conflict of interest for a representative of the Deutsche Bank to sit on the supervisory board of, say, BASF and Bayer, two companies in the same sector of industry. But where is the conflict? The Deutsche Bank has a vested interest in the well-being of both companies; it has put its money into the two companies and wishes to see a return on that investment from both, so it will not be inclined to favour one more than the other. In fact, it could be argued that the presence of the man from the Deutsche Bank actually avoids conflicts of interest.

The supervisory board of a West German company has two sets of clearly-defined duties. It hires and fires the management board, and it gives or withholds approval for major financial decisions. In the example above, let us assume that BASF decides, with the assent of its supervisory board, to make a major investment in plant in Country X. Let us further assume that Bayer has been thinking along similar lines. Once the decision has been taken at BASF, the man from the Deutsche Bank would advise against such action by Bayer, and since he is the representative of a major shareholder he would be listened to. Conflict, in the sense of competition between two West German companies, would thus have been avoided.

The presence on large West German companies' supervisory boards of representatives of the Deutsche Bank, Dresdner Bank and Commerzbank is also advantageous in terms of consortium formation and consortium management. Each of the Big Three has shareholdings in a whole range of companies, so consortium formation from within that circle of companies is relatively straightforward. Moreover, in the unlikely event that the companies forming the consortium fail to cooperate satisfactorily, the bank could apply the ultimate sanction.

Approximately 400 large West German companies have banks' representatives on their supervisory boards, and the management boards of these companies welcome their presence. They bring to the manufacturing companies a high degree of financial expertise and, what is more, a high degree of financial security. A predatory takeover bid for one of these large companies is virtually out of the question because the banks' equity holdings are tantamount to a corporate poison pill. In conditions such as these, manufacturing companies can operate, plan, invest and train for the long term, without worrying about the effects of a bad set of figures on their share price.

When subjected to criticisms of excessive power, the Big Three defend themselves in the following terms: as for proxy votes, the banks state that shareholders are at liberty to cast their votes as they see fit, and not to follow the recommendations made by the bank in question. They claim further that many of their large shareholdings in manufacturing companies arose from company rescues, when debt was turned into equity. The bailout of Klöckner & Co in 1988 by the Deutsche Bank was a case in point; the rescue of AEG-Telefunken at the beginning of the 1980s, when a banking consortium stepped in to stop the country's second largest electricals group going to the wall, was yet another. Finally, the banks maintain that seats on supervisory boards give them better radar with which to detect companies' problems.

Each of the Big Three is already a so-called universal bank, i.e. heavily involved in virtually all aspects of banking, from company financing, personal lending and deposit-taking, to foreign exchange dealing and stockbroking. But one of the latest trends for the private commercial banks has been to diversify even further. Led by the Deutsche Bank, they are entering the fields of mortgage finance, property broking, management consultancy, venture capital and insurance, with the aim of offering their clients **Allfinanz** (all-inclusive financial services).

At the end of 1988, the Deutsche Bank decided to establish its own life insurance company. Although this move inevitably resulted in a clash with Allianz, West Germany's largest insurance company in which it had a major shareholding, the leading member of the Big Three felt it had little choice. In 1987, West Germans invested 30 per cent of their savings in insurance policies, up from less than 20 per cent in 1977, with premium income totalling approximately DM 120 billion. Life insurance made up the largest segment of this premium total, which does not include reinsurance. In March 1989, the Dresdner Bank announced that it was also diversifying into the insurance market through a cooperation with Allianz, which has 14 per cent of the life and 16 per cent of the non-life market.

Diversification at home and expansion abroad, with the Deutsche Bank buying Banca d'America e d'Italia, an Italian commercial bank in 1986 and Morgan Grenfell, the British merchant bank in 1989, and Commerzbank taking a 10 per cent holding in Banco Hispano Americano of Spain in 1988, are the hallmarks of the Big Three in anticipation of the completion of the European Community's single market. They wish to secure their home market against ever-increasing penetration by foreign banks, especially from Switzerland, and to position themselves in expanding markets abroad. There is very little to stop them – certainly no lack of financial clout.

Stock markets

In sharp contrast to the private commercial banks, the West German equity markets are tiny. Attempts to foster 'equity-mindedness' among business people and investors alike have met with only limited success. Nevertheless, change is in the air, and this is an aspect of the business culture in the country which could embrace significant developments in the near future. There is certainly plenty of scope for innovation and reform.

The minor role played by share financing, and the relatively heavy dependence on bank finance, have been typical of the country's industry. Broadly speaking, debt-to-equity ratios have traditionally been about twice as high as in the USA or comparable European countries. Of the two million or so companies in West Germany, approximately 2000 are AGs, or public limited companies, with a joint stock capital structure. At the end of 1987, only 574 domestic companies were actually listed on the markets of the stock exchanges, and companies themselves owned about half of the country's equity, often through complicated cross-holdings. The market's capitalization represented only about 20 per cent of GDP, compared to around 85 per cent in the United Kingdom.

The structure of the market reflects the emphasis of West German industry, with services underrepresented. According to the *Investor's Chronicle* of 7 April 1988, chemicals, including the world's three biggest firms, Hoechst, Bayer and BASF, were responsible for 25 per cent of the market's capitalization. Banks and insurance accounted for another 16 per cent. The vehicles and engines sector (another 16 per cent) was dominated by Volkswagen, Daimler-Benz and BMW. Utilities (11 per cent), electricals (mainly Siemens with 9 per cent) and engineering (9 per cent) were the next largest sectors. Shares in advertising, financial services and consumer goods did not feature significantly.

Apart from a handful of blue chips, most of the shares are traded so infrequently that share prices are fixed for the day. Not surprisingly, therefore, the equity market is small relative to the bond market.

Prior to the start of 1987, the level of equity investment by individuals was low, with only some 5 per cent of households owning shares, and insurance companies holding only about 6 per cent of their funds in equities. In addition, relatively few pension funds exist in West German, a remnant of the post-war period when companies had little spare cash for such luxuries. Although individual West Germans have traditionally been good savers, squirreling away on average some 14 per cent of disposable income, they have also been conservative and risk-averse. The convention has been for them to put their money into local and regional savings banks or hold government bonds. Since the beginning of 1987, however, the number of shareholders in West Germany has jumped by more than two million to almost six million, or about 10 per cent of the population. Many of the newcomers are in their twenties and early thirties, more cosmopolitan than their parents and less cynical about shares. Moreover, they belong to a generation in West Germany which, for the first time this century, will inherit wealth not diminished by war or hyperinflation.

The West German equity market is the world's fourth largest, and concern about **Finanzplatz Deutschland** (Germany as a financial centre) has at last brought about a number of changes. 1983 was declared the Year of the Share, and 11 new companies were launched onto the market. This number rose to twenty-seven, worth some DM 4.9 billion, in 1986. Before the stock market crash in October 1987, nineteen maiden share issues and thirty-seven capital stock increases were made. A total of eighty-nine new issues in five years may not sound impressive, but this has been accompanied by other significant developments.

One helpful factor was the introduction in May 1987 of a new tier to the market. This might appear strange, in a market which already distributes a low turnover over three tiers, but there were good technical reasons. The top tier, **amtlicher Handel** (full listing), involves heavy costs. The next, **geregelter Freiverkehr** (regulated free market), has modest reporting requirements but is hardly policed. The bottom tier, **ungeregelter Freiverkehr** (unregulated free market) has no rules governing disclosure or admission and consists entirely of off-the-floor trading between banks. The new **geregelter Markt** (regulated market) comes immediately below the topmost tier. It involves about half the costs of a full listing, imposes fewer admission and reporting requirements, and is open to firms with a lower minimum nominal capital. The new market immediately attracted more than fifty existing shares and many of 1987's stock market newcomers.

The best news of all came for the stock markets in January 1989, when the cabinet in Bonn approved a bill to revamp the Stock Market Act, which goes back to 1896, and to set up a **Deutsche Termin-Börse** (options and futures exchange). The bill passed through the Federal Parliament in autumn 1989, so that the new-look stock exchange and the new futures market could start operating in 1990. Although other financial centres have futures exchanges, in West Germany such trading was long regarded as tantamount to gambling. So why the change? The West German experience has been that the absence of an effective hedging instrument was magnifying the swings in their stock market, and foreign competition was taking business away from Frankfurt. The new Act also implements EC guidelines under which a company accepted for a stock market listing in one member state can be listed in West Germany without further bureaucracy.

However, if the Federal government is serious about promoting Finanz-platz Deutschland and making it a true competitor with Japan, the United States and the United Kingdom, it should abolish the notorious **Bör-senumsatzsteuer** (stock market turnover tax). The tax is levied at a rate of 0.1–0.25 per cent on all local market secondary trading in West German stocks and bonds. This it promised to do years ago, but instead it reintroduced in January 1989 a 10 per cent **Quellensteuer** (withholding tax) on dividend and fixed-interest payments. The move was bitterly resented by the financial community and seen as positively harmful to Finanzplatz Deutschland at a time of growing competition between international financial centres. After intense lobbying, the withholding tax was abolished in July 1989.

Business and the labour market

Business activities in West Germany in the 1980s have been conducted against the background of a declining and ageing indigenous population. In contrast, the working population has been increasing, thus contributing to higher unemployment than might be expected from such a strong economy. Special groups within the working population have been disproportionately affected by the scourge of unemployment, and towards the end of the decade they have been joined on the labour market by large numbers of **Aussiedler** (returnees of ethnic German origin from Eastern Europe) and **Übersiedler** (refugees from East Germany).

Demographic trends

The last national census was held in West Germany on 27 May 1987. On that day the country had a population of 61,083,000, nearly a million fewer than expected, composed of 31,758,000 women and 29,325,000 men. 4,100,000 inhabitants were foreigners. The actual number of West Germans is declining. In 1970, there were 58,200,000; in 1987, the total was 56,900,000. Over the same period, the number of foreigners in the country rose by 70 per cent from 2,400,000 to 4,100,000, or from 4 per cent to 6.85 per cent of overall inhabitants.

The population is also ageing. In 1970, 23 per cent of the people were under 15 years old; in 1987, the proportion sank to 14.6 per cent, West Germany having the second-lowest birth rate in Europe (1.4 children per woman). From 1970 to 1987, those aged over sixty-five increased by a fifth from 13.2 per cent to 15.3 per cent. In 1990, the so-called 'pensioner quotient' or dependency ratio (the number of old-age pensioners in relation to the number of people paying in pension contributions) was 50 per cent. In other words, two persons in employment were making contributions for every retired person receiving a pension. However, in the year 2000 this ratio will be 62 per cent; in 2010, 74 per cent; and in 2030, 117 per cent, i.e. by then every 100 employees paying in contributions will be supporting 117 pensioners!

Unemployment

The declining population figures have not been reflected in low unemployment rates (Table 1.4), partly because the working population actually increased from 26.3 million in 1970 to 28.2 million in 1987.

Table 1.4 *West German Unemployment Rates (1979–89)*

Year	(%)
1979	3.8
1980	3.8
1981	5.5
1982	7.5
1983	9.1
1984	9.1
1985	9.3
1986	9.0
1987	8.9
1988	8.7
1989	7.9

Source: OECD

There is no single factor that can be blamed for the high percentages of the dependent labour force out of work in West Germany. At the beginning of the 1980s, the effects of the second oil crisis of 1979 and the worldwide recession are clearly 'reflected in the steep rises in the unemployment statistics. In the mid-1980s, factors common to most OECD countries, such as rapid technological change and fierce Japanese competition, combined with particular West German circumstances to produce in 1985 the worst annual set of unemployment figures since the proclamation of the Federal Republic.

Low growth rates in the West German economy throughout most of the 1980s have already been noted, and these have no doubt been partly responsible for the high unemployment figures. So why was no attempt made to reflate the economy and thus reduce the number of jobless? The test of reflation is whether greater domestic demand would improve output rather than increase prices. In addition, between 1965 and 1985, the country witnessed a rise in the rate of unemployment relative to capacity utilization. This indicates, as *The Economist* observed on 26 October 1985: '. . . that even if capacity were fully used, unemployment might remain high. The reason is familiar: too much capital deepening (men replaced by machines) and too little capital widening (expansion of capacity) because of what the OECD calls West Germany's "real wage rigidity".' In effect, West German wages are less flexible than those in most European countries, and inter-industry wage differentials are virtually negligible.

Towards the end of the decade, higher growth rates did contribute to a dip in the unemployment rates, and between 1983 and 1988 one million new jobs were created. The increase in employment originated in the gradual expansion of the services sector, which has been slower to grow than in most comparable countries on account of the overregulation already noted.

Guest workers

One segment of the labour market in West Germany which has been disproportionately affected by unemployment during the 1980s is that formed by the **Gastarbeiter** – guest workers (Table 1.5).

The percentage of unemployed guest workers was lower than the national average until 1974, the year following the first oil crisis. Thereafter, it has always been significantly higher. This is because most of the guest workers are unskilled and thus regarded as more dispensable in a harsher economic climate.

The first agreement on the recruitment and placement of foreign workers was signed with Italy in 1955. Further agreements followed with Spain (1960), Greece (1961), Turkey (1964), Portugal (1967) and Yugoslavia (1968). Although the signing of an agreement with a particular country inevitably confirmed the status quo, it did not mark the date of the arrival of the first immigrant worker from that country.

Table 1.5   *Gastarbeiter (June 1987)*

	Employed	Unemployed
Turks	518,423	99,884
Yugoslavs	292,054	20,997
Italians	181,696	37,931
Greeks	100,913	14,610
Spaniards	64,046	6,956
Portuguese	35,802	3,244
Others	395,925	80,684
Total	1,588,859	264,306
Total Gastarbeiter Population		1,853,165

Source: Bundesanstalt für Arbeit (Federal Labour Office)

The guest workers originally came to West Germany on account of the push factors in their countries of origin (high unemployment, low wages) and the pull factors prevailing in the Land of the Economic Miracle. Here they perform tasks which indigenous workers are increasingly unwilling to undertake: they work in tedious jobs (assembly lines); in dirty jobs (street-cleaning); in dangerous jobs (coalmining); and weather-sensitive jobs (building and allied trades).

The guest workers in West Germany are very unpopular with the native population. A poll in 1981 revealed that two-thirds of West Germans believed that the guest workers should return to their countries of origin. They are accused of: defiling West German cities by living in ghettos; bleeding the country dry by sending home a high proportion of their wages; failing to integrate in society; and above all, taking the jobs that rightfully belong to West Germans.

One of the fundamental reasons for the unpopularity of the guest workers is the mismatch between original expectations and reality. When they first arrived, the guest workers were perceived by many West Germans as a simple solution to a simple problem. The country needed workers, and the guest workers needed jobs. In addition, the guest worker was regarded as ideal economic man. He would be a healthy individual in the prime of life, come to West Germany without his family, stay for a few years, and then return home. Young and fit, he would require no medical support services; without a family, he would exert no pressure on social or educational facilities. He would naturally pay taxes and social security contributions, but he would be long gone before any benefits fell due. The reality has been quite different: although some guest workers have returned home, most have stayed. What is more, they have been joined by their wives and children, and they have had further children 'made in Germany'. In fact, they have become a permanent feature of the West German labour force, and are overrepresented in the unemployment statistics through little fault of their own.

Graduates

Another group for whom employment prospects look bleak are the graduates of West German **Fachhochschulen** (polytechnics) and universities. The total number of unemployed graduates passed the 100,000 mark in 1984, and increased fivefold from 1980 to 1985. Among the graduates registered as unemployed in 1985 were:

- 29,546 teachers.
- 22,010 engineers of all types.
- 13,168 economic and social scientists.
- 6,722 natural scientists.
- 3,728 doctors of medicine.
- 3,348 lawyers.

Unemployment rates among graduates in West Germany have continued to rise throughout the decade, and there is little hope of improvement in the situation. In fact, matters could get much worse. According to the **Institut für Arbeitsmarkt- und Berufsforschung** (Institute of Labour Market and Vocational Research), there were in the country in 1980 a total of 1,501,000 graduates, 874,000 of whom will still be employed by the year 2000. There will also be a demand for an additional 627,000 graduates on account of retirements in the interim. But by the year 2000, total graduate supply will have reached 2,983,000, leaving 1,482,000 graduates unemployed!

Patterns of graduate employment are also forecast to change. Hitherto, 60–70 per cent of graduates have found employment in the public sector. But in view of government determination to cut public-sector spending at both Federal and individual state levels, it is doubtful whether such take-up rates will ever be achieved again. Economic growth rates would have to be truly phenomenal for the private sector to absorb such large increases in graduate supply.

Perhaps the best prospects for West Germany's unemployed graduates lie outside the country. Their chances of taking up employment in another EC state will be enhanced greatly by the completion of the internal market, one of the provisions of which is the free movement of labour between member states (see also page 191).

Returnees and refugees

The fall in unemployment towards the end of the 1980s was accounted for by higher economic growth rates and, to a disproportionate extent, by the labour force under twenty-five years of age, a group in which the labour supply is declining perceptibly for demographic reasons. This relief for the labour market contrasted with the increase in the labour supply resulting from a strong rise in immigration into West Germany. Thus the number of returnees of ethnic German origin from Eastern Europe, totalling 240,000 in 1988, was twice as high as in 1987. At the beginning of 1989, only 40,000 of these returnees were registered as unemployed, but this figure did not include recent arrivals who had not started to look for work. 300,000 more returnees were expected in the course of 1989.

In the autumn of 1989, the returnees were joined in West Germany by an estimated 200,000 refugees from East Germany. Their prospects on the labour market are much brighter than those of the returnees because German is their native language, and they are mostly young, skilled, or at worst semi-skilled workers. They are likely to be snapped up very rapidly by West German companies, and their most pressing problem will probably be adjustment to the faster tempo of work in the West.

Heinrich Franke, President of the **Bundesanstalt für Arbeit** (Federal Labour Office), is pessimistic about medium-term developments on the West German labour market. In an interview with the **Westdeutscher Rundfunk** (West German Radio) on 15 February 1989, he said that unemployment in the country would remain at high levels, between 1.5 and 2 million, until the second half of the 1990s. According to Heinrich Franke, the advent of the EC's single market by the end of 1992 will only serve to exaggerate movements on labour markets. Assuming West German annual economic growth of 2.5 per cent, the number of people in employment by the year 2000 will total just over 26 million, a level similar to 1988.

Business and trade unions

The trade unions in West Germany can look back over the 1980s with a certain satisfaction. Despite the presence in Bonn for much of the decade of a centre-right coalition ostensibly committed to free markets and deregulation, the strength of the unions remains virtually unaffected. In 1988, approximately 42 per cent of the dependent labour force was still organized in unions. Although the unions' reputation as entrepreneurs in their own right has suffered severe setbacks, they have achieved notable gains in collective bargaining, and successfully contributed to the system of **Mitbestimmung** (worker codetermination). However, their demands for a 35-hour week and commitments to certain rigid working hours are coming under pressure from employers. Moreover, the trade unions are concerned about the completion of the EC's single market. Not only the significance of 1993 for manufacturing jobs in West Germany but also its implications for the rights and agreements which they have established over so many years are giving rise to anxiety.

Organization

After the Second World War, the tradition of a multiplicity of small craft unions was abandoned in West Germany, and blue-collar workers were organized in sixteen large unions, one for each major 'industry'. Every one of these industrial unions affiliated to the **Deutscher Gewerkschaftsbund** (DGB) (Confederation of German Trade Unions), as subsequently did the **Gewerkschaft der Polizei** (Police Trade Union).

The DGB was formed in Munich in 1949 and is now located in Düsseldorf. As the umbrella organization for the seventeen industrial unions, its role is to coordinate the activities of the member unions, provide advice on legal and social security matters, contribute to education and training programmes, and to act as spokesman for the unions in national affairs. It is not affiliated to any of the political parties, nor is it associated with any of the churches.

The DGB is run by its Federal Board, which consists of twenty-eight members: the President of the DGB; two Vice-Presidents; the seventeen Presidents of the member unions; and eight full-time DGB officials, who are the heads of its special committees, and two of whom have usually been card-carrying members of the CDU or CSU. The DGB meets every three years for its Federal Congress, which is attended by 504 delegates.

Entrepreneurial activities

One of the features which distinguishes the trade unions in West Germany from those in comparable countries is, or rather was, the extent of their activities as entrepreneurs. Although union subscriptions, at 2 per cent of gross wages or salary, and unions' individual contributions to the DGB, at 12 per cent of revenue, are in themselves modest enough, the DGB and its affiliated unions had succeeded, by the early 1980s, in building up considerable business interests. Through a holding company, they controlled, inter alia, the Volksfürsorge life insurance company, the third largest of its type in West Germany; Neue Heimat, the biggest construction company in Europe; the Bank für Gemeinwirtschaft, the fifth most powerful non-state bank in the country; and the co op based in Frankfurt.

The trade unions justify these large company interests by referring to them as an attempt at an alternative form of business activity based on the cooperative principle – **Gemeinwirtschaft.** They point out that their experiments at capitalism with a human and acceptable face date back to the early part of the century, with the foundation of the Volksfürsorge in 1912 to combat the high premiums being demanded by existing insurance companies. Neue Heimat, founded in 1950, was established in order to alleviate catastrophic conditions on the post-war housing market.

In the mid-1980s, however, the whole concept of Gemeinwirtschaft received a series of blows from which it might never recover. Neue Heimat was shattered by allegedly corrupt management practices to such an extent that this massive company was sold in September 1986 to an obscure West Berlin bakery-owner, Horst Schiesser, for a token DM 1. The banks, however, to whom some DM 12 billion were owed, out of total liabilities of DM 17 billion, forced the trade unions to take it back. Because of the financial effect on them of the Neue Heimat affair, the unions were obliged to sell 51 per cent of the Bank für Gemeinwirtschaft to the Aachener und Münchener insurance group.

Mismanagement on a massive scale, including alleged presentation of falsified balance sheets, credit fraud, and tax evasion shook another union-owned company, the Frankfurt-based co op, in 1988. Total debts were estimated at some DM 600 million, and a consortium of foreign banks bought 72 per cent of the shares. The evident inability of the trade unions to manage their companies adequately has thus forced the DGB to rethink their strategy on Gemeinwirtschaft. Current plans include the proposed sale of 25 per cent of the unions' holding in the Allgemeine Hypothekenbank and even the disposal of 75 per cent of their stake in the Volksfürsorge. At the beginning of the 1990s, Gemeinwirtschaft may not be dead, for the DGB and the unions still hold considerable assets, but to all appearances it is terminally ill.

Collective bargaining

A high percentage of employees in West Germany are covered by collective agreements. Such agreements are primarily industry-based and, sometimes, also regional within an industry. There are basically two types of agreements: the **Lohn- und Gehaltstarifvertrag** (wages and salary agreement), which affects solely pay; and the **Manteltarifvertrag** or **Rahmentarifvertrag** (framework conditions agreement), which regulates in addition such matters as hours of work, holidays, benefits, dismissal and redundancy provisions. The former has traditionally been concluded for 12 months at a time; the latter for several years. Recently there has been a move towards longer-term pay agreements.

Collective bargaining for industry-level or sector-level agreements takes place between the trade union and the corresponding employers' association. Once signed, these agreements are legally binding on companies and employees alike. An agreement can, however, be extended to cover all employees in the relevant sector by being declared **allgemein-verbindlich** (generally binding). This can be done by the Federal Minister of Labour or the state Minister of Labour if companies employing at least half of all the employees in that sector have signed it. In practice, however, employers apply the terms of an agreement to all employees regardless of union membership.

Pay agreements for some 14 million employees came up for renegotiation in 1987. New arrangements provided for increases ranging between 3.4 per cent and 3.8 per cent. In several major negotiations pay was linked with hours cuts in longer-term awards, and pay increases were predetermined for each of the years of the agreements' validity.

Industrial democracy

The business culture and the business climate in West Germany have both been favourably affected by the degree of integration of the trade unions into corporate structures. Although this integration was not always welcomed by employers, at least not initially, they have come to accept it as a fact of business life. Moreover, possibly as a result of close trade union involvement in corporate decision-making processes, employers and trade unions in West Germany refer to themselves collectively as **Sozialpartner** (social partners), thus avoiding at least the adversarial rhetoric encountered in other countries, and indicating a higher degree of consensus than is found elsewhere.

Industrial democracy in Germany looks back over a long history:

1920: Works' councils recognized as bargaining counterparts of employers in companies with more than twenty employees.
1951: Parity codetermination introduced for the mining, iron and steel industries. Capital and labour representatives have equal voting strength on supervisory boards. Voting deadlock is prevented by an additional 'neutral man', appointed by the state, if the board is split.
1952: Companies with over 500 employees forced to allocate one-third of the seats on their supervisory boards to labour representatives.

1972: Companies with five employees permitted to have a works' council. In addition, works' councils are given full codetermination rights on issues of working hours and the introduction of new technology, unless these matters are already covered by wage negotiations between unions and employers' associations.

1976: **Mitbestimmungs-Gesetz** (Codetermination Act) passed through Parliament. It embraces AGs and GmbHs normally employing over 2000 persons, which must have a supervisory board composed of half shareholders' and half workers' representatives. Companies with between 500 and 2000 employees have supervisory boards with one-third worker representation.

The trade unions are not entirely happy with the 1976 Act for several reasons. First, it affects only relatively few, large companies, and not the vast majority of small and medium-sized firms in the country. Second, the unions claim, the Act does not deliver true parity codetermination. It ensures that, in the event of voting deadlock, the capital owners will prevail because the chairman of the supervisory board is always a shareholders' representative with a casting vote. Moreover, one of the worker representatives must be a 'senior manager' who, it is alleged, is likely to side with the shareholders.

The employers were not happy with the 1976 Act either. In June 1977, just as the Act was due to come into force, nine companies and twenty-nine employers' associations submitted a complaint to the **Bundesverfassungsgericht** (Federal Constitutional Court) in Karlsruhe to the effect that it contravened the **Grundgesetz** (Basic Law). In March 1979, the Court published its decision and rejected the employers' injunction.

Since 1979, West German companies have come to terms with the provisions of the Codetermination Act, which has been the subject of minor amendments in the interim. Most will admit that worker representatives on the supervisory board make a positive contribution to the smooth operation of companies. This has been achieved both through their direct inputs in the decision-making process and through the dissemination of information on decisions taken at high levels in the company, although the works' councils in West German companies were already privy to large amounts of company information. Indeed, for the ordinary worker in the average West German company, the focus of industrial democracy lies neither with his representatives on the company supervisory board, nor with his trade union, but with the works' council. Works' councillors need not belong to the trade union represented in a company but most of them do.

Areas of disagreement

The social consensus between trade unions and employers in post-war West Germany, as graphically illustrated by the relatively few working days lost through strikes, continued throughout the 1980s (Table 1.6). Moreover, it is significant that the issues which divided them most over that decade are those concerned with working hours. This is undoubtedly a reflection of the sea-change taking place today, away from the erstwhile **Leistungsgesellschaft** (high-performance society) and towards the **Freizeitgesellschaft** (leisure society).

Table 1.6   *Working days in West Germany lost through disputes (1980–89)*

Year	Working days lost
1980	128,386
1981	58,398
1982	15,106
1983	40,842
1984	2,921,263
1985	34,505
1986	27,964
1987	33,325
1988	41,880
1989	100,409

Source: Bundesministerium für Arbeit (Federal Ministry of Labour)/Bundesanstalt für Arbeit (Federal Labour Office)

The older generations in the country rarely tire of recalling how West Germans used to work: women in headscarves passing bricks from hand to hand as they toiled in the rubble to rebuild a country devastated by war; men who laboured long hours in the factories and fashioned an economic miracle; unions that used to sit down with employers, not to argue over a shorter working week, but to hatch out strategies for greater efficiency and higher output. But as West Germany has prospered and achieved the **Wohlstandsgesellschaft** (affluent society) attitudes have changed. People are taking things easier. They want more time to spend the money they are earning, and are more interested in holidays abroad than in overtime in factories at home. What has happened to the good old West German hard-work ethic?

Opinion polls provide an answer of sorts: young people are more interested in being with their families. They do not believe that they should produce ever more and work ever harder; and they are increasingly unwilling to trade off leisure for more pay. Such findings have led some commentators to deduce that the West Germans are becoming idle, a notion abhorrent to the older generation. But this is not even part of the real answer. The circumstances of the post-war reconstruction period were very special. Not only were enormous efforts necessary to make the country habitable again; hard work was a form of guilt expiation for the atrocities of the war, a way in which West Germans could regain their dignity in their own eyes, and the respect of the rest of the world. The nature of work in the 1980s has, however, changed radically. The introduction of large numbers of numerically-controlled machine-tools and industrial robots into West German manufacturing plants has alienated many and left them feeling ill at ease at the workstation.

It is against this background that the altercations between employers and trade unions over shorter working hours should be viewed. In 1984, the **IG Metall** (Metal Workers' Union) went on a strike lasting eight weeks for the 35-hour week. They successfully broke the 40-hour week barrier and settled for 38.5 hours. Since then several other unions have wriggled through the same barrier, and in 1988 over 50 per cent of the workforce were on a sub-40 hour week, with some even down to 36.5 hours.

Holiday entitlement has also continued to rise throughout the decade. In 1987, average basic entitlement was 32.6 working days, while the average maximum entitlement was 35.3 days. Where age is used as a criterion, thirty, thirty-five or forty is the age at which employees usually attain their maximum holiday periods, while maximum service-related entitlements are between five and fifteen years' service. Overall, 99 per cent of all employees had at least four weeks' annual holiday in 1987; 94 per cent had at least five weeks; and 66 per cent had six weeks or more.

In 1987, 94 per cent of employees received additional holiday pay in one of three forms. 42 per cent of all employees averaged 47 per cent of basic pay; 33 per cent of employees were given a flat-rate cash payment to cover the entire holiday period amounting to DM 677 on average; 19 per cent of employees received a flat-rate cash payment for each day's holiday, which averaged DM 25. Moreover, some 92 per cent of employees received an annual bonus, usually expressed as a percentage of a month's salary (the so-called thirteenth month's salary), and in 1987 this percentage averaged 68 per cent of gross monthly pay. Taken together, additional holiday pay and thirteenth month's salary averaged 92 per cent of a month's normal salary, while about two-thirds of all employees received a total bonus equivalent to at least one month's salary.

Given fringe benefits such as these, it is hardly surprising that an area of growing strife is that of weekend working. Working on Saturday or Sunday separates not only employers and unions but has also sown divisions amongst unions themselves and between unions and local works' councils. In the 1950s and 1960s, the unions succeeded in gaining acceptance of the 40-hour, five-day working week. Recently, there has been renewed pressure by employers to reintroduce weekend working, particularly Saturday working.

In 1988, both Opel in its Kaiserslautern plant and BMW in the new Regensburg works brought back Saturday working. Similarly, Siemens and IBM introduced weekend working to permit continuous production of megabit chips at their factories in Regensburg and Sindelfingen respectively. Goodyear insisted that a DM 100 million investment at Fulda was made dependent on the acceptance of Saturday working by the works' council.

Article 139 of the Basic Law states: 'Sunday and the public holidays recognized by the state shall remain under legal protection as days of rest from work and of spiritual edification.' Exceptions included in the **Gewerbeordnung** (Trading Regulations) cover mainly utilities, transport and health services, as well as the leisure sector. In contrast, there are no legal restrictions on Saturday working: wage agreements expressly stipulating a Monday-to-Friday working week apply to some 265,000 employees only.

Employers maintain that weekend working is necessary because overall working hours have become shorter, thus leaving expensive equipment idle for long periods. This, they say, places West Germany at a competitive disadvantage in relation to other countries. The inclusion of Saturday as part of the normal working week would allow employers to incorporate more effective equipment working times. Dr Werner Stumpfe, President of **Gesamtmetall** (Engineering Employers' Federation), has stated that, whereas the incorporation of Saturday as a normal working day was a necessity, Sunday working was required for technical reasons and not on economic grounds.

The engineering and print-workers' unions are opposed to either Saturday or Sunday working. They claim that weekend working isolates employees from friends, sport and culture; disrupts family life; and places further strain on the environment. The chemical workers, traditionally a more moderate union than the engineers or printers, maintain that although works' councils initially rejected the introduction of weekend working, in many cases ensuing arbitration found in favour of employers. The union consequently decided that where Saturday working seemed likely, it would attempt to trade this off against shorter working hours and reductions in overtime.

In view of the large differences between the various parties, it appears unlikely that this conflict will be resolved in the short term. At present, the employers appear to be winning, partly because they can often drive a wedge between official union policy and local works' councils. They can also point to increased competition not only from the Far East but also from other countries in Europe post-1992.

Medium-term concerns

The West German trade unions are also anxious about the implications of the completion of the EC's single market, but for different reasons. As the *Financial Times* observed on 31 October 1988: '. . . with the highest pay and best fringe benefits in Europe, they have most to lose from the greater mobility of capital.' They are confident that they can retain most of the skilled-labour and high-value-added jobs on account of their outstanding system of education and vocational training – a theme to which further reference will be made (see below). But they worry that many lower-skilled manufacturing jobs could be exported to relatively low-cost countries such as those in the Iberian peninsula.

Many of their fears could be groundless. Since the very large companies, particularly in the car industry, have already moved to Spain and Portugal, 1992 will probably not have much of an effect. Similarly, the swift modernization of these two countries in the south of Europe will probably also entail an equally swift increase in labour costs. But 1992 might inspire some smaller companies, particularly the car-component makers, to emigrate south after the multinationals.

Finally, the West German trade unions are worried about what they call the 'social dismantling of Europe'. They claim that 1992 merely marks the advent of a 'Europe of capital' and focus on the opposition of such countries as the United Kingdom to the Community Charter of Fundamental Social Rights as tabled by Jacques Delors (see page 197). They point to the rejection of the Vredeling initiative in the early 1980s, which incorporated much of the West German system of worker participation and fear that, yet again, what will be adopted in Europe is the lowest common denominator.

Business, education, training and development

The business culture in West Germany has been constantly enriched by the presence in the country of a highly-trained and well-educated workforce. Education at school, vocational training in the Dual System, job-related courses at polytechnics and universities, and management development in companies all make their own unique contributions to the formation of this 'human capital'. Currently an attempt is being made to have the widespread training ethos underpinned yet further by the concept of longlife learning through extra paid holidays for self-improvement. The concept itself is welcomed by the employers but they are putting up stiff resistance to the notion of even more holidays!

Vocational training

The vocational training system in West Germany is the envy of many of its competitors and a cornerstone of the country's success in business. It also helped to keep youth unemployment down to approximately 5 per cent during the 1980s. In 1987, almost 650,000 young people embarked on apprenticeship courses which mostly last three years and link in-company training with specialized and general education in **Berufsschulen** (vocational schools) – the so-called Dual System. In 1987, there were approximately 1,800,000 apprentices undergoing initial vocational training.

Of the young people taking up vocational training after leaving school in 1987, 40 per cent came from **Grundschulen** (general schools) – in 1977 the figure was 54 per cent – 45 per cent had attended **Realschulen** (intermediate schools) (40 per cent), and 15 per cent of applicants for such traineeships had gone to a **Gymnasium** (grammar school) (6 per cent). The apprentices entering such schemes had behind them eight, ten and thirteen years of education at the respective schools.

In the Dual System, the individual states run the vocational schools, but the **Industrie- und Handelskammern** (Chambers of Industry and Commerce) or the **Handwerkerkammern** (Craft Chambers) are responsible for inspecting the approximately 500,000 approved training firms on a regular basis as well as for monitoring the training content of the 439 recognized training occupations. Apprentices are also registered, supervised and examined by the Chambers.

As the *Financial Times* of 25 August 1988 revealed, a comprehensive system of vocational training such as this is not cheap. AEG, for instance, spent almost DM 70 million on apprenticeship training in 1987. Training just one apprentice costs AEG approximately DM 24,000 per annum. 'Multiply this throughout the economy and the annual sum spent by industry on **Ausbildung** (initial vocational training) for its 1.8 million trainees is around DM 35 billion, though the net figure is around DM 25 billion allowing for trainees' contribution to production.'

At the end of the apprenticeship courses, in which 90 per cent of candidates pass the final examination at the first attempt and the drop-out rate over the average three-year course is less than 5 per cent, the erstwhile trainees become **Facharbeiter** (qualified skilled workers). Now they have gained social status and possess a qualification which they can show to their present, or any future, employer. Qualified skilled workers also earn more than the unskilled, even when working in trades or crafts not their own. But equally important, the possession of this qualification gives access to a range of higher vocational awards.

In theory, any qualified skilled worker with two years' experience of his or her trade could go on to **Fortbildung** (higher vocational training) and take one of the higher qualifications; in practice, the average age for those taking the **Industriemeister**, **Fachwirte** or **Fachkaufleute** examinations is approximately thirty years. In 1987, 7231 qualified skilled workers passed the Industriemeister, 5642 the Fachwirte and 4144 the Fachkaufleute examinations. The possession of a higher vocational award affords opportunities for career progression into supervisory and even management positions. In fact, the presence in lower and middle management ranks of practice-oriented employees who have emerged from the apprenticeship system, alongside more theory-oriented graduates from the country's polytechnics and universities, represents one of the major strengths of West German management.

Management education

Most of West Germany's managers come from the polytechnics and universities, where they will have studied a subject which is directly related to their future careers in business. The emphasis is, therefore, firmly placed, from the outset, on the acquisition of relevant knowledge and functional skills. The average age of a graduate leaving polytechnic at diploma level is twenty-six years, and twenty-eight years for university graduates. The 14,000 continuing their studies at university to the doctorate level are aged thirty on completing their dissertation.

In the 1960s, some 100 polytechnics were established in the country offering shorter (three to four-year), more vocationally-oriented courses than universities. In 1987, there were approximately a quarter of a million students at polytechnics, with 1 per cent per annum more students with the tertiary level entrance qualification opting for a polytechnic in preference to a university. The main subjects in order of popularity are: mechanical and production engineering; economics and **Betriebswirtschaft** (business economics); and social studies. In most programmes, there is a period of placement in industry or commerce. To distinguish polytechnic from university awards, some of the states insist that their polytechnic graduates designate themselves **Diplom-Ingenieur (FH)** or **Diplom-Kaufmann (FH),** the abbreviation in brackets denoting **Fachhochschule.**

There are, in West Germany, some sixty-eight universities which were attended by 1,250,000 students in 1988, giving a grand total of 22 per cent of age group in tertiary education. University courses are more academically demanding and thus longer than their polytechnic equivalents, with economics students taking 6 years and engineering students 6.5 years to complete to diploma standard.

Business regards university graduates with the diploma as good abstract thinkers but believes that they require two years of 'apprenticeship' before they become really useful to the company. In contrast, the more practically-educated polytechnic graduates are considered to hit the ground running from the very start of their careers. This is possibly why such a high percentage of polytechnic graduates find employment in medium-sized companies where induction training is rare, while university graduates tend to be recruited by large companies.

If a university graduate aspires to the topmost ranks of West German management, he would be well advised to take a doctorate in a relevant subject. In 1985, 36.7 per cent of management board members in all the country's **Aktiengesellschaften** (AGs) (corporations) possessed the doctor title; 41.5 per cent of management board members in the AGs quoted on the stock exchange also sported the title; and 53.8 per cent of the management board members of the 100 largest AGs had the right to be addressed as 'Herr Doktor'.

Management development

Large companies in West Germany conduct most of their **Weiterbildung** (management development) programmes in-house. They are fully committed to the training and development ethos and firmly believe that nobody can develop their managers more effectively than they can. Moreover, they possess their own lavishly-equipped short-course centres and are resolved to make maximum use of them. In addition, they perceive their own programmes as a means of stressing their particular corporate culture and thus persuading the individual manager to identify more closely with this culture. In other words, one of the spin-offs of in-house development programmes is their usefulness as a management retention tool.

The pattern in large companies is for lower management to receive more development than middle or senior managers. Among the lower managers would also figure the Industriemeister, Fachwirte and Fachkaufleute who have come up from the shop floor. Programmes at this level would be product-specific or function-specific. Typical examples for Industriemeister would be courses on safety at work or quality assurance. Programmes for middle managers would be company-specific and have a high management information content. Senior managers concentrate on objective management techniques, subjective management behaviour and, increasingly, the company and its environment – another theme to which further reference will be made (see pages 46–51).

Medium-sized companies lacking the appropriate human, physical and financial resources look outside the firm for their management development courses. Indeed, the cost of management training starts to become significant for this size of company, and here the programmes run by the Chambers of Industry and Commerce are particularly attractive. Since all companies paying **Gewerbesteuer** (trade tax) must be members of their local Chambers and must pay membership fees, these value-for-money programmes are particularly popular.

The Chambers offer a range of development programmes for all levels of management from entrepreneurs to lower managers. Teaching staff are bought in from large companies, polytechnics or universities. Programmes are taught either in the Chambers' own short-course centres or in hotels.

The management development programmes organized by the Chambers should not be regarded as second best to those run by the large companies. In fact, the Chambers have very sensitive radar for company development needs because of their close contacts with firms of all sizes. They are ideally placed to identify the latest development trends in the large companies and subsequently to provide similar, or even better, programmes for other large, medium-sized and small companies.

Indeed, the Chambers of Industry and Commerce and the Craft Chambers in West Germany represent the key element in training and development for so much of business activity. As was noted earlier, they are closely involved in initial vocational training and higher vocational training, and the natural progression of their activities into the field of management development during the 1980s met with almost universal acclaim inside the country.

If management education and management development in West Germany can be faulted at all, criticism would have to focus on the heavy emphasis on functionality found in both areas. There is little room in West German management for the generalist: the whole system is geared to producing functional specialists. MBA (Master of Business Administration) courses turning out generalist managers do not exist. Nor perhaps were such courses necessary in the past when companies were operating mainly within their own business culture, but in the light of increased outward investment by West German companies a more generalist approach to management education and development has now become desirable.

Lifelong learning

Higher vocational qualifications and management development programmes should be viewed against the background of a concerted attempt
in the country to promote the concept of lifelong learning. It is claimed
that 25 per cent of the population between the ages of nineteen and sixty-
five take part every year in some form of continuing education.
Participation rates are, however, disproportionate. Only 8 per cent of
unskilled workers were in any way involved in 1985, and in the same year
there were six times fewer participants with the general school-leaving
certificate than with tertiary level entrance qualifications.

To rectify these imbalances, the notion of **Bildungsurlaub** (extra paid
holidays for self-improvement) has been mooted. Five of the individual
states and West Berlin have legislated in favour, and Bildungsurlaub has
formed part of a few tariff agreements between trade unions and
employers' associations. While welcoming the concept of lifelong learning
and actively supporting the process of adjustment to new technologies,
the vast majority of companies oppose the notion of extra paid holidays.
They argue that their employees already work the shortest number of
hours in Europe, enjoy the longest holidays, retire as pensioners at the
lowest age, and receive the best education, training and development. It is
difficult to disagree with them.

Business and the environment

In the past twenty-five years, the business culture in West Germany has
become increasingly affected by issues connected with the environment.
Although this concern is perhaps most visibly evidenced in the country at
large by the presence of Europe's most successful ecological party, The
Greens, all West Germans are worried about air, water and ground
pollution. Business now shares this concern. While West German
companies were never exactly ecstatic about the massive investments they
were forced to make to clean up their act, they now realize that this capital
expenditure has placed them at a competitive advantage vis-à-vis many of
their neighbours in Europe. The issue of the environment will not go away
in any of the European countries, and foreign companies will subsequently
be obliged to purchase pollution control equipment, much of which has
been researched, designed and made in West Germany.

The origins of the problem

West Germany is one of the most densely-populated countries in the world. More than 60 million people inhabit the 250,000 square kilometres between the North Sea and the Alps, giving 247 persons per square kilometre compared with 24 in the United States of America. Approximately 10 per cent of the land is built up and there are only 120 areas measuring 10 kilometres by 10 kilometres which are not crossed by main roads or rail networks.

After the Second World War, industrial reconstruction progressed at a rapid pace. Economic growth rates in the 1950s and early 1960s were phenomenal; ever more manufacturing industries were set up; increasing numbers of citizens moved from the land into the new conurbations. The economic miracle duly occurred. But the miracle was built on the steel, steel-processing, chemical, pharmaceutical, and machine-tool industries, all of which took their toll of the physical environment.

In addition, the affluent society created in West Germany permitted the citizenry to indulge in a love affair with the motor car, and the high-performance car in particular, matching the high-performance society in which they were living. One of the results is that even today there is no general speed limit on the country's motorways. Another is that there are some 29 million private cars on the roads.

The political response

The first voices were raised in protest at the damage being done to the environment in the mid-1950s, but they were ignored. The initial hesitant response came from the legislators in the mid-1960s.

1965 First Clean Air Act passed by the Federal Parliament. Fears were still widespread about the effect which more radical legislation might have on the competitiveness of West German industry.

1969 Protection of the environment accepted for the first time in a Federal government declaration in Bonn.

1971 First comprehensive environmental programme published by a Federal government. In the course of the 1970s, a whole series of Acts were passed for the protection of the environment. The lead content of petrol was reduced; refuse disposal was placed under legal controls; the use of certain additives in detergents was restricted.

1975 Environmental consciousness began to spread rapidly through large sections of the population. The number of citizens' initiatives grew considerably.

1980 The Greens established themselves as a political party.

1983 The Greens entered the Federal Parliament for the first time.

1986 The **Bundesministerium für Umwelt** (BMU) (Federal Ministry of the Environment) was founded. It is supported in its work by two Federal agencies, the **Umweltbundesamt** (Federal Environment Office) and the **Bundesforschungsanstalt für Naturschutz und Landschaftsökologie** (Federal Research Institute for the Protection of Nature and Countryside Ecology).

Environmental damage

The passing of laws, the establishment of an ecology-oriented political party, the founding of a dedicated Federal Ministry, even enhanced public consciousness of the importance of a clean environment represent only the first steps in the struggle to reintroduce equilibrium in the balance of nature in West Germany. So much was destroyed or damaged in pursuit of the ideal of the affluent society via the high-performance society that the damage is truly immense.

In the opinion of many experts, 50 per cent of the bird species in West Germany's Central Uplands are threatened with extinction. The damage done to the woods and forests by air pollution is responsible for their plight. In 1982, approximately 8 per cent, in 1983 approximately 34 per cent, and in 1989 approximately 50 per cent of all the country's woodlands were either damaged or suffered from reduced vitality as a result of the effects of acid rain. This is caused after the combustion of coal, petrol and heating oil, when sulphur dioxide and nitrogen oxides combine in the air to descend as an acidic precipitation on the leaves, needles and roots of trees.

Air pollution has contributed in its turn to water contamination. Precipitations have deposited phosphates, heavy metal and halogen compounds in rivers and lakes. The nitrates used in intensive farming and present in factory effluents have only served to exacerbate the problem. The worst-affected areas in West Germany are found in the Bavarian Forest, the Fichtel Mountains and the Northern Black Forest. In some of these areas, the water has become so acidic that the ph-value has fallen by one or two degrees since the 1950s, which corresponds to a ten to twenty-fold rise in acidity.

Every inhabitant of West Germany produces annually 375 kilograms of refuse which have to be disposed of, domestic waste accounting for approximately 32 per cent of the country's total refuse of 250 million tons per year. The 365 domestic refuse disposal areas can no longer cope with such quantities, and many towns and cities have begun to incinerate on a large scale, using the excess energy for district-heating schemes. The disposal of industrial waste products is, however, more problematical, and the construction of incineration plant for special industrial waste has led to protests from the citizens most immediately affected.

The first successes

According to the Federal Environment Office, crimes against the environment are responsible for DM 20 billion of damage every year. Here not only large companies which introduce poisonous effluent into a river or stream are to blame; equally culpable are those drivers sneaking off into the woods to change the oil in their cars and tipping the waste onto the ground. West German police statistics in 1987 registered approximately 18,000 cases of air pollution, water contamination or environmentally-harmful waste disposal. The clear-up rate for the approximately 16,000 cases in 1986 was 75 per cent.

The most spectacular successes have been achieved in the area of air pollution (Table 1.7).

Table 1.7   *Emissions in West Germany (in millions of tonnes)*

	1966	1974	1982	1986
Sulphur dioxide	3.4	3.6	2.9	2.2
Carbon monoxide	12.3	13.7	10.1	8.9
Nitric oxide	1.9	2.6	2.8	2.8
Dust	1.8	0.9	0.6	0.5

Source: Globus

Mainly responsible for the improved air quality in West Germany are the 165 so-called desulphurizer plant which had been installed at the seventy-two sites for coal-burning power stations by 1988. The operators of such plant will have spent DM 22 billion by 1995 on the installation of sulphur dioxide and nitric oxide filters. By 1993, these measures will have led to reductions of sulphur dioxide emissions of 33 per cent and nitric oxide emissions of 37 per cent. What is more, the technology was invented, designed and refined in West Germany, with Deutsche Babcock being particularly successful in this field.

The reaction of business

Even at the beginning of the 1980s, protection of the environment was considered by both employers' associations and trade unions to be hostile to employment. It was assumed that the additional costs of measures for the protection of the environment would lead to reductions in the incomes of employees if not actually to job losses. In the meantime, there has been a change of heart on both sides. Protection of the environment is no longer regarded as a job-killer but as job-neutral, and latterly even as job-creating.

In 1985, it was calculated that approximately 300,000 employees were engaged directly or indirectly in work connected with protection of the environment. The sector of the economy associated with environmental protection was growing at 14 per cent per annum above the average for other sectors. Even back in 1980, gross sales of DM 16 billion had been achieved, 25 per cent of which were exported. This resulted in the preservation of 170,000 to 180,000 jobs.

In March 1985, the Confederation of German Trade Unions presented its programme on protection of the environment. It demanded for the following five years environmentally-effective investments of DM 50 billion. The aim of the demands was to avoid further stress on the environment and to bring about a drastic reduction in existing stresses. Protection of the environment was, according to the Confederation of German Trade Unions, to be achieved by 'quality growth', and not by a virtual renunciation of industrial society as proposed by The Greens.

The myth that protection of the environment, because of the expense involved, destroys jobs was finally laid to rest in West Germany by 1989 at the latest. It was revealed then that the immediate production of goods for environmental protection accounted for 190,000 jobs in the country. The production value of goods and services connected with the environment was estimated at DM 23 billion annually. Again in 1989, 7.2 per cent of total investments by manufacturing industry was earmarked for investments in environmental measures. A total of 440,000 jobs were associated either directly or indirectly with protection of the environment. Growth estimates for further employment in this sector of the economy were approximately 16 per cent per annum.

It is predicted that, by 1993, 50 per cent of West Germany company capital expenditure will be devoted to the environment and to safety. Moreover, West Germany currently has the highest standards for pollution control in the EC. As legislation throughout the EC becomes harmonized, this is one area where standards will not be reduced to the lowest common denominator. On the contrary, standards will be forced to rise as the degree of environmental consciousness common to the citizenry in West Germany spreads to other EC countries and beyond. What West Germany is investing today, others will eventually have to match – and almost certainly at higher costs. Moreover, the West Germans were the first in the field and are better placed than anyone else to export not only their products but their services as well.

The response of business to the EC's single market

The response of the West German business community to the completion of the EC's **Binnenmarkt** (single market) appears to have been a muted one. Up to March 1988, there had been no large-scale publicity campaign, and a French business journal even went so far as to accuse the West Germans of a 'conspiracy of silence' on the subject. But such accusations ignore the discretion favoured by the business culture in the country. Despite the late start to the nationwide publicity campaign, preparations have been going ahead quietly at the individual state level, with conferences organized by employers' associations and trade unions. Moreover, coordinating efforts at the national level have been placed in the all-pervasive hand of the Chambers of Industry and Commerce. Nothing could be more certain: the West Germans will be ready for the challenges posed by the end of 1992 and beyond.

Many West German business people perceive little need for large publicity onslaughts. They are confident of their strengths; aware of their weaknesses; look forward to the opportunities; and are only mildly concerned about the threats. What is more, certain strategies have already been put in place and appear to be successful.

Strengths

The Germans have fostered a strong domestic manufacturing base ever since the country first became industrialized. They never ruled over a large colonial empire, and very few industrial goods were actually produced in the colonies which they did possess. Production was retained back home in Germany. The consequence today is that manufacturing in West Germany and exporting from West Germany represent two of the country's undeniable strengths.

The concept of Technik, the art and science of manufacturing useful artefacts, is so widespread in the country that West Germany can be regarded as a manufacturing-friendly society. Indeed, this is borne out by the contribution of manufacturing to the economy which, together with construction, accounts for some 42 per cent of GDP. Moreover, the lion's share of the 2.8 per cent of GDP spent on R & D is targeted at applied research in manufacturing, thus underpinning the production orientation of the economy.

Manufacturing and exporting are synonymous for firms of all sizes, so the completion of the EC's single market holds few terrors for the country's production companies. West Germany is already responsible for over half of all intra-EC exports, and companies are confident that the figure of 53 per cent can be maintained or even improved. Given that West Germans export more per capita than any nation in the world, including the Japanese, this confidence appears to be justified.

A third area of strength is to be found in the country's financial institutions. The record of the Bundesbank in protecting the currency and in combating inflation is probably superior to that of any other central bank in the twenty-four OECD countries. Moreover, the Big Three private commercial banks are held to be among the fourteen most powerful banks in the world in terms of their financial strength and security. Nor have they been dilatory in adopting certain strategies for the completion of the single market, as has already been seen.

Human capital represents a fourth area of strength. West Germany's workforce is probably the best equipped in Europe to withstand the challenges of the future. Starting with an excellent public education system, and continuing with either vocational training or entry into higher education, only some 5 per cent of young people fail to progress to one or the other. In addition, the whole of the education and training effort in the country is supported by business through a deep commitment to the development ethos of its employees.

Perhaps this same commitment is partly responsible for a West German strength in a fifth area – that of industrial relations. Here the consensus between employers and trade unions, though brittle at times, has produced a business climate which is envied by many other countries. The West German record on industrial disputes is matched in Europe only by Switzerland and Austria. Moreover, the country's long-established tradition of industrial democracy through powerful works' councils has been reinforced by a system of worker codetermination on supervisory boards which, despite initial serious misgivings on the part of employers and trade unions alike, has accomplished much over the decade in which it has been in existence.

A final area of strength is represented by West Germany's geographical location at the very heart of the EC. The country has common borders with five of the EC member states – Denmark, the Netherlands, Belgium, Luxembourg and France. The physical proximity to markets, with all its implications for transport and distribution costs, could assume even more significance if Austria and Switzerland, another two of West Germany's immediate neighbours, eventually join the EC. Indeed, West Germany could become without question the dominant economic power in Europe if Hungary and Poland, let alone East Germany, succeed in forming closer economic links with the EC.

Weaknesses

The country's weaknesses in the manufacturing sector are primarily associated with a decline in profitability over recent years. Here high corporate taxation at 70 per cent of retained earnings contributed little to the attraction of West Germany as a location for industry. Company profitability, especially in the manufacturing sector, is not enhanced either by high real unit labour costs or by inflexible labour markets. Small wonder, then, that domestic companies have recently failed to match erstwhile high rates of investment, and foreign companies did not invest proportionately during the 1980s.

Taxation is also detracting from West Germany as a financial centre. The 0.1–0.25 per cent stock exchange turnover tax and the on-off 10 per cent withholding tax on dividend and fixed-interest payments have both prevented Frankfurt from competing effectively with London as Europe's premier financial marketplace.

The services sector is bedevilled by overregulation. The **Güterfernverkehrsamt** (Road Haulage Office) has a staff of 900 to monitor the activities of domestic and foreign trucking companies. Similarly, the Bundespost still enjoys a virtual monopoly in the telecommunications field despite recent changes in its status. These are just two of the areas of the service sector which must be opened up to international competition by the completion of the EC's single market.

While the manufacturing and finance sectors were expecting some fiscal relief from the much-vaunted 'tax reform of the century', which was due in 1990, the companies in the services sector were looking forward to the report of the deregulation commission, which was also awaited in 1990. Federal government action would then follow after due consideration and consultation. By then, however, the services sector might have been affected more by legislation arising from Brussels than from Bonn.

One area of weakness in the West German business culture which is reputed to be as serious as any concerned with the individual sectors of the economy relates to the alleged lack of a spirit of entrepreneurship. Critics point to the country's entrepreneurs at the bottom of the management buyout league in Europe, with only thirty-six recorded by the end of 1988, and speculate that West Germany might fail to take full advantage of the single market because the business community is risk-averse.

The critics are wrong. The West German business culture was enriched after the Second World War by many entrepreneurs. Without them there would have been no economic miracle. But in West Germany today the older entrepreneur is sometimes regarded as a capitalist, exploiting workers and bribing politicians. Nevertheless, many older entrepreneurs still exist throughout the country, and they want to leave their businesses to someone! These are the entrepreneurs who developed their businesses after the Second World War and who now wish to retire. Very often they have no members of their family willing to continue their businesses because their younger relations have taken up different careers. But they do want their businesses to survive, and here opportunities present themselves for domestic or foreign companies to acquire these firms.

The attitude of the manager towards entrepreneurship is different. The manager's overriding attribute is loyalty to the company-owner. He – and it is predominantly he – would never dare ask the owner if he wanted to sell the company to him because this would be construed as disloyal and could constitute grounds for dismissal. Moreover, the manager is looking for security for both himself and his family. Being a manager means belonging to the workforce and enjoying the same privileges of security. Finally, contemporary West German society values the social standing of a senior manager more highly than that of an entrepreneur. A position as a member of the management board of a large company is more prestigious than being the owner of a medium-sized company.

Nonetheless, the number of new businesses established in West Germany has been rising steadily over the past decade, though many quickly fail. In 1980, there were approximately 160,000 start-ups; in 1985, 290,000; and in 1989, 300,000. West Germams, it would appear, still possess an entrepreneurial spirit, but prefer to set up their own businesses rather than indulge in complex buyouts.

Opportunities

Large companies, it is commonly believed, will be the ones to profit most, at least initially, from the completion of the EC's single market. Here West German business is well placed, with 3600 officially-designated major companies. Apart from the sheer number and critical mass of these companies, it must not be forgotten that the equity holdings of the Big Three banks in many major firms render them virtually immune from hostile takeover bids. Conversely, many large West German companies are cash-rich as a result of the country's accountancy and taxation provisions, so they can take over companies at home or in other EC countries without recourse to either bond or equity markets, provided they do not fall foul of mergers and acquisitions legislation. If the big spend on R & D by the country's major companies does not produce the desired results, then ideas or even brands can be bought with cold cash.

Although successes will differ from one sector to another, most large West German manufacturing companies are supremely confident of their chances in a free market. To name but one sector, the large chemicals companies, Hoechst, Bayer and BASF, are absolutely sure that they are unbeatable in the EC's single market.

Threats

In contrast, the **Mittelstand** (small and medium-sized businesses) are slightly more anxious about prospects in the single market. Here, 1,900,000 companies, each with fewer than 500 workers, are responsible for roughly half of the country's GDP, employ two-thirds of the workforce, train four-fifths of all the apprentices, and register most of the patents. Although they may have been innovative, resilient and export-oriented in the past, they are now mildly nervous about the new competition which they will face in their home markets. They worry about foreign penetration of these markets and are only just beginning to realize how protected they have been hitherto by standards and norms so painstakingly concocted.

To date West Germany has rigorously enforced a plethora of competition-frustrating industrial standards, the most notorious of which are the **Deutsche Industrie-Normen** (DIN) (German Industrial Standards). Any country wishing to export manufactured items to West Germany has been obliged in the past to have the product tested for compliance with the appropriate standard. In the single market, industrial standards will be harmonized, so that exporters from one country do not feel disadvantaged by spurious regulations imposed by others.

Some small and medium-sized West German companies feel threatened because the protection of their standards may be taken away from them. They fear that, in the harmonization of industrial standards, agreement will be reached, yet again, at the level of the lowest common denominator. But here the West Germans have taken pre-emptive action: they have seen to it that over half of the 120 separate EC standards committees are chaired by their fellow-countrymen!

Strategies

The strategies of West German companies in anticipation of the single market appear to be two-fold: secure the home base by diversification and expand abroad, especially in other EC countries.

To secure the domestic position, acquisitions and mergers rose steeply in the late 1980s. There have been few takeovers anywhere in the world in recent years as phenomenal as Daimler-Benz's of AEG, Dornier, MTU and MBB, but the number of smaller deals has also been on the increase. In 1987, there were some 887 completions, and in 1988 1100 mergers and acquisitions were registered with the Federal Cartel Office, with concentration becoming particularly intense in the food sector. They have been occasioned by the conviction that size is what is needed to face the challenges of the single market.

Expansion abroad saw seventy-eight acquisitions by West German companies in 1986, 137 in 1987, and 180 in 1988. The focus of much of the merger and acquisition activity has been France. Feldmühle, Europe's largest paper manufacturer, bought out two competitors there; Klein, Schanzlin & Becker, market-leading pump-makers, acquired Pompes Guinard; Bosch took a holding in Jeumont-Schneider; Degussa purchased Sarget; Daimler-Benz acquired a holding in Matra.

West German companies have not been the most active in Europe in terms of acquisitions in other countries in anticipation of the single market, but they have been very selective. Circumspect as ever, they have been at pains to play to their strengths. In general, however, they appear very confident of their prospects in the single market. As the Bonn correspondent of *The Economist* pointed out in the 12 November 1988, issue of the journal: 'West German businessmen seem pretty smug about 1992. Many companies reckon they are so good at selling to foreigners (hence Germany's chronic trade surplus) that the creation of a single EC-wide market will mainly mean scope to sell more.'

References and suggestions for further reading

Ambrosius, G. (1984), *Der Staat als Unternehmer*, Göttingen: Vandenhoeck and Ruprecht.

Ardagh, J. (1987), *Germany and the Germans*, London: Hamilton.

Böhler, W. (1984), *Betriebliche Weiterbildung und Bildungsurlaub*, Düsseldorf: Centaurus.

Burtenshaw, D. (1984), *The Economic Geography of Germany*, London: Macmillan.

Capital, various issues between 1982 and 1989.

Childs, D. and Johnson, J. (1981), *West Germany – Politics and Society*, London: Croom Helm.

Conradt, D. P. (1978), *The German Polity*, New York: Longman.

Cullingford, E. C. M. (1976), *Trade Unions in Germany*, London: West View Press.

Economist, The, various issues between 1982 and 1989.

Economist Intelligence Unit (1989), *West Germany Country Profile 1989–90*, London: The Economist Intelligence Unit.

Economist Intelligence Unit (1989), *West Germany Country Report*, London: The Economist Intelligence Unit.

Financial Times, various issues between 1982 and 1989.

Handy, C. et al. (1988), *Making Managers*, London: Pitman.

Hübner, E. and Rudolfs, H-H. (1989), *Jahrbuch der Bundesrepublik Deutschland 1988/89*, Munich: Beck/DTV.

Investor's Chronicle, various issues between 1982 and 1989.

Jäkel, E. and Junge, W. (1978), *Die Deutschen Industrie- und Handelskammern und der Deutsche Industrie- und Handelstag*, Munich: Droste.

Kloss, G. (1989), *West Germany: An Introduction*, Basingstoke: Macmillan.

Koch, K. (1989), *West Germany Today*, London: Routledge.

Lawrence, P. (1980), *Managers and Management in West Germany*, London: Croom Helm.

Manager Magazin, various issues between 1982 and 1989.

OECD Economic Surveys, West Germany, various years between 1982 and 1989.

Oldham, K. M. (1981), *Accounting Systems and Practices in Europe*, London: Gower.

Owen-Smith, E. (1983), *The West German Economy*, London: Croom Helm.

Price Waterhouse (1988), *Doing Business in West Germany*, London: Price Waterhouse.

Römer, K., Dreikandt, U. K. and Wullenkord, C. (1987), *Facts about Germany*, Gütersloh: Bertelsmann.

Schuster, D. (1977), *Der Deutsche Gewerkschaftsbund*, Düsseldorf: Droste.

Smith, G. (1982), *Democracy in Western Germany*, Aldershot: Gower.

Spiegel, Der, various issues between 1982 and 1989.

Times, The, various issues between 1982 and 1989.

Wall Street Journal, The, various issues between 1982 and 1989.

Wirtschaftswoche, Die, various issues between 1982 and 1989.

Witte, E., Kallmann, A. and Sachs, G. (1980), *Führungskräfte der Wirtschaft*, Cologne: Poeschel.

Zeit, Die, various issues between 1982 and 1989.

2 The business culture in France
Colin Gordon

Introduction

As in the United Kingdom, over the last decade business in France has been faced with a drastic upheaval in both the political and economic environment. In the United Kingdom, emphasis on the supply-side of the economy throughout the Thatcher years has led to the enterprise culture with companies experiencing fewer and fewer constraints particularly in terms of finance and labour relations. In France, however, the sea-change has been of a different order which is typified by the French obsession with the idea that since the first oil shock of 1974, France has been in a state of **crise** (crisis) from which it is only now just emerging.

During that time business had to come to terms with the realization that the **Trente Glorieuses**, thirty years of constant growth since 1945, which in the 1960s even exceeded that of West Germany, were over. Profits and investment rapidly declined in a country which obstinately refused to wake up to reality and to cut back on paying its citizens enough to maintain their sacrosanct standard of living. Businesses, and not individuals, were made to pay for this 'crisis' through indexed wages and spiralling debt and social charges.

An ill-timed reflation of the economy by a Socialist government in 1981 brought yet more grief and it was only at the end of the 1980s that French business began to recover slowly from the changed circumstances. Hence, there is a general awareness that there is some considerable catching-up needed, as France has lagged behind its major industrial competitors.

So business culture in France has not been characterized by gradual change, but by a long period of deeply-disturbing events shaped both by external developments and domestic policies.

Yet despite this setback to an economy which, according to a Hudson Institute report of the early 1970s, was set to become the Japan of Europe, France is bouncing back energetically and has underlying strengths on which to draw:

- The fourth-largest economy of the OECD countries behind the USA, Japan and West Germany, but ahead of Italy and the United Kingdom.

- A rate of inflation in 1989 of 3.5 per cent, growth of 3.5 per cent, increase in exports of 15 per cent.
- Investment levels back to those of 1973, due to the sharp upturn in companies' profitability.
- A nationwide consensus on the importance of education and training, proof of which is the fact that France is one of the few EC countries actually increasing expenditure on education.
- A degree of cooperation between industry and government.
- A concerted effort by many companies to become more internationally-oriented. Overseas investment has increased by a factor of five over the last five years, as companies favour size as their number one objective.
- Political stability with policies more of a centrist, social democratic hue than of a distinct right or left dogmatism (the ruling Socialist party having no overall majority, for example).
- A greater willingness to take risks – management buyouts are now common currency – in a general climate of public opinion which has grown to be enthusiastic about the business world after a long tradition of aversion.
- The emergence of a new type of self-made business leader to challenge the highly-élitist structure of French management.
- Increasing use by large companies of share capital in preference to debt, thus creating an upsurge in the importance of Paris as a strong financial centre.

Considerable concern and question marks remain, however, in a number of areas:

- Is French industry still less competitive than its main industrial competitors? (Reducing the costs of materials, labour and inventories is hence the major preoccupation of manufacturing concerns.)
- Although numerically weak, trade unions have begun to flex their considerable muscle in the public sector, particularly over increased pay after some five years of wage control. This movement is now spilling over into the private sector and the political and social peace in France may be shattered by industrial unrest.
- Although temporarily stabilized at 9.5 per cent of the working population in 1989, unemployment may be difficult to contain without sustained growth.
- The élitist management education system may not be turning out the right calibre of flexible, international manager, capable of responding quickly enough to shorter product life cycles.
- The same system, with its rigid equation of qualifications with hierarchical grades, is suppressing the aspirations of the supervisory and lower grades to management status.

- Many French companies, albeit dynamic, are undercapitalized and lack the critical size necessary to compete in the European and global markets post-1992. They are, therefore, easy prey to foreign corporate raiders.
- In spite of the increased overseas investment, managers lack the international vision and experience of their counterparts in West Germany, the United Kingdom, USA, etc.
- A worrying increase in the trade deficit in manufactured goods indicates a failure to concentrate on certain important sectors in both consumer and capital goods.
- The level of R & D investment in private companies is insufficient.
- In its attempt to reduce its budgetary deficit, the state is short of cash to inject into the sizable nationalized sector to enable it to make necessary overseas acquisitions.
- Is the state, in its commitment to 'no more nationalizations, nor more privatizations' going to continue to pursue an industrial policy or are market forces going to be allowed a freer rein?

The scene is set in France, however, for an almost complete restoration to full health of the economy and for a transformation of traditions, values and strategies which will enable France to benefit more substantially not only from the single European market but from the globalization of markets.

Business and government

It has often been said that in France market forces have never been allowed to function freely due to a long succession of interventionist policies in all aspects of economic and industrial activity. Perhaps more than in any other OECD country, central government, therefore, has played a crucial and all-pervasive role in determining the major directions in which business activities have moved. Decentralization in the 1980s has shifted some of the centres of decision-making but, nevertheless, central government continues to be the major determinant of policy.

Central government

Three features in particular stand out when examining the role of central government since the Second World War. First, the importance attached to a system of five-year economic plans, especially during the Trente Glorieuses. Second, largely in response to the West German economic miracle and the American challenge of the 1960s, the French authorities devised a system of industrial policies specifically designed to convert inefficient industries and develop industries of the future. This took the form of mergers and takeovers engineered by a policy of tax incentives, medium and long-term credits allocated through a state-directed financial sector and direct government intervention. This was the policy of national champions, and such present-day companies as CGE, Péchiney, Saint-Gobain, Rhône-Poulenc and SNIAS (Aérospatiale) were all moulded during this period. Third, the fact that from 1958 until 1981, with one or two minor exceptions, France enjoyed an uninterrupted period of one-party rule, the rise of the Socialist party as an alternative government being of quite recent date – the early 1970s.

The initial plans were limited to building up industry after the devastation of war but in the boom years of the 1960s they became so sophisticated and all-embracing – they covered not only all macroeconomic variables but also industrial inputs and outputs – that they generated much interest abroad, and France was considered to have discovered the secret of managing effectively the complexities of a national economy. Internal crises – the return of one million **pieds noirs**, the white settlers of Algeria, in 1962, for example – and international constraints such as that imposed by the first oil shock, eventually blew some of the later plans off course. Planning lost much of its importance and the 1970s were typified by erratic stop-go policies implemented in reaction to the new conditions of reduced growth. Under ex-President Giscard d'Estaing and his Prime Minister, growth slumped to -2 per cent in 1975 (the first minus figure since the war), investment fell sharply and both bankruptcies and unemployment increased dramatically. Under Raymond Barre, Chirac's successor, there was an attempt both to combat the immediate crisis with an austerity programme of higher taxation and a temporary freeze on wages and prices and to initiate a longer-term restructuring of the economy to bring it more into line with the country which increasingly became France's obsession, West Germany. (Even today, all leading indicators are compared avidly with those of West Germany.)

The result was a dramatically high level of unemployment (1½ million in 1981) and the austerity programme did not reduce inflation (13 per cent in 1980). The franc held steady, however, due partially to a growth rate slightly above the Western average (GNP grew by 1½ per cent in 1980). A healthy surplus in the trade balance was wiped out by the second oil crisis of 1979.

This, then, was the situation inherited by the in-coming Socialist government, with François Mitterand as President. There is some argument about the opportuneness of the economic policy of reflation which he then decided to pursue. Most observers consider reflation against the stream of a severe world recession was akin to harakiri. Others, particularly the French themselves, deem it to have been purely unlucky in its timing. Certainly, its objectives were clear and laudable: increased growth, reduced unemployment, reduced wage differentials and maintenance of purchasing power. To achieve these objectives there was an increase in the legal minimum wage (the SMIC), an increase in social benefits, a reduction in the working week, retirement for all at sixty, and a fifth paid holiday week – a heady cocktail which rapidly led to increased production costs, yet more inflation, and the resulting loss of competitiveness combined with the increase in demand led to a chronic trade balance deficit and three devaluations of the franc. For the business world, the effects were catastrophic. Profits and investment levels had been steadily declining throughout the 1970s and the recourse to crippling bank borrowing to cover ever-increasing costs led to a lack of profitability from which companies have only just emerged.

One other aspect of Socialist policy must be mentioned: the extension of the already considerable, nationalized industrial and financial sectors. Classical Socialist ideology no doubt played its part but there was also some sincerity in the conviction that private industry had failed to invest in the 1970s and that the state would have to take control, if France was to maintain a powerful industrial presence in the world with the necessary financial support to sustain it.

Nationalization was no stranger to France. Whereas the issue aroused passionate opposition in the British parliament in the immediate post-war years, a similar programme in France during the same period aroused little debate, a **dirigiste** industrial policy (whether through planning or nationalization) becoming an acceptable, even desirable, norm to back up private industry. Even under the continuing domination of parties of the right in government, and particularly during the 'national champion' years of the 1970s, nationalization via takeovers by existing state companies continued unabated. Despite their shortcomings the existence of state companies was never challenged, particularly since investment was considerably greater in the state than in the private sector (especially in energy and telecommunications) and many firms depended on it as subcontractors. But in 1982–83, the process reached its zenith with eventually, in 1984, the public sector representing:

- 16 per cent of the working population (excluding agriculture).
- 28 per cent of turnover.
- 36 per cent of investment.
- 23 per cent of exports.
- 91 per cent of bank deposits.

The whole vast experiment of the early Socialist years failed catastrophically, however, and in 1983, the Socialists were forced to execute a spectacular U-turn by freezing prices and incomes, tightening exchange controls and increasing taxation, including a compulsory loan. Many jobs created in the state sector were precisely those to go first and perhaps the greatest sign of the true significance of the U-turn was the new-found belief by the Socialists that only companies, not the state, could create wealth and therefore jobs. Indeed, it can be said that the recent love affair of the French with the world of business can be traced to this period. They would not have believed parties of the right but if Socialists said business was acceptable then they would accept it.

By the time of the general election in 1986, then, the economy was being nursed back to health with the slower rate of increase in costs of the factors of production and the fall in imported raw material prices gradually contributing to lower inflation. Reduced demand plus an effective policy to reduce energy imports through the substitution of nuclear energy (80 per cent of electricity in France is now generated by nuclear means) transformed the trade deficit in both goods and services into a surplus by 1986.

The new right-wing government under Jacques Chirac (with a Socialist president still in power, however) was an ardent advocate of less state spending and deregulation and liberalization. Privatization of not only the newly-nationalized companies but also of those which had been in the state sector since immediately before or after the war, became a burning issue, with CGE, Saint-Gobain in the industrial sector, Société Générale and Paribas in banking, Agence Havas (advertising) and the television channel TFI reverting into private hands before the October crash of 1987. Since then Indosuez and Matra have also been privatized.

Liberalization in particular meant a dismantling of supply-side rigidities, particularly the necessity for companies to seek the authorization of the local Inspector of Labour before shedding labour, reduction in taxation and total freedom in prices except for pharmaceuticals and oil products. The reduction of the government deficit, business efficiency and market forces became the driving forces, and many in France, with its long tradition of dirigisme, became concerned whether these were right policies for France.

The highest marginal rate of personal income tax fell from 72.4 per cent in 1986 to 56.8 per cent in 1988, the rate of corporation tax was reduced from 50 per cent to 42 per cent (now 40 per cent if dividends are paid, 38 per cent if not) and the **taxe professionnelle** (payroll tax) has been progressively cut. Offset against this, however, social insurance contributions were increased in 1987 and these, combined with other forms of taxation, both direct and indirect, contribute to France having the heaviest burden of taxes among the major OECD countries.

The resolve to continue a public-sector pay policy which has a knock-on effect in the private sector increasingly led to business making greater profits and beginning to reach investment levels of the early 1970s. Unemployment still stubbornly refused to fall, however, as growth in 1986–7 remained sluggish and France failed to take as much advantage of the upturn in the world economy as other OECD countries. Fear of another dramatic turn of events as witnessed in 1983, together with the chastening discipline of membership of the European Monetary System and being hence locked into West Germany's own meagre growth performance, forestalled any idea of expansion through reflation.

In 1988, President Mitterand was elected for a second term and a general election was called. A landslide victory was predicted for the Socialists but they surprisingly failed to win an overall majority and are forced to seek the support of members of the Centrist parties. Right-wing parties, particularly the Gaullists, are in a state of complete disarray, the Communists are a spent force and hence France is governed in 1990 by the politics of moderation and consensus.

In industrial policy terms, Mitterand has declared there will be no more nationalizations or privatizations, but there is much evidence to support the view that, although management of the state sector is at arm's-length, the government still takes vital strategic decisions, particularly those concerning acquisitions where further capital is needed.

In economic terms, France considers itself to be back on the road to complete fitness, provided the international environment remains favourable. Stocks are low, demand is high with domestic supply increasingly capable of coping with it. As long as prices and salaries hold steady, increasing competitiveness and extra capacity will begin to relieve import penetration. Growth rates show much improvement (Table 2.1).

Business investment stood at 9.3 per cent for 1988 (in comparison with an average annual rate of −0.2 per cent in the period 1980–6) and the inflation rate of 3.5 per cent remains well below that of other OECD countries and similar to that of West Germany (see page 21). If wages continue to be controlled successfully (4 per cent in the private sector) it is predicted that this figure could dip under 3 per cent.

The main question marks remain over whether more sustained growth will contain unemployment, forecast by INSEE to rise to 14 per cent, 3.5 million by 1993, despite the creation of 500,000 new jobs in 1988–9; worsening social discontent in most state and some private sectors as workers tire of wages depressed by the rigour of government policy; and the steadily-worsening trade deficit on manufacturing goods (the first ever was recorded in 1987) as France slowly loses market shares and remains insufficiently specialized in its exports. These facts point to how much France has come to be highly exposed to the world economy, and the years

Table 2.1   *French growth rates (1979–89)*

Year	(%)
1979	3.2
1980	1.6
1981	1.2
1982	2.5
1983	0.7
1984	1.3
1985	1.7
1986	2.1
1987	2.3
1988	4.3
1989	4.0

Source: OECD

until 1993 will decide whether it is capable of meeting the challenge of increasing external forces, both within the single market and worldwide. A recent report by the Bain Consulting Group in Paris suggests that although aware of the challenge and determined to compete fiercely on the world stage, French companies suffer a number of handicaps. Reference will be made to this report later (see page 103).

Business and the economy

The tertiary sector, as in the United Kingdom but less so, has grown rapidly in France to represent some 60 per cent of GDP. Manufacturing industry has inexorably declined to around 30 per cent of GDP but France has not allowed whole swathes of industry to go to the wall, considering it strategically vital to retain interests not only in aircraft manufacturing, electronics and defence equipment but also in space, consumer electronics and a sizable indigenous car industry.

Manufacturing

Unlike West Germany, however, French products are losing market share, due partially to poor price competitiveness but *more* particularly to lack of domestic capacity capable of meeting export demand and stemming import penetration. Failure to invest in the 1970s and early 1980s on account of excessive wage costs, as has been seen, is one direct cause of this situation. Another is the hitherto poverty of capital, resulting from lack of profitability and limited external sources. Whereas West Germany's manufacturing investment increased between 1975 and 1987 by 44 per cent, France could only manage 14.3 per cent. R & D has fared better in recent years rising from 1.46 per cent of GDP in 1975 to 2.28 per cent in 1987, figures which again are a poor comparison with West Germany's 2.1 per cent and 2.71 per cent between the same two years. This is only part of the picture, however, since a large proportion of that R & D expenditure has been by the state in a highly-targeted narrow band of industries (e.g. electronics) and has not been across the board by both state and private companies, as in West Germany. Small and medium-size companies (**Petites et Moyennes Entreprises** – PME) in particular have lost out, with very little benefit accruing to them from vast national projects. In 1983, however, the government introduced a research tax credit scheme which has increased the number of PMEs investing in R & D. In 1989, there was yet more discussion of how to bring PMEs' efforts up to West German standards, with priority areas being JESSI, high-definition TV, the 'lean-burn' engine, agribusiness and new materials. Other forms of investment, in marketing, for example, have been inadequate, too, with French goods not enjoying good press in either West Germany or Switzerland in terms of sales promotion and advertising.

Compared with other major OECD economies, France has few real strengths in the manufacturing sector, except in transport equipment and metalworking. Indeed, France's gradual loss of comparative advantage reveals another weakness of its manufacturing sector – failure generally to spot in which sectors world demand was growing and prices falling. According to the OECD it has thus had a tendency to remain specialized in exporting highly-priced, high-technology goods for which world demand is relatively declining. In addition, it has shunned head-on competition in the more dynamic markets of the USA, Europe and Japan in favour of the often captive markets of its former colonies in Africa where a greater relative percentage of its high-technology goods are exported.

Iron and Steel

Although hard hit by Barre's attempt to restructure industry in the late 1970s and in spite of record losses in 1983, France's and Europe's leading steelmaker in terms of production, Usinor Sacilor, can now match the profits of British Steel (4.5 billion French francs in 1988). 1987–9 were boom years throughout Europe but the 1990s could see casualties in a sector still suffering from overcapacity, particularly in West Germany.

Hence Usinor Sacilor, like its major European competitors, is banking on increased specialization and market share via overseas acquisition to protect itself against an eventual downturn.

Vehicle building

Despite domestic shares of 24.2 per cent for Renault and 35.3 per cent for PSA (Peugeot-Citröen), leading positions amongst the European car manufacturers (number 6 with 10.5 per cent and number 3 with 12 per cent respectively) and a return to healthy profits, the French car industry still faces a number of problems.

Protected by a 3 per cent annual limit on new Japanese registrations, Peugeot and Renault have fought a losing battle to keep out British-made Nissan Bluebirds. They have accepted the inevitability of a sharp increase in Japanese penetration to maybe 8–9 per cent with the dismantling of trade barriers, but are still pressing for some transitional quota after 1992 to enable them to adopt new manufacturing methods, speed up product development and launch more joint ventures. Both firms support higher debt levels than their other European counterparts and despite drastic labour reductions and other cost-cutting measures, may well be vulnerable over the next three to four years, particularly if unrest in Peugeot over wages and conditions spills over into Renault, too. Finally, underlying all this, there is an already perceptible increase in import penetration (40 per cent) by foreign makes, giving the lie to the often-heard statement that 'the French only buy French'. An interesting comment on the situation is that any merger between the two is considered completely out of the question in Paris, with each side preferring joint ventures with foreign manufacturers in preference to attempting a marriage between the state-run, highly-centralized Renault and the private, more dispersed Peugeot.

In commercial vehicles, France shows a weakness characteristic of many other sectors, its overconcentration on the domestic market, with RVI, Renault's truck division, having 42 per cent of the French market, but only 12.3 per cent of the European market. Despite a creditable comeback from the abyss of the early 1980s, and being Europe's number two manufacturer in production terms, both technically and in terms of reliability, RVI trucks are not up to Mercedes and Volvo standards. In addition, if **cabotage** (permission to pick up and set down loads within another country) is allowed in the EC, this will particularly favour Dutch road haulage firms with their lower labour and fuel costs and therefore their vehicle suppliers DAF, Mercedes, Volvo and Scania, to the detriment of RVI.

Electronics

With an annual turnover of FF 50 billion, Alcatel (part of CGE) is the world's second-largest manufacturer of telecommunications equipment and represents one of the flagships of the French economy.

Thomson, now world number two behind Hughes-General Motors in defence electronics and number one in Europe for radar and sonar equipment, again is considered to be too French, with 95 per cent of its employees in France and 60 per cent of production exported in a sector where customers are requiring more and more local production and where not only overall size counts, but also size per market.

A major disadvantage arising from France's policy of the 1960s to withdraw from NATO and to plough its own furrow for reasons of national independence has been that French arms manufacturers have not had access to NATO specifications. While Third World markets were buoyant, this situation was of less significance but as they become more and more saturated, French companies must turn to acquisition in Europe (e.g. Thomson's takeover of Philips' defence interests) to plug the gap. Certainly France sees the whole defence industry as one of its strengths to be pursued, as other leading manufacturers are divesting themselves of their defence interests in a climate of greater détente and arms limitation talks.

Aerospace

The recent merger of Thomson's and Aérospatiale's avionics divisions puts the new company Sextant Avionique in fourth position in the world and points to the state's role (both companies are nationalized) in galvanizing key industries into assuming internationally competitive positions.

The sector as a whole represents one of the stars of the French economy (number three in the world, number one in Europe in terms of turnover and exports) and remains firmly in state hands (Aérospatiale, SNECMA, Dassault). France's resolute intention to remain in the space sector with the Ariane launcher points to its deeply-held conviction that Europe cannot neglect its spin-offs (manufacture in space of new products) unless it wants to become a mere subcontractor of the USA (the old bogey of the 1960s and the 'American challenge').

Chemicals

The chemical industry in particular was one of the industries completely restructured by the Socialist government in 1982 but in spite of now showing a profit after many years of losses, there is still a considerable gap between the French chemical industry and its main competitors. Rhône-Poulenc, the largest of the French companies is, for example, only half the size of BASF, Bayer and Hoechst. Size is less important, however, than position in each speciality market, but even here France is not so strong. Paradoxically, therefore, France is the second-largest producer of plastics in Europe but no one French group is number one or number two in its field. In pharmaceutics, Rhône-Poulenc is only number twenty in the world.

The industry is destined for yet another bout of restructuring, therefore, with Rhône-Poulenc aiming to be number five in the world and, as has been seen to be a recurrent theme in French industry, a general intention to break out from being too concentrated on the French market. With Europe restructuring, France sees it imperative to be part of the trend but, fearful of losing its independence, is not seeking alliances with other European companies, particularly the West German companies.

Here again, the state has the whip hand, owning six French chemical companies (Rhône-Poulenc, Atorkem, Orkem, Entreprise Minière et Chimique, Total Chimie, Société Nationale des Poudres et Explosifs): a neat illustration of the ambiguity and dilemma of state control in France. The government is determined to allow heads of state companies to use their initiative in restructuring the industry as long as competitiveness is reinforced. Heads will roll if it is thought that companies are sitting back on old protected positions – **chasses gardées**, as they are known in French, the term for protected hunting grounds. Thus the autonomy of the chairmen of these state companies has its limits, with the government determined to have the final say, and particularly since it has to stump up extra capital.

Luxury goods

Perfumes, bags, scarves from companies such as L'Oréal, Yves St-Laurent, Hermès, Vuitton – for many, these are the traditional image of France at its best and certainly recent results and trends underline French strength. With the explosion of sales worldwide, turnover in the sector in France increased by 18 per cent in 1988, with value added standing at 40 per cent of turnover and gross trading profits at 13 per cent. In 1988 luxury goods as a whole (including château-bottled wine) showed a positive trade balance of FF 36 billion, considerably more than the FF 25 billion for military equipment. When Yves St-Laurent sought a listing on the Paris Stock Exchange, it had to be delayed because the issue was oversubscribed some 260 times! Indeed, the wheel has turned full circle: French ministers once considered that modern France had much more serious things to offer than perfume and wine but are now so alarmed at seeing the jewels of the French luxury industry falling into foreign hands that they are blocking Japanese attempts to buy into the distribution of the exclusive Romanée Conti wine. But the nature of the industry has changed, moving to a blend of high-tech processes and traditional craft skills with companies generally preferring to reinvest profits than distribute dividends. It is also breeding a new generation of managers, typified by Bernard Arnault the mercurial head of LVMH (Louis-Vuitton-Möet-Hennessy), which is ousting the old family owners and replacing maintenance of traditions with more emphasis on modern management techniques and profitability.

Whereas, as a percentage of exports, the figure for manufactured goods has remained absolutely stable over the last ten years (77 per cent), OECD reports show that the corresponding figure for manufactured goods as a proportion of imports has risen dramatically (from 54 per cent to 73 per cent). There has been, therefore, an inexorable decline in the export/import ratio, with drops in exports recorded, not only to both EC and other OECD countries, but also to non-OECD countries. The forecast for the deficit on manufactures in 1989 is FF 40 billion, up from FF 20 billion. Possible reasons for this have already been discussed but there is firm conviction in government circles that capacity investment in the right areas is enough to narrow the deficit over the next three to four years, although this may seem optimistic in view of the fact that for capital goods alone, the real export/import ratio fell from 143 per cent in 1984 to 106 per cent in 1987.

But according to a report in *L'Usine Nouvelle* if domestic investment is picking up, as far as inward investment is concerned, government officials are beginning to talk of missed opportunities: 'We wanted to safeguard our jobs and our industry by limiting foreign investment in France in sensitive areas like cars. The result? We've got neither the jobs nor the added value. And in three years time, the Japanese will be spraying us with cars from Great Britain.' There is much talk of Japanese investment in France, but in reality there is very little, according to the national planning agency DATAR (Direction de l'Aménagement du Territoire). Point-blank refusals and the imposition of draconian conditions have meant that the Japanese invested a meagre FF 1.7 billion in France in 1988, whereas the three car-manufacturing groups, Toyota, Nissan and Honda, alone spent FF 18 billion in the United Kingdom, with Honda preparing to invest another FF 3.3 billion (see page 171). In contrast, Subaru have been negotiating for the last 3 years to build a site near Angers but have now thrown in the towel, in spite of the last minute and ironic concession by the Ministry of Industry to reduce the amount of local content demanded from 80 per cent to 60 per cent.

In spite of this setback, however, France succeeded in attracting FF 32 billion of inward investment in 1988. In terms of acquisitions, France is the second-largest target for foreign investors in Europe, but still way behind the United Kingdom ($2.3 billion compared with $6 billion). According to the French Ministry of Industry, one company in nine is now under foreign control (20 per cent of capital).

According to the same report, last year American (22 per cent of total), West German (20 per cent) and Swiss (15 per cent) investments 'created or preserved' 13,000 jobs in France as opposed to 44,000 in the United Kingdom.

Opinion is divided over the potential benefits of such investment. Some see it as nibbling away at French industry whereas others point to the better performances recorded by foreign-controlled companies where productivity is some 20–25 per cent higher than in their totally French counterparts. In 1986, FF 35,000 per employee were invested in foreign-controlled companies, as against FF 27,000 in French companies. Their export record is far superior, too: 32 per cent of production compared with 26 per cent.

The biggest constraint on inward investment has no doubt been the Ministries of Finance and Industry. They may well vaunt their policy of selectivity as having served French interests well but the severity of the policy has been enough to dissuade many overseas companies from bringing yet more investment to France. In order to improve this situation the Ministry of Finance has abolished the procedure requiring potential investors to submit a prior declaration and the right exercised by the Treasury to defer any decision. Such procedures caused Northern Telecom to wait thirteen years before building a plant in Eastern France.

One barrier has been removed, but another has appeared in its place – a monthly meeting of a Treasury committee to discuss investment by foreign companies in France, particularly those involving acquisition of more than 20 per cent of French companies. The avowed objective is to find a Franco-French solution. An example of what may occur is that investment opportunities in France were hawked by the Minister of Finance, Mr Bérégovoy, in New York only for a proposed takeover of Spontex by 3M to be rejected in favour of the nationalized group, Total.

One further possible factor in deterring potential investors and one which seriously constrains the competitiveness of French companies are social charges. France is one of the most heavily taxed of the OECD countries (45 per cent of GDP compared with 38 per cent for West Germany and the United Kingdom, 35.8 per cent for Italy and 29 per cent for USA). For every 100 Francs of direct wage paid, companies in reality spend 146 Francs just to cover social charges. If paid leave, (five weeks' annual entitlement) a thirteenth month's salary, payment to 'mutual' societies to top up social security coverage, and, for companies in the Paris

Table 2.2   *Employers' social insurance contributions*
(as percentage of GDP in 1986)

	(%)
France	12.1
Italy	8.9
West Germany	7.2
United Kingdom	3.6

Source: OECD

region, a 50 per cent contribution to the transport season ticket (**carte orange**) are all included, the figure climbs to 182 Francs.

In its determination not to allow the Americans, Japanese, British and even Swedes to invest in Europe without doing the same, France is the largest investor in Europe in terms of mergers and acquisitions, the major purchases being:

- BSN's acquisitions of pasta-making concerns in Italy, of HP and General Biscuit in the United Kingdom.
- Compagnie Générale d'Electricité's acquisition of Kabelmetale and ITT Europe.
- Carnaud's purchase of Metalbox.
- Various purchases by Pernod, Elf, Rhône-Poulenc, SGS-Thomson.

In addition, in 1988, France was the fourth biggest international investor behind Japan, USA and the United Kingdom and ahead of West Germany. In five years overseas investment has multiplied by a factor of five, from FF 14 billion in 1983 to FF 71 billion in 1988. This growth of investment is undoubtedly explained by the better profits being turned in by private companies but against this background must be seen the ability of state companies to make similar purchases. Most have become profit-making but profits have been used more to repay debt than to build a war-chest. The undercapitalization of these large groups makes them financially dependent on the state.

If domestic investment is beginning to pick up, its geographical spread remains highly uneven. Efforts by DATAR since the war have ensured that there is no North-South Divide and that, apart from parts of the Lille-Tourcoing conurbation and Marseilles, there are no real areas of great urban decay or deprivation. Some regions have inevitably progressed faster than others and there are some signs that a French version of the Sun Belt is being created along the French coast from the Pyrenees to the Italian Border. Montpellier has, for example, the highest rate of start-ups and the most successful of the **technopoles** (science parks) is at Sophia

Antipolis near Nice. Technopoles are a good example of the way in which decentralization has loosened the grip of Paris as the centre of all decisions, particularly regarding regional development aid. Regions and municipalities now enjoy greater financial freedom, through a redistribution of state tax income, and now compete fiercely to set up the latest technopole, with its attendant research centres, university or business school and small company 'nurseries'. Many may well find success difficult for two reasons.

First, the communication infrastructure in France is still such that many regions, if not inaccessible, at least require lengthy journey times to reach them. This explains why France has embarked on such a massive programme of improvement in all areas of transport, but particularly in road and rail. More East-West motorway links are planned, as is a comprehensive network to link the French end of the Channel tunnel both to the rest of France and to its immediate neighbours. 20 September 1989, in France, witnessed the inauguration of a new 300 kph TGV (high speed train) service between Paris and Le Mans, costing FF 18 billion. This TGV-Atlantique will eventually link the capital with the West and South-West and, it is hoped, bring the same advantages as the present TGV has created for passenger traffic to Lyon. Deregulation of air transport constitutes a major threat to the French national railway company, SNCF, which it is countering with a vigorous policy of extending the TGV network which includes links to the major capitals of Northern Europe and a by-pass system around Paris and Lyon to ensure more rapid transit to the South. By 1993 not even some of the most far-flung cities of France (Toulouse, Perpignan, Nice, Biarritz) will be more than five hours by train from Paris. The whole project represents a considerable challenge to France's biggest employer (200,000 employees), not only in terms of better communication but also in terms of the technological spin-off for transport equipment of France's most important industrial sectors.

Second, for the same population as the United Kingdom (approximately 56 million), France is three times the area with only six towns having more than half a million inhabitants. There are large, wide open spaces between its small and medium-size towns and therefore the ready markets of concentrated hinterlands as in the Ruhr, Northern Italy and in the South (and parts, too, of the North) of the United Kingdom do not exist. However, many companies, particularly those from the Scandinavian countries are beginning to see France as a European crossroads giving particularly good access to the booming Mediterranean markets. But commercial reasoning will decide where to invest. Saint-Gobain's decision to build a new float-glass factory in the Grenoble area has more to do with the desire to be near its markets in South-East France and Italy than to benefit a particular region, either at the behest of the state or a technopole.

The same applies to the car manufacturers compelling their subcontractors to set up close to their assembly plants; to Pechiney installing new plant at Dunkirk to benefit from ease of delivery by sea of raw materials and access to cheap nuclear power; to Coca-Cola setting up, again in Dunkirk, to serve the whole of the European market; and to Arthur Andersen software going for the proximity of analogous industries in Sophia Antipolis.

One striking feature of the present upsurge in investment, particularly in the production of basic materials is the new lease of life being given to the old smokestack areas of the North, a welcome move for the area ahead of completion of the Channel Tunnel. Coca-Cola and Pechiney at Dunkirk have already been mentioned. Usinor-Sacilor is renovating its steelworks, Saint-Gobain its glassworks in the Aisne département.

But despite DATAR's past achievements, the present blossoming of the South-East and South-West, the incipient renewal of the North and the energetic attempts of technopoles to attract customers, the Paris region still acts as a magnet, especially in the area of services. There still has not been in France a spreading of high-level functions between several towns as in West Germany, the United Kingdom, Switzerland and Italy. In 1964, Paris had 14,766 group headquarters with only 1325 in Lyon, the second largest town in France. Twenty years later, the geographical concentration of power still remained very strong. Paris still had 77 per cent of top management posts in the tertiary sector, 83.5 per cent of the headquarters of the top 200 French companies. In terms of investment credit, the greater Paris region (Ile-de-France) accounted for 59 per cent across all sectors, 66 per cent of all loans to the service sector, 84 per cent for transport and telecommunications and 91 per cent for energy. 89 per cent of export credit alone also went to the region, up from 79 per cent in 1975.

In industry, the Ile-de-France region lost a third of its workers between 1962 and 1985, but unemployment remains at 8.4 per cent below the national average of 9.5 per cent and the region's contribution to national added value has remained at a steady 22 per cent, thus underlining the fact that although other areas have benefited from industrial growth, there has been no real deindustrialization of the Paris region.

In education, too, Paris remains preponderant, having 34 per cent of the university population and in R & D, although the region's share of public-sector research has fallen from 61 per cent in 1973 to 52 per cent in 1983. In the private sector there has been virtually no change (62.4 per cent to 61.7 per cent).

All of which points to the continuing monopoly of the Paris region in many areas and to the relative failure to develop sufficient regional poles of activities to attract particular services away from Paris. Only the signing of the Single European Act has compelled France to realize that not only countries but regions will be competing with each other, hence the decision to implement the overall policy to improve the basic infra-structure and thus open up more space to allow more regions on the margin of industrial and economic activities to benefit more fully from a Europe sans frontières.

Services

As in most other industrialized countries the contribution of the services sector to added value has grown rapidly in France, standing at 63 per cent in 1986, compared with 55.2 per cent in 1973. 60.4 per cent of the working population were in service industries, compared with 49.3 per cent in 1973. The most spectacular growth has been in the retail sector, where concentration has been the most prominent feature, with the rise of Europe's largest retailer, Carrefour and other groups such as Casino, Auchan and Mammouth. Yet, in spite of the presence of 747 hypermarkets, the retail sector still remains more fragmented than in the United Kingdom (see page 173). No one group has more than 5 per cent market share and the top forty groups account for only 37 per cent of the retail trade's total turnover. Independent retailers as a whole still account for 46 per cent of retail distribution as opposed to 25 per cent in the United Kingdom, thus underlining the fact that whereas in the United Kingdom the chief buyers of the top twelve major chains need to be persuaded to buy a product before it appears on shelves from Lands End to John O'Groats, in France even contacting all of the top purchasing organizations will not ensure that a product will reach the twenty-five largest centres of population.

It is a sector, too, where there is very little sense of mutually beneficial cooperation between manufacturers and retailers. Relations are on more of an open war-footing as price margins are pared to the bone in a highly-competitive sector. In its drive to contain inflationary pressures, the government is not displeased to see advantages gained from manufacturers passed on to the consumers by the large hypermarket groups. Profits are consequently low: for the same turnover as Carrefour, Marks & Spencer makes seven times more profit (although profits are understated in France, accounts being prepared only for the tax authorities). The average profit margin can be as low as 1 to 1.5 per cent with as much as 80 per cent of this profit margin deriving from managing the cash flow. On average, hypermarket stock rotates once every twenty-four days, while sixty days are normally taken to pay suppliers, thus providing thirty-six days of cash to invest.

The **Loi Royer** of 1973 established regional commissions to regulate the building of new hypermarkets and, as a result, the commission being heavily weighted in favour of local small retailers, a firm brake has been put on any extension to the market. This had led most major groups to set up abroad with no fewer than 100 French hypermarkets to be found as far apart as Brazil (15) and Spain (53). French hypermarket chains have indeed excelled precisely in countries with a highly-fragmented distribution system, but on the whole failed in the more concentrated systems of North Europe (e.g. the United Kingdom and West Germany).

The question of Sunday trading brings into sharp relief how the public authorities shape economic policy. Shops already open for some 100 hours in France, as opposed to sixty hours in West Germany, but there has been a strong lobby to increase this even further by allowing Sunday trading. A report published in August 1989 suggested that hypermarkets should not be allowed to open, but furniture hypermarkets should, restricted, however, to those in the Ile-de-France region! The Swedish group Ikea is particularly pleased since 25–28 per cent of its turnover is taken on Sundays, in a market which is generally stagnant (+ 1.5 per cent in 1988) but where the hypermarket groups have a market share of 33.6 per cent and annual growth rates of 4.6 per cent. The trade balance in furniture was negative in 1988 by FF 11 billion so what easier than to allow Ikea to continue trading on Sundays, particularly since the group is purchasing ten times more from French sources than in 1984? A decision made all the more desirable since French manufacturers are beginning to adapt to selling to the large discount stores.

In the tourism sector, record revenues of FF 90 billion were expected in 1989 with a healthy foreign trade surplus which has remained stagnant since 1984, however. This has greatly benefited French hotels and particularly the largest hotel group Accor (Sofitel, Novotel, Ibis, Mercure) which currently ranks as number four in the world. Despite its presence, however, the hotel market remains highly fragmented with 55 per cent of hotels having less than twenty-five rooms and 65 per cent of the French never, or rarely, staying in a hotel. Only 18 per cent of hotels are in the hands of the mega-chains, compared with 60 per cent of the market in the USA. The pattern of holidays in France is anarchical, too, not so much in terms of the periods in which they are taken – no other nation seems to compress its holidays into so short a time between mid-July and August, plus a week's skiing during the winter – but in terms of the type of holiday the French take. France has one of the highest numbers of people going on holiday, but 80 per cent take their cars and go and stay with friends or relatives. By contrast, 43 per cent of Germans go to hotels. Only 16 per cent of the French go abroad, as against 33 per cent for the rest of Europe.

Of those going abroad, only three million take package tours as against ten million in West Germany and the United Kingdom. The top four national tour operators – of which there are over 200, again, in a highly fragmented market – only account for 29 per cent of total demand as against 80 per cent in West Germany. Thus, lacking the commercial clout of the big West German and British tour operators, Touropa of France, for example, charges 73 per cent more than Thomson in the United Kingdom for the same holiday, half-board in the same hotel in Benidorm in Spain.

Vertical integration is the key, the most important aspect being air transport. Most tour operators have their own fleets (Britannia, owned by Thomson is the largest of its kind in the world) and if deregulation becomes a reality in air transport, these same operators could well take a long, hard look at the French market where both tour operators and charter airlines are much smaller. As with road haulage, cabotage could be the key. It is not too fanciful, for example, to imagine a Britannia airliner taking off half-full from Luton and landing at, say, Beauvais to pick up the other half of its passengers, en route for Spain. A new trend on the part of the largest United Kingdom tour operators to move up-market could be another spur.

As for travel agents, there are some 3000 points of sale in France (Havas Tourisme, Wagon-Lits and Selectour being the largest) but 1000 of these are forecast to go by 1992, either through restructuring from within the industry itself or through acquisitions by foreign predators. They live off 10 per cent commissions, have low levels of productivity and are generally of a poor quality of service, with a low penetration rate. As has been seen in connection with other sectors, size is the all-important factor again (with the exception of Club Med), together with less navel-contemplation on the domestic market. In-fighting is another problem, too – it has been recently said that, generally speaking, there is a lack of solidarity amongst French industrialists, compared with their West German counterparts. Whereas in West Germany links between distributors and producers are important, the French are almost proud to sell out to a foreign purchaser and thereby thwart a domestic rival, particularly if it is felt that the foreign purchaser is a leader in its field, that it has the right level of technical and professional know-how and is not just a financial holding company.

Business and the law

In West Germany the concept of the Rule of Law is emphasized: the same is true of France, except that having devised a whole series of complex and arcane laws and decrees, the French are most anxious to find ways round them! Written detailed contracts are paramount in business but whereas the British are content with accepting more general and simple rules, the French business person will constantly be seeking reinterpretation and

⨍ loopholes. This legalistic environment holds good for the system of public administration (ultra-bureaucratic in nature), commercial law and labour law to which further reference will be made later.

The advent of 1992 has brought the legal profession into sharper focus, particularly in matters concerning cross-border mergers and acquisitions. At present, the profession is fairly compartmentalized with each sector having different areas of responsibility and expertise. There is a general feeling that the system, particularly in terms of ease and accessibility is very backward in comparison with its Anglo-Saxon and West German counterparts. The legal environment of French companies has indeed been recently described by the journal *L'Entreprise* as 'underdeveloped, incoherent, ill-adapted and archaic'. Whereas a West German competitor may go to one organization to carry out a simple legal act, a French director has to go through the hands of many different professionals who are often all necessary and all jealous of their prerogatives. Overall, France has fewer legal experts than any other Western countries (1 per 2000 inhabitants, as against 1 per 1200 in West Germany and 1 per 500 in the USA) who in the main, still look after individuals whereas corporate law is most lucrative. The **avocats** provide advice in all areas of the law and have a monopoly of pleading before the courts. The **notaires** have a monopoly in drawing up an **acte authentique** (authentic document) necessary for all transfers of property, wills and marriages. They enjoy no monopoly in matters of consultancy or advice. Anyone can become a **conseil juridique** (legal adviser), however, who enjoys no monopoly and does not necessarily have to belong to one of the liberal professions (**avocat** or **notaire**), hence banks, insurance companies, chambers of commerce and employer organizations will offer such a service. This is also true of the big eight accountancy firms which in France are allowed to carry out both legal and accounting work, whereas they are kept rigidly apart in the United Kingdom and USA. Fidal is the largest legal advisory firm in France and is a subsidiary of KPMG which claims that no confusion arises between the two professions. Whereas its legal activities only represent 15 per cent of turnover, it is considered that while the auditing side is coming up to maturity, legal advice shows the biggest potential in the present climate of acquisitions, takeovers, etc.

Looking forward, urgent reform of the profession is seen to be sorely needed with the most likely outcome being a merger of the conseils juridiques and the avocats, thus establishing a monopoly in legal advice and a new profession similar to that in the USA.

The most common forms of business enterprise are:

1 Société Anonyme – SA (corporation)

This is the most common form adopted by large companies and may be quoted or unquoted. A minimum of seven founder shareholders is required with a minimum legal share capital of FF 250,000 of which 25 per cent must be paid in at incorporation. Most corporations issue one class of common shares, but two other classes exist: preferred and non-voting, the latter being limited to 25 per cent of share capital. It is possible to limit the number of votes per shareholders' holding of the same class of share, and double votes are also possible, but limited to fully paid-up registered shares for at least two years by the same shareholder.

The issuing of double voting rights is quite frequently used as a defence mechanism against takeover bids (**Offre Publique d'Achat – OPA**) together with the right to buy back shares (**autocontrôle**) as long as they are for cancellation (reduction of capital) or for employees' share acquisition plans. Cross-shareholdings also exist up to ceilings of 10 per cent.

As recently as 1987, very few financial directors or heads of companies were concerned about their shareholder structure but since that time acquisitions both by French and foreign companies have snowballed to such an extend that even the French President issued a dire warning of possible consequences for French industry early in 1989. The facts are, however, that French companies have not been slow in going over to the offensive making 143 acquisitions in France, as opposed to 129 by foreign companies. Most have been straight, friendly acquisitions since takeover bids are still comparatively rare in France, in spite of the media attention surrounding such companies as LVMH, Bolloré and the insurance company Victoire, recently the subject of a bid by Suez, the largest ever seen in France. In 1988 there were only twenty-nine stock exchange battles in France, compared with 186 for British companies in London.

French companies do not enjoy the same solid backing of banks as they do in West Germany and defence measures are therefore more limited. Some have already been mentioned, the following are other examples.

- The Act of 7 June 1987 allows companies to write into their statutes the obligation for all shareholders above 0.5 per cent of share capital to be declared. Only some 5 per cent of listed companies have not availed themselves of this provision.
- It is perfectly legal to limit the number of votes. In CGE individual shareholders arc not entitled to more than 8 per cent of votes, whereas in Lafarge-Coppée, now the world's second largest cement producer, the limit is as low as 1 per cent. The technique is common in West Germany, the Netherlands and Switzerland but hitherto has only been used in France by the two companies quoted.

- BSN, Schneider, Lafarge-Coppée and Saint-Gobain have used another far more expensive ploy, that of buying as a financial institution (**Etablissement de Crédit**). Under French law, any raider making a bid for a company owning more than 10 per cent of such an establishment must have the prior backing of the authority which oversees all backing operations, the **Comité des Etablissements de Crédit**. Companies using the method thus kill two birds with one stone. They gain time to marshal their defence and they provide themselves with an efficient tool for managing their treasury or juggling with exchange controls.

- The last resort for many companies are the institutional investors (**les zinzins**). The main problem here, however, is that the French institutional investors are not as rich as their West German counterparts, for example, to be able to afford significant shareholdings in French companies, mainly due to undercapitalization. The insurance companies, however, precisely though their insurance activities, do have capital to invest. These are the state-owned companies, UAP, AGF and GAN, which between them held a share portfolio of some FF 60 billion at the end of 1988, in 140 different companies. These sums are small, however, in relation to the capitalization of French companies and hence their room for manoeuvre is accordingly limited. Their objectives are twofold: either purely to make a trade investment like unit trusts or involvement in the management of a company, in which case they ask to take a seat on the board of management. Even here, however, holdings are of the order of 4–6 per cent. French insurance companies do not have the financial clout to own 50–60 per cent of a company's capital, like British insurers.

Banks find themselves in a similar position for the same reason of lack of capital, with BNP, Crédit Lyonnais and Société Générale having holdings of a total value of FF 32 billion. Such activity is increasing rapidly, however, (Société Générale has increased its shareholdings by 179 per cent in three years) both to defend their clients and to help them make their own acquisitions. The fact that the three insurance groups and two of the banks are State-owned must be of considerable importance here and it is difficult to believe that certain governmental preferences are not stated in those boardrooms where State representatives are present. This is particularly true, given the close-knit nature of the relationships between senior managers in large groups, both state and private, senior civil servants and government ministers. This relationship is a key ingredient in France's business culture and will be discussed at greater length later in the chapter (see page 97).

Of the top 200 companies, sixty-two are still actively family-controlled including such names as Michelin, Peugeot, Carrefour, Casino, Matra, LVMH, Pernod, l'Oréal. Foreign companies are slowly but surely making their presence felt with forty-four French companies in 1987 and sixty-one in 1989 controlled by overseas concerns (mainly American and West German).

As far as management structure is concerned, French commercial law allows for SAs to have either the two-tier management structure of a Supervisory Council (**Conseil de Surveillance**) and Directorate (**Directoire**), based on the West German model or a single Board of Directors (**Conseil d'Administration**) whose chairman (**Président**) is often general manager as well (hence **Président Directeur Général**).

In reality the two-tier structure is virtually confined to the state sector in which the trade union movement is more powerful and is allocated seats on the supervisory councils.

2 **Société à Responsabilité Limitée – SARL** (limited liability company)
The SARL, the most popular form of company, is suitable for small French business. Registration requirements are identical to those for SAs but, in contrast, a SARL need only have a minimum of two and a maximum of fifty shareholders, with a minimum share capital of FF 50,000. When a SARL has only one shareholder it may be transformed into an EURL (**Entreprise Unipersonnelle à Responsabilité Limitée**) in which the single shareholder exercises all the rights and powers of shareholders in general meetings. Shares (**parts sociales**) are freely transferable among existing shareholders but cannot be transferred to third parties without the assent of three-quarters of the shareholders. There is no board of directors in this form of company which is managed by one or more managers (**gérant**). Statutory auditing requirements depend on size in terms either of turnover or of numbers employed.

3 **Société en Nom Collectif – SNC** (general partnership)
All partners in an SNC are called **commerçants** and have unlimited liability for all debts and obligations of the partnership. They may appoint a manager (**gérant**) who is not necessarily a partner.

Since reporting or regulatory standards of SAs and SARLs are almost identical, interest in SNCs and other structures has been rekindled, principally because of the great degree of control which can be exercised.

4 **Société en Commandite** (limited partnership)
This may take one of two forms: by guarantee (**société en commandite simple**) or with shares (**société en commandite par actions**). It is a form

rarely used in recent times and considered to be antiquated, but the prestigious manufacturer of luxury goods Hermès has recently decided to adopt the form to guarantee family control over the company. The principle is simple: the law provides for a **commandité**, the representative of the shareholder, to have the sole right to oversee the managing body and cannot be relieved of its powers unless 75 per cent of the shareholders so decide, a provision which guarantees almost total security. In the case of Hermès, the commandité is an SARL controlled by members of the Hermès family. Along with Yves St-Laurent, which decided on the same route to avoid the fate of LVMH, the subject of tough takeover bids, Hermès is determined to remain private to provide more long-term management of a quality product and not to fall prey to institutional investors in search of short-term profits which have become more accepted in France with the gathering strength of the **Bourse** (Stock Exchange).

5   **Groupement d'Intérêt Economique – GIE** (economic interest grouping)
     This is a form of joint venture with a legal personality. Generally they are cost and not profit centres and are used for exports, R & D, joint sales or distribution agents for their members who set their rules by agreement.

6   **Entreprise Individuelle** (sole trader)
     The sole proprietor of such an entity is personally liable for all debts and obligations and must be registered with the Clerk of the Commercial Court (**Tribunal de Commerce**).

Business and finance

Two notable changes have occurred in the French financial scene in the 1980s: a gradual but fundamental reform of the banking sector and a general shift away from reliance on debt towards equity as a source of external finance. These two changes have been underscored by a whole paraphernalia of new financial instruments and engineering methods which are leading to radically-changing views on ownership, management and structures of companies.

  The period of greatest expansion in the banking sector occurred between 1967 and 1975, following the reform of 1966 which allowed banks more flexibility to set interest rates and to open new branches, with the aim of shifting the burden of providing investment funds from the state to the banking sector. Until the 1960s some 80 per cent of investment financing emanated from state sources. During the late 1960s and 1970s the financing of investment by banks increased from 38 per cent (1965) to 60 per cent (1974), while the capital markets played a very minor role. The banks were essentially the main financial intermediaries.

The concentration of industry was mirrored by a similar process in the banking sector, as many local banks disappeared (245 in 1945 and 63 in 1975), together with a number of merchant banks (43 in 1946, 17 in 1975). The period was dominated by the deposit banks Banque Nationale de Paris, Crédit Lyonnais, Société Générale (all nationalized) and the two merchant banks Paribas and Indosuez, but the mutualist and cooperative banks also expanded rapidly to compete both on interest rates and number of branches.

By the 1980s, there was a growing crisis in the financial system:

- The increasing number of clients using cheques (for which there is still no charge in France) was rapidly increasing overheads.
- There was growing unemployment in banks as those hired in the 1960s and 1970s were laid off to make way for new technology.
- There were some sixty-five privileged loan schemes, sixty-eight different types of subsidy being offered by different privileged compartments of the system (e.g. Crédit Agricole which had a monopoly of preferential loans to agriculture), which led to 48 per cent of credit to the economy being allocated through specialized and diverse lending establishments. All had so many different statutes, rights and privileges that competition became hopelessly distorted with a resulting high cost of credit. Because of such distortions the task of the Banque de France regulating the economy by interest rates was infinitely more difficult than that of its much more independent West German counterpart, the Bundesbank (see page 21). France's attempts in controlling inflation have hence been much less successful (see Table 2.3).
- The growing importance of the capital market, particularly after the tax incentives of 1979, started a gradual tendency for savings to move from shorter to longer types of investments (unit trusts – SICAV – became particularly attractive and still represent one of the most vigorous markets in Europe).
- The low equity base of French banks was of continuing concern.

This crisis was characterized by a gradual process of disintermediation, i.e. less indirect and more direct financing via the capital markets which large companies were finding more profitable. French firms increasingly switched to building up equity and reducing debt, with the result that the proportion of new equity issues rose from 8.4 per cent of new external resources in 1982 to 25.5 per cent in 1987, although in 1988 and 1989 there was a sharp upturn in short-term credit after the October crash in 1987.

All this meant less custom for the banks at a time of growing costs

Table 2.3   *French inflation (1982–9)*

Year	(%)
1982	9.7
1983	9.3
1984	6.7
1985	4.7
1986	2.1
1987	3.3
1988	2.8
1989	3.5

Source: OECD

(labour in the early 1980s representing two-thirds of overheads) and led to an overall drop in profitability.

Most of the banking sector was nationalized in 1982, a process which involved thirty-six banks (thirty-four deposit and two merchant banks) and provided the state with control of over 80 per cent of both loans and credits. Reasons for such nationalization were partly classical Socialist ideology, but there was a genuine concern to introduce a more efficient system of monetary control, by decompartmentalizing the system and allowing all of the various types of establishment to offer the same services in terms of loans and deposits. This process had already started under the previous government in 1979 with the introduction of the savings accounts and the Livret d'Epargne Populaire (LEP) and the Compte de Développement Industriel (CODEVI) which all banks were entitled to offer. Two acts, one in 1982 and a second in 1984, made all establishments covered by the same law, excluding the Treasury, the Banque de France and the powerful Caisse des Dépôts et Consignations (a State financial institution responsible for the collection and distribution of all funds through the Caisses d'Epargne – national savings banks – and a major institutional investor). In reality, the many different networks have not disappeared, but they can all offer the same products. There are still four big categories:

● The high street and merchant banks.
● The mutualist and cooperative sector.
● The Sociétés Financières, specializing in leasing, hire purchase etc.
● The specialist state-controlled financial institutions e.g. Crédit Foncier, Crédit National which are still the main distributors of state credit for industrial investments and whose loans are often subject to the National Plan.

The final main chapter in the recent history of French banking was the bout of privatization under the right-wing Chirac government of 1986 under which it was planned to sell off Société Générale, Crédit Lyonnais, BNP, Paribas, Indosuez and Crédit Agricole. Only three reverted to the private sector – Société Générale, Paribas and Indosuez. As has been seen, it is essentially these six banks together with the insurance companies which make up the major institutional investors. The partial success of the privatization programme, however, posed the fundamental question of how effective the programme could possibly be when some of the major shareholders of these same privatized companies were still in state hands and thus subject to a degree of inevitable manipulation. To this issue was added another, that of the **noyau dur**, the hard-core of faithful investors approached by the Chirac government to acquire stakes in the newly privatized-companies. The incoming Socialist government of 1988 accused the Chirac government of approaching those companies which gave financial support to the right-wing parties, and as a result there has been some debate over ways of dismantling the noyau dur before the expiry of the legal time limit imposed on these shareholders to retain the shares. Certainly the ensuing saga points to the very thin line which exists between the influence of political and financial clans and the workings of the marketplace in France.

Life for the two **vieilles dames** (old ladies) – Crédit Lyonnais and BNP – still left in state hands has not been made easy by the difficulty of finding new capital from a government intent on reducing its central borrowing requirement in a climate of tax harmonization (and hence loss of tax revenue as France will inevitably be forced to lower its VAT rates). Crédit Lyonnais' failed attempt at an equity swop with Commerzbank in Germany was a clear example of the difficulty. But state-owned companies can now issue up to 25 per cent of their capital in non-voting **certificats d'investissements** (the original target of 49 per cent has been dropped) and are now experimenting (e.g. Rhône-Poulenc) with perpetual notes which are considered as close to equity.

In spite of recent attempts to bring some order into banking and finance, France still has a bewildering array of specialist financial institutions ranging from leasing companies to the newly-formed **banques de trésorie** whose prime function is to improve the workings of the reorganized financial markets by market making and arbitraging.

But although the 1970s saw an opening of so many bank branches that many began to talk of France as being overbanked, foreign banks are particularly anxious to buy into the number of small but rich regional deposit banks. The savings rate of French households at present stands at 12.2 per cent of disposable income and indicates a market of some potential, particularly for medium-size banks capable of offering more sophisticated services to their customers. In addition, it was considered to be the only way to have a presence in France in the run-up to the single market.

Although there is not the same degree of closeness between banks and industry in France as in West Germany, as holders of equities in companies (see page 23), it has been seen that some measure of influence over corporate strategy is possible. During takeovers special arrangements often exist whereby banks have an option to issue special subordinated loans which count as equity.

In addition, bilateral consultation and exchange is extensive together with multilateral consultation through the national planning bodies. Banks also share a common feature with large industrialized groups in that their PDGs are often ex-top treasury officials, thus pointing to an even closer triangular relationship between banks, industry and government, such a big feature of the business culture in France.

Stock markets

The growing importance of the Bourse has already been alluded to as the direct result of tax changes favouring equity investments by individuals (particularly through unit trusts) and of disinflation and the consequent switch by companies from debt to equity. The privatization issues of 1986 greatly swelled the ranks of private investors from 1.5 million in 1986 to 7.5 million in 1988. Major structural reforms have accompanied this evolution with the addition of new financial instruments and markets, one of the overall major aims also being to make Paris the major financial centre for Europe, after London, and to attract back securities business which has leaked to London.

France has seven stock exchanges: one in Paris (the seventh largest in the world) and six in various towns and provinces, the second most important being Lyon. In Paris, the old outcry method on the forward market (**à terme**), which accounts for the greatest value of trading, has been replaced by a computerized system giving continuous quotations. Prices are still fixed daily on the spot or cash market (**comptant**) which comprises a greater number of stocks, although capitalization is less than the forward market. For those companies wishing fewer strict formalities, there is the over-the-counter market (**marché hors côte**).

The big success story, however, has undoubtedly been the equivalent of the unlisted securities market – the **second marché** which was set up in 1983. Its popularity has largely been due to the less onerous conditions imposed on companies than on the official market. Only a minimum of 10 per cent of shares have to be offered and a complete prospectus is not required. New issues have been frequently oversubscribed many times, making it the largest market of its kind in Europe.

There have been changes, too, in the system. The previous stockbrokers (**agents de change**) were all appointed by the Ministry of Finance which also fixed commissions. They alone could deal in shares on the Stock Exchange – there were no market makers – and they also monopolized the market for French government bonds. The break-up of their monopoly started under the Socialists but to speed the process of reform a new market was set up in 1987 to deal with government bonds. This business, transacted by twelve market makers, is now proving more lucrative than the equivalent London market shared by double the number of dealers. Since 1988, any French or overseas concern has been able to buy one of the stockbroking firms (now called **Sociétés de Bourse**) whose monopoly is set to end in 1992 (fixed commission having ended in 1990). Many are in dire need of such an injection of funds, having lost vast sums of money on the new futures market, the MATIF, whose regulations have now been accordingly tightened up. Principal buyers of the stockbrokers have been the banks which have long fretted at the commission they paid the brokers although the majority of orders come through the banks.

Other financial instruments now commonly used by banks and industrial companies are commercial paper (**billets de trésorerie**) and certificates of deposit (**certificats de dépôts**).

The Paris financial scene is much changed then, since the early 1980s with many expecting it to be the most important financial centre in Europe after London. But old traditions and cultures die hard, and foreign banks have great difficulty in making money in Paris, unless their staff are completely French and fully conversant with the close network of treasury officials, bankers and industrialists who will all have been educated and trained in the same élite establishments.

To complete this picture of dramatic metamorphosis, according to *Science, Vie, Economie* junk bonds may be beginning to make a halting entrance onto the financial scene in France. Unlike the USA, only companies which are sufficiently well known and powerful issue bonds. These are mainly the state-owned or newly-privatized concerns. Most of the others, particularly the small and medium size-companies, borrow from banks. The idea of rating agencies is also in its infancy, only one being in existence thus far, the Agence française d'évaluation financière which was established in 1986 and hitherto has rated just forty-seven issuers of bonds.

In addition, whereas such bonds are commonly used in the USA for hostile takeover bids, such bids, as has been seen, are rare in France where it is forbidden to endanger the existence of a company which one does not yet own and therefore to guarantee a raid with the assets of the target company.

Junk bonds are commonly used for leveraged management buyouts (RES – **rachat d'entreprise par ses salariés**) however, and it is in this activity that the French equivalent of junk bonds are appearing. Such LMBOs have rapidly increased since 1986, both in numbers and value. In 1986, no LMBO was greater than 400 million francs. In 1988 three operations (Darty, Saunier-Duval and Fruehauf-Trailor) exceeded this sum, using financing similar to that used for LMBOs in the United States, although only one true junk bond has been recorded so far in France, that issued for the SICLI group (industrial cleaning, maintenance) when buying the American company, HP Cleaning. Any 'mezzanine' transactions are mainly in the form of bank loans rather than bonds.

But the potential market is thought to be small in France (several hundreds of millions of francs) compared with the United Kingdom (FF 2 billion), these two being the only two European countries where there are experiments with the formula. Such issues require a liquid market, and hitherto most institutional investors in France seem unwilling to invest their clients' money in such risky ventures. With an increasing number of mergers and acquisitions, a market for subordinated debt may well emerge, and Paribas is seriously contemplating a special investment fund for this purpose. Of significance is the fact that Moody's, the credit-rating agency, has set up in France, thus considering it a country which is increasingly prepared to envisage financial innovation.

Indeed, there is a new, younger generation of managers in France who refuse to adopt the negative attitude of those who blame la crise for France's ills and carp continuously about the Socialist experiment of the early 1980s and its effect on the competitiveness of industry, but who have a growing and passionate faith in industry and in growth. The number of heads of companies aged over fifty-five has dropped by 13 per cent since 1980, proof that this generation is taking over the reins. In so doing they are not hesitating to use the most up-to-date methods of financing: management buyouts, stock options, second market, venture capital, etc.

Business and the labour market

Demographic trends

According to the national statistical office, INSEE, 1 January 1988, the population was estimated at over 55.7 million persons, compared with 55.5 million in 1987, thus growing at a rate of 0.4 per cent, compared with − 0.2 per cent in West Germany and 0.1 per cent in the United Kingdom. The fecundity rate at 1.8 children per woman has dropped since the 1960s, but if this rate continues the population will grow to 58 million in 2000. As in West Germany and elsewhere, the population is ageing, however: in 2000 there will be 15 million people less than twenty years old, 1.1 million less than 1990, 12–13 million aged more than sixty, representing 2 million more and 1 million aged over eighty, compared with 680,000 in 1983.

The geographical spread will look different too, with 35–36 per cent of households living in rural communities, compared with 27 per cent at present. Taking the population as a whole, nearly 40 per cent will live in rural communities, contrasting sharply with 1990's 29 per cent.

The number of immigrants is growing too. In 1985, France had 3.8 million foreign inhabitants, 21 per cent more than in 1972 and representing 8 per cent of the total population.

Unemployment

The working population has been increasing at a rate of 1 per cent annually, reaching 24.5 million in 1987. 190,000 more seeking work are predicted annually until 1991, and more than 100,000 annually until 2005. The working population will then stabilize at around 26.5 million and decline slowly thereafter. One of the key current questions about the French economy is, therefore, how to create enough employment for these new arrivals on the job market when growth rates, although much improved, need to maintain a strong upward trend. This is particularly disturbing to a nation which has seen its unemployment figures obstinately refuse to fall during the 1980s, as they have in many other European countries (Table 2.4).

The working population is growing, as has been seen, but not at the same pace as in other countries and this cannot therefore explain higher unemployment. According to OECD reports the underlying cause is a failure to create enough corporate employment in the 1980s due to rigid labour costs (high social charges, indexed wages, the minimum wage – SMIC), in marked contrast to France's main trading partners. Such employment picked up in 1988, but mainly in the tertiary sector, whereas only in 1989 did industry start to create jobs with the upsurge in investment in production capacity (particularly in metalworking, rubber, plastics and building materials).

Youth unemployment causes the most concern. In 1990 23 per cent of the 16–25 age group were out of work (7.8 per cent in West Germany, 17.4 per cent in the United Kingdom). Various youth employment schemes have been funded by government schemes such as the TUC (**Travaux d'Utilité Collective** – community work contracts), work familiarization placements

Table 2.4   *French unemployment rates (1979–89)*

Year	(%)
1979	5.8
1980	6.3
1981	7.3
1982	8.3
1983	8.3
1984	9.9
1985	10.2
1986	10.4
1987	10.5
1988	10.0
1989	9.5

Source: OECD

and social security relief for employers hiring young people, but such schemes are unlikely in the long run to halt rising unemployment. Apprenticeship schemes are far fewer in France than in West Germany and hence a larger proportion of young people either leave the education system with no qualification at all, or with unwanted qualifications. Generally speaking, for example, there is a shortage of engineers, technicians and skilled workers as production techniques progress but a waning demand for unskilled workers, hence explaining the apparent contradiction between industry beginning to create jobs and unemployment remaining at 10 per cent.

Particularly disadvantaged at present are the PME (small and medium-size companies) which are most in need of more labour and increasingly having to employ managers (**cadres**) and technicians, often for the first time. They are losing out, however, to the large companies towards which cadres and technicians naturally gravitate.

One rigidity in the labour market which was removed in 1986 was the obligation for companies to seek the authorization of the local inspector of labour before making employees redundant 'for economic reasons'. A new Act, the so-called **Loi Soisson** has modified the measures enacted in 1986 and allows a labour court (**Conseil des prudhommes**) not to have an *a priori* check on redundancies but to seek *a posteriori* justification of their necessity. French employers could now face the real prospect of checks on all redundancies after the event, following the principle that the benefit of the doubt is with the employee.

Paris has a significant role to play in the labour market, too. In spite of its continuing economic significance, French managers are beginning to show considerable signs of disenchantment with life in the capital and to express growing preferences for a pleasant lifestyle in the South and South-East where sun, sea and the ski-slopes offer obvious attractions. In a recent survey, Aix-en-Provence, Toulouse, Montpellier, Annecy and Grenoble were put at the top of a list, ahead of Paris, of towns where managers would accept to live. Towns of the North and North-East (Lille, Reims, Le Havre, Nancy, Amiens, Calais) were, not surprisingly, the least popular.

One of the main reasons for this trend is the cost of a career in Paris, both in terms of energy and money. Two-thirds of housing is in the East of Paris, two-thirds of offices in the West. Constant traffic jams and annual strikes in the public transport system make life hard for workers in Paris, with the rush-hour increasing by a quarter-hour annually since 1985. Rents are three times those to be found in the provinces and not surprisingly therefore, there has been a move away to villages and towns of less than 20,000 inhabitants. 36 per cent of managers still live and work in the Paris region, however, with the Rhône-Alpes and Mediterranean areas still way behind with 18 per cent.

These are various reasons for the pull of Paris:

- By accepting a job elsewhere, a manager might greatly reduce his potential on the labour market.
- Selling a house in some areas of Paris could bring some into the bracket of wealth-tax payers. Paris prices are also increasing dramatically, making it difficult to return and buy housing.
- Children's education in a city in which there is a disproportionate number of both universities and particularly of the highly prestigious and élitist engineering and business schools.
- The tradition that unless a manager has done a stint in Paris his career could suffer thereby, particularly in the large companies in the banking and insurance sector. Amongst the young, if any preference is given for working elsewhere, it is not in the provinces but abroad, with the USA far ahead of the EC countries as the main preference.

Once again, improvements in the transport infrastructure are bringing about change. With the Paris-Lyon TGV full at the beginning and end of the day, commuters in both directions are now quite commonplace, with managers living in Lyon and working in Paris and vice versa. Passenger traffic between Paris-Lyon-Grenoble has increased by 7 per cent yearly, with over a quarter being managers.

Immigrant workers

By far the largest group are those from the Moslem countries of North Africa – Algeria (780,000), Morocco (520,000) and Tunisia (212,00), although there are considerable numbers of Portuguese (860,000), Italians (425,000) and Spaniards (380,000). Although many will have entered the country quite legally, mostly after 1945, a considerable number were illegal, a situation which particularly suited employers who could thus pay lower wages, hire and fire at will and pay less attention to working conditions.

Many of the original immigrants also arrived without their families, hoping to find a job and save up enough money to go home and set up in business. The majority stayed in France and were later joined by their families (as was also to be later the case with many illegal immigrants who regularized their position). Thus family groupings are on the increase, with women representing 38 per cent of the Algerian and Tunisian population. More than 80 per cent of immigrants in France today have residence permits and work permits valid for ten years, but automatically renewable.

The bulk of the immigrants arrived in France without qualifications and took jobs on building sites, as unskilled workers on assembly lines, particularly in the car industry or the less salubrious jobs, such as emptying dustbins, which the French disdained to take.

With the onslaught of la crise, many immigrants were the first to suffer, representing two-thirds of redundancies in the construction industry and the greater part of the massive lay-offs in the car industry, particularly at Talbot, in 1983. Today, more than a third of them are to be found in local grocery stores or as waiters in cafés and restaurants.

The immigrant is often the first to be laid off and the young often leave school with few qualifications and hence find it difficult to secure jobs. For the older ones, reconversion is difficult, at times impossible, as many are still unable to read or write French. This led directly to the failure of plans to reconvert Talbot workers and miners recruited directly in the Atlas mountains.

In the Ile-de-France region, 30 per cent of the long-term unemployed are immigrants and hence, in 1977, the government introduced its first plan to encourage immigrants to return home. Some 60,000 – mostly Portuguese and Spanish – took advantage of the scheme between 1977 and 1982, and in 1980 50,000 Algerians benefited from a special Franco-Algerian agreement to provide travelling expenses and training centres in Algeria. The scheme was revived in the car industry in 1984 but, after some initial success, rapidly ran out of steam, most immigrants viewing acceptance of aid to return home as acceptance of failure and preferred to stay in a country in which they were not always welcome. Racial friction often erupts. Islam is now France's second religion and this alone is a source of much tension, particularly over the recent claim to the right for girls to wear the traditional Islamic headscarf, the tchador, in schools – anathema to the highly anti-clerical teachers' union which jealously protects a lay state system and brooks no recognition of religious affinities. Islamic fundamentalism is taking a firm grip in the Algerian education system and many see the tchador affair as being a fundamental exercise in surreptitiously spreading Islamic propaganda. The numbers of immigrants are still being swollen, too, by illegal entrants who prefer indignities at the hands of unscrupulous employers to poverty in their native lands.

Business and trade unions

The trade unions in France experienced a dramatic dwindling of their numbers in the 1980s, down from a fairly low figure of 20 per cent in the early 1980s to around 10 per cent in 1989. Too close an identification with the hard-line Communist party which refused to condemn the Russian invasion of Afghanistan was one reason for the decline. Other causes put forward have been:

- Growing unemployment in large sunset industries more likely to employ unionized labour.
- The unions being out of step with the aspirations of an increasingly wealthy working population.
- Unions are too fragmented to be effective.
- Unions being generally too politicized.

Although the law provides for various forms of worker representation, overall the picture of labour relations in France is far from being one of basic agreement between management and employees for the good of the company, as in West Germany. But there are growing signs that neither the unions nor employees are happy with this state of affairs as industrial conflict begins to increase in France, particularly in the public sector.

Organization

The bodies representing workers are confederally organized and have no umbrella organization to which they jointly belong, such as the DGB in West Germany and the TUC in the United Kingdom (see page 34 and 194).

Each confederation comprises separate unions and federations which horizontally represent different industrial sectors and vertically the administrative units, from the **département** through the region to national level. The three largest, in order of size, are:

- The CGT (**Confédération Générale du Travail**) founded in 1895, which is particularly strong in most of the state-owned sectors such as steel, electricity and gas (EDF and GDF) and the railways. Its leaders are members of the Communist party.

- The CFDT (**Confédération Française Démocratique du Travail**) which has strong Socialist allegiances and is still committed to workers' control (**autogestion**), a principle rejected by both the other unions, unless ownership of the company is shared too, as in state companies (in which employees' representatives sit on the board), cooperatives, local government, etc. This latter point underlines a basic tenet which the FO shares with the other unions and that is of complete opposition to capitalism.

- The FO (**Force Ouvrière**) is the most moderate of the three, believing in direct negotiation rather than conflict with government authorities.

Before 1982 it was possible to create a union branch only in companies employing more than fifty persons but since then, even in the smallest companies, there exists the right to establish a branch. The only condition laid down is that one or several employees notify the head of the company, who must agree to meet the unions at least twice yearly. Japanese and other investors cannot demand single unions and must therefore resort to creating a small company or one in a low-unionized region.

At shop floor level, the unions nominate a shop steward (**délégué syndical**) and all workers in companies employing more than ten people elect a **délégué du personnel** whose task it is to solve individual problems, but not negotiate with employers as does the délégué syndical.

At plant and company level, a works' committee (**comité d'entreprise**) is necessary in companies of over fifty people and must be informed on planning, results and changes in organization and consulted on redundancies, working hours, wages and health and safety.

All of these different representatives are protected by law, are allocated specific hours to conduct their business and cannot be fired. Over and above these representatives, new laws (**les lois Auroux**) in 1982 allowed for 'expression groups' which the government (even though Socialist!) considered necessary to counteract what they saw as too much potential influence of the unions in the existing structures and to give the shop floor more effective consultation at company level. They were intended as a means whereby workers could talk directly to management without necessarily going through the unions. In this they resemble quality circles and both bodies aroused the hostility of the unions, particularly the CGT. Quality circles have become extremely widespread, particularly since 1985 when France had more than the rest of Europe together. In 1987 there were 30,000 such circles which varied considerably in their degree of effectiveness. One particular problem is that they threaten traditional hierarchies in the firm – particularly middle managers and hence cadres are often accused of being indifferent to them.

Collective bargaining (conventions collectives)

Many salaries, rights and conditions are laid down in collective agreements drawn up either on an industrial sector or local/regional basis. Employers bound by these agreements, either through their employers federation or through being a direct signatory to them, must respect their minimum provisions.

Such agreements lie at the very heart of a form of traditional corporatism in France which perpetuates a highly-fragmented patchwork of rights and privileges pertaining to all forms of profession, trade and even employee status. The very composition of the workforce is made up of a scale of coefficients which correspond to levels of specified duties and tasks and specific qualifications enabling those duties and tasks to be fulfilled. A nightwatchman in the oil industry who does no rounds is coefficient 100, for example; one who does have rounds is coefficient 120; a fork-lift driver is 130; light-vehicle driver is 150. The minimum salaries, periods of leave, seniority, bonuses and promotions sanctioned by these agreements are fiercely defended by unions and non-union workers alike and not infrequently cause stoppages, particularly if a company wishes to rescind an agreement covering one industry to sign an agreement covering a different industry, affording more flexibility and lower costs.

Such a system leads to rigid hierarchies which can prevent advancement of workers on merit and no more clearly is this seen than in the case of technicians aspiring to managerial grades, a case which will be discussed later in the chapter (see page 100).

Until the mid-1980s nearly all salaries rose by the same fixed amounts according to the industry, but this system, much to the chagrin of the unions, and again particularly the CGT, is progressively being replaced by two-part awards, one part being fixed and the other based on merit and performance. In addition, an Act of 1986 has enabled companies to pay generalized bonuses based on a whole new set of flexible criteria: productivity, quality improvement, cost reductions, sales, etc. Such money (called **intéressement**) is immediately available, unlike profit-sharing schemes (**participation**) which are frozen for five years before any payment is made. In general, the unions favour such payments, except for those linked to productivity which are still taboo to the CGT.

Industrial relations in the public sector

Many jobs in the public sector – SNCF, PTT – are guaranteed for life since they confer the status of civil servant on their holder. Other privileges include advantageous pension and health schemes, automatic advancement, but in strict line with the hierarchy laid down in the **convention collective** and various bonuses. Wages are often low, however, and since the rigorous deflationary policy pursued by the government since 1983 has particularly held down salaries in the public sector, many state sectors – banks, air-traffic controllers, taxmen, nurses, teachers, postmen, railwaymen – are undergoing a period of extreme social tension. Add to this the fact that the unions are numerically strongest in these sectors, and there is reason for some concern. Whatever the strength of the unions, however, the unrest is characterized by outbreaks of spontaneous stoppages called by groups of individuals determined to voice their grievances. Such outbreaks the unions are finding hard to control and, indeed, there is a growing conviction amongst some employers that a strong and ordered union is easier to deal with than 10,000 individual grievances.

Unrest is also leading to difficulty in making necessary structural changes in certain sectors. This is particularly true of the combined postal and telecommunications organization, PTT-France Telecom, which is still officially a government department (but the world's fourth-largest tele-communications operator). Its head and five principal senior managers are appointed by the Council of Ministers, negotiations on salaries, staffing levels are at state level and even the state representatives in the regions – the **préfets** – have a say in its affairs. Prices are set by the state, not only for basic telephone call units, but also for telephone equipment (while FNAC and DARTY, two large consumer electronic retailers, are offering special deals on the same equipment). It needs new investment but can only obtain it from the Ministry of Finance which has continuously milked its profits since 1982 for national budgetary purposes and for investment in the electronics sector, an industrial policy priority area.

Reform is needed, therefore, if it is to compete with companies which have already adapted to global competition, particularly through deregulation and privatization as in the United Kingdom, Spain, Italy and the Netherlands. France is the exception in Europe and one of the major reasons holding it back is its highly-unionized labour-force (430,000 employees) who adamantly refuse to accept any split between the post and telecommunications sectors or, worse still, any attempt to turn the organization into a company, albeit state-run (a **régie** like Renault), which would possibly herald loss of their sacrosanct status, rights, privileges and rigid hierarchies.

Business, education, training and development

In line with its 'dirigiste' tradition, France has a unique higher education system which was originally designed to produce the engineers and administrators needed to implement state policy. The universities were seen as too mediaeval and uninterested in the realities of state requirements, and hence in the middle of the eighteenth century, the 'Ecole des Ponts et Chaussées', the engineering school, was created, the first in a whole succession of so-called **grandes écoles** (there are now over 170) which provide education specifically geared to technical, administrative and business needs in the civil service, and state and private industry.

Unlike the universities to which any student with a baccalauréat (the equivalent of British 'A' levels, but more broadly based) can gain access, competition to enter these grandes écoles, particularly the top engineering and business schools, is fierce and eliminates all but the very best – that is, in terms of mathematical prowess (a French obsession and the main admissions criterion) and abstract, logical thinking. Only 6 per cent of those going on to higher education make the grade, some 15,000 graduating annually from the engineering schools and 8000 from business schools. There is some pressure to increase the output of engineers but the argument that some form of *numerus clausus* is needed has won the day. It is argued that demand should exceed supply otherwise there will be unemployment amongst engineers, as there is amongst doctors.

Large companies focus their graduate recruitment on the grandes écoles, on a student population which is highly gifted and trained, although much criticism is often heard of their arrogant view of their own infallibility and their lack of some of the 'softer' personal skills. This is the price to be paid in a system which breeds a narrow élite, which has been and still is to some extent the lynchpin of French economic and industrial activity and a vital constituent part of the business culture.

The élite is not purely intellectual, however. It has been argued by John Ardagh in *France Today* that the French failed to do away with its aristocracy in 1789 because the meritocracy which replaced it has not eliminated power and privilege. To this extent the management class has become far more of a hereditary class than in comparable countries, with one-quarter of managers in the top 200 West German firms coming from rich families, just one-tenth in the USA, but over three-quarters in France. The grandes écoles system perpetuates this situation with a student population which is overwhelmingly middle class and Parisian. With over 80 per cent of senior managers in large companies having a grande école qualification, it is not hard to see the true extent of the power and privilege which the system bestows.

State service has long been a laudable and acceptable goal in France and top civil servants are as much a product of the grandes écoles as their counterparts in industry. Indeed, it is still a current tradition for civil servants, particularly Treasury officials, to move over into banking and industry, whether state or private and to retain the right to revert to government service as members of one of the **grands corps** which resemble collegiate bodies acting as old boys' clubs and dominating selection of the upper echelons of the civil service. So contact between business and government is close, with the main actors being cast in the same mould of the grandes écoles and preserving a lasting web of interlocking formal and informal relationships, which have served France well over the last three to four decades.

And these relationships are used. Before the world of business was rehabilitated, to reach the top of the civil service was a primary career ambition for the young, for top civil servants who were noticed by their Ministers, ran departments, formulated policy and influenced decisions to nominate heads of both public and private companies. Both sectors existed in a mixed economy in which the grands corps pulled the strings through personal relationships and positions of influence and power. Such a system underlines the strength of **colbertisme** in France, the idea of a strong, interventionist state which, particularly back in the 1960s and 1970s, had to be researcher, investor and financier. It alone had the necessary global vision. The heads of major companies connived with this view – it allowed them to share out markets between them, fix rules to avoid competition and constitute monopolies to serve the state. Hence even nationalization was seen in a different light. An interventionist industrial policy which it implies was to their advantage in sustaining the incestuous relationship with the state.

With the accession of the Socialists to power in 1981, nationalization assumed a new ideological hue, however, although there were solid grounds for believing that, with a virtually non-existent Bourse and no banks as in West Germany to provide major sources of funding, the state had to make up for the growing deficiencies of the private sector. The enthusiasm of the ideology of a party dominated by a majority of ex-teachers led to a fundamental disturbance of the hitherto cosy relationship between the state and private industry and, although some nationalized companies recovered dramatically from near bankruptcy in 1981, overzealous interference replaced mutual self-interest. Imperious commands were substituted for arm's-length surveillance.

The success of the privatizations of 1986 forced the Socialists to realize to what extent they had cut themselves off from reality with their brand of nationalization – many of the valid arguments of 1981 had gone, with a reinvigorated Bourse capable of bringing capital to companies requiring it. The recent Société Générale affair (one of the top deposit banks privatized in 1986) revealed, however, that even privatizations in France were potentially unhealthy, with the formation of a hard core of friendly investors which supported the Gaullist RPR party and would prefer a return to the comfort of the 1960s and 1970s, when the Establishment which they constituted went hand in glove with the state, and takeovers, markets and strategies were decided by a few civil servants and heads of companies behind closed doors. A failed attempt to split up this hard core of investors and replace it with a group more amenable to the Socialist position pointed to the opposing view of state intervention in France. During the affair, Jean Peyrelevade, head of UAP, one of the three nationalized insurance companies, refused to submit to a request by the Minister of Finance to buy shares in Société Générale and for some commentators, this constitutes a highly-significant turning point in the history of state intervention in France. The head of a state company refuses to be the lackey of ministers and civil servants and this could well be a marked shift to a more Anglo-Saxon view of business with its concepts of raising capital independently on the Bourse and enjoying freedom to determine strategy on purely business grounds. The stage is set for a battle between this new view of running a business and the all-pervading wisdom of a narrow clique of civil servants and the Establishment determining major directions of industrial policy – a battle which could well see the demise of the remaining nationalized companies and their eventual privatisation.

The élitist nature of the management of large companies is also prevalent in the number of places held on different boards of directors by heads of both state and private companies. Jean Peyrelevade, for example, also sits on the board of the private Banque Stern, of which he was once chairman, of the Lazard group, Roussel-U claf, BNP and CGE. Jean-Marc Vernes, head of the Compagnie Industrielle, sits on the board of no less than twenty-six companies and Ambroise Roux, head of Générale Occidentale, has seats on the boards of CGE and nine other companies. Between them, they symbolize the concentration of power which is characteristic of large French companies and acts as another powerful tool in the event of unwanted takeover bids. This power is reinforced by the role of the boards and their chairmen. General meetings of shareholders have virtually no teeth and the board is only formally answerable to its shareholders. In their turn, members of the board are only there to back up the chairman (**le président**). The system is almost a

carbon copy of the French parliamentary system, with extensive powers
vested in the state President. Some have called it management by divine
right with chairmen not answerable to anyone – votes are rare and,
indeed, if a proposal is put to the vote, it is seen virtually as a sign of no
confidence in the chairman and time for him to resign.

By law, no more than eight seats on different boards may be held by any
one person, but in reality many get round this by representing people who
do officially have a seat. The inevitable result in many cases is only scant
knowledge of the detailed workings of a company's business and hence
greater reliance on the authority of the chairman. Absenteeism is rife, as in
French law there is no obligation to mention attendance at board meetings
in annual reports. The notion of working committees is also virtually
unknown, and board members are very rarely taken to court for
negligence. Add to this the fact that in both private and state companies,
the main decisions are not taken during board meetings, but as a result of
discussion between a few key board members, and the picture of the
extensive cross-linking powers of board chairman is complete.

Élitist status is nowhere better exemplified then in the distinction
between technician and engineer. Whereas the word 'manager' in English
is informal and loose, the corresponding word in French, cadre is stricter
in definition. To become a cadre, employers may come up through the
ranks (but usually with no transferability of the status to another
company); graduates may join a company directly but with a qualification
gained after four (increasingly five) years of study after baccalauréat (bac
+4/5 in French parlance); or after some years on technician grade (with
the qualification of BTS – **Brevet de Technicien Supérieur** – or DUT –
Diplôme Universitaire de Technologie: both bac +2). The latter are
increasingly sought after with the increasing emphasis on automation of
production and the designing and running of automated systems. They
have virtually cornered production management jobs which engineers
shun for design offices and R & D. They are highly praised by employers
and there is little unemployment at this grade. Precisely because of their
increasing importance, however, they have aspirations to cadre status and
that is precisely where the shoe pinches, because having reached the top
of the technician grade, the majority find it impossible to become
engineers, i.e. cadres. Companies prefer their engineers to have the
generalist's more theoretical training of a grande école – 'You can't have a
plethora of generalists in a company, you've got to have some rank and
file.' However good a technician they are, a technician is what companies
want them to stay. Many drift towards the small and medium-size
companies where they immediately become cadre. Some large companies
have grasped the nettle, however, and instigated training programmes
allowing technicians to gain an engineer's qualification (IBM, in particular)

or have implemented a policy of bringing their status close to that of engineer and cadre, even if they do not have the same responsibilities. Rigid differentiation is still the order of the day for most companies, however, and is yet one more symbol of the attachment the French feel for rights and privileges accorded to status and positions. Even the French language allows for such distinctions, the form *tu* being used instead of *vous* in some design offices by engineers when talking to non-cadre technicians, to denote their inferiority (tu was always used to address servants and is still used to insult). The situation has even caused considerable industrial unrest in some companies and as individuals demand more and more responsibility and freedom in the workplace in France, such attitudes could well provoke some discontent in the future.

Perhaps the last comment on this aspect of élitism lies with the company spokesman who said, '*un technician supérieur ne pourra jamais faire valoir les compétences d'un Supélec*' (a senior technician will never be able to display the same abilities as a Supélec engineer [the grande école for electrical engineers]).

The response of business to the EC's single market

France was almost certainly the first of the EC countries to start public awareness campaigns on the subject of 1992. Every business and every individual in the land has hence been long aware through national, regional and local conferences, debates and seminars of the issues involved. The Chambers of Commerce and the employers federation (CNPF – **Confédération Nationale du Patronat Français**) have been particularly active. The coping stone has been the Xth National Plan which is entitled 'France and Europe' and which devotes separate commissions to seven different areas: technology in Europe, finance, social policy and employment, social protection, education and training, quality of life and State efficiency. Various luminaries from the other EC countries have been appointed to an advisory European board (Robert Maxwell and Theodore Zeldin from the United Kingdom, de Benedetti from Italy, Hahn from Volkswagen in West Germany amongst others).

Initially, 1992 was spoken of in France in tones of fear and foreboding, particularly given certain structural and economic weaknesses. As economic strength appears to be growing, so optimism is now more characteristic of France's approach to 1992. Optimism, that is, tinged with the knowledge that weaknesses there still certainly are, together with certain real threats but that the opportunities will outweigh them both, as industry begins to invest again to reorganize and expand. The confidence lacking in 1986 has been refound.

Strengths

Many sectors still show the traces of a long history of fragmentation, late development and protectionism. But of late, through increased levels of investment engendered by greater profits, there has been a strong industrial recovery, particularly in some of the basic industries such as steel, chemicals and aluminium. In the strategic high-technology areas, too, such as aerospace, nuclear and telecommunications, investment and restructuring are proceeding at a fast pace. Agribusiness, luxury goods, civil engineering, transport equipment and computer software continue to maintain their traditional strength and this investment brings new capacity to increase exports and stem haemorrhaging imports. The Ministry of Finance firmly believes that the 1990s will see France ceasing to lose world market share because its supply capacity is too narrow. Overall, France is the world's fourth largest industrial power.

Second, French society has been reconciled with business. The image of companies has been rehabilitated and the new entrepreneurs enjoy the same limelight as actors and footballers, as they juggle with the new instruments of financial engineering offered by a rapidly-developing capital market. Control of inflation, principally through containment of wage increases, has added to the attraction of increased profits.

Third, France will not suffer the same effects as West Germany and other countries as their ageing populations dwindle. While not completely renewing its generations, its fecundity rate is higher than in any other European country, except Ireland. The presence of sizable populations of North Africans, however, is not without significance in this respect.

Fourth, the level of concertation between top civil servants, government and the heads of large state and private companies, which is such a prominent feature in the economic and industrial management of the country, is ensuring that areas of weakness are recognized and acted upon in a cohesive manner.

Fifth, France's geographical location is seen as an area of strength and explains in part the government's determination to provide the country with a much improved and expanded road and rail network. Its central position between North and South Europe, particularly the dynamic markets of Spain and Italy is seen as an advantage to be nurtured. The Channel Tunnel and the importance which this will bestow upon the North Eastern area of the Nord-Pas-de-Calais for combined manufacturing and distribution purposes is also often stressed and explains the whole-hearted enthusiasm expressed by France for the tunnel.

Weaknesses

In stark contrast to its high technology industries, which some commentators would conclude that France has emphasized too much, many others are inward-looking, fragmented and small by world standards. The state oil companies, Elf and Total, are still too firmly entrenched in their domestic markets and are dwarfed by such giants as BP and Shell; Rhône-Poulenc is half the size of the West German chemical giants BASF, Bayer and Hoechst; the car industry is protected by a 3 per cent import limit of Japanese cars; the Renault Truck Division's sales are predominantly concentrated in France; even in aerospace, there is some doubt whether France can afford two major airframe manufacturers, Aérospatiale and Dassault, particularly as the latter goes it alone with the construction of the 'Rafale', France's alternative to the European Fighter Aircraft and for which there is no other market as yet, except the French Air Force. In the tourist sector, too, the tour operators are small and lack the vertical integration of their United Kingdom and West German counterparts: the top four companies account for only 29 per cent of a market of three million taking package tours, compared with the top four in the United Kingdom and West Germany, accounting for 80 per cent of a market over three times the size. Overall there is no French company which figures in the world's ten largest companies and only fifty in the top 500. A recent survey conducted by Bain Consultants in Paris, for the Ministry of Industry, amongst 300 companies in the turnover range FF 1–35 billion (i.e. between the top twenty groups and the PME) showed that the average turnover of the top 250 French companies is 35 per cent and 40 per cent less than that of United Kingdom and West German companies respectively. 52 per cent of this turnover was generated in France and 60 per cent of their manpower worked in France. Hence the realization that they must quickly become more international, particularly since the companies concerned realized that only one-third of their growth would come from France over the next three years.

Second, as a result of this preoccupation with the domestic market, relatively few French managers enjoy the international experience and vision of their British and West German colleagues.

Third, the managerial class is well trained but the general workforce overall lacks the right training and qualifications, a fact underlined by the high unemployment amongst the young.

Fourth, France has pursued certain elements of its industrial policy up a blind alley. Some regret is now being expressed, for example, that Japanese investment, especially in the car sector, has been kept out. The 3 per cent limit on Japanese car imports will have to go post-1992, which will inevitably lead to job losses.

Fifth, a high level of VAT on luxury goods (25 per cent), plus withholding taxes on all forms of savings might well create a situation of some panic if France, West Germany and the Benelux countries implement their Schengen agreement to form a frontier-free zone.

Sixth, low levels of trade union membership are leading to anarchical claims on the one hand, and on the other, the strong concentration of membership in some state sectors is stifling long-overdue reform and flexibility in the labour market.

Finally, as appears quite plainly in the Bain report, French companies intend to compete with price/performance and niche strategies, whereas the overriding priority of their major competitors is cost/low price and brand strategies. There is thus some appreciable gap between the perceptions of the exact nature of the competition ahead.

Opportunities

The large companies, in many sectors, have primarily appreciated the opportunities an enlarged EC market will bring, as a springboard for global markets. Indeed, perhaps in realization of their former weakness, French companies are at present the biggest investors in Europe in terms of mergers and acquisitions, the United Kingdom being their number one target. France is investing more overseas than is being invested by overseas buyers in France but it still only ranks as number six in terms of overall international investment. Thomson, in defence equipment, GCE in both telecommunications and transport equipment, Rhône-Poulenc in chemicals, Lafarge in cement, BSN in food manufacturing and Financière de Suez in banking and insurance, are some of the big names which have moved fast to reach critical size and market share via acquisition of brands, joint-venture agreements and mergers.

Threats

The main threat is to the myriad of small and medium-size companies which are top of the range through their high-value-added and often incomparable know-how. France is viewed as a veritable goldmine for brands and labels built up over many generations in a wide spectrum of sectors from baby soaps (Monnot) to ladies' stockings (DIM). British companies have been most avid, quadrupling their acquisitions to a value of FF 12.5 billion in 1988, followed by the Italians and Americans. Because, in the main, French companies are not as cash-rich as many of their West German and United Kingdom counterparts, they cannot afford some of the prices being offered. Many, indeed, may disappear themselves through lack of size: in plastics, for example, out of 3800 companies, only thirty have more than 500 employees and only 1500 exceed ten employees. In public lighting, three of the major companies are in British hands in an area rapidly expanding with the construction of new motorways and where, being subject to national and local procurement traditions, trading under a French name is crucial.

Strategies

The larger French companies are having to pursue a parallel course of action embracing consolidation at home and acquisition abroad to enable them to reach the critical size they so often lack. Thomson, for example, merged its avionics interests with those of Aérospatiale while at the same time acquiring the defence interests of Philips in Europe. Reydel, Plastic Omnium and Sommer-Allibert in the automotive equipment area have all installed major sites near car manufacturers in the United Kingdom, thus shadowing a move already made nearer car manufacturers in France. The chemical groups, Rhône-Poulenc, Alsthom, Orkem, etc., are regrouping in France but also seeking overseas partners – not in Europe, however, and particularly not in West Germany, as they value their independence! The plastics side of the chemical industry is indicative of a common French problem – France is the second-largest producer in Europe but no one group is number one or number two producer.

In the Bain report quoted above, all companies intended to go over to an offensive strategy in search of expansion, better performance and innovation. Concern was expressed over the need to catch up, and over their vulnerability, in terms of both their size and convalescent profits. A sense of urgency is common to them all, as they face stiffer competition both at home and abroad. The years from 1990 to 1993 will be critical for these French companies as France attempts to keep up with the major industrial powers on the international scene.

References and suggestions for further reading

Albertine, Jean-Marie (1988), *Bilan de l'Economie Française*, Seuil.
Ardagh, John (1987), *France Today*, Penguin.
Baliste, Marcel (1989), *L'économie Française*, Masson.

Drevet Jean-François (1988), *1992-2000 Les Régions Françaises entre l'Europe et le Déclin*, Souffles.

Eck, Jean-François (1988), *Histoire de l'Economie Française depuis 1945*, Armand Colin.

France 300 (1989), Bain et Compagnie, Paris.

L'Entreprise, various issues in 1988 and 1989.

L'Expansion, various issues in 1988 and 1989.

L'Express, various issues in 1988 and 1989.

L'Usine Nouvelle, various issues in 1988 and 1989.

Le Nouvel Economiste, various issues in 1988 and 1989.

OECD Economic Surveys, France (1988/1989).

Price Waterhouse (1989), *Doing Business in France*, London: Price Waterhouse.

Science, Vie, Economie, various issues in 1988 and 1989.

3 The business culture in Italy
William Brierley

Introduction

Business culture in Italy is informed by three principal factors: the size
and importance of the state sector (and the concomitant importance of
politics and client–patron relationships); the large number of family
concerns (and hence a preoccupation with social values including, but also
beyond those of, the profitability of the enterprise); and the scale of the
small firms sector (which requires for its survival a finely balanced mix of
both highly cooperative and highly competitive attitudes). These factors
have led to an extraordinarily rich mix of corporate cultures, with
interesting spillover effects for both the big and small industrial sectors:
for example, in the recent large-scale reorganization of the public-sector
industries, profit rather than social engineering has emerged as the
driving force, but in striving to retain the synergies identified as the
benefit of being big, the newly-reorganized companies are also seeking to
achieve the flexibility of smaller companies and thus the ability to respond
more quickly to shifts in market demand. Business culture must, therefore,
be explored in relation to these basic factors. But first an overview of the
Italian economy is called for.

In the mid- to late-1980s the Italian economy presented a bewildering
and at times paradoxical spectacle. Italy had:

- High unemployment (the national average is 12 per cent, but ranges
  from 8 per cent in the North, to 20 per cent in South).
- Relatively high interest rates (prime lending rates stood at 22 per cent
  in 1982, and fell to 14 per cent in 1989, but are consistently among the
  highest in Europe).
- High labour costs.
- Relatively high inflation (16 per cent in 1982, falling to a fairly constant
  5 per cent since the end of 1986).
- Vast public expenditure (in 1988 the budget deficit was 13 per cent of
  GDP).
- A staggering public debt (in 1988, 93 per cent of GDP).

At the same time, however:

- Exports are at an all-time high.
- State industry has undergone a relatively successful process of restructuring and reorganization.
- Italy's large private firms are European leaders (Fiat, Olivetti, Montedison, Ferruzzi).
- Its small and medium-sized enterprises bedazzle observers (Benetton is the best known, but far from only, example).
- An air of prosperity now pervades the country.

At the end of the 1970s, after a decade of terrorism, political and social strife and obvious industrial weakness, the words most commonly used to describe the state of Italy were 'chaos', 'shambles' and the most common of all, 'crisis'. Yet, by the end of the 1980s, the scourge of both left- and right-wing terrorism had been eliminated, industrial restructuring involving the loss of 700,000 jobs in manufacturing had been accomplished with relatively little pain, and a new relationship had been established with the trade union movement. All of this despite a political and administrative system which remains the least adapted to the needs of modern and efficient government in the late twentieth century, where clientelism and political patronage are rampant in every sector from nationalized industry to the arts and media. These contradictions and paradoxes became particularly apparent when, in November 1987, by including the 'black economy' in the official statistics, the Italian economy overtook the British economy as the third largest in Europe and the fifth largest in the Western world, yet the Italian President, Francesco Cossiga, had to cancel a state visit to the United Kingdom because he had to stay at home to sort out the collapse of the forty-seventh post-war government. How, the question was asked, can a country have such an apparently strong and resilient economy and at the same time such a weak and unstable political system and a corrupt and inefficient bureaucracy?

Business and government

One often-expressed view suggests that the success of the Italian economy is all down to the geniality, imagination and flair of the individual Italian entrepreneur. In fact, the picture is a good deal more complicated and much relies on an understanding of the relationship between the public sector and private sector in Italy and how the public sector has been used to provide a basis for the growth of the private sector. It is necessary, therefore, to understand how this system works.

Istituto per la Ricostruzione Industriale (IRI) was set up by the Fascists in 1933 as a temporary measure to handle a number of bank insolvencies and industrial bankruptcies. The agency was to take temporary control of these concerns and sell them back to the private sector when conditions had improved. By 1937, when it had become clear that reselling the firms would be impossible, IRI was given a new role in the autarchy objective – that of reinforcing the state's direct control over the economy. After 1945 its role became one of sustaining the national economy, maintaining the basic sectors considered crucial for the development of the country's *private* manufacturing capability. IRI now accounts for three-quarters of employment in the state holding system, and is the largest service and investment company in Europe (see Table 3.1). Its activities are so vast that they are split up into sectorally-defined subholding companies, the most important of which are Finmeccanica (mechanical industries), Fincantieri (shipbuilding), Finmare (shipping lines), STET (telecommunications) and Italstat (infrastructure construction). Finsider (the steel group) has recently gone into voluntary liquidation.

Ente Nazionale Idrocarburi (ENI) was set up in 1953 with the initial objective of disposing of the assets of AGIP (Agenzia Generale Italiana Petroliferi), which had also been founded by the Fascists. Under the dynamic leadership of Enrico Mattei, by 1962 AGIP had expanded into an organization dealing with oil exploration, drilling, importing and marketing, natural gas exploitation and petrochemicals. In 1978, ENI accounted for 13.5 per cent of state sector employment and 29 per cent of its fixed capital investment.

Ente Partecipazione Finanza Industria Manufatturiera (EFIM) deals with manufacturing industries in difficulty and is the least purposeful and least profitable of the state holding companies. It seems to owe its existence to the fact that, in the carve-up of the public sector, it has traditionally been the preserve of the Social Democrats.

There is little logic to the activities of the three companies; their activities are as much a result of historical accident as political (but never industrial) design. All three are involved in informatics and tourism; and duplications occur in railways, air transport, construction and insurance.

The state holding sector, of which IRI, ENI and EFIM are the principal components, has a basically pyramidal structure. At the top is the **Ministero per le Partecipazioni Statali** (Ministry of State Holdings), which issues directives and is responsible to Parliament. Below the Ministry come the principal **enti** (boards), which are wholly government controlled in the sense that all their equity capital is put up by the state. At the base of the pyramid come the various firms and enterprises in which the enti have a controlling interest but whose capital can also be partly privately subscribed. Given the fragmented nature of private shareholding in many firms, the state can maintain a controlling interest with as little as 15 per

Table 3.1   *IRI employment (1970–85)*

	1970	1980	1985
Manufacturing			
Steel and iron	84,625	120,652	86,323
Cement	2,073	2,265	1,741
Mechanical	59,086	97,329	74,145
Electronics	22,339	46,175	41,467
Shipbuilding	19,055	31,165	24,515
Food	10,803	18,503	8,828
Others	12,650	12,670	8,911
Total	210,631	328,759	245,830
Services			
Telecommunications	53,713	76,777	80,896
Sea transport	14,119	11,006	10,275
Air transport	15,157	20,178	20,473
Broadcasting	13,301	15,403	15,962
Others	3,532	12,552	16,324
Total	99,822	135,916	143,930
Infrastructure and construction			
Motorways	4,905	15,108	13,198
Construction	5,317	13,969	15,366
Total	10,222	29,077	28,564
Banking and finance			
Banking	35,162	60,952	63,088
Finance	1,245	1,957	2,302
Total	26,407	62,909	65,390
Total	357,082	556,659	483,714

Source: Bianchi, Patrizio (1987), 'IRI', *West European Politics*, no. 1.

cent of the equity capital. Thus the state holding sector differs from the Italian nationalized industries which are wholly state financed.

This network of public and semi-public bodies dominates every aspect of Italian life: state corporations control 80 per cent of Italy's banking, 25 per cent of industrial employment, 50 per cent of fixed investment. The state sector is a vast array of hypothetically-independent entities (some with private shareholders), but in receipt of public funds and, since the late 1950s, increasingly under the control of political appointees. Other western states have large public sectors, but none has such a breadth of economic power with such a depth of national influence.

The achievement of lRI and ENI was that they succeeded in the 1950s and 1960s in establishing those industrial infrastructures essential for rapid economic growth (cheap steel, cheap petrochemicals, cheap energy, a motorway system). Thus the public sector, instead of competing against private monopolies and/or adopting a strategy in favour of collective needs, ensured instead the expansion of the private sector.

By the 1970s, however, the state sector had become a political instrument in the hands of **Democrazia Cristiana** (the Christian Democrat party – DC), its economic functions entirely subordinated to the objective of enabling the survival of the party and the kind of economic structures which had grown with it. Between 1965 and 1977, the DC factions were estimated to have received $100 million from public corporations. Between 1974 and 1984, IRI ran a $200 million slush fund largely for the benefit of the DC.

Thus, from being the foundation stone of the economic miracle in the late 1950s and early 1960s, the public sector had by the mid-1970s become a major drain on the country's resources and an authentic power centre in its own right. Most of the public corporations are now in permanent debt. There have been major scandals in the banking sector (the collapse of Italcasse in 1980 and the Banco Ambrosiano in 1982 are the best-known examples) and the DC has seen its grip on the public sector loosened. Nevertheless, the DC has to keep supplying the public sector with state funding, which it hopes will continue to be used to ensure political support for the DC.

The captains of Italian industry (not unnaturally) object because private enterprise is being squeezed:

- High wages in the public sector create high demands in the private sector.
- Wage indexation has constrained bargaining power.
- Excessive union power has constrained the ability of management to manage.
- High social costs have been imposed on employers.

Hence the increasingly strident demand for the break up of the public sector which eventually got under way with the sale of Alfa Romeo to Fiat in 1986.

Romano Prodi, professor of economics at Bologna University and former economics minister (DC), was appointed to head IRI in 1982. His strategy for dealing with the holding company was in the medium term to re-establish control over the management and solvency of IRI firms while in the longer term seeking to take IRI out of sectors in which private industry could do better than the state, in order to concentrate on service networks and high technology in which, because of the huge investment involved he ('unlike the rest of the world', comments *The Economist*) believes the state still has a part to play. In pursuing this latter objective, Prodi had to move towards an internationalization of the public sector in order to improve efficiency, especially in advanced sectors. The new IRI strategy required at the outset the privatization of firms acquired during the period of crisis which were not crucial for (or were counterproductive to) the achievement of IRI's objectives.

Two early attempts at privatization were made, both of which failed. In 1982 the proposed sale of Maccarese (agricultural holdings) was blocked by the trade unions, and in 1983 the proposed sale of the SME food conglomerate to Buitoni-Perugina (part of the De Benedetti group) was blocked after disagreement within the government. The SME sale would have made SME-Buitoni the largest food group in Europe and by far the largest in Italy but it fell through after sustained pressure from Barilla and Ferrero provoked the opposition of the **Partito Socialista Italiano** (Socialist Party – PSI). This sort of party political interference in the management decisions of big industry is typical. For example, Marisa Bellisario, Italy's top woman executive and managing director and chief executive of Italtel (the Milan-based telecommunications switch gear manufacturer) was blocked by Fiat's managing director as chief executive of a joint venture with Fiat's Telettra because of her Socialist party affiliation.

Alfa Romeo had been in trouble since the early 1970s. Originally Alfa had produced higher-class cars and aimed at a lower volume market, unlike Fiat which had always targeted a mass market. In the late 1960s, however, Alfa was required as part of the government's policy of direct investment in the South, to build a new production plant. Construction of the new plant at Pomigliano d'Arco near Naples began in 1968, and production of the new Alfa Sud came on line just in time to coincide with the slump in demand which followed the first oil crisis. In 1986, Alfa Romeo was employing 36,000 people (28,832 in the automobile sector). Despite gradually increasing sales the company was running huge losses.

Alfa was sold to Fiat in November 1986 for 1,050 billion lire, although payment for the company in five annual instalments is not due to start until 1993, by which time the cost in real terms will have halved and Alfa should in any case be paying for itself. As a result of this successful and the previous failed privatizations a number of ground rules for future privatizations in Italy seem to have been established:

- It is up to the agency that effectively controls the stock of the company to be privatized to work out an agreement with the purchaser.
- This agreement must meet objective criteria.
- IRI has to ratify the sale based on an overall evaluation of the objectives of the public sector.

- The government must agree to the deal based on a consideration of the overall economic well-being of the country.

Privatization, however, is not the answer to all the public sector's problems. IRI and ENI have been controlled by technocrats (Romano Prodi (DC) at IRI and Franco Reviglio (PSI) at ENI), and some restructuring has taken place. Prodi and Reviglio have turned the sector round: in 1983 IRI and ENI between them lost 4,000 billion lire, but in 1987 they made a profit of 900 billion. IRI shed 125,000 jobs in six years (1983–8), privatized twenty-nine 'non-strategic' companies and as a result of mergers and internal streamlining, the number of IRI-controlled industrial concerns was reduced from 467 to 361 and the number of banks from eighty-two to fifty-four. The share of IRI equity held by private shareholders has increased to 37.7 per cent. Prodi and Reviglio have, nevertheless, had their difficulties. Prodi's major failure was his inability to sell SME, the food conglomerate, to De Benedetti. Reviglio's moment of torture was in the Summer of 1986 when a dangerous manoeuvre in the exchange market failed, causing a sudden collapse of the dollar–lire exchange rate.

These difficulties apart, the periods in office of Prodi and Reviglio have been generally judged a success. But as their mandates ended in October 1989 the old party struggles for the succession began. Now that the companies are profitable again, they represent rich pickings for the parties and the DC and the PSI have already demonstrated that they have become tired of the independence of their nominees and they wish to give the jobs to more amenable candidates.

Issues remaining to be resolved include the choice of foreign partner for Italtel, the telecommunications equipment manufacturer; the rationalization of telecommunications services under STET (currently divided among SIP, the telephone company, Italcable, the international carrier, and ASST, a telephone company which is part of the postal service); a swop of IRI's Alfa Avio aeroengine components company for Fiat's Savigliano subsidiary which produces railway bodies and rolling stock; an agreement between IRI and ENI over the production of gas turbines; the rationalization of aerospace and defence equipment manufacturers (Aeritalia (IRI) and Agusta, Oto Melara and Galileo (EFIM)); and a regrouping of Termomeccanica (EFIM), Italimpianti (IRI) and Snamprogetti (ENI) in the heavy plant and equipment sector. Discussion of the industrial logic of these proposals has been swamped by political objections to their main effect – the strengthening of DC-controlled IRI.

The extent to which the government is capable of resolving these problems must remain open to discussion. The latest (forty-eighth post-war) government crisis is a case in point. Ciriaco De Mita (DC) resigned the premiership in May 1989 having endured the sniping of the right wing of his own party for over a year and after being attacked at the PSI Party Congress by Bettino Craxi, former Prime Minister and leader of the PSI, the second largest of the five coalition parties. Craxi was demanding tougher action on the economy (despite the fact that the government's main economic programme was the work of Giuliano Amato, Treasury Minister and himself a Socialist) and several institutional reforms, including direct election of the head of state and a 5 per cent threshold for party representation in Parliament. These demands came a month before the elections to the European Parliament (18 June 1989) and the period was used by all the parties to attempt to bolster their strength with the electorate. The Italian electorate, however, demonstrated a magnificent indifference to their manoeuvrings, barely shifting in its voting from the preferences expressed in the 1987 general election (see Table 3.2).

Table 3.2

Party	General election 1987 (%)	Euro election 1989 (%)	% change
DC	34.3	32.9	− 1.4
PCI	26.6	27.6	+ 1.0
PSI	14.3	14.8	+ 0.5
MSI	5.9	5.5	− 0.4
PSDI	2.9	2.7	− 0.2
PRI-PLI-FED	5.8	4.4	− 1.4
Others	10.2	11.3	+ 1.2

DC = Democrazia Cristiana, Christian Democrat Party
PCI = Partito Comunista Italiano, Communist Party
PSI = Partito Socialista Italiano, Socialist Party
MSI = Movimento Sociale Italiano, extreme right-wing party
PSDI = Partito Socialdemocratico Italiano, social democrats, currently undergoing a split
PRI-PLI-FED = an electoral alliance of liberals (PLI), republicans (PRI) and federalists. The PRI and the PLI present separate lists in national elections.
The current members of the governing five-party coalition are the DC, PSI, PSDI, PLI and PRI.
Source: *Corriere della Sera*

The European election results weakened the position of De Mita (and of the left-wing faction of the DC which he leads), without apparently strengthening Craxi's. When Giulio Andreotti (veteran DC politician, in parliament since 1947, in and out of government since 1954, five times

Prime Minister in the 1970s, and Foreign Minister since 1983) eventually formed his sixth government in July after over two months of 'crisis', he made no promises of institutional reform and Amato's programme of economic reform was shelved and its author removed from the government to be replaced by Guido Carli (DC Senator, Governor of the Bank of Italy between 1960 and 1975, then president of Confindustria, the Italian employers' confederation, and Senator since 1983). Carli's appointment to this government position was welcomed in many financial and business sectors as an indication that at last the government was getting serious about dealing with Italy's financial problems and the debt crisis. Carli is well known for his outspoken views on US mismanagement of exchange rates, the lack of action by the EC in regard to a European system of central banks and the failure of the Bank of Italy to take action over the credit system. Carli also favours lowering interest rates soon – an opinion not shared by the present Governor, Carlo Azeglio Ciampi.

As always, the Italian government 'crisis' was a rather protracted way of carrying out a government reshuffle. Of the thirty-three members of De Mita's government, thirteen stayed in the same job under Andreotti, nine changed jobs and eleven ministers were replaced. The same five parties were involved in the coalition before and after the crisis, with almost exactly the same number of ministries each (the DC had sixteen ministers before, fifteen after; the PLI had one before, two after [losing Defence, a 'big' ministry, and gaining two smaller ones], the PSI had eleven before and after, the PRI three, and the PSDI two).

Interpreting such reshuffles and predicting the stability of the resulting coalition is a notoriously difficult task. The combination of the removal of De Mita from the premiership (so soon after losing the secretaryship of the DC party to Arnaldo Forlani) and of Amato as Treasury Minister seemed to indicate a defeat of the left within the government, and therefore of Craxi's hopes of returning to the premiership. The elevation of Gianni De Michelis (PSI) to Foreign Secretary (to replace Andreotti) and the nomination of PSI rising star Claudio Martelli as Deputy Prime Minister contradict this view, however. It may rather be that De Mita, having set out to change the DC by consensus had simply fallen victim to a faction-ridden party which did not wish to change. (Eugenio Scalfari, editor of the daily *la Repubblica*, comments on this laudable but ultimately pointless exercise, saying: 'The DC is the suit that best fits Italy's deformities. . . . The deformities of the DC are those of the country as a whole, so it is useless to expect renewal from it; it would be against its nature.' – 24 July 1989.) It may rather be that a new Forlani-Craxi power axis is being forged which will see Craxi back as Prime Minister in the not too distant future with Andreotti elevated to the Quirinale Palace and the State Presidency. Shortly after presenting his government, Andreotti said that he hoped it would be durable: 'We are looking towards 1992.' Cossiga's term as president ends in 1992; but a government which lasted two and a half years would be no mean achievement: of Andreotti's five previous governments, the longest lasted 536 days, the shortest only nine.

Businessmen trying to read the runes will find it just as diffficult as election pundits. Andreotti's campaign against De Mita was largely based on accusations that De Mita was guilty of bowing to big business concerns and forgetting his Catholic roots. Carli's appointment, therefore, probably represents a balancing act, a desire by Andreotti not to alienate big business too much (Carli is also a member of the board of Fiat). Andreotti's political acumen and his ability to hold a coalition together are undoubted; whether he will have the energy left to bring forward the necessary economic reforms is another question. His major problem is the enormous government debt.

The current national debt is over 100 thousand billion lire – more than Italy's annual GDP and in comparison with the national income three times the national debt of the United States. Interest payments on the debt account for 8 per cent of GDP. This is a significant problem on its own, but it is compounded by the requirement, as part of the 1992 project, for Italy to lift its remaining exchange controls in July 1990. This is particularly difficult for Italy because the government deficit is funded almost entirely by domestic private sector saving which is traditionally higher in Italy than in other countries. When all restrictions have been removed Italian capital may start to leave the country either because of a lack of confidence in the government's economic policy, or simply because investors see the possibility of better returns elsewhere. In either case, the exchange rate will come under pressure and the government will be required to act to sustain the value of the lira within the Exchange Rate Mechanism (ERM) of the European Monetary System (EMS). Given these sorts of pressures, a traditional approach would be to raise interest rates. By so doing, however, the government would be shooting itself in the foot: since the Italian debt is largely (80 per cent) held by Italians, paying higher interest on the debt would strengthen domestic consumption while at the same time reducing industrial competitiveness thus worsening the balance of payments problem. There is a real fear, therefore, that the scale of the problem could force the lira out of the ERM and reimpose capital controls. In any case, the problem will be as severe a test of the effectiveness of the EMS as it is of Italian government policy.

Proposals for dealing with the problem in 1990 aimed to limit the deficit to 133 thousand billion lire (10.4 per cent of GDP), by raising revenues by 15 thousand billion lire and cutting expenditure by 5 thousand billion. There are still no credible restraints being placed on health and pensions expenditure but at least a start has been made and there is greater optimism than for some time. Providing Parliament approves this proposal, it will increase confidence in the government's economic policy and help to smooth the relaxation of exchange controls and the narrowing of the lira's band in the ERM from 6 per cent to 2.5 per cent, and second it will limit consumer demand. This explains the Bank of Italy's present willingness to allow the lira to appreciate against other currencies, which has the effect of forcing up the price of imported goods and thereby limiting consumer demand. All of this must be achieved while at the same time controlling inflation (see Table 3.3).

Table 3.3   *Italian inflation rates (1979–89)*

Year	%
1979	14.1
1980	21.2
1981	17.8
1982	16.5
1983	14.7
1984	10.8
1985	9.2
1986	5.9
1987	4.7
1988	5.0
1989	6.3

Source: OECD

The cabinet and government face other immediate and urgent problems of relevance to the industrial sector, such as:

- Whether to give priority to a new draft law for the small business sector.
- How to build up and make more effective Italy's low spending on research and development (currently only 1.5 per cent of GDP).
- Who to appoint to replace Prodi and Reviglio at IRI and ENI.
- Whether to force a showdown with the unions over pay and organization in the civil service and local government.

A 'window of opportunity' now seems to exist provided by a degree of consensus in the Andreotti government. Carli and Ciampi may have their disagreements (for example, about whether industrial companies should control banks), but they agree on the reform of the Italian economic system through the introduction of more effective market mechanisms.

Table 3.4   *Italian growth rates (1979–89)*

Year	%
1979	4.9
1980	3.9
1981	1.1
1982	0.2
1983	1.1
1984	3.2
1985	2.9
1986	2.9
1987	3.1
1988	3.7
1989	3.2

Source: OECD

Business and the economy

Manufacturing

The private sector economy is proportionately the smallest in Europe, accounting for only 35–40 per cent of production. It is also remarkable for its large number of small producers (90 per cent of firms employ fewer than 100 employees, the average number of employees in an Italian firm is 7.6). Italy has the largest number of shopkeepers in Europe. In the 1980s the private sector blossomed, to an extent replacing the state sector as the dynamic segment of the Italian economy. But the private sector, despite the vast number of small firms, is dominated by a handful of dynamic industrialists: Gianni Agnelli (nicknamed **l'Avvocato**, the lawyer, at Fiat), Raul Gardini (**il Contadino**, the farmer, at Ferruzzi-Montedison), Carlo De Benedetti (**l'Ingegnere**, the engineer, at Olivetti) and Silvio Berlusconi (**Sua Emittenza**, his 'emittence' – a pun on a Cardinal's honorific – owner of the TV network Canale 5 and the supermarket chain Standa, amongst other things). A review of the activities of these extremely influential men and their organizations is therefore appropriate.

Agnelli and Fiat

Fiat had to face the same crisis in the 1970s as all the other European car producers, but the company emerged in the late 1980s as the largest and most successful European car manufacturer. Fiat's problems were of two types: one to do with the management of the workforce, the other to do with production of the right product.

Along with other big employers after 1969 Fiat found itself beset by the problem of handling a well-organized and disruptive workforce. Fiat's response to this problem was to develop and perfect its subcontracting strategy: unable to reconstruct the social peace of the 1950s inside the factory after 1969, the firm opted for the fragmentation of labour power into a multitude of small supplying firms. Fiat decentralized many of its subprocesses and components to subcontracting firms. In the early 1970s, for example, Fiat had been criticized for not investing in the South. When it finally did begin to invest, three years after Alfa, it was able to learn from Alfa's mistakes (principally, setting up a large factory in an urban industrial area). Fiat took better advantage of regional incentives and rather than setting up large plants in urban industrial areas it opted for smaller factories in conservative rural areas with high unemployment, creating a scatter of medium-sized plants in a range of locations. This multi-plant strategy, which also includes plants outside Italy, prevents a strike from suddenly paralysing the whole of production, since major components such as engines or gearboxes can be obtained from several sources.

It is estimated that there are now some 8000 supporting satellite firms which are in some way subordinate to the main industry; Fiat determines the supply of these firms' products, the level of prices and, by implication, the investment and staffing levels. Together with the introduction of robots in labour-intensive tasks such as welding, this has meant a large reduction in the Fiat workforce. Fiat laid off 23,000 workers in 1980. The lay-offs were bitterly opposed by the unions, but in October of that year, 40,000 workers marched through Turin, in defiance of their union leaders, demanding the right to work. This moment was a significant one in worker–management relations at the national level as well as at the level of the company. It signalled the end of the militant postures adopted by the unions since their victories of 1969 and marked the beginning of the end of trade union unity. The significance of the event was noted all over Italy. Industrial tribunals began upholding dismissals for absenteeism and Confindustria challenged the **scala mobile** (wage indexation system) which had been in operation since 1975.

Fiat, then, has an important role in the national political scene as well as in the industrial scene – this is hardly surprising, given that the company . accounts for 4 per cent of Italy's GNP. In the 1950s Fiat worked closely with the political authorities and was able to influence the economic strategy of the DC and hence of the government. The Italian state helped Fiat by providing the infrastructure for the development of a large car market: building motorways, keeping down the price of petrol, running down public transport. Externally, Fiat presented a progressive image, but internally it was repressive towards the unions, especially the Communist-inspired CGIL. Throughout the 1960s and 1970s, however, Fiat dissociated itself from the DC, attacking the clientele system and demanding (when Agnelli became President of Confindustria in 1974) a central role for industry in the management of the economy, planning and a clear separation between the state and the private sector. Agnelli's line did not prevail, mainly because the sheer size of the public sector makes it difficult for private industry to emerge as a political protagonist. Nevertheless, Agnelli is not averse to making his political views known, and he has expressed enthusiasm for Craxi's 'modernizing' approach.

Much of Fiat's commercial success is due to the ability of the car section to capture larger market shares, mainly through its new models, the Uno and the Tipo. 60 per cent of Fiat's 38 thousand billion lire turnover in 1988 came from cars, and cars generated 2 thousand billion lire profit – two-thirds of all Fiat's profits from 48 per cent of its 270,000 employees. In 1988 Fiat became Europe's largest car manufacturer with over 2 million sales (Table 3.5).

Table 3.5   *European car sales 1988*

Company	(%)
Fiat	14.9
Volkswagen	14.6
Japanese	12.7
Peugeot-Citroën	11.6
Ford	11.3
General Motors	10.5
Renault	9.8
Others	14.6

Source: L'Espresso

Agnelli's announcement in November 1988 that Vittorio Ghidella, the managing director (**amministratore delegato**) of Fiat Auto and previously tipped to succeed Cesare Romiti as the chairman of the Fiat Group, was to leave the company and his functions to be assumed by Romiti himself, may seem puzzling in the light of Fiat Auto's success. In fact, 1988, as well as being a year of outstanding success for the company, was also a year of deep and bitter internal struggle over the basic strategy of the group. Ghidella believed that to survive and prosper into the 1990s, a successful car producer would have to be able to compete in 'two out of three' of the world's major markets (Europe, the USA and Japan). Fiat's domination of Europe would not be enough to safeguard its future. The group would therefore have to concentrate more of its resources on car production and/ or enter into large-scale production and commercial agreements with US manufacturers. Fiat's agreement with Lee Iacocca's Chrysler was a start in this direction, but for Romiti, this was already too much. For Romiti, car production is a 'mature sector' and investment should be limited to that strictly necessary to maintain market share. Romiti is much more interested in the financial sector and banking, media and telecommunications, and diversification into other industrial sectors (operations such as Snia-Bnp who produce missiles and munitions – Table 3.6). Ghidella had been supported by Umberto Agnelli in demanding restrictions on Japanese imports, but such demands were out of step with political developments and unlikely to find favour in government circles.

Table 3.6   *The Fiat Group, 1988*

Sector	% of operation
Cars	59.5
Commercial vehicles	16.8
Vehicle components	7.7
Tractors	6.0
Snia-Bnp	5.2
Metal products	3.3
Industrial components	2.5
Production systems	1.7
Civil engineering	1.4
Telecommunications	1.4
Aviation	1.2
Lubricants	0.9
Publishing	0.7
Railway products	0.6

These figures exclude the activities of Rinascente, Toro Assicurazioni and Gemina.
Source: L'Espresso

Under Romiti, Fiat will not buy out other car manufacturers (BMW was mooted at one time), but rather will diversify into electronics and aerospace, even though its experience and success in these sectors are limited (a modest agreement with IBM produced less than expected, Fiat withdrew from Westland after less than two years). Even more, Fiat will attempt to expand into banking and finance. Romiti wants to put together a bank from Nuovo Banco Ambrosiano, Banca Cattolica del Veneto and Banca Nazionale dell'Agricoltura, which would have 25 thousand billion lire in deposits. Fiat has the money to buy these banks (it has 10 thousand billion lire, but in Fiat Auto) mainly because its recent acquisitions have cost it very little (see the Alfa purchase above) but the group must first overcome the strong resistance of the Bank of Italy, which is firmly opposed to the mixing of industrial and financial interests.

Many have questioned the wisdom of dispensing with such a successful manager as Ghidella, and of concentrating the whole of Fiat management in one person's hands, and of radically changing a strategy which has paid such dividends in recent years, particularly at a time when the highly-protected Italian car market (car imports from Japan have been limited to a meagre 14,000 units per year) is being opened up as a result of Project 1992. But Romiti has responded vigorously to the challenge, signing an historic deal with the Soviet Union in November 1989 to build a £1 billion car plant in the USSR, setting up a merger between Lancia (Fiat's luxury car subsidiary) and the car division of Sweden's Saab to create the largest luxury car manufacturer in the world, as well as making the running in two other deals, the first to take over the Spanish state-owned truck manufacturer, ENASA, and the second to build a replacement for the existing Fiat-backed FSO factory in Poland.

Gardini and Ferruzzi-Montedison

The Ferruzzi agribusiness group, headed by Raul Gardini, is the major shareholder in the Montedison chemicals company. In 1988, Gardini, with the not inconsiderable assistance of Enrico Cuccia at Mediobanca, put together a consortium to refinance Montedison and consolidate the chemicals activities of the state-owned Enichem and of Montedison into a new company, Enimont. Before the reorganization, Ferruzzi and Montedison had combined debts of 12,000 billion lire; rationalization and the selling off of many of Montedison's assets have given the group considerable liquidity and greatly reduced debts. Enimont (by adding Enichem and Montedison's market shares together) has 34 per cent of the domestic Italian chemicals market and employs 52,000 people (7–9,000 jobs are set to go in rationalization). Sales are estimated at about $10 billion per year.

De Benedetti and Olivetti

Carlo De Benedetti resigned as Chief Executive of Fiat Auto in 1976 (at the age of forty-one) when his plan for revitalizing the auto group was rejected by Agnelli. He immediately bought CIR (Compagnie Industriali Riunite) and used it to start buying small manufacturing companies. He took over the loss-making ($8 million a month) typewriter manufacturer in 1978 and transformed Olivetti into Europe's second biggest information technology company, after IBM, with sales in 1988 of $4.8 billion. Just under half of Olivetti's sales are in Italy, followed by France, West Germany, the United Kingdom, Spain and Switzerland. Olivetti has 40 per cent of the domestic personal computer market (25 per cent to IBM) and 23 per cent of the minicomputer market (33 per cent to IBM). Olivetti's relationship with AT&T (who own 21 per cent of Olivetti's shares and distribute Olivetti PCs in the US) has proved problematical especially on the issue of technical standards. De Benedetti has dreams of a Europe-wide industrial and financial empire to which diversification is the key, and in the pursuit of which he has been repeatedly frustrated, first in his failed attempt to take over Société Générale de Belgique, then in the SME fiasco, and more regularly in competing with the West German Siemens, who produce almost everything that Olivetti produce. Olivetti went through a shakeup in 1988 both in production and in organization: with a new corporate structure and a new product range the prospects for Olivetti in the 1990s are brighter.

Berlusconi

The Berlusconi empire is built on suburban housing and B-grade television. Silvio Berlusconi began his career in the early 1970s building Milano 2, a development just outside Milan which claims to have 'everything to cater for the social, commercial and leisure interests of man'. In 1976, he bought a small commercial TV station for Milano 2, more or less at the same time as the Italian high court was ruling that private local TV stations could compete with the national RAI network. Berlusconi succeeded where many others failed by buying local stations up and down the country and shipping out to them prerecorded programmes on cassettes, thereby creating a pseudo-national network to compete directly with RAI. Having established this national network Berlusconi hammered home the advantage by offering advertisers twice as much time for their money. By buying out two competitors who tried to beat him at his own game, Berlusconi created the three networks he now owns.

Berlusconi is now diversifying his activities. The purchase of the Standa supermarket-department store chain in 1988 (for details see below) puts Berlusconi in a unique position with a mutually supportive advertising, distribution and sales network. By giving TV advertisers guaranteed shelf space he is attempting to gain a stranglehold on large areas of consumer retailing.

Textiles and clothing

Textile manufacturing is Italy's third biggest business after engineering and construction. Textile sales account for almost 14 per cent of the value of Italian manufacturing and one third of the entire textile turnover of the EC. Exports account for 20,000 billion lire, more than double the value of textile imports. Italy has about 840,000 textile workers. Italy is also Europe's leading exporter of clothing, with exports in 1987 totalling 5,360 billion lire. Italy accounts for 38 per cent of the clothing imports of the members of the EC.

The jewel in an already glittering crown of clothing manufacturers and exporters is Benetton. Addressing the casual market, rather than the fashion market, Benetton's annual sales are over $1 billion, of which about 35 per cent are in Italy, 15 per cent in North America, 13 per cent in West Germany, 11 per cent in France and 6 per cent in the United Kingdom. Benetton's current group strategy in the clothing market is to achieve a geographical spread of sales that will see one-third of its revenue coming from North and South America, one-third from Europe and one-third from the Far East.

The fashion market is smaller but no less sparkling. The top five fashion houses – Valentino, Armani, Versace, Krizia and Ferre – have combined sales of about $1 billion, of which just over half comes from the sale of clothes. The business strategies of the top fashion houses do not differ greatly: they have all realized that there is money to be earned both in Italy and abroad by lending their names to the manufacture of an array of goods, from sunglasses, watches and perfumes to less exotic umbrellas and even kitchen tiles. And almost all have also launched cheaper secondary lines in ready-to-wear clothes as well as the ubiquitous designer jeans.

The food industry

The food industry in Italy is small scale, fragmented and wide open to foreign takeovers (Table 3.7).

The inability of the industry and the government to handle the privatization of SME is an indication of the fragmentation of the sector and the dangers of government interference. The original proposed sale of

Table 3.7 *European and Italian food companies (sales in billions of lire)*

European	Sales	Italian	Sales
Unilever (British-Dutch)	12,000	Eridania	4,370
Nestlé (Swiss)	11,700	Ferrero	2,100
BSN-Danone (French)	7,500	Barilla	1,634
Allied Lyons (British)	5,900	SME*	1,590
Grand Met (British)	5,000	Galbani	1,360
Guinness (British)	4,800	Star	850
United Biscuits (British)	4,200	Parmalat	816
Heineken (Dutch)	3,400	Lavazza	502

* Not including supermarket activities
Source: *L'Espresso*

SME (which includes companies like Cirio, Motta, Allemagna and Pavesi) to Carlo De Benedetti's Buitoni-Perugina company was blocked in government by the Socialists. Having been frustrated in his efforts, De Benedetti sold off Buitoni to Nestlé. SME's profits between 1984 and 1987 rose from 65 billion lire to 115 billion. The IAR group (an alliance of Barilla, Ferrero and the broadcasting magnate Silvio Berlusconi) began to show interest in acquiring SME. Berlusconi, having acquired the Standa national department store chain from Raul Gardini in 1988 was seeking to build up a supermarket and store network to rival Rinascente (part of the Fiat group). He was interested in the highly-profitable Autogrill (which has a monopoly of motorway cafés) and Generale Supermercati supermarket chain. Berlusconi was not interested in the food-producing side (presumably to be left to Ferrero-Barilla), but sought to take his profits from advertising (food producers now spend more on TV advertising than car manufacturers, and Berlusconi has Canale 5 ready to provide them with air time), and distribution via the GS supermarket chain. Berlusconi was too keen, however, and his close relationship with the Socialists antagonized the Christian Democrats, who will almost certainly ensure that the deal does not go through. All this as the foreign competitors amass their forces for a concerted onslaught. (BSN-Danone and Nestlé have already made inroads into pasta production.)

Design

Italian designers and Italian design are among the most celebrated in the world. The names of car designers like Pininfarina and Giugiaro are well-established throughout Europe and the US. Pininfarina designs cars for Fiat and for General Motors too. Giugiaro has designed some of Europe's best-selling models: the VW Golf, the Fiat Uno, the Audi 80 and the Saab 9000.

Although industrial design may be big business in image terms, in revenue terms individual designers tend to be small and compact operations. Giugiaro, for example, had a turnover in 1987 of 65 billion lire. Small-scale home and office furniture designers are proliferating as all the major companies now farm out their design problems to an army of creative individuals.

The recession of the early 1970s restricted the expansion of industry in the North, but the effect on the South was even more dramatic. As the recession hit both the north Italian and the European economies, leading to higher unemployment in these areas of traditional labour shortage, the usual safety valve for southerners – emigration – was blocked. At the same time both the population and the labour force in the South continued to grow faster than in the rest of the country. The slowdown in economic growth was accompanied by high inflation which limited the effectiveness of public expenditure programmes on which the Southern economy had come to depend. As the scale and value of investment stagnated, so did growth in the South. Between 1974 and 1988, the South's overall contribution to Italy's GDP remained between 23 and 24 per cent (whereas the Southern regions account for 36 per cent of Italy's population). More significantly, per capita GDP declined from 69 per cent of the Italian average to 64 per cent, whereas in the Centre-North per capita GDP rose from 116 per cent of the Italian average to 120 per cent. The South's contribution to Italy's exports also declined, from 13.7 per cent to 9.6 per cent, while imports from both the Centre-North and from abroad continued to grow. The effect on employment has been dramatic: employment in agriculture, industry and construction has continued to decline, but has not been balanced by the expansion of employment in the service sectors, as has happened in the Centre-North. In 1987 Italy's average unemployment rate was 12 per cent, average unemployment in the South was running at almost twice that rate, and in the fifteen–thirty age group it reached 36 per cent (Table 3.8).

Government policy to address the problems of the South has seen some changes but the main arm of policy throughout has been the development of infrastructures. In the 1950s and 1960s (with the creation of the semi-autonomous regional development fund, the **Cassa per il Mezzogiorno** [Fund for the South]), as Italy transformed from a rural to an industrial economy, there seemed to be sense in a policy of infrastructure development to facilitate private industrial investment. Of the 94 thousand billion

Table 3.8   *Italian regional unemployment and income*

Region	Unemployment rate	1987–8 GNP % variation
Abruzzo	9.8	3.2
Molise	12.6	3.5
Campania	23.7	3.7
Puglia	17.2	4.5
Basilicata	21.5	3.4
Calabria	25.0	− 1.3
Sicily	21.6	2.5
Sardinia	19.8	5.3
South	20.6	3.9
Centre-North	7.8	4.2
Italy	12.0	3.9

Source: SVIMEZ

lire (at 1987 prices) spent between 1974 and 1988, almost 70 per cent was spent on infrastructures and only 23 per cent on direct investment in production. Even so, much of this money was wasted in ineffectual bureaucratic monitoring procedures: by 1988, of the 39,000 public works programmes initiated under government intervention schemes, only 13,000 had reached completion. Moreover, the regions had been unable to spend all the money allocated to them, some 25 thousand billion lire remaining in regional treasuries.

Of the major problems facing the South, perhaps the most dramatic is organized crime in its various manifestations (**mafia** in Sicily, **'ndrangheta** in Calabria and **camorra** in Naples), which poses a grave threat to civil life and a major disincentive to legitimate entrepreneurial activity in some areas of the South. These criminal forces not only threaten public order, but they also destablize the economy. They have now become dominant forces in these three regions; they control bidding on public works projects and launder money obtained illegally (especially from drug trafficking). Estimates of the scale of organized crime and of its significance in economic terms vary widely, from $750 million per year (equivalent to a company the size of ITT) to $10 billion (equivalent to the activities of Exxon). These would seem to be conservative estimates, given that the value of heroin traded in Italy in 1988 is put at $35 billion, and the trade seems set to continue to grow to satisfy the demand from Italy's 300,000 addicts (three times as many as the United States, on a per capita basis).

The traditional pattern is for the organization to make money from prostitution, protection and more recently and more lucratively from drug trafficking and to 'invest' their gains in property speculation and construction work. A cosy relationship has existed in the past between the mafia families and the political parties, particularly the Christian Democrats, but this has recently been torn apart as the government and regional authorities have been forced to confront the organization with bloody consequences. Political leaders and senior policemen, once considered immune from the attacks of the assassins of the **onorata società** (honoured society), now fall victim with sickening regularity. Just three tragic examples will suffice to demonstrate that no part of the establishment is now safe: 1980, Pier-Santi Mattarella, Christian Democrat leader of the Sicilian region; 1982, Pio La Torre, leader of the Communist group in the Sicilian parliament, prominent opponent of cruise missiles and mafia involvement in the building contracts at the nuclear base at Comiso in Sicily; 1982, Carlo Alberto Dalla Chiesa, Prefect of Palermo, sent to Sicily to take on the mafia after defeating the **Brigate Rosse** (Red Brigades terrorist group). The list of murdered magistrates would fill pages. The arrest of 'supergrass' Tommaso Buscetta in 1984 led to a series of **maxi processi** ('super trials') as cracks in the wall of **omertà** (the rule of silence) began to appear. But the mafia is deeply rooted in the social fabric and its extirpation is a matter of social and cultural renewal, not only of criminal investigation and prosecution. Organized crime is a plague on the South, creating a negative business atmosphere and blocking useful investment. Concerns about the criminal ramification of the completion of the European internal market entered national consciousness recently when the Governor of the Bank of Italy told a parliamentary committee that the mafia had billions of dollars ready for laundering and investment throughout the European Community. Antonio Gava, then Minister of the Interior, revealed how the mafia was underwriting Italy's national debt by buying up treasury bonds through foreign banks. The **Guardia di Finanza** (Finance Police) believes that the mafia has enough of a representation on the Italian stock market to manipulate companies and even destabilize the lira.

For the rest, the South suffers all the problems of modern Italy but in a more concentrated form – urban degeneration is more pronounced, the transport network is less efficient, the banking system is more costly and less efficient, research and development is almost nonexistent (of Italy's already low R & D investment, only 7 per cent is spent in the South), vocational training is declining in all regions except Sicily and Sardinia.

Some rays of hope do exist: the high quality of the potential labour force, for example. Of the 758,000 young unemployed in the South, 45 per cent have diplomas or degrees. Also, the population in the South continues to grow, while that in the Centre-North is declining (it is projected that the South will account for 45 per cent of Italy's population by 2005). The South is, therefore set to repeat its role as source of labour for the North as the North fails to produce sufficient labour for its growing economy. Southerners also display great flexibility and very high productivity – often diverted into the black economy and therefore not revealed in official statistics.

The **Cassa per il Mezzogiorno** has recently been wound up and replaced by a new **Azienda per il Mezzogiorno** and a series of special provisions including law 64 of 1986, which allocated 120 thousand billion lire to the South over a nine-year period. Few improvements are to be expected as a result, however, since the problems of bureaucracy and lack of control which prevented the old system from being effective have not been addressed. Some large-scale investments are taking place, for example Fiat and Olivetti have been given 2,500 billion lire for projects in the South (a state contribution of 60–70 per cent of the total investment), but the impact on employment will be limited: Fiat proposes to provide only 1,200 new jobs (each job therefore costs 1.5 billion lire) and Olivetti will use its money simply for restructuring just to preserve the current jobs. The prospects for Southern Italy are not encouraging.

Business and the law

The means of incorporating a business enterprise as a legal entity in Italy are laid down by the **Codice Civile** (Civil Code).

The most usual types of company are as follows:

- **Società per Azioni** (SpA), which is the same sort of organization as a United Kingdom public limited company. The minimum share capital is 200 million lire with special permission being required from the Italian Treasury if the capital is to exceed 2 billion lire.
- **Società a Responsabilità Limitata** (Srl), which is similar to a United Kingdom private limited company. The minimum capital requirement is 20 million lire, but otherwise the formation procedures are the same as for a public limited company. For both the SpA and the Srl, 30 per cent of the initial capital must be paid up on incorporation. There is no restriction on foreigners being shareholders or directors.
- **Partnerships** – There are three main types of partnership: a general partnership in which the liability of the partners is not limited (**Società in Nome Collettivo**, Snc); a partnership in which the liability of individual partners is limited by agreement to the amount of their capital contribution (**Società in Accomandita Semplice**, Sas); and an incorporated partnership in which the liability of certain partners is unlimited (**Società in Accomandita per Azioni**, SapA). In a partnership

there must be at least two partners, but there is no legal maximum. There is no legal minimum of capital to be subscribed except in the case of the incorporated partnership which follows the same rules as the corporations and must have the same minimum capital of 200 million lire. This latter form of partnership is very rare.

All business concerns in Italy must be registered with the local Chamber of Commerce (**Camera del Commercio**). Taxes on companies are levied both by central government and by local authorities. The rate for corporate income tax (IRPEG, which is levied on all income whether produced in Italy or abroad) is 35 per cent and for local income tax (ILOR) 15 per cent. There are withholding taxes on dividends, interest and royalties. A double taxation agreement exits between Italy and the United Kingdom.

VAT (**Imposta sul Valore Aggiunto** – Iva) was introduced in Italy in 1973 and is levied at a basic rate of 19 per cent (raised from 18 per cent in July 1988) with special low rates for food and other essential products and higher rates of 20 and 38 per cent for luxury goods.

Labour law and social security legislation are complex and extensive. Italian law recognizes four basic categories of employee: **dirigenti** (senior managers); **quadri** (middle managers); **impiegati** (staff employees, white collar workers); and **operai** (manual workers, blue collar workers). A range of laws regulates employment conditions and individual and collective rights, the most important of which is Law 300 of 1970, the **Statuto dei Diritti dei Lavoratori**, (Law on Workers' Rights). Other legislation regulates the engagement and dismissal of employees; maximum normal working hours (forty hours for a five day week) and overtime; employees' rights to reasonable remuneration, annual bonus, one day's rest per week, annual paid holidays and severance pay. In general, firms employing more than three persons must recruit their employees with the approval of the local Employment Office of the Ministry of Labour, and half of all recruits are nominated by their offices. Grounds for dismissal are limited by statute, especially for firms with more than fifteen employees. Discrimination in employment on grounds of race, sex, or religion is illegal, as is discrimination based on trade union membership or activity.

Business and finance

One of the anomalies of the Italian economy is that while the nation's industry is moving forward, its financial markets are 'backward, incestuous and dangerously underregulated' and the financial system is 'anachronistic, even feudal' (Alan Friedman, in the *Financial Times*).

Banking system

Italy has some 1200 separate banks with around 12,000 branches. The system is the least concentrated in the world and the least competitive, not least because a large proportion of the banks are in the public sector and most top jobs are handed out as part of a division of political spoils (**lottizzazione**).

The need to rationalize the system, demanded by the Governor of the Bank of Italy, Carlo Azeglio Ciampi, and by the then Treasury Minister, Giuliano Amato (PSI), awoke in the minds of the two main government coalition parties not the need to find the best people for the jobs, but simply the need to carve up the jobs between themselves at the expense of the smaller political parties and to ensure that their relative political strengths would be preserved in any future rationalizations (Table 3.9).

Table 3.9   *Italy's top banks and their political controllers (1988)*

Rank	Bank	Assets ($ million)	Political control
1	Banca Nazionale del Lavoro	96,072	PSI
2	Istituto Bancario S Paolo	73,477	DC
3	Monte dei Paschi di Siena	67,183	DC
4	Banca Commerciale Italiana	62,539	Technocrats
5	Banco di Napoli	59,343	DC
6	Banco di Roma	56,361	DC
7	Cariplo	53,891	DC
8	Credito Italiano	50,448	Technocrats
9	Banco di Sicilia	31,140	PRI
10	Istituto Mobiliare	23,386	Technocrats

With the exception of the Cassa di Risparmio di Venezia (PSI) all the other major savings banks were also controlled by Christian Democrats
Sources: The Banker and *L'Espresso*

Despite the political shenanigans, some rationalizations were planned in early 1989. The model on which restructuring was to take place was the so-called 'universal' banks of West Germany (see page 23). The Italians use the term **plurifunzionale** (polyfunctional) to describe the new system: holding companies control commercial banking, medium-term corporate finance, securities underwriting, investment banking and financial services including insurance. Links were to be established between Istituto

Bancario San Paolo and Crediop, Hambros and Guardian Royal Exchange (UK); between IMI and the troubled Banco di Roma and Banco di Napoli; between Banca Nazionale del Lavoro and INA (insurance group); and between Credito Italiano and Banca Nazionale dell'Agricoltura (the largest private sector bank).

So, the banking houses seem to be getting in order, but they have a long way to go in providing an acceptable retail banking service. As any tourist knows, the service offered to bank customers in Italy is appalling. Lengthy queues and indolent bank clerks are the order of the day. In-built inefficiencies abound, such as the civil service status of bank employees; the difficulty of achieving restructuring by means of redundancies; and the way banks have got used to the easy money earned on cheques which take up to a month to clear. A nationwide cash dispenser system (Bancomat) has recently been introduced, which should have helped, but has not been fully utilized: customers are supposed to be able to use their cards at other banks' machines, but often find their cards rejected because not all the banks follow the rules of the system. New technologies have also been introduced haphazardly into bank branches; labour-saving computers have been introduced without labour reductions. Before things can improve, top bank executives must undergo a cultural change in the way they perceive individual retail customers. Italian bankers have not yet recognized that value-added retail services can generate substantial revenues, as well as improving efficiency and reducing cost structures.

Such a sea-change seems unlikely in the near future, given that most interest in the financial sector seems to focus on the more glamorous aspects of corporate finance. Most major Italian industrial companies are flush with cash and everyone recognizes the need for Italian banks to be made more efficient post 1992. Why, then, not allow the industrialists to take over the banks and run them as efficiently as they have been running their companies? This is the question posed by Cesare Romiti of Fiat (though he always wears his hat as chairman of Gemina when talking about banking), Raul Gardini of Ferruzzi-Montedison, Carlo De Benedetti of Olivetti and Silvio Berlusconi. The principal obstacle to their ambitions is the Governor of the Bank of Italy. Ciampi does not oppose the idea of industrialists buying minority shares (up to 15 per cent) of banks, but he sees the possibility of serious conflicts of interest if their shares go higher and they start to control the banks. The debate has been very heated and critics have said that Italian industrialists could better use their time and company cash balances to concentrate on achieving Europe-wide economies of scale, while the central bank could make better use of its resources to press for priorities such as faster cheque-cashing, a stronger interbank market, and more cuts in government spending. One cannot help feeling that the critics might have a point.

In all this, the **Banca d'Italia** (Bank of Italy) has managed to maintain a reputation as the most authoritative, least political, most independent and internationally experienced institution in Rome. The Bank is an organ of government and cannot, therefore, always behave as though it were immune to the caprices of politicians and powerful corporate interests. Unlike politicians and managers of state industry, however, the Governor of the Bank of Italy is appointed for life, and he therefore enjoys a greater deal of security than many of his opponents. This security lends him authority and also allows him to take a longer view of the timescale for change. The Bank in recent years has encouraged greater competition among banks and relaxed its rules on the freedom of banks to alter their branch networks. It has promoted improvements in the efficiency of the payments system and tightened restrictions on general purpose loans to industry (loans which were then relent on the financial markets). The Bank has also been active at the international level on issues such as Third World sovereign debtors and the European System of Central Banks. The fact that Governor Ciampi enjoys the fierce opposition of both politicians and industrialists is the surest sign that he is doing a good job.

At the other end of the banking spectrum lies the relationship between small firms and their local banks. In this area, as in so many others, Italy shows a marked difference from the United Kingdom. A large part of the banking system is made up of local savings banks (**Casse di Risparmio**). These banks derive their funds from local investors and savers and lend to local firms. They have a strong local identity. Their directors and managers have a close working relationship with the firms in their area and a personal knowledge of anyone setting up in business and needing to borrow money to do so. In some cases the bank may be involved in the decision-making of the business and may even lend staff. Some banks subsidize centres to provide specialist services to small firms, but equally important is the fact that the decisions of the bank will be based on an understanding of the local economy rather than on rules laid down by a distant head office. There are clearly implications for this system, which is obviously of benefit to Italy's small firms, in the moves to rationalize the banking system post 1992.

Stock market

In 1985 fewer companies were quoted on the Milan bourse than in 1975 (145 compared with the earlier 155), but in the next two years the number jumped by over 40 per cent to 210. However, to say that the Italian stock market is now the fifth largest in Europe, after the United Kingdom, West Germany, France and Switzerland, is to give the wrong impression.

Milan's total market capitalization in 1988 stood at around 160,000 billion
lire. This represents between 16 and 17 per cent of Italy's GNP, whereas
the capitalization of the London Stock Exchange is equivalent to 98 per
cent of UK GNP and Wall Street amounts to 55 per cent of US GNP. The
Italian stock market's value is equivalent to only 12 per cent of the
country's total financial assets. But even this may mislead. Among the 200
or so quoted companies, the average proportion of company stock that is
actually traded on the Milan bourse – the float – is 25 per cent of issued
share capital. So the actual capitalization of Milan could be considered to
be one-quarter of its total 160,000 billion lire. Moreover, the market sees
active trading in only forty or fifty shares – again one-quarter of the total.
Some forty quoted companies do not even have as much as 25 per cent of
their shares available on the market, even though this is the legal
minimum. The stock market regulatory body believes it would be
'unrealistic' to suspend trading in so many shares just to conform with a
legal nicety. Final confirmation of the limited nature of the bourse, if such
were needed, is given by the fact that a third of the stock market's value is
accounted for by just two companies, Fiat and Generali. In macroeconomic
terms, then, the Milan bourse is tiny. It is also riddled with insider
dealing.

The retiring Chairman of the Milan Stock Exchange, Ettore Fumagalli, in
December 1988 said: '. . . the bourse in Milan is a club of insiders, made
up of the big groups, a few shareholders and the brokers. . . . The big
groups have manipulated the market, prices have been rigged and the
share deals have generally hurt the small investor.'

Consob, the stock market and securities industry regulatory body, was
founded in 1974, but it still remains without the legislative backing which
might allow it to play a more positive role in protecting the interests of the
four million small investors on the Milan bourse. Italy still has no anti-
trust legislation, no monopolies and mergers commission, no rules on
company takeovers, no laws to restrict insider trading and no law that
would even require companies to put out full results including net profit
figures on a half-yearly basis. One example should suffice: when
Berlusconi bought 70 per cent of the stock of the publicly-quoted Standa
retail chain from Ferruzzi he paid nearly double the quoted market share
price. United Kingdom law would have required a public offer to be made.
Italian law does not, so thousands of small investors were left holding just
under 30 per cent of the shares at a price well below that paid in the
takeover.

The Milan bourse, is not, therefore, an attractive place for Italian
investors. As a result a real fear exists that, post-1992 and the relaxation of
restrictions on investing abroad, Italian investors will be looking to bigger
and better markets elsewhere. The 'corner shop' image of the Milan bourse

will be reinforced when the major Italian companies are also quoted on other exchanges as they seek to gain access to international finance.

A solution to this problem may lie in persuading some of the estimated 800 Italian companies which are legally qualified but not quoted to float themselves on the stock market. If only half of them decided on this course of action, the market would become immediately more varied, more attractive and more competitive. It is unlikely that they will be persuaded, however, for mainly cultural reasons: most of the companies are family businesses, in the black, and quite happy with the way things are; quotation on the stock market brings with it lots of obligations such as providing information for shareholders and for regulatory authorities, without any immediate and obvious return. These smaller family firms have never seen or appreciated the value of, or need for, a stock market quotation. Perhaps elsewhere the banks might have played a greater role in this development, but as we have already seen, the relationship between small firms and the banks is quite cosy too.

Business and the labour market

Demographic trends

In 1988 Italy had the lowest birth rate in the world. Zero growth rate implies a birth rate of 2.05 children per woman: Italy's national average was 1.29 children per woman. At this rate, Italy's population would fall from its current 57.4 million to 41.6 million by 2033. Such a decline would imply dramatic burdens on the social and economic structure of the country: by 2033 more than half the population would be over 70 years old; there would be one pensioner for every person of working age. These predictions may be too dramatic, however, since attitudes in the present child-bearing generation have changed rapidly. In 1983 most Italians thought a falling birth rate was 'a good thing'; now more than half see it as a problem, and 90 per cent of Italians think that the 'ideal family' should have two or more children (2.2 on average).

Employment and unemployment

Although the economy has shown a sustained growth rate over the last three or four years, total employment has grown only slowly. A sharp decline in the rate of dependent employment creation in the services sector, together with the continuing decline in manufacturing employment has

Table 3.10 *Italian unemployment rates (1980–9)*

Year	%
1980	7.1
1981	7.9
1982	8.5
1983	9.2
1984	9.8
1985	10.1
1986	10.9
1987	11.8
1988	12.1
1989	11.9

Source: OECD, ISAT

led to a decline in employment of about 1 per cent. Since 1987, unemployment has remained static at about 12 per cent (Table 3.10).

The figures in Table 3.10, however, disguise sizable differences according to region and age group. While unemployment declined in the North and Centre, and virtually full employment has been reached among prime-age males (twenty-five to fifty-nine-year-olds), unemployment in the same age group in the South was 7.8 per cent and in 1987, and the rates among unemployment-prone groups (women and young people) were much higher (for example, 35.5 per cent of the youth labour force, compared to 15 per cent, which is the OECD average). Since sectoral wage agreements are negotiated nationally and labour mobility is low, wage pressure in the North spreads throughout the economy, thus making employment prospects in the South even worse (see page 127).

Migration

Labour migration is no longer the easy answer to Italy's problems that it was in the 1950s, at least in part because welfare assistance is now so much more adequate and available in the South. More investment is required directly in the South if the country is to make full use of its labourforce. Some believe this will happen automatically as labour markets tighten in the North, but it could equally be that with the opening of the single European market, investors will look to place their capital in more productive and accessible regions in the centre and north of the Community.

Graduates

In 1987-8, 19.8 per cent of the Italian population was in full-time education, of whom 10 per cent (1.1 million) were at university. 13.7 per cent of the nineteen-twenty-four age group was attending university. 67 per cent of high school graduates go on to university. The most popular faculty is economics and social studies (29 per cent of the first-year intake), followed by literature (19 per cent), law (17 per cent), engineering (15 per cent) and science (11 per cent). The intake to economics and social studies is growing steadily, while intakes to literature and law are slowly declining.

This rosy picture is belied, however, by an examination of the number of graduates produced. More than two-thirds of the first-year intake of over 250,000 drop out, to leave an annual graduate cohort of about 75,000. This happens because there is no selection of university entrants. To some extent, first-year exams constitute the selection procedure, but in fact studies have indicated that as many as 70 per cent of first year drop-outs do not even take these exams.

The distribution of graduates is, as a consequence, rather different from the distribution of first-year intake. Literature accounts for the largest proportion of graduates (20 per cent) followed by medicine (16 per cent of graduates, but only 4 per cent of the intake), economics and social studies (also 16 per cent), science (13 per cent) and engineering and law (both 12 per cent). The drop-out rate in economics should concern business employers, but they may find consolation in the fact that the number of economics graduates has more than doubled over the past ten years.

A study carried out by IBM Italia in 1987, and confirmed by subsequent studies, showed a considerable imbalance between the supply and demand for graduates in industry, especially for graduates of scientific and technical disciplines. Generally speaking, the university system does not produce the types of graduates in the sorts of subjects that industry believes it needs. (See below for a discussion of business, education and training.)

Women and part-time work

Part-time work is growing in all western economies and now accounts for about 15 per cent of total employment on average, but reaches 25 per cent in some north European economies. Part-time work has been seen as one of the weapons in the battle against unemployment, especially amongst women. It is also seen as attractive to other previously marginalized groups (older workers, the disabled); and it may also appeal to a growing number of people more concerned with the 'quality of life', in search of a new relationship between work, pay and leisure. In this sense, part-time work has actually opened up new areas of the labour market, rather than offering a solution to the problem of traditional 'official' unemployment. But the growth in part-time work cannot be explained simply by changes in the labour supply. It is also dependent on a change in the type of work demanded, the new flexibility in production, and therefore a demand from employers for new working methods and practices.

Part-time work in Italy has had formal recognition and legal control only since 1984 (law no. 863). (The concept is still both new and foreign, such that Italians refer to **il part-time**, rather than using the Italian phrase **il lavoro a tempo parziale**.) The law was clearly intended to provide an entry point into the labour market for young people, and also to provide a less traumatic (and cheaper to the state) alternative to laying workers off when industries restructured. This clouds the discussion of part-time work, since the ILO definition of part-time work includes the notion of choice, where the Italian legislation dealing with part-time work is aimed at resolving employment difficulties. It is, therefore, dealing with the problem of underemployment rather than with part-time work as such.

Even so, the phenomenon in Italy is less well developed than in other European countries. In 1985 Italy had about one million part-time workers (5 per cent of the total workforce), compared with the United Kingdom's 5 million (21 per cent) and West Germany's 3.3 million (13 per cent). In the 1980s throughout the rest of Europe, both unemployment and part-time work increased at the same time as the proportion of women in the workforce also increased. In Italy, however, the entry of women into the labour force had a less dramatic effect on full-time employment. In fact, women are entering the full-time labour market in Italy, rather than the part-time market. Participation rates among the group normally most attracted to part-time work (married, middle-aged, middle-class women) are particularly low (only 80 per cent of the EC average), and part-time employment in Italy is found more commonly in the industrial and agricultural sectors, rather than in the service sector where it is encountered in the rest of Europe.

In terms of business culture, part-time work is seen not so much as a factor contributing to flexibility and modernization, but rather as a way of reducing the size of the workforce and the attendant labour costs.

Business and trade unions

Employers' organizations

Most employers in the private sector belong to the appropriate employers' association:

- Confindustria (liberal, free market orientation)
- Confcommercio (merchants)
- Confapi (small firms)
- Confagricoltura (agricultural producers)
- Confartigianato (craft industries)

Intersind is the employers' organization for public sector employers.

Confindustria, led by Gianni Agnelli (1972–6), promoted political consensus and accommodation with the PCI and the trade unions. Since 1980, first under Guido Carli and then under steel producer Luigi Lucchini (1984–8), a conservative counterrevolution has taken place, with a demand for the re-establishment of free-market principles. The current president of Confindustria is Sergio Pininfarina.

Organized labour

There are three main trade union confederations in Italy, the **Confederazione Generale Italiana del Lavoro** (CGIL, basically Communist (PCI) but with a substantial Socialist (PSI) minority), the **Confederazione Italiana Sindacati Lavoratori** (CISL, basically Catholic (DC)), and the much smaller **Unione Italiana del Lavoro** (UIL, an amalgam of the Socialists (PSI) and the smaller lay parties). In 1983, 45.5 per cent of Italy's 14.8 million wage earners were members of trade unions. The working members of the trade unions totalled 6.75 million divided as follows: CGIL 46.8 per cent; CISL 34.9 per cent; UIL 18.3 per cent. There is also a philo-fascist trade union, CISNAL, which has 2–300,000 members.

The issue at the heart of Italian trade unionism is: how to reconcile political power and responsibility with the partisan defence of workers' wages and conditions. The influence of the unions in the political and economic spheres has shifted periodically.

1945–48 The unions were strong politically but weak economically.
1948–62 Weak in both respects.
1963–69 Weak politically, strong economically.
1969–80 Strong in both respects.
1980–   Declining influence in both spheres.

These shifts need some explanation.

Land workers from the south flooded into the northern factories in the late 1950s and 1960s. Permanent employment in the prosperous factories did not easily come to them, however, and when it did they discovered that the work bore little relationship to that to which they were accustomed. They felt they were treated as unskilled and resented strangers who were putting pressure on the already scarce stock of housing resources. The southern immigrants wanted to be accepted and to have some sort of social standing which at that time no union or political party offered them. They needed to make a convincing gesture to show that they were willing to take on the values of northern industrial workers and to do this they adopted a militancy and a trade union loyalty not known in the north before. In their militancy they had four main objectives:

- To become accepted by northern workers as good trade unionists.
- To demand and obtain better working conditions and better housing (demands for better working conditions and higher wages were always bound up with wider demands for better living conditions, better housing, better public services).
- To remove the (to them) wounding distinction between skilled and unskilled work, at least by removing wage differentials (hence the demand throughout the 1970s for flat rate increases which naturally reduce differentials).
- To ensure that wages were high enough for them to transfer residues to families left behind in the south.

The great achievement of trade union militancy, and especially of the **autunno caldo** (hot autumn) of 1969, was the **Statuto dei Diritti dei Lavoratori** (Statute on Workers' Rights) of 1970. The Statute was the first of a series of legislative measures which provided almost cast-iron security of employment in larger firms (small firms were exempt from many of the provisions of the Statuto, see below) and also gave unions the right to organize elections in factories and set up factory councils.

Throughout the 1970s, the united CGIL-CISL-UIL Confederation achieved a series of major victories including the extension of the **scala mobile** (wage indexation system), significant wage increases, the forty-hour week, the reduction of wage differentials (**ugualitarismo** – partly the result of the flat rate increases awarded under the wage indexation system), the establishment of a common job classification system (**inquadramento unico**), and the setting up in 1975 of the **Cassa Integrazione Guadagni** (CIG – a national government fund to make up the wages of workers who were temporarily laid off). The CIG was of at least as much benefit to industrialists as it was to workers. Much industrial reorganization in the late 1970s and early 1980s was made possible by the CIG, which paid laid-off workers up to 95 per cent of their wages. By September 1985, 436,000 workers were in receipt of CIG benefit. Such funding will not be available to Italian industry post-1992, as state subsidies of this kind will be outlawed under the EC's competition rules.

Trade unions also won the right from 1975 onwards to have access to information about the firm's economic condition and investment programmes. As a basis for worker participation, however, these rights were never built upon, since, though the unions could agree that some form of worker participation was a good thing, they could not agree on what form such participation should take. The CGIL took a global view, saying that the union should have an input into factory plans, but that these factory plans should form part of a wider strategy of economic planning. The CISL and the UIL took a narrower view, believing that all trade union action should be directly related to shopfloor demands.

By 1978 the trade unions were increasingly identified as one of the major contributing factors to the chaotic state of the Italian economy. Their position (to demand a role in the management of the economy as a whole) was seen as untenable in the light of their refusal to moderate their claims for higher wages which the nation could not afford. In an impressive display of unity and restraint they modified their position (the so-called **svolta dell'EUR** of 1978), indicating a willingness to exercise restraint in bargaining over wages and conditions in return for an increased say in national economic policy making, but for many it was too late. Government and industry were already beginning to regain the upper hand.

The most significant moment in this struggle came in 1980 when Fiat announced the dismissal of 14,000 workers, in an attempt to re-establish the profitability of its automobile division. The FLM (the metalworkers section of the unified CGIL-CISL-UIL Federation) called an all-out strike which lasted thirty-five days but which was ended when 40,000 workers marched in protest against the strike, demanding the right to return to work. The terms negotiated for the return to work – 23,000 workers to be laid off with 93 per cent of their wages to be paid by the CIG – were drastic and the reaction of the workforce was violent, since the call for a return to work had been far from unanimous. But the tide had clearly turned. After protracted and bitter disputes between the unions and the employers, the scala mobile was eventually dismantled in 1984, and the acrimonious break-up of the trade union federation followed. Demoralization set in: between 1981 and 1987 membership of the CGIL fell by 23 per cent. New autonomous trade unions and Cobas (**comitati di base** – grass roots committees) also sprang up, fragmenting the union movement.

It is too early, however, to write off the Italian trade union movement as a force in Italian industry and the economy as a whole. 1988 saw an upturn in membership and new ideas are emerging, at least in the union leadership. The new general secretary of the CGIL, Bruno Trentin, identified a failure to understand the implications of new technologies as the major failing of both unions and management in the 1970s. New technologies were misunderstood by management (who often sought to take advantage of the situation by increasing pressure on workers) and by unions, who failed to grasp the fact that the implicit drawbacks (mobility of labour, discontinuity of employment) could also be opportunities for workers to construct more varied professional careers.

Managers and workers are clearly in search of a new culture for industrial relations to replace the aggressively conflictual culture (on both sides) of the 1970s, a culture which made **c'è sciopero** (there's a strike) the commonest excuse for the inefficiency of production or the inadequacy of public services. One view, inspired by Romiti at Fiat, would see the unions having a recognized role in the firm, but as representatives of the lowest paid and defenders of minimum conditions, leaving other issues to direct negotiation between managers and individual workers. (At least part of the reason for Ghidella's marginalization at Fiat was his desire to see a more participative form of management in response to the introduction of new technologies. This view conflicted with Romiti's predominantly financial view of things.) In recent years, several companies have put forward ideas for linking a part of wage increases to the performance of the company. The idea was first floated by Fiat but has since been taken up by other employers: Zanussi, Olivetti, Aeritalia, Enichem, Snia, etc. All want to go further than old-fashioned production bonuses but stop short of a direct link between salary and company profits. Olivetti, for example, wants to link profits to its **margine operativo lordo** (MOL – net operating margin) which is the value which is obtained by subtracting from the value of company sales the cost of materials, labour, fixed costs and stocks. Part of the annual wage increase would be made dependent on Olivetti's MOL being above the average of its international competitors. The MOL is not the same as the company's profits, and De Benedetti says that company profits should not be used as a measure for awarding even a part of wage increases because the unions are not yet ready to deal with the problems of company balance sheets that this implies (amortization policy, management of financial resources, company tax strategy, etc.). The unions, in particular the CGIL, reject the notion of linking wage increases to company profits and even less to company competitivity, because these things are influenced by management decisions, investment strategies, by the market and by the behaviour of the firm's competitors far more than by anything the individual worker can do.

However this debate turns out, it will not lead to the complete marginalization of unions in Italy. The Italian world of production offers a wealth of possible solutions. The worst culture (both for the management and for unions) would be one which simply defends past practice. An alternative might be what Bruno Trentin calls *'una codeterminazione in una fase sperimentale'* (experimental worker participation) where unions and management share responsibility for new work practices, training programmes, job enrichment and greater efficiency. Whether the workforce is ready for these new responsibilities when all the pressures of the system are for sectoral retrenchment is an open question. But the question has at least been asked, and it will remain an issue while the discussions surrounding the European Company Statute and the writing of a European charter of workers' rights remain a part of Project 1992.

Collective bargaining

Pay and most other terms and conditions of employment are negotiated nationally between the national trade union confederations and the relevant employers' federation. Contracts are negotiated nationally, industry by industry, though supplementary plant level agreements may also be negotiated, especially where minimum rates do not attract skilled personnel. National sectoral agreements last for three years and also stipulate annual holidays (normally at least four weeks plus ten statutory public holidays), working hours and permissible levels of overtime. Most national agreements also stipulate thirteen months' wages (fourteen in the case of commerce). Although the national agreements are binding only on those employers and unions who sign them, they tend to be applied to other analogous occupations, either because of custom and practice, or because of court judgements, or because Employment Offices are required to ensure that terms and conditions on offer are no worse than in the appropriate national agreement before authorizing recruitment.

Indirect labour costs

Non-wage labour costs are among the highest in Europe (over 40 per cent of total labour costs according to the OECD). Contributions to the social security agency (INPS) for pensions and to the Cassa Integrazione Guadagni for ompulsory lay-off insurance are the lagest element. The main burden of contributions falls on employers. Normal retirement age is sixty for men and fifty-five for women, but pensions may be drawn when thirty-five years' contributions have been paid. Employers are also required to pay in full during sickness or maternity leave, though partial offset may be available from INPS. The burden of severance payments is also heavy: since 1982, $2/27$ of annual pay for each year of service, subject to inflation-proofing. The entitlement to severance pay is virtually guaranteed, no matter what the grounds for termination of employment.

Business, education, training and development

Education

Compulsory schooling in Italy lasts for eight years: five years of elementary education (**scuola elementare**, 6–11), followed by three years lower secondary education (**scuola media inferiore**, 11–14). The minimum school leaving age is 14. Upper secondary education (**scuola media superiore**) is extremely diversified, but the basic categories are:

- Academic (*liceo scientifico, classico*)
- Technical (*istituto tecnico-commerciale, tecnico-industriale, tecnico-agrario, tecnico femminile*)
- Teacher training (*magistero*).
- State vocational training schools (*istituto professionale statale alberghiero, IPS industriale* and *artigianale*).

The **istituti professionali** used to have three-year cycles of study but now most adopt a five-year cycle like the other schools, except the **magistero**, which runs for four years. Any student obtaining the school-leaving certificate (the **maturità**) is automatically qualified to attend the university of their choice.

The secondary education system is complex. There are clearly overlaps between what the education system is trying to do and what a vocational training system might want to do, but the secondary education system is generally acknowledged to be failing to provide adequate preparation for the world of work.

Vocational training

Most of the problems which beset vocational training in Italy have existed for years. Essentially, conflicts and overlapping responsibilities between the central government and the regions (both of whom run employment services and provide vocational training), and between the Ministry of Labour and the Ministry of Education, and between the unions and the employers over the purpose and form of vocational training, coupled with the need to reform the secondary education system, have made it impossible to establish an effective and coherent system for vocational training. While some areas of vocational training within industrial firms are covered more or less adequately, major deficiencies exist in sectors such as vocational training for agricultural workers, apprentice training, vocational training for adults (as opposed to young people) and continuing education. Both the vocational training set-up and the adult education system are underdeveloped in Italy – the courses lack variety, there is no established system of leaving certificates, there are no clearly-defined aims and the opportunities for using what has been learned are limited.

High unemployment in the immediate post-war years made the promotion of vocational training necessary and led to legislation which placed the system of vocational training under the Ministry of Labour. Many firms and public companies offered specialist courses at their own vocational training centres, some of which attracted large government subsidies. Law no. 264 of 1948 enabled the Ministry of Labour to finance training courses organized by firms or other institutions for the purpose of retraining their workers, or those looking for their first job. Although the law was quite exceptional for its time because of the prospects it opened up, its power to produce a workable system of vocational training was limited by the lack of planning for the courses, which were financed indiscriminately on the basis of applications received rather than in response to identified training needs. Development was also hindered because Italian industry, in the moderately industrialized areas, was able to achieve high profits with low wages and relatively modest technology. Furthermore, the trade unions, after the suppression endured under the Fascists and still involved in the struggle for recognition, concentrated on security of employment and wage increases, giving less priority to other objectives such as the implementation of a vocational training scheme. As a result the system which emerged was more concerned with patronage and using vocational training as a semi-educational form of welfare than with responding to the training needs of industry.

At the same time, a parallel training system was developed under the Ministry of Education, but the state institutes for vocational training, developed in the 1960s within the education system had not been devised as a means of implementing labour market policies. In fact, they were usually attended by people looking for more highly-skilled jobs.

Another reason for the lack of development in the 1960s was the failure to implement regional reform. The 1948 Constitution (articles 117 and 118) gave the responsibility for vocational and craft training to the regions. The regions were not established until 1970, and it was not until 1972 that the regions were finally given responsibility for training outside the education system. Even then, the Ministry of Labour retained responsibility for distributing resources, for relations with the EC, for social security contributions for apprentices, for the training of teaching and training personnel and for training for special measures associated with the reorganization of production or the establishment of new industries. These functions were to be carried out by the **Istituto per lo Sviluppo della Formazione Professionale dei Lavoratori** – ISFOL, Institute for Workers' Vocational Training. Other public bodies concerned with training were disbanded and their functions transferred to the regions.

At the same time, some potentially innovatory steps were being taken in the area of educational leave. Educational leave for workers was included in nearly all wage agreements after 1973–74. This is the so-called **150 ore** (150 hours) entitlement to workers in many industrial sectors to attend school in work time to pursue studies leading to the **licenza** of the **scuola media inferiore** (middle school leaving certificate). Provision is based on use of the school system. The exact nature of access to this system depends on the collective agreement between the trade union for the industry concerned and the employers. The job of selecting which workers are to enjoy educational leave is left to the **consiglio di fabbrica** (works' council), and the trade unions have developed selection criteria to ensure fairness in the selection procedure.

The '150 hours' system was set up to respond to certain needs as identified by the trade unions: in 1971 76.6 per cent of Italians had not obtained the **licenza media**, and the figure was much higher among women, senior citizens and in the South. The '150 hours' courses were therefore aimed at correcting the deficiencies of the schooling system by making up for the general lack of educational qualifications among many employees, and also by increasing pressure for the reform of the school system as a whole. The system specifically excludes the possibility of the 150 hours being used for vocational training. The effects of educational leave provisions on the labour market in Italy are consequently virtually nil.

A 1977 law on youth unemployment acknowledged the regions' responsibilities for vocational training agreements and in general for all measures to encourage the development of training. The results have not, however, come up to expectations because of the inadequacies of the training system. An outline law was adopted in 1978, for example, which linked training to employment, made clear the distinction between vocational training and academic education and gave the regions an opportunity to plan vocational training. By 1985, thirteen of the twenty regions had adopted legislation in the area, but six had failed to take steps to bring existing legislation into line, and one region had no legislation in the area at all (Table 3.11).

Initial vocational training in the non-agricultural sector is conducted in vocational training centres.

Between 60 and 70 per cent of trainees are male, aged between 18 and 20.

Table 3.11 *Vocational Training in Italy (1984)*

Region	Training Centres		Trainees		Population	Workforce
	(no.)	*(%)*	*(no.)*	*(%)*	*(%)*	*(%)*
North West	413	28.0	58,366	28.9	27.6	28.9
North East	346	20.6	43,317	21.5	18.5	20.6
Centre	233	15.8	28,820	14.3	19.0	19.3
South	632	35.6	70,924	35.2	34.9	31.2

Source: CEDEFOP

The long-overdue reform of the system cannot take place without an equally long-overdue reform of the secondary education system.

Information in the area of vocational training for adults is hard to come by, but the picture that emerges is not an encouraging one: there is no established system of vocational training for adults comparable with systems in other EC member states. This is the result of:

- The general pattern of development of firms, and small firms in particular, which have tended to resist the introduction of new technologies and have therefore side-stepped the issue of retraining.
- The priority given by trade unions to equality of educational opportunity, and therefore the linking of demands for paid leave for education to the completion of compulsory general education. Unions have traditionally not demanded vocational training as part of their general demands on wages and conditions.
- Firms have been discouraged since it has not been possible to offset the costs of vocational training against grants or tax concessions.

Training activities

Only a few large private firms (Fiat, Olivetti, Montedison) and the large public enterprises have their own training services for their employees. Run mainly by personnel departments, these services take three forms:

- Training for new workers, for workers in line for promotion or transferring to a different section within the firm.
- Retraining required as the result of company or section reorganization.
- Management training, either in-house or provided by external agencies.

There has been a basic change in the relationship between small firms and their larger sisters in the matter of training: up to the 1960s it was the small firms which provided executives for the larger firms, but nowadays, the reverse is the case. Large undertakings function as centres where skilled workers acquire initial training and social skills. They then usually find better prospects on the external market. Some of the major companies have reacted to this state of affairs and have reorganized their training departments, converting them into training agencies which cater both for the group and for the external market. Most of these activities are self-financing and are therefore not subject to external control and are difficult to quantify and assess, but it is generally thought that the qualitative level is good and well matched to the needs of the labour market.

Apprenticeships have virtually disappeared from industrial firms in Italy, though they still exist in the craft industries. Trade unions objected to the apprentice system as a form of exploitation of young labour through underpayment. Law no. 25 of 1955 established the framework for apprenticeships, combining training at work with instruction outside for eight hours per week, but the law was never properly implemented because of disagreements between the employers and the unions. In 1984 the regions stopped financing the additional eight hours' tuition and such apprenticeships as survive are now conducted entirely within the firm.

Incentives to employ young people have been made available via training-work contracts (**contratti di formazione-lavoro**) provided for by Law no. 863 of 1984. This law gives firms special concessions to employ young people (aged 15–29) for a limited period before either taking them on permanently or returning them to the labour market. 108,000 people were on the scheme in 1985. About 60 per cent of young people on the scheme are in industrial employment, the remainder in the service sector. Over 70 per cent are in small firms (with fewer than fifty employees).

Continuing training, in the sense of publicly-financed vocational training not specifically linked to workplace activities or reorganization, does not exist. There is no legislative framework, nor any separate agency, nor, in some respects, sufficient expertise.

The ineffectiveness of vocational training in Italy has been at least in part the result of intransigence on the part of both trade unions and employers. The collective bargaining system is both conflictual and politicized and this has led to a disjuncture between the individual who requires training and the 'social partners' who see training either in terms of basic education, an instrument for general human and cultural betterment and for the promotion of the general political awareness of the workers, or in terms of the promotion of a narrow industrial culture, on-the-job training exclusively for the improvement of immediate profitability. Inevitably, the system as it stands satisfies none of even these narrow objectives.

Given that the unions and the employers have been unable to agree on the objective of vocational training, but given also that training must be happening because the nature of work has changed so radically, it follows that a two-tier system of training has developed: a rather ineffective explicit institutional system (that described above), and a more successful, but still inefficient, implicit submerged system based on the decentralization of production, precarious employment in small subcontracting firms, the learning implicit in the creation (or more precisely, the creative destruction) of firms. The challenge of the 1990s is to institutionalize the submerged system, both to give a greater role to the employers and the unions in negotiating training programmes and to make the training system more effective.

There are signs that developments are occurring in this direction: trade unions are becoming more involved in in-firm training to handle restructuring (Fiat, Italtel, Alfa Romeo); large firms are reassessing their own training centres (Elea-Olivetti, Isvor-Fiat); vocational training is becoming associated with industrial democracy (the Protocol agreements between the unions and the public sector employers, Intersind, in 1984, 1986 and 1987). Such developments need now to be consolidated.

Management training in small firms

Despite a few prestigious exceptions, like the private Luigi Bocconi University in Milan with its **Scuola di Direzione Aziendale** (Business School), Italy is a country without a supporting network of major business schools. Support services for updating and training managers are provided by private consultancy firms. There is still a feeling, though, that either managers are born (and therefore do not need training) or that experience is the best teacher (therefore management skills are acquired in the process of managing a company, and cannot be acquired through abstract or theoretical study). In recent surveys, 47 per cent of managers of SMEs had never attended any training course. The managers showed an awareness of a need to update their professional knowledge, but the fact that there were so few managerial staff in small firms made taking time off to attend courses very diffficult. 30 per cent of managers saw nothing to be gained from management courses. The remaining 70 per cent viewed training as a luxury to which they could treat themselves only in times of prosperity. These findings disguise the fact that many firms draw solely upon their own resources to provide training, since they doubt the ability of outside public- or private-sector training providers to make a useful contribution towards solving their problems. Given the reluctance of small firms to release employees for training, one might have expected to see the development of a distance-learning system. A CEDEFOP report of 1986 cites Italy as the only industrialized country which as yet has no distance-training system.

The rise and rise of the small business

One of the problems facing Italian entrepreneurs in the 1970s was how to circumvent the gains achieved by the working class in 1969–70 by reorganizing the system of production in such a way as to maintain the production of traditional goods while resisting Third World competition. It should be remembered here that Italy has never been strong at producing high-technology goods, but rather medium-technology, like televisions and washing machines, or low-technology, like clothes and shoes; electrical and non-electrical machinery and appliances accounted for 24 per cent of Italian exports in 1987, clothing and shoes accounting for a further 11.6 per cent. But how do small firms producing low-technology goods survive in a market which is elsewhere dominated by large corporations in fierce competition with each other and with low cost Third World exporters? The answer to this question is complex, but it begins with the decentralization of production.

The basic theory of the firm suggests that a firm is a system whose purpose is the organization of the factors of production. These factors are human resources (the labour market), technology, capital, raw materials and energy. In the classical theory of the firm, there exists 'one best way' to combine these factors, but this management approach has never been accepted in Italy. But we are no longer in the Ford production ethos, nor are we beset by Taylorist principles of scientific management. To the extent that the firm consists of basic operations such as planning and design, production, sales, all supported by services, any one of these operations can be subcontracted out. The first thing to go is production, in favour of sub-contracting a semi-finished product (the entrepreneur no longer has the problem of controlling the workforce). Planning and design can also be decentralized. And so the cycle continues.

This phenomenon exploded in the 1970s. Why?

- Labour costs: increased rapidly after 1970.
- Raw materials and energy: Italy is a transformation economy, it is deeply affected by the rate of exchange and the price of oil.
- The cost of money went up: 1973–4 the interest rate rose from 4 per cent to 14 per cent.
- Technology also became more expensive.

Given the explosion in costs, the entrepreneur seeks to maintain his market share by first of all adding value to his product through design. But this is not enough on its own. Production shifts from large industrial concerns to an array of small firms and cottage industries, using domestic labour, juvenile labour, part-time and casual labour. Pressures towards this type of reorganization also come from the desire to escape from:

- Trade union constraints.
- Health and safety regulations.
- Strikes.
- Taxes and social security contributions.

Many of these constraints on industry were the direct result of the Statuto dei Lavoratori, and in fact small firms now enjoy major concessions from the Statuto. Small firms (originally defined as employing fifteen or fewer workers, later raised to twenty) were exempted from the main provisions of the Statuto, especially those relating to trade union representation. They were exempted from VAT up to a generous limit, and from social security payments and they were to be assessed for local taxes at a lower rate than larger firms. Local authorities were also empowered to set up small trading estates and to designate certain areas as 'depressed zones' and to provide subsidies for small firms to set up in them.

In Italy there are firms which start small and remain small. The existence of small firms is permanent and structural (not always the same small firms, obviously, the turnover of small firms is very rapid). And small firms are an essential ingredient of Italy's success: almost 60 per cent of employment in Italy is in companies with fewer than 100 employees, and these firms account for 26 per cent of total manufacturing exports. Small firms dominate totally in the traditional manufacturing areas such as fabrics and clothing, shoemaking and leather goods, ceramics, carpentry and furniture.

In some areas and sectors, new low wage economy conditions were created – but these were acceptable because wages in the black economy are often used to top up wages in the formal economy (women adding to the man's wage, moonlighting – an estimated 54 per cent of state employees have second jobs). But the survival of the small firm in the traditional low-tech industries is not solely a function of low wages and a deregulated labour market.

The flourishing of small enterprises reflects both the fragmentation of the industrial system, with specialized manufacturing and services increasingly contracted out by large companies to smaller operations, but also a creative entrepreneurialism in an increasingly decentralized country. At best, regional and family loyalties combine in local networks which embrace trade unions, bankers, businessmen and politicians to produce cultures that both facilitate and reward initiative. The Italian small firm is therefore more of a cultural entity than its British equivalent.

It has familial, social and artistic aspects as well as economic ones, offering its workers a wide range of satisfactions besides that of simply earning a living. There are no sleeping partners or equity shareholders in the majority of small firms, so the possibility of takeover is unlikely, and small firms cannot be considered as fodder for larger, growing firms to feed on. Neither growth nor profit maximization can be considered the principal reason for existence of the small firm.

Various models have been developed to explain the phenomenon of small firms. One such is the Emilian model (King 1987). The principal features of this model are: decentralized production in small and medium-sized rural towns; geographical specialization in the kind of product made; and a high degree of mainly female sweated labour in small factories, craft workshops and homes. In Emilia-Romagna, the region to which the model is said to apply, there are no industrial concerns employing more than a couple of hundred workers, with the exception of the petrochemicals plants at Ferrara and Ravenna, the fruits of outside investment. But the characteristics of independent enterprise, product distinctiveness and hard work based on solid traditions of peasant farming and generations of craft skills have made the region into one of the richest in Italy. In 1983 Modena overtook Milan as the richest province in Italy.

Another model is that of 'flexible specialization' (Goodman *et al.* 1989). This model suggests that within a productive system characterized by the decentralization of various stages of the production process, the small and medium-sized firm will tend towards specialization in a limited number of phases of production, but for many different types of goods. According to the model of flexible specialization radical changes in the production environment are the cause of this new structure of the industrial system. Technological innovation is no longer to be found principally in the large firms, and its effects are to be felt throughout the productive system. It helps to make machinery more efficient and more flexible, and allows the progressive substitution of machinery for human labour in the more repetitive areas of work. Above all, it enables firms to react more quickly and more efficiently to changes in product demand. The advantages which large firms have traditionally derived from economies of scale have been outweighed by the growing demands of the workforce in large firms and by the reduction in the minimum efficient size of the firm, brought about by changes in the production process as a result of the introduction of new technology.

The resulting small firms, grouping together into industrial districts, display certain characteristics:

- Flexibility of production, made even more possible by the falling costs of modern technologies.

- A dualism of competition and collaboration; in other words, the same firms may collaborate closely on the development of new tools or techniques, but will compete fiercely for contracts.

In general terms, the success of the small firm system in central and north-east Italy seems to be based on three principal factors:

- Maintaining competitivity on international markets, where demand is determined as much by quality (and here design, 'Made in Italy', plays a significant role) as by price. Advantages that other producers may gain from long runs at high volume are offset by the ability of the Italian small industry system to produce non-standard goods and to respond quickly to short-term demand.
- Flexible production and division of labour between firms. A system of complex subcontracting allows costs and risks to be shared out among a number of firms, but it also allows production to be based on short-term contracts which can rapidly be adjusted to market requirements by switching between subcontractors when a particular type of good is required or by raising or reducing the subcontracting when the level of demand fluctuates. In turn, this system depends on the efficient circulation of goods and information between the producers. This is guaranteed by the geographical proximity of the firms as well as the frequent use of microcomputers to communicate information sometimes even to domestic out-workers.
- The unique local, social and institutional conditions provided by the relationship between the modern market town and its once agricultural hinterland.

Within this model, the particular culture of individual firms (the way they recruit, use or remunerate labour, the technologies they apply, the marketing skills of the entrepreneurs) is of limited relevance. More important is the way the firms operate within a system of production. The firms are not free operators in a free market but part of a complex and integrated system of production. The firms derive their resilience from the stability achieved by the system as a whole. The firms described here are not independent small firms in the traditional sense, nor are they simply subcontractors for larger firms. They are interlinked but independently-owned production units, within an industrial system. The uniqueness of the system does not derive from the economic and social organization of production within the individual firms, but rather from the economics of the vertical disintegration of the production process, which has created a new set of interfirm relationships.

Generalization about the small firms sector is difficult and dangerous, though, since within the category a highly diversified situation is to be found. The models described in the previous paragraphs, for example, are more or less geographically confined to the regions of north-east and central Italy. But even here, and especially in other areas, highly-innovative firms operate alongside technologically-backward firms. It must also be said that in their process of reorganization, large firms may take advantage of new technologies to reunite the various phases of the production process within medium and large plants. These factors may place limitations on the small firms sector and may signal the beginning of a new phase of domination by the large firm. Similar questions remain about the durability of the Emilian model. It is becoming more and more difficult to increase or even maintain the level of exports; increasing labour costs can no longer be counteracted by devaluation; markets supplied by many of these firms are becoming saturated both at home and abroad; competition from other sectors – agriculture, tourism, the construction industry – for both land and labour is intensifying; and finally, the reserves of marginal labour are also drying up.

Is it realistic to expect the small firm to continue to flourish in the face of financial pressures and inducements that are likely to arise over the next few years? One of the threats to the political economy of the small firm comes from developments within the EC. Among the changes brought about by the single market will be the removal of restrictions in Italy which prevent foreign firms from owning more than 49 per cent of an Italian business. Possibly more alarming is the prospect of foreign banks freely entering the Italian market, and the consequent 'rationalization' of the Italian local savings bank system which, as we have seen, gives vital support to small businesses.

The response of business to the EC's single market

All of Italy's top entrepreneurs from both the public and private sectors (Agnelli, Gardini, Prodi, Reviglio, De Benedetti) are vocal in their enthusiasm for 1992 and the completion of the single market. They believe that they are strongly placed to take advantage of industrial development which will result from the complete integration of the European national economies. They also claim, with justification, that their companies are already well-established in the European marketplace and that there is no need for them to be taking additional preparatory measures before 1922.

A 1988 survey of opinion among Italian and European industrialists, however, revealed that the Italians, although sharing the enthusiasm of the top entrepreneurs for the principle of a single market (72 per cent thought it represented an opportunity rather than an obstacle), were far more pessimistic about their ability to take advantage of the opportunity.

64 per cent of those interviewed thought that other European countries would benefit more from the single market than Italy, and a further 11 per cent thought that non-European countries would do better too. In other words, only one in four thought 1992 was looking good for Italy. In this respect, Italian industrialists were the most pessimistic in Europe, and the gravest misgivings were expressed by those in the motor car and electronics industries. Only 12 per cent of industrialists saw exporting to the EC as a natural path of development for their company. Among their greatest fears (felt by 23 per cent of Italians, a greater proportion than in any other country), was the withdrawal of state subsidies. Seeking partnerships with other EC companies was not seen to be an answer to the problem: in the sample as a whole, 62 per cent would actively seek partnerships with other EC companies, 23 per cent with companies from their own country, and 15 per cent with companies from outside the EC, but in Italy 53 per cent thought allying with other Italian companies was the answer, only 27 per cent seeking allies in Europe and a further 19 per cent outside. Even where companies had taken action in response to the challenge of 1992, the responses had been largely confined to the marketing function; other functions such as commercial planning, production, company organization and personnel had been largely ignored.

From the preceding outline of Italian business culture it will be obvious that the threats to Italian industry posed by the completion of the internal market are not insignificant:

- Will small and medium-sized businesses cope with international competition?
- Will the country's relative shortage of high technology industries be a handicap?
- Can the fragmented and relatively underdeveloped banking and financial services sector hold its own against foreign competition?
- Will political controls on the public sector turn out to be its undoing?
- How will it be possible to prevent parts of the Mezzogiorno from falling even further behind industrially?
- Will industry as a whole be able to withstand the withdrawal of state aid (a 1989 European Commission report showed that in 1988 Italian state aids to industry amounted to £5.3 billion – nearly nine times the amount of United Kingdom state aid to industry)?
- Can the political system deliver the necessary reforms of the economy and the bureaucracy?

And it is this final point which, at the end of the day, may be the most telling. Italy's failure in the past to apply EC directives and even to spend its allocations from Community funds have been the despair of Brussels. Henceforth, failure on the part of government, Parliament and the bureaucracy promptly to apply Community legislation will lead directly to competitive disadvantage to Italian industry.

In more general terms, there are underlying weaknesses in the Italian economy which must cause concern in the business sector. The development of the 1980s has not been coordinated, so the effects have been unevenly distributed, the rewards unevenly spread between the social classes and between North and South. Thus the dualisms which were identifiable in Italy immediately after the war are still there, and must remain a cloud over the undoubted successes of the Italian economy:

- Territorial dualism: which sees a prosperous industrial North expanding despite or at the expense of a poorer, agricultural South.
- Industrial dualism: which sees a coexistence of an advanced, modern, highly-productive sector together with a fragmented, undertechnologized sector.
- Labour market dualism: wherein well-paid, secure sectors coexist with badly-paid, marginal and precarious sectors.

The problems remain. They will not be solved by the flair and imagination of the individual Italian entrepreneur alone. The real opportunities for business in Italy lie in finding a new accommodation between the public and private sectors, and between the government, the employers and the workers. This accommodation must be found soon if Italy's economic success is to last.

It would be beguiling and perhaps comforting in a Thatcherite climate to conclude that the Italian experience shows us that small really is beautiful and that a culture of democratic flexible specialization as typified by small firms in North-East Italy is the right response to the problem of post-Fordist socioeconomic systems. More realistically, it has to be seen that, having been on the defensive in the 1970s, large firms in Italy have recovered their dynamism and determination. They have undertaken intensive restructuring, invested heavily in new technologies and inflicted a series of defeats on their workforces and on the trade union movement generally.

Italy will remain an exciting arena for the clash and interplay of business cultures and systems for a few years to come, but the conclusion may well be that though small continues to be beautiful, big is more viable.

References and suggestions for further reading

Beltrami, Ottorino (1989), *I Neolaureati in Azienda*, Milan: Edizioni del Sole 24 Ore.

Bianchi, Patrizio (1988), 'Privatisation of industry: the Alfa Romeo case', in Nanetti, Rafaella, Leonardi, Robert and Corbetta, Piergiorgio (eds), *Italian Politics: A Review*, vol. 2, London: Frances Pinter.

Boldizzoni, Daniele (1985), *La Piccola Impresa*, Milan: Edizioni del Sole 24 Ore.

Bracalente, Bruno and Marbach, Giorgio (1989), *Il Part-time nel Mercato Italiano del Lavoro*, Milan: Franco Angeli.

Ciarrocca, G. (1987), *Come Investire in Italia* (How to Invest in Italy), Milan: Pirola.

Department of Trade and Industry (1988), *Italy: Country Profile*, London: Exports to Europe Branch, Italian Desk, Department of Trade and Industry.

Economist Intelligence Unit (1989), *Italy: Country Report and Country Profile*, London: The Economist Intelligence Unit.

Friedman, Alan (1988), *Agnelli and the Network of Italian Power*, London: Harrap.

Garonna, P. (ed) (1987), *The Role of the Social Partners in Vocational Training in Italy*, Berlin: CEDEFOP (European Centre for the Development of Educational Training).

Goodman, Edward and Bamford, Julia with Saynor, Peter (eds) (1989), *Small Firms and Industrial Districts in Italy*, London: Routledge.

King, Russell (1987), *Western Europe: Economic and Social Studies – Italy*, London: Harper & Row.

de Michelis, Gianni, and Scognamiglio, Carlo (1989), *Come Guidare l'Italia nel Duemila. Le Riforme del 1992*, Rome: Sperling e Kupfer Editori.

OECD Economic Surveys, Italy, Paris: OECD.

Onida, Fabrizio and Viesti, Gianfranco (eds) (1988), *The Italian Multinationals*, London: Croom Helm.

Sassoon, Donald (1986), *Contemporary Italy – Politics, Economics and Society since 1945*, Harlow: Longman.

Spotts, Frederic and Weiser, Theodore (1986), *Italy: A Difficult Democracy – A Survey of Italian Politics*, Cambridge: CUP.

4 The business culture in the United Kingdom
Colin Randlesome

Introduction

Business people in the United Kingdom do not have it easy. As a nation, the British are taught in school to deplore the vulgarity of wealth; in much of English literature, the villain of the piece is exposed as a ruthless businessman either deceiving aristocrats or exploiting workers. Prince Charles apart, the leading members of the Royal Family do not appear to be particularly interested in business; while the established Church of England gives the impression that it is actually anti-business. Indeed, the Archbishop of Canterbury, Dr Robert Runcie, in an interview with *Director* magazine in 1989, castigated the country for being too materialistic and warned of the emergence of a 'Pharisee' society based on self-interest and intolerance. In short, the country at large has never really learned to love business.

As a result, British business people have hesitated to proclaim their business activities as denoting something inherently good or to trumpet their many achievements. They have also been reluctant to lend an air of permanence to their business activities, too often giving the notion from their job-hopping tendencies that they are 'just visiting' rather than representing an established feature of a company. They have even tolerated for far too long the absurd caricature of the British business person as someone who indulges in protracted lunches and rounds of golf in company time.

Such values, attitudes and downright distortions have exerted a profound influence on the business culture in the country. Above all, they have contributed to the much-criticized short-termism which continues to haunt the culture. Short-termism manifests itself still in the British fascination with financial engineers in the City rather than the real thing in the country's manufacturing industries; in the preference for asset holders rather than product makers; in the exposure of the country's leading industrial companies to hostile takeovers by financial manipulators.

It is short-termism that forces British company boards to concentrate on profits now rather than investment for the future. Thus there has been a signal failure by the country's companies to invest in human capital. Company directors have been reluctant to train their employees and develop their managers because the companies which do adopt the longer-term view and educate their workforces are actually punished. Their shares are marked down, they are accused of damaging cash flow, and their skilled workers are poached by other companies. The result is that the United Kingdom probably has one of the poorest-trained workforces of any of the major industrial countries.

Equally, short-term thinking is responsible for a lack of investment by British companies in R & D. Between 1981 and 1985, British firms spent £250 per annum per employee, compared with £300 in France and £400 in West Germany. Of the top ten industrial nations, the United Kingdom ranked ninth in terms of R & D spending by industry. If rate of growth is taken into account, the country came last. Nor has business been helped in this respect by government. In fact, the government's share of civil R & D funding declined from 30 per cent in 1981 to 23 per cent in 1986, with a further fall in real terms of 3 per cent between 1986 and 1987.

At the same time, the business culture in the United Kingdom has always been one which is receptive to new ideas, innovative and adaptable. It has inevitably been the first to try out new concepts – the good as well as the bad – originating from the acknowledged home of free enterprise, the United States. Nor has it been slow in inventing its own concepts and systems.

Perhaps, however, the outstanding positive feature of the business culture in the country is its sheer adaptability. Indeed, business in the United Kingdom has had to be adaptable just to survive the many changes visited upon it since the Second World War by different governments of the left and the right, and by swings in economic policy brought about by political expediency. In recent times, the adaptability of the business culture has been demonstrated nowhere more clearly than in its response to the 'enterprise culture' since the return to power of the Conservatives in 1979. The number of companies in the United Kingdom almost doubled during the 1980s; more jobs have been created in the country than in the rest of the EC countries put together; profitability has improved out of all recognition. Indeed, business must be doing something right: why else would Japanese direct investment in the United Kingdom constantly outstrip that in any other European country and total some £4 billion per year?

At the end of the 1980s, business in the country was doing much that was right. Fixed investment by non-oil companies in 1989 had reached record levels (more than double what it was in 1986), and even expenditure on training and development had increased spectacularly.

Moreover, the country's contribution to world manufacturing exports revealed a rising tendency, probably for the first time this century.

The highly-adaptable business culture in the country has changed radically during the 1980s. If business is to rise to the challenges of the 1990s, including the completion of the EC's single market by the end of 1992, it will have to continue the process of adaptation, but with an even greater sense of urgency.

Business and government

After the strike-ridden 'winter of discontent' of 1978–9, European newspapers and magazines appeared to be competing with one another to paint the blackest possible portrait of business in the United Kingdom. *Le Monde* forecast that the United Kingdom was on the verge of becoming 'an underdeveloped country'; *Der Spiegel* ran a whole series on 'sick England'. In May, 1988, by contrast, *Fortune* magazine was declaring in its cover title that 'Britain is back' and even speculating that the comeback might qualify: '. . . as a full-blown economic miracle'. If the cold economic indicators over the period from 1979 to 1989 are compared with the country's long-term past performance, there was no miracle in the United Kingdom. However, the business climate, for which government in any country is mainly responsible, did change radically and for the better, and with it the business culture.

In May 1979, the Conservatives regained power from Labour, and their leader, Margaret Thatcher, became the United Kingdom's first female prime minister. On 6 June 1979, in a speech in Cambridge, she said: 'The mission of this government is much more than the promotion of economic progress. It is to renew the spirit and solidarity of the nation.' Economic progress, especially in terms of economic growth, has been promoted in the interim, and the spirit and solidarity of much of the business community, but not of the nation as a whole, have been renewed.

One of the ways in which business confidence has been bolstered is through continuity. Margaret Thatcher has retained office in two general elections since 1979, thus becoming the longest-serving prime minister this century, and the longest in continuous office since Lord Liverpool in the first quarter of the nineteenth century. The stability afforded by her continuous tenure of 10 Downing Street has enabled business to plan, invest in capital goods and equipment and indeed make profits, in a way which the country has seldom witnessed. While not all sectors of business have flourished equally under what has come to be known as **Thatcherism**, profit is no longer held to be a dirty word, and managers have been given the freedom to run companies in the way in which they, and not the trade unions, think fit. They have also received the rewards for doing so.

Since 1979, the Conservative government, led if not actually dominated by Margaret Thatcher, has pursued policies which are founded on a political and economic philosophy of free enterprise, competition and less state intervention. The Conservatives' top priority, from the outset, has been to furnish a framework within which private business can succeed. Margaret Thatcher's three periods of office have attempted to loosen business people, the creators of wealth, from regulations and constraints, and let market forces prevail. Only in this way, she believes, can power be returned to individuals. According to Margaret Thatcher, there is no such thing as society!

The state of the United Kingdom's economy was indeed gruesome in the year that the Conservatives resumed government:

- Economic growth for 1979 measured 2.6 per cent.
- Inflation was high at over 13 per cent, and on the increase.
- Unemployment registered 5.1 per cent according to OECD figures and 4 per cent on the Department of Employment's admission, but rising.
- The current account was in deficit.

The overriding macroeconomic priority of the first government under Margaret Thatcher was the **defeat of inflation**. However, the policies chosen to reduce inflation by the Chancellor, Sir Geoffrey Howe, did little to enamour the Conservatives to large sections of business, especially manufacturing. A tight monetary policy was adopted, with high interest rates and a lofty exchange rate for sterling. By the end of 1980, the pound cost approximately $2.40, making imports relatively cheap but rendering the country's exports uncompetitive. These measures prompted Sir Terence Beckett, erstwhile Director General of the **Confederation of British Industry** (CBI), in his closing speech to the 1980 conference, to call upon the leaders of industry to take up a 'bare-knuckle fight' with the government. One month later, he warned that industrial companies were 'disappearing down the plug-hole faster than we can stop them'. In 1981, as industrial output reached its nadir, 264 eminent economists signed a letter published in *The Times* demanding a change of policy.

But in many ways the first three years of Conservative government from mid–1979 to mid–1982 appeared to be a denial of much that Margaret Thatcher stood for. Despite the frequent utterances of **TINA** ('There is no alternative'), government succumbed to the threat of a coal miners' strike, conceded a 50 per cent rise in civil servants' pay over the 1979–80 period, and continued to subsidize nationalized industries such as British Steel, which was losing £1 million per day at the time. With unemployment approaching three million, 'job-creation schemes' were concocted which amounted to the complete antithesis of the Conservative philosophy. It seemed ironic in the extreme that the successful Conservative slogan in the 1979 election had been 'Labour isn't working'.

By mid–1982, there were clear signs that the worldwide economic recession was coming to an end. Inflation in the United Kingdom began to fall, as did the number of days lost through industrial disputes (see pages 180 and 195). These achievements, though modest enough in themselves, taken in conjunction with the 'Falklands Factor', helped the Conservatives to victory in the 1983 general election. They also helped mask the fact that many of the pledges on which the Conservatives had regained power in 1979 remained unfulfilled. Despite the sales of several state-owned concerns, i.e. privatizations, to which further reference will be made (see page 163), and of dwellings previously owned by local government to occupiers, the size of the public sector and public spending were increasing; and despite certain cuts, the tax burden on the majority of the working population was greater than when the Conservatives took over from Labour.

Although they do not win general elections, the leading economic indicators for 1983, with the exception of the unemployment figures, did show an improvement on 1979.

- Economic growth for the year registered 3.6 per cent.
- Inflation was below 5 per cent and falling.
- Unemployment amounted to 10.7 per cent according to OECD figures and 10.5 per cent on the Department of Employment's, with both rates still showing a rising trend.
- The current account was in surplus, thanks to North Sea oil.

The Conservative victory in 1983 was facilitated by a high level of internal dissent in the Labour Party, and the emergence of the Liberal/SDP Alliance as a real political force served to deprive Labour of some of its traditional supporters.

It was only during Margaret Thatcher's second period in office, from June 1983 to June 1987, that three of the key policies affecting business – trade union reform, privatization and tax reform – were perceived as approaching fruition.

Victory over the coal miners in March 1985 after a strike lasting 14 months appeared, to the public at large, to vindicate the **1980 Employment Act** which had outlawed secondary picketing. Victory over the print unions at Wapping in 1986 justified the Conservatives' struggle to introduce a measure of flexibility into the country's labour markets, which had found its expression in the **1982 Employment Act**. The Conservatives' trade union reforms, including those passed in 1984 incorporating measures to make unions more democratic and in 1988 to tighten up the circumstances under which a 'closed shop' can operate, are discussed in full in a separate section of this chapter (see pages 192–198).

One of the most radical policies implemented by the Conservatives under Margaret Thatcher, and one which came to prominence in her second term of office, has been the **selling of state-owned concerns to the private sector.** Just as the sales of local council homes to occupiers (1,300,000 by 1989) were used to foster a nation of property owners, privatization was the Conservatives' main method of creating a share-owning democracy. Among the public-sector companies sold were: 50.2 per cent of British Telecom, which brought in £3.9 billion in November 1984; British Gas for £5.6 billion in December 1986; the Government's 31.5 per cent stake in British Petroleum, sold for £7.2 billion in October 1987; British Steel for 2.5 billion in December 1988; and the water authorities for a further £5.2 billion in December 1989.

By the turn of the decade, over 42 per cent of 1979's nationalized industries sector, or roughly 6 per cent of GDP, had been transferred to the private sector. In addition, the Conservatives propose to privatize the electricity supply industry by the next general election, due in June 1992 at the latest. The sale of electricity could raise a further £18 billion. There is also speculation afoot that British Rail and British Coal might be privatized if the Conservatives were to win the next election.

The privatization policy has proved to be one of Margaret Thatcher's most controversial. The Conservatives contend that companies in the private sector are more efficient than those in the public sector because they produce a better level of service, due to market forces, and have to meet profit targets. Government critics counter that, especially in the cases of British Telecom, British Gas, and water and electricity supply, private monopolies have merely replaced public monopolies, thus necessitating the establishment of watchdog bodies to protect consumer interests. Critics have also claimed that government revenue from privatizations, 'selling the family silver' as it was called by the late Lord Stockton, a former Conservative prime minister, distorts public accounts. They point to future problems once this source of revenue dries up.

The third area of policy with important repercussion for business has been that of **tax reform.** When Labour left office in 1979, the basic rate of income tax was 33 per cent and the top marginal rate 83 per cent. In his first budget in June 1979, Sir Geoffrey Howe set the tone for the Thatcher era, reducing the basic rate by 3 per cent to 30 per cent, widening the tax bands and cutting the top rate to 60 per cent. Personal allowances were also increased. In 1986, Nigel Lawson, Sir Geoffrey's successor as Chancellor, brought the basic rate down to 29 per cent and indexed personal allowances. He followed these cuts one year later to bring the basic rate down to 27 per cent, and in 1988 to 25 per cent. Five higher tax rates up to 60 per cent were replaced by a single rate of 40 per cent for taxable incomes over £19,300.

Reforms of company taxes were also initiated under Sir Geoffrey Howe's chancellorship and continued under that of Nigel Lawson. A reduction of 1 per cent in the hated National Insurance Surcharge was announced in the 1982 Autumn Statement, and further reductions were made in 1983 prior to final abolition in 1984. At the same time, cuts were introduced in the main corporation tax rate, which fell from 52 per cent to 50 per cent in 1983–4, then to 45 per cent in 1984–5, 40 per cent in 1985–6 and to 35 per cent in 1986–7. The rate for small companies was reduced from 38 per cent to 30 per cent in 1983–4, then 29 per cent in 1985–6, 27 per cent in 1987–8 and to 25 per cent in 1988–9.

Despite the Conservatives' attempts to create a property-owning democracy, by the time of the 1987 general election over a quarter of all householders were still public tenants; despite their attempts to create a share-owning democracy, only a fifth of the adult population aged sixteen or over possessed shares. A third of all workers were in the employment of the state, more than in West Germany or France. Worse still, government expenditure was increasing in real terms and the state was responsible for as large a share of GDP as under the last Labour administration. The popularity of the legislation introduced to curb trade union powers and the tax cuts probably constituted the most successful elements of the Conservatives' record in government, especially with business people. Managers had been afforded the freedom to manage companies and were in receipt of the rewards as well.

The leading economic indicators for 1987 were much more auspicious than in 1983, and even the unemployment rates were falling.

- Economic growth registered 4.6 per cent for the year.
- Inflation was below 3.8 per cent.
- Unemployment measured 10 per cent according to both OECD and the Department of Employment.
- The current account showed a slight deficit.

Once again, the opposition vote was split between Labour and the Liberal/SDP Alliance, which benefited the Conservatives, who remained in government with a reduced but comfortable majority. The Labour Party, however, mounted its most professional campaign in living memory.

After the 1987 election victory, the United Kingdom probably witnessed the most radical programme of change since 1945. The continuing policies of trade union reform, privatization and tax reform were joined by fresh government initiatives in rates reform, the National Health Service (NHS) and education.

Possibly the most controversial of the initiatives was **rates reform**. The government had been committed for some considerable time to abolishing rates, the tax based on nominal property values levied to fund local authority services such as education, police and fire services, refuse disposal and roads. Under the new legislation, domestic rates were replaced by a community charge payable by all adults. The former system of rates on commercial properties was changed to a uniform business rate. The government argued that the community charge would render high-spending local authorities more accountable to those who vote for them. Critics preferred to call the community charge a poll tax, maintaining that it was a regressive tax which disproportionately affects the poor in society. They also claimed that the poll tax is expensive to collect and difficult to administer. Despite the distinct unpopularity of the community charge, the government went ahead. It was introduced in Scotland in 1989 and in England and Wales in 1990.

Another area of government policy in Margaret Thatcher's third term which brought forth much opposition, from the public at large and the medical establishment in particular, was the **reform of the NHS**. The aim was to promote efficiency and competition within the NHS by means of a three-phase package due for completion by 1991. This is a politically sensitive issue and will need careful handling before the next general election by Kenneth Clarke, who was appointed Secretary of State for Health in the July 1988 cabinet reshuffle. His initial attempts at pushing through the NHS reforms were not auspicious, encountering stiff resistance from virtually all sections of the medical establishment.

The Conservatives' education reforms are discussed in full in a subsequent section of this chapter (see page 199).

In macro-economic terms, the most outstanding achievement of the Conservative Governments between 1979 and 1989 was probably their record on economic growth (Table 4.1).

The *1987–1988 OECD Economic Survey* commented as follows on the post-1979 cycle: 'Measured from peak to peak, the division of nominal GDP growth between output growth and inflation was much more favourable over the 1979/1988 period than during the 1973/1979 cycle and similar to earlier experience, suggesting that there have been policy-induced improvements in supply performance. Other economic indicators confirm this picture: the deterioration in performance in the 1970s has been reversed; and, compared with other Member countries, there has been a relative improvement. Economic growth during the 1981–8 recovery, at over 3 per cent per annum, was not outstanding compared to previous upswings, but the upturn was unusually long.' In other words, peak-to-

Table 4.1   *United Kingdom growth rates (1979–89)*

Year	(%)
1979	2.6
1980	− 2.7
1981	− 1.7
1982	2.0
1983	3.6
1984	2.2
1985	3.5
1986	3.2
1987	4.6
1988	3.7
1989	2.3

Source: OECD

peak sustained growth outstripped the rates recorded in West Germany, France and other countries but fell short of the United Kingdom's own long-term trend rate. Growth was good, but not miraculous.

What was almost miraculous is the growth in company profits. During the 1980s, profits grew more quickly in the United Kingdom than in any other industrialized country, albeit from a low base. Average growth in gross trading profits (net of stock appreciation) of United Kingdom firms outside the North Sea oil sector was 21.7 per cent per annum in the period from 1981 to 1987. The real rate of return on capital rose to its highest level since the 1960s and was in 1988 broadly in line with that of other major competitor countries.

Provided the Conservatives can bring down the overheated economy to the much-vaunted 'soft-landing', business confidence will remain high. The new optimism and new business ethos engendered in the Thatcher era, in which the creation of wealth is not merely accepted but actually applauded, will then be afforded time in which to permeate the whole of the business community, including manufacturing. The sooner the new optimism and the new business ethos become permanent features of the business culture at large, the better for the citizenry of the country. Business and government in the United Kingdom can then proceed to address an issue which has yet to enter the country's business culture in any significant fashion – protection of the environment.

Business and the economy

The United Kingdom was the 'workshop of the world', the leading manufacturing nation, in the nineteenth century. Although the value of the output of the country's manufacturing sector has been surpassed in the interim by the United States, Japan, West Germany and France, it still came as a shock when, in 1983, the United Kingdom registered a deficit in manufactured goods for the first time since the Industrial Revolution. Despite great improvements in productivity and large increases in inward investment, a record trade gap remained at the end of the decade, when manufacturing accounted for only 24 per cent of GDP. Nor has an impressive increase in the size of the service sector of the economy been able to offset fully the decline in manufacturing industry.

Manufacturing

'Mrs Thatcher prefers people who make money to people who make things', was a complaint by one of the delegates to the CBI conference in 1988 which was widely reported in the business press. While it is not beyond the bounds of possibility that Mrs Thatcher likes both, Sir John Harvey-Jones, former chairman of Imperial Chemical Industries (ICI), has frequently pointed out that manufacturing is still perceived, in the United Kingdom, as a less important and laudable aspect of the business culture than making deals in the City.

Almost immediately after the Conservatives regained power in 1979, manufacturing industry began to feel disadvantaged. While exchange and dividend controls were abolished by the incoming government, the detested National Insurance surcharge remained in force. In addition, interest rates were maintained at a high level, as was the sterling exchange rate, making the country's exports uncompetitive. Whereas the index of industrial production registered a record 107.1 in 1979, it had plunged by 1981 to 96.6 as two million jobs were lost. The government's anti-inflationary policies combined with the worldwide recession to thrust manufacturing industry into deepest gloom.

In 1980, nationalized British Steel entered *The Guinness Book of World Records* with the largest annual loss recorded up to that time – some $4 billion. It subsequently cut its workforce by two-thirds. In March 1981, Guest, Keen & Nettlefolds (GKN) reported an annual trading loss for the first time ever. In three years, GKN reduced its workforce from 69,000 to 37,000. A similar pattern was repeated throughout industry as demand plummeted and companies found themselves severely overmanned. Some of the most illustrious names in British industry went into liquidation or were taken over.

One of the effects of the recession in manufacturing industry was to exacerbate the **North-South Divide** . Between 1971 and 1984, the number of people employed in manufacturing industry in the Newcastle-upon-Tyne area dropped from 147,000 to 77,000. The biggest falls were in shipbuilding and engineering but practically all manufacturing sectors shed labour. A few miles away in Consett, County Durham, in six months in 1980, the unemployment rate rose from 12.3 per cent to 22.4 per cent, the highest in mainland Britain. But hardest hit of all in the recession was Northern Ireland, with its clothing industry. By November 1981, unemployment in Londonderry was 23.1 per cent and rising. Many parts of the South East of England, with their service-based industries, were relatively unaffected.

Table 4.2

	Regional real gross product % change from previous year (excluding North Sea oil)			Regional unemployment rates % of working population	
	1979	*1985*	*1988*	*1985*	*1988*
North	1.1	3.8	6.1	16.5	12.2
Yorkshire/Humberside	1.2	5.5	6.4	13.0	9.8
East Midlands	4.0	3.8	6.9	10.5	7.4
East Anglia	1.7	1.7	8.0	8.6	4.9
South East	2.5	3.6	6.5	8.6	5.4
South West	2.7	3.0	7.7	10.0	6.5
West Midlands	− 0.3	4.8	6.3	13.6	8.8
North West	0.0	2.8	6.2	14.8	9.7
Wales	1.2	5.0	5.9	14.8	9.3
Scotland	1.1	3.0	5.5	14.1	11.7
Northern Ireland	1.9	1.3	6.0	17.4	16.7
UK (including North Sea oil)	3.0	3.5	4.3	11.8	8.3

Sources: Business Strategies and Employment Gazette

As Table 4.2 above indicates, the North West, Wales and the West Midlands, after suffering particularly heavily during the recession, made strong recoveries towards the end of the 1980s. Scotland and Northern

Ireland remain problem regions. According to forecasts published in 1989, East Anglia, which topped the gross domestic product growth charts from 1986, will continue as the fastest-growing region (4 per cent per annum), together with the East Midlands (3.7 per cent). The South West and South East (outside London) will also expand faster than average. London, which is already suffering from skills shortages (see also page 190), will probably witness an outward drift of companies. Without a significantly higher level of investment, Scotland and Northern Ireland are expected to achieve levels below the country's growth averages.

One of the reasons for the re-emergence of certain traditional manufacturing regions such as the North West and the West Midlands was the remarkable **rise in productivity**, and with it competitiveness, in the 1980s. Productivity in manufacturing industry increased by an average 5–6 per cent per annum in 1980–8, faster than in any other developed industrial economy, including Japan. The annual strike rate dropped to the lowest for fifty years (see page 195). Even in terms of what is called 'total factor productivity' or the efficiency with which business uses both capital and labour, the United Kingdom surpassed the achievements of other industrialized countries. In a study comparing the six years from 1979 to 1985 to the preceding six-year period, the OECD established that only the United Kingdom had registered a sizable increase. There were also some amazing turnarounds. British Steel increased productivity by almost 13 per cent per annum in 1979–88 and moved from that world record loss to an operating profit of £472 million in 1988.

Industry's critics, however, have pointed out that manufacturing output exceeded the 1979 level only in 1987, and fixed investment in manufacturing reached its pre–1979 level, in real terms, only in 1989. They have stressed that despite the rise in labour productivity in manufacturing, by 1988 the country's share of world trade in manufactured goods had dropped to 6.5 per cent in volume terms and roughly 6 per cent in value terms, compared with 8 per cent on both counts in 1979. There has also been greater import penetration in manufactured items. While finding it impossible to deny the vast improvements in labour productivity, critics have turned to the 'batting average' argument which shows that a cricket team's overall average automatically improves if several of the worst players are excluded from the calculations. It follows that if the least efficient companies go bankrupt, the performance of the survivors must appear to be better.

On balance, however, it is generally recognized that manufacturing industry emerged from the horrors of recession much leaner and fitter, if not actually large enough to satisfy domestic demand. Some of the sectors of manufacturing industry in which the most successful companies operate are as follows:

Chemicals

The United Kingdom's chemicals industry is the third largest in Western Europe and the fifth largest in the non-communist world. Almost half of its output is exported. One company, ICI, is responsible for half of the industry's production and is the fourth biggest chemicals company in the world.

Iron and steel

The United Kingdom is the world's ninth largest steel-producing nation in terms of volume. The country's manufacturers delivered 15 million tonnes of finished steel in 1987, 61 per cent of which was sold on the domestic market and the rest exported. British Steel is the third largest steel company in the world and accounts for approximately 75 per cent of crude steel production.

Electrical and electronic engineering

This sector of manufacturing industry suffered less than others in the recession, and output has risen steadily since 1982. In fact, sales of electronic data-processing (EDP) equipment trebled between 1983 and 1987. Expenditure in the country on EDP as a proportion of GDP is the highest in Western Europe, and leading overseas manufacturers, such as IBM, Wang, Seiko and Unisys, have established manufacturing plants in the United Kingdom.

Mechanical engineering

Much of the output in this sector is capital equipment, and it suffered particularly during the recession. However, from 1984 it began to recover. Over 40 per cent of sales go overseas, and exports of mechanical engineering equipment were responsible for 13 per cent of all visible exports in 1987.

Motor vehicles

The production of cars is dominated by five groups which account for over 95 per cent of the total. They are Rover, in which the government had a majority stake prior to the company's sale to British Aerospace in 1988, Ford, Vauxhall, Peugeot-Talbot and Nissan. In recent years the industry has suffered from increased import penetration, but it remains a major exporter. In 1987, Jaguar alone exported cars to the value of £785 million.

Aerospace

The United Kingdom's aerospace industry is the third largest in the world. In 1987 its turnover was £9 billion, with exports amounting to £5.6 billion. Almost half of the export effort was provided by British Aerospace (BAe). Rolls-Royce, which was privatized in 1987, is one of the three largest manufacturers of aeroengines in the world. The company order book at the beginning of 1988 stood at £4 billion.

Leaner and fitter supplier companies account for some of the country's attraction as a target for **direct inward investment**. Direct investment, i.e. setting up or acquiring companies in another country as opposed to portfolio investment, which is the buying of foreign equities or overseas government bonds by financial institutions, reached record levels in the 1980s. In 1986 foreign companies invested £4.8 billion in the United Kingdom; in 1987 £8.1 billion; and in 1988 £7.1 billion in some 320 different projects. Since the beginning of the 1980s, total direct foreign investment in the United Kingdom has been in the region of £29.6 billion.

Much of the direct foreign investment has come from Japan. The first Japanese company to invest in the United Kingdom was YKK zip fasteners at Runcorn in 1972. By February 1987 the number of Japanese firms investing was fifty; by April 1989, the total had risen to 100 when Toyota announced that Burnaston, near Derby, was to be the site of its new European assembly plant, at a cost of £700 million. But it is not only the giants of Japanese industry such as Nissan, Toyota and Fujitsu which have invested in the United Kingdom. Citizen wristwatches opened a factory in Scunthorpe. Nikken, an engineering company, has settled in Rotherham. Union Chemicar, a carbon ribbon manufacturer, has opted for Barnsley.

The reasons for the Japanese investment in Europe in general are first the prospects of the EC's internal market. Second, the Japanese fear that 'Fortress Europe' might make it more difficult to sell in this market of 320 million Europeans. While other countries such as the United States would also suffer from a fortress mentality in Europe, most US multinationals already have a substantial presence here. The reasons for the Japanese investment in the United Kingdom in particular, which attracts 30 per cent of total investment in Europe, are held to be: the English language, which is compulsory in Japanese schools; low corporation taxes; an efficient distribution system; relative ease of access to mainland Europe; improved labour relations; and competitive labour rates.

A definite cause for concern in terms of its attractiveness for inward investment is the country's **infrastructure**. Government investment in road and rail transport in the 1980s fell behind that in West Germany, France, Italy and Spain, and the transport infrastructure was the single most worrying issue in 1988 for the thirteen regional chairmen of the CBI. Though the government published a White Paper in 1989, promising a virtual doubling of expenditure on the road-building programme, the most glaring omission was any provision for motorways along the east and south coasts linking the ports there with the industrial heartland.

In 1987 the road network in the United Kingdom totalled some 376,100 km, of which 2990 km were trunk motorways. While motorways and trunk roads account for only 4 per cent of road mileage, they bear 33 per cent of road traffic, including almost 60 per cent of heavy goods traffic.

Railways were pioneered in Britain, and the four large railway companies were nationalized in 1947. In 1962 the British Railways Board was established to manage railway affairs. In 1987, the length of the route open for traffic measured 16,633 km, about 25 per cent of which was electrified, including British Rail's busiest InterCity route linking London, the West Midlands, the North West and Glasgow.

Construction work started on the Channel Tunnel in 1988, which entails the provision of twin single-track rail tunnels with a shuttle service for cars, coaches and heavy goods vehicles. The project, which is being undertaken by Eurotunnel, is estimated to cost some £7 billion at 1989 prices. It is the largest civil engineering project in Europe financed by private enterprise.

The country's inland waterways make only a limited contribution to freight carriage. In 1986 an official survey of freight traffic reported that some 69 million tonnes of freight were transported on inland waterways and estuaries, constituting only 1.4 per cent of freight traffic tonne-km.

There are over 300 ports in the United Kingdom, but many are small harbours which do not handle freight on a regular basis. In 1987, traffic through the ports totalled 457 million tonnes. The main ports with total tonnage throughput in 1987 were: Sullom Voe, 50 million tonnes; London 48.9; Tees and Hartlepool, 33.9. Milford Haven 32.7; Grimsby and Immingham 32.2; Forth 30; and Southampton 27.2

Total capacity offered by British airlines in 1987 amounted to 15,853 million available tonne-km. Additionally, the airlines transport 28.5 million passengers a year on regular, scheduled services and 23.5 million on charter flights. The main airports are London (Heathrow) with 34.7 million passengers in 1987; London (Gatwick) 19.4; Manchester 8.6; Glasgow 3.4; Luton 2.6; Belfast (Aldegrove) 2.1; Edinburgh 1.8; Aberdeen, 1.5; Newcastle-upon-Tyne 1.3; and East Midlands 1.3.

Services

As the United Kingdom's manufacturing industry has contracted, an increasing share of GDP has been taken up by services. In 1960, services accounted for approximately 45 per cent of GDP and 48 per cent of persons in employment; in 1987, services contributed about 60 per cent of GDP and employed 68 per cent of those in work. Foreign trade in services has also grown, particularly in financial services (see page 183), and in 1987 overseas revenue from services totalled almost half the value of exports of manufactures. The fastest-growing service sectors, measured by employment, were leisure and personal services, finance, distribution, hotels and catering. A study by the University of Warwick suggests that by 1995 services will account for over 70 per cent of employment.

A significant factor in the expansion of services has been the growth of real incomes; personal disposable income has increased since 1948 at an annual rate of 2.8 per cent. As spending power grows, consumers tend to spend a greater proportion of their income on services. For example, increased motorization and expenditure on the running costs of cars are important factors in the rise in expenditure on services. Other changes in the country have also encouraged the growth of services: the increasing number of elderly people in the United Kingdom (see page 186) has expanded the demand for medical services; and the fall in the average number of hours worked has created the need for more leisure services.

Among the major private sector services is tourism, which has become increasingly important and is a large employer, especially in London. Spending by British residents and overseas tourists amounted to approximately £18 billion in 1987. It is calculated that about 1.4 million people were employed in 1987 in jobs directly or indirectly related to the tourist industry. 15.4 million people from abroad visited the United Kingdom in 1987, an 11 per cent rise on 1986, spending some £6.2 billion. The largest single nationality group were citizens of the United States, followed by France and West Germany.

A further growth area in the services sector is to be located in the retail trades. In 1987 retail sales were 8.3 per cent greater than in 1986, representing a 6 per cent increase in volume. The number of businesses in the retail trade is approximately 250,000, and turnover in 1987 was in the region of £100 billion. While the large multiple retailers with ten or more outlets have expanded and diversified, there has been a decline in the number of small retail businesses and outlets, with independent businesses and retail cooperatives most affected. The largest multiple retailers in the grocery market are the retail cooperatives, Sainsbury, Tesco, Asda, Dee Corporation, Argyll Stores and the Kwik Save discount group. The major mixed retail companies are Marks and Spencer, F. W. Woolworth, Boots, Great Universal Stores, John Lewis Partnership, Burtons, Littlewoods, Sears and the House of Fraser.

Towards the end of the 1980s, an expanded services sector had failed as an adequate substitute for a slimmed-down manufacturing base. While manufacturing achieved extraordinary increases in productivity during the 1980s, it suffered a massive reduction in size. The result was a capacity gap, with domestic suppliers incapable of meeting demand, leading to record trade deficits. In early 1989, the country was consuming more than it produced by the equivalent of 4 per cent of GDP. Most of the excess was in manufactured items. In turn, capacity shortages, and employers taking the opportunity to raise profit margins to international levels, contributed to rises in inflation. It is estimated that investment in capital stock by domestic suppliers would have to increase by 20 per cent above the level in the 1980s to close the gap.

Widespread neglect of the special needs of manufacturing in the United Kingdom remains a disturbing feature of the business culture which looks set to continue into the 1990s.

Business and the law

English law differs fundamentally from the other legal systems to which reference is made in this book. The English common law emerged as a series of devices aimed at settling disputes or controversies; Continental law originated as a system instructing which rights and duties ought to be accepted in society as an ideal of justice. Similarly, the attention of English lawyers was focused for centuries on the types of action which could be claimed from a common law court. Although great changes have taken place over time, a high degree of significance still attaches, under English law, to procedures such as 'due process' and 'fair trial'. Scottish law is different again.

The common law was developed in England by the courts and thus a case law emerged where legal rules and certain procedures are linked with the facts of a particular case; on the Continent, by contrast, legal rules were constructed and laid down by legal scholars and writers. In the fullness of time, these legal rules were then codified.

A further difference is noteworthy which is of significance for the business culture. Legal studies in England are still, for the most part, pursued separately from studies of political science, public administration or management; on the Continent it is not uncommon to find university courses which embrace all three aspects of scholarship. Thus it is quite rare to meet a business person in England who has studied law in any depth, while on the Continent a legal background is often held to be an ideal preparation for business.

The law in the United Kingdom admits a range of different business organizations. At one end of the scale are the sole proprietorships; at the other the huge public limited companies. The principal forms of business entities in the United Kingdom are sole traders and partnerships; limited liability companies; and branches of foreign companies. A more comprehensive account can be found in the Price Waterhouse *Guide to doing business in the United Kingdom*, but the essential points are as follows:

1 **Sole traders**
   The sole trader is the simplest legal entity within which to conduct business. It consists of one person carrying on business who may employ other persons to work for him or her. The sole trader is entirely responsible for the conduct of the business and has unlimited liability for business debts. Normally there is no requirement for registration or the independent auditing of accounts.

2 **Partnerships**
   A partnership is defined under the **1890 Partnership Act** as: '. . . the relationship which subsists between persons carrying on a business in common with a view to profit.' Under English law, a legal personality separate from the partners is not accorded to a partnership. Although the partners may be referred to collectively as a firm, the firm does not have the legal status of a company. Under Scottish law, a partnership does possess a legal status separate from the partners. But the partners in a Scottish firm are ultimately, like those in an English firm, personally responsible to the creditors for the debts and obligations of the firm. One of the few regulatory controls stipulates that a partnership may not consist of more than twenty persons unless they are lawyers, accountants, or members of a recognized stock exchange.

   The **1907 Limited Partnership Act** provides for a general partnership with one or more general partners who conduct the firm's business and have unlimited liability, and one or more limited partners with liability limited to their capital contribution to the firm. The limited partners must not partake in the management of the firm otherwise their limited liability status is forfeited. Because of the latter stipulation, limited partnerships have not proved to be popular forms of business entities.

3 **Limited liability companies**
   The most common type of company in the United Kingdom is the limited liability company incorporated by statute, of which the most recent is the **1985 Companies Act**. Limited liability companies are

companies limited by guarantee or companies limited by shares. A company limited by guarantee is one where members' liability is limited to such amounts as they pledge to contribute in the event of the company being wound up. Such companies are, however, rarely encountered. A company limited by shares is one where the members' liability for the company's debts is restricted to the amount paid or unpaid (if any) on their shares. Since companies limited by shares form the vast majority of business entities in the United Kingdom, the remaining remarks under this heading will refer to companies thus limited.

A company may be incorporated either as a public or as a private company. Only a public company may offer shares or debentures to the public, but they need not necessarily be quoted or traded on a stock exchange. Where a company seeks public-company status, it must include a statement to this effect in its memorandum of association. A public company must have an allotted share capital of £50,000, of which at least one-quarter of the shares' par value must be paid up. It must possess a name ending in 'public limited company' which may be abbreviated to 'plc', or their Welsh equivalents. All other companies are regarded as private companies. There is no authorized minimum share capital for a private company, but such a company must include as the last part of its name either the world 'limited' or the abbreviation 'ltd', or their Welsh equivalents.

A public company must have at least two directors; a private company need only have one. Unlike a public company, a private company need not acquire a trading certificate and can do business or borrow as soon as it is registered. There exist other legal requirements from which private companies are exempt, but the requirement to file annual accounts, which are thus made available for public inspection, applies to all limited companies. If the company is only small or medium-sized, it may file modified accounts, though these accounts must contain all the information specified by the 1985 Act.

The document by which a company is incorporated is the memorandum of association. It provides details of the company's name, the country in which its registered office is to be located, the limited liability of its members, its public-company status if appropriate, its authorized share capital, subscribers and objects. The objects clause is normally so widely drafted that it gives the company the powers necessary to conduct any business it may wish. Usually the articles of association are drawn up by lawyers at the same time as the memorandum of association. The articles lay down the internal rules for a company and its members. They set out provisions on voting rights, transfer of shares, the powers of directors and many other items. In fact, Table A in the Companies Regulations 1985 may be adopted as the articles, with or without modification.

A company's authorized share capital and the division of the capital into shares are specified in the memorandum of association. Issued share capital is held to be that part of the authorized share capital which has actually been issued to members. It may not exceed the authorized share capital. Shares may be of any fixed amount, usually £1 or smaller denominations. Shares of no par value are not allowed. They may be of different classes having different voting, dividend and other rights. Issued shares may be fully or partly paid. Shares may not be issued at a discount in relation to their par value, but may be issued at a premium. Each company is required to keep a register of members, recording details of the shareholders and the quantities of shares they hold. Public companies must also maintain a register of shareholders with an interest of 5 per cent or more of the company's voting shares. Anyone acquiring such a stake is required to notify the company affected. Companies may issue debentures as well as share capital. Debentures are normally issued as security for a loan. They usually bear rights to interest at a specified, often fixed rate and repayment at some future date.

The conduct of the company's business is the responsibility of the directors. A director need not be a shareholder in the company but sometimes articles of association require of a director a so-called share qualification. The directors often appoint one or more of their number to executive positions in the company, such as managing director. They also appoint one of their number as chairman, who may or may not hold a full-time executive position. The company's articles of association define the powers and duties of directors. Important among the latter is the obligation under company law to ensure that proper information about the company is divulged to the public and to potential and existing investors. In addition, directors must take into consideration the interests of employees as well as shareholders. Every company must appoint a secretary who may also be a director, but a sole director may not also be secretary. The secretary is regarded as an officer of the company and is usually the person responsible for ensuring that the company complies with the requirements of company law.

A company's dividend policy is the responsibility of the directors. The shareholders may either ratify or reject the directors' recommendations or propose that the amount be reduced. No dividend can exceed the amount recommended by the directors.

Every company must hold an Annual General Meeting (AGM) in each calendar year. At least twenty-one days' notice of the meeting must be given in writing to every member entitled to vote at the meeting. Business at the AGM is regulated by the company's articles of association and normally takes in: the accounts of the most recent financial year, including the directors' report; the auditors' report on the accounts; approval of the dividend proposed by the directors; the election or re-election of directors; the appointment of auditors and the fixing of their remuneration. A simple majority of votes will carry an ordinary resolution. Unless the articles of association specify otherwise, a shareholders' meeting may be held anywhere, and not, necessarily in the United Kingdom.

4   Branches of foreign companies

Branches of foreign companies, i.e. companies incorporated outside the United Kingdom which set up places of business in the country, must comply with the provisions set forth in Part XXIII of the **1985 Companies Act**. Similar legislation is applicable in Northern Ireland. Within one month of establishing a place of business in the country, the company must file with the Registrar of Companies: certified copies of the company's charter, statutes, memorandum and articles; particulars of the directors, such as names and addresses, nationalities and business occupations; a list of one or more British residents authorized to accept notices served on the company's behalf; and a declaration showing the date on which the place of business was established in the United Kingdom. Where the required documents are not in English a translation must be filed. Overseas companies must submit the same accounts as would be required if they were incorporated in the United Kingdom but in most cases it is possible to obtain permission from the Department of Trade and Industry to file the accounts as published in the company's own country, or an English translation of those accounts.

An influential factor in company law in recent years has been the EC. One of the objectives of the EC's industrial policy is: 'The creation of a unified business environment involving the harmonization of company law, and the creation of a community capital market.' The advent of the EC's single market by the end of 1992 has lent fresh impetus to such objectives, and existing company law in the United Kingdom could be affected most profoundly by changes currently under discussion.

Business and finance

The United Kingdom is one of the leading financial centres in the world. Concentrated mainly in the City of London, the financial institutions provide services for business in this country and overseas. More international deposit and lending business is done in London than in New York or Tokyo, and more than in the rest of the EC put together. The stock market in the United Kingdom is three times larger than in West Germany; four times larger than in France; seven times larger than in Italy and the Netherlands; and even ten times the size of Spain's. Indeed, the City has latterly exerted a profound influence on the United Kingdom's business culture, appearing to enjoy most-favoured status with Conservative politicians, attracting more of the brightest young people that the country produces than ever before, and rewarding them most generously. Nevertheless, the Bank of England, the Big Four clearing banks and the financial markets are not without their critics.

The Bank of England

Founded in 1694 to furnish money for the government during the War of the Grand Alliance against France, the Bank of England is the central bank in the United Kingdom. Since its establishment, it has undergone several changes in status which have involved modifications to its responsibilities. Perhaps one of the most significant of the changes for the country's business culture occurred when, with the election of the first post-war Labour government, it was nationalized under the **1946 Bank of England Act**.

The Act contained the clearest possible message that the government of the day was henceforth responsible for the country's monetary policy. In fact, Section IV of the Act provides that the Treasury can give such directions to the Bank as it thinks appropriate in the public interest, after consultation with the Governor of the Bank. In its turn, the Bank has the power to issue directives to clearing banks and other financial institutions.

All the banks operating in the United Kingdom are subject to the supervision of the Bank of England. In addition to its supervisory role, it controls the issue of bank notes (the Scottish banks also enjoying limited rights to issue notes), manages the national debt, acts as a banker to Government and the banking system itself, and controls the official reserves.

It is, however, the Bank's association with the Treasury in their joint failure to keep inflation within tolerable limits that has raised most comment during the Thatcher years.

At first glance, it would appear that monetary policy under the Conservatives has succeeded in suppressing inflation. During the 1980s, the figures revealed a declining tendency, even if they were on the rise again towards the end of the decade (Table 4.3). But if the United Kingdom's record on inflation is compared with West Germany's (see page 21), the figures appear much less impressive.

Table 4.3   *United Kingdom inflation (1979–89)*

Year	(%)
1979	13.5
1980	16.3
1981	11.3
1982	8.8
1983	4.8
1984	5.1
1985	5.3
1986	4.2
1987	3.8
1988	5.1
1989	7.8

Source: OECD

One possible solution to the United Kingdom's inflation problems which has been widely canvassed is for the country to become a full member of the **European Monetary System** (EMS). Established in 1979, the EMS consists of three elements – the Exchange Rate Mechanism (ERM), the European Currency Unit (Ecu) and the Monetary Cooperation Fund. Sterling forms part of the Ecu and contributes to the cooperation fund. There are nine full members of the EMS, with only the United Kingdom, Greece and Portugal not yet (1990) part of the ERM.

Although full membership of the EMS has been openly advocated by two of Margaret Thatcher's Chancellors of the Exchequer, Sir Geoffrey Howe and Nigel Lawson, she has insisted that the United Kingdom will not join until the time is right. She remains unconvinced that there are significant benefits for the country stemming from full membership. Her critics point out that: the existing full members of the EMS have all achieved a low inflation rate; the EMS has furnished a discipline in monetary policy which has been lacking in the United Kingdom; the EMS would protect against the possibility of a falling pound bringing with it higher inflation; EMS members have benefited from lower interest rates than the United Kingdom; currency stability encourages trade; and currency stability leads to greater investment because business has the confidence to plan ahead.

Margaret Thatcher's supporters claim that the year from March 1987 to March 1988, when the pound was informally pegged to the West German DM, was a resounding failure in terms of financial management. Credit ran out of control during this time, preparing the ground for the serious deterioration in the balance of payments from mid-1988 and for a rise in inflationary pressures. Among others arguing against full membership of the EMS are the Bruges Group, set up after the Prime Minister's speech in September 1988 which was highly critical of the European Commission. They contend that full EMS membership would require the reinstatement of the country's exchange controls, abolished in 1979, and jeopardize the City's position as the leading financial centre in Europe. The Bank of England also joined the argument by publishing technical objections to full EMS membership in May 1989.

Despite her misgivings, Margaret Thatcher reluctantly agreed, at the EC's Madrid summit in June 1989, that she could accept stage one of the report by Jacques Delors, French socialist President of the European Commission, on Economic and Monetary union (EMU). Stage one foresees the United Kingdom joining the ERM at some as yet unspecified date. Although Robin Leigh-Pemberton, Governor of the Bank of England, together with the governors of the other EC central banks, had sat on the committee which framed the Delors report, Margaret Thatcher refused to recognise any automaticity between stage one and stages two and three which eventually envisage the EC adopting a common currency.

Fundamental to Mrs Thatcher's objections to EMU and all that such involves is a fear of loss of sovereignty in matters of monetary policy. In a paper on 'Europe: Fortress or Freedom?', Dr Brian Hindley agrees that the EMS cedes a large degree of control of members' monetary policy to the West German Bundesbank. But he adds: 'I think it very likely . . . that the British economy would have been better off had its money supply been controlled by the Deutsche Bundesbank over the past two or three decades. And given a choice between the Bank of England and the Deutsche Bundesbank for the next two or three decades, I would be inclined to choose the latter.'

The Big Four

Domestic banking business in the United Kingdom is dominated by the Big Four clearing banks – Barclays, Lloyds, Midland and National Westminster. These banks are called clearing banks because they were members of the London Banks' Clearing House which originally administered the cheque-clearing system in the country. There are now seven banks which form the Committee of London and Scottish Bankers (CLSB), and this body has replaced the Committee of London Clearing Banks as the trade association for the major 'high street' banks.

Each of the Big Four, which are among the largest banks in the world, has an extensive network of branches throughout the country and is thus well located to provide financial services to businesses operating anywhere in the United Kingdom. The most frequently-encountered service for business offered by the Big Four has been the provision of current accounts, i.e. non-interest-bearing cheque accounts permitting companies to effect payments in a quick and convenient manner. In addition, clearing banks have also lent to their corporate customers, either in the form of flexible overdrafts but with relatively high, floating rates of interest; or in the form of term loans with lower and, usually, fixed rates of interests.

In recent years, the relationship between the clearing banks, whose traditional mode of operation was to borrow short and lend short, and business has changed radically. Business customers have turned increasingly to banks not only for working capital but for capital to expand over medium and longer-term periods. Indeed, the range of financial services offered by all the clearing banks has become so diverse that the former clear-cut distinctions between these and other types of banks have become blurred. The clearing banks now offer export finance, factoring, insurance, stockbroking, leasing, investment management advice, and almost any other financial activity.

Towards the end of the 1980s, the Big Four had, however, succeeded in alienating both shareholders and personal customers alike. Their shareholders felt aggrieved because, by October 1989, Barclays, Lloyds, Midland and NatWest announced that they had written off as irrecoverable debts of £1,938 million. Moreover, they were committed collectively to provision against further debt of £6.7 billion. The debts arose as the result of loans to the governments of Second and Third World countries. By the autumn of 1989, Midland had already written off £846 million; Lloyds £464 million; NatWest £395 million; and Barclays £235 million. The sheer size of the write-offs had quite naturally affected the banks' trading figures, with the result that the Midland revealed a £531 million loss for the year. In fact, someone even went so far as to calculate that if the £1,938 million were converted into £5 notes and the money were laid end to end, it would stretch for 30,000 miles!

About the same time, the clearing banks announced that they were considering a charge for the use of credit cards. The charge would be levied either for the purchase of the card itself or on those customers who pay their credit card bills promptly, or both. Coming after the banks' practice of refusing to pay interest on current accounts and levying charges on the movements on these accounts under certain conditions, which lasted for many years, this announcement is likely to drive even more customers into the arms of the building societies. Unless the Big Four improve their services for the private customer, including items so mundane as opening hours, they could well see many of their future activities restricted exclusively to the corporate sector.

Stock market

As has been observed, the financial markets appear to have enjoyed special treatment under Thatcherism. The tone was set right at the outset when Sir Geoffrey Howe abolished exchange and dividend controls in 1979, thus giving the City the kind of freedom in which it is held that markets work best. Privatizations then furnished the stock market with excellent business. Nigel Lawson's reforms of corporate taxation also did much to encourage a recovery in company profits, which in turn increased the attraction of the shares of these firms.

Perhaps, however, the most significant single event for the financial markets occurred when Cecil Parkinson, Secretary of State for Trade and Industry at the time, reached an agreement with Sir Nicholas Goodison, Chairman of the Stock Exchange, to break the jobbers' monopoly and the brokers' cartel. The eventual outcome was the **Big Bang** on 27 October, 1986. This particular piece of reform appeared appropriate because first it was in line with the government philosophy of deregulation throughout the economy, or letting market forces hold full sway. Second, it was convenient because the City needed to adapt to new trading systems elsewhere if it was to remain a global player and exploit to the full its position between the time zones of New York and Tokyo.

Although the changes in regulations and trading practices culminated in the Big Bang, they were only the last in a series which revolutionized the operations of the stock exchange. The most important changes can be summarized as follows:

- Fixed minimum commissions on the buying and selling of securities were abolished.

- Corporate membership of the stock exchange, with 100 per cent outside ownership, was introduced.
- All firms were allowed to act as broker/dealers or to act as agents for clients and as buyers or sellers in their own right.

One effect of the Big Bang was to induce a rush of mergers and acquisitions as banks and other financial institutions bought into traditional jobbing and brokering firms. Another was to create such a demand for staff in the City that recruits were sometimes welcomed not only with inflated salaries but also with 'golden hellos' which assumed the shape of Porsche cars! This state of affairs did not last for long. Within a year, sanity was restored with an even bigger explosion. City firms' combined losses in 1988 totalled approximately £500 million, and it is estimated that some 20,000 redundancies were declared with a net loss of 4,000 jobs.

The even bigger explosion, which occurred on 19 October 1987, was **The Crash**. After a bull market which had lasted for seven years, 22 per cent of the value of shares was wiped off the London stock exchange within one week. Despite the losses suffered by its shares, manufacturing industry in the country found it difficult to suppress a feeling of *Schadenfreude*. The City was now taking some of the medicine which manufacturing had been obliged to swallow during the recession. Surprisingly enough, United Kingdom firms in the City overcame the difficulties very well. In 1989 the two clear market leaders in the equity and gilts markets remained British: Barclays de Zoete Wedd and S. G. Warburg. The leading foreign-owned stockbroker, UBS-Phillips & Drew, reported a loss in excess of £100 million in 1988.

Towards the end of 1989 the stock market was approaching its pre-crash peak, the £5.2 billion privatization of the water authorities having provided a welcome fillip in December. For much of the year, however, it had been sustained by takeovers and rumours of takeovers (Table 4.4).

In the first six months of 1989 over 1600 United Kingdom companies took part in mergers and acquisitions, worth a total of 238 billion – more than twice the 1988 sum. The largest of the bids, Hoylake's £13 billion offer for BAT Industries, which was to be financed mainly by junk bonds, must persuade all British public companies, even the largest, that none of them are safe from corporate raiders. Hitherto, it had generally been assumed that the giants among the country's companies were too complex in structure to be the target even of hostile takeover bidders intent on unbundling, or breaking up the company.

Indeed, there is a distinct threat of the arrival in force of the highly-leveraged buyout as pioneered in the United States of America by firms such as Kravis Kohlberg Roberts, Bankers Trust and Wasserstein Perella.

Table 4.4   *Top ten British takeover bids January–July 1989*

Target	Bidder	Value, £million
BAT Industries	Hoylake	13,000
Consolidated Gold Fields	Hanson	3,500
Gateway	Isosceles	2,050
Sea Containers	Tiphook/Stena	505
UEI	Carlton Communications	495
Coalite	Anglo United	478
Ward White	Boots	474
William Collins	News International	402
Tootal	Coats Viyella	395
NEI	Rolls-Royce	316

Source: *Acquisitions Monthly*

All three specialist firms now maintain offices in London. Leveraged buyouts may represent good news for institutional fund managers, but their targets are usually large, diversified manufacturing companies with strong cash flows and undervalued assets. Such buyouts are as yet uncommon in the United Kingdom: by the end of 1989 only one leveraged bid had succeeded – the £1.1 billion offer by Isosceles for Gateway, the supermarket chain. Nonetheless, it has been calculated that approximately forty-four of the stocks which constitute part of the FT-SE 100 Index could become the targets for leveraged bids.

Towards the end of the 1980s, high interest rates were discouraging highly-leveraged buyout activity by necessitating large interest payments on the mountains of debt which support these companies and deterring consumers from purchasing their products. Once interest rates ease, however, there is every sign that such buyout activity could take off rapidly as merchant banks boost their buyout funds. Potential profits are simply too attractive for such buyouts simply to go away (see page 205).

Then managers in manufacturing industry in the United Kingdom will have to call upon all their expertise to beat off the challenge from hostile predators. If the political and economic philosophy remains as it has since 1979, cries of 'foul' at yet another attack on the country's manufacturing base will go unheeded. The business culture will continue to be dominated by short-term considerations, such as profit forecasts by stockbrokers' analysts and the interests of institutional fund managers seeking the maximum possible return on investment in the shortest possible time. None of this is conducive to long-term thinking, which is vitally important if manufacturing industry is to plan, invest, equip and train for the future.

Business and the labour market

Business in the United Kingdom in the 1980s had to feed an increasing and, as in most European countries, an ageing population. Similarly, the civilian labour force continued to grow appreciably, thus making its own contribution to high levels of unemployment during the severe recession. However, from 1986 to 1989 unemployment fell by a million, partly due to the fact that the United Kingdom's economy created as many new jobs as the rest of the EC countries combined. Nevertheless, the labour market in the United Kingdom in the future will be affected by certain disturbing demographic developments.

Demographic trends

In 1981, when the last national census was taken, the population of the United Kingdom numbered 56.4 million. By 1987 it had increased to 56.9 million, comprising 27.7 million males and 29.2 million females. The population is projected to grow steadily to reach 57.5 million by 1991, 59.0 million by 2001 and 60 million by the year 2025.

The age structure of the population has changed perceptibly over recent years. The number of people aged sixty-five or over (8.8 million in 1987) was more than 50 per cent greater than in 1951 (5.5 million). This age group represented 15 per cent of the population in 1987 compared with 11 per cent in 1951. The overall size of this segment of the population is expected to rise to 11.3 million by the year 2025.

At the lower end of the age range, in 1971 there were some 12.4 million children aged under fifteen compared with roughly 10.8 million in 1987, when they formed only 19 per cent of the total population. By the year 2025, this proportion is expected to remain unchanged. The implications for the labour market of this fall in the numbers of children under fifteen will be the subject of subsequent discussion (see page 190).

In recent times there has been net immigration to the United Kingdom of some 30,000 persons per annum. Averages for 1983–7 reveal 220,000 new residents each year (including British citizens) and 190,000 leaving the country to take up residence elsewhere.

Unemployment

The civilian labour force in Great Britain increased at an average rate of 140,000 per year during the 1970s and reached 26.2 million in 1980 and 1981. It fell by over 300,000 between 1981 and 1983, but the upward trend was then resumed, and in 1989 it reached 27.6 million. The net increase in the labour force between 1979 and 1989 of some 1.4 million is, naturally, reflected in the United Kingdom's unemployment rates during the period (Tables 4.5 and 4.6).

Table 4.5   *Unemployment rates in the United Kingdom*

Year	(%)
1979	5.1
1980	6.3
1981	10.3
1982	10.6
1983	10.7
1984	11.1
1985	11.3
1986	11.4
1987	10.0
1988	8.0
1989	6.4

Source: OECD

The reason for the discrepancies between Tables 4.5 and 4.6 is that unemployment can be measured in several ways. The OECD unemployment rates up to 1986 were based on the percentage of the total labour force each month without paid jobs who said they were available to start work in the next fortnight and had sought work at some time during the past four weeks or were waiting to start a job already obtained. This definition of unemployment is consistent with the guidelines of the **International Labour Organization** (ILO). It would appear, however, that since 1987 the OECD has been willing to accept each individual member country's definition of unemployment.

The fundamental measure of unemployment used by the Department of Employment changed six times from 1979. Since 1982 the figures have been based directly on the claimant count, i.e. the number of people

Table 4.6   Unemployment rates in the United Kingdom

Year	(%)
1979	4.0
1980	5.1
1981	8.1
1982	9.5
1983	10.5
1984	10.7
1985	10.9
1986	11.1
1987	10.0
1988	8.0
1989	

Source: Employment Gazette

claiming benefits at Unemployment Benefit Offices. The figures are derived almost entirely from computerized administrative records. They include those people who claim unemployment benefit, supplementary benefits and national insurance credits. They also include some of the severely disabled. However, the figures exclude students claiming benefit during a vacation but intending to return to full-time education when the new term begins, and the temporarily stopped. The latter are held to be people who had a job on the day of the monthly unemployment count (usually the second Thursday of each month) but were temporarily suspended from work on that day and were claiming benefits.

No matter which of the two tables is used, the figures clearly show the unemployment rates rising from 1979 to 1986. In fact, the United Kingdom suffered its worst recession this century in 1980–1. Unemployment increased to a recorded three million, and industrial production fell further and faster than even in the inter-war years. The jump in unemployment in the 1980s was largely the result of a labour shake-out, particularly in the manufacturing sector.

Between 1979 and 1981, manufacturing output dropped by 14.2 per cent; between 1979 and 1982, 385,000 men in manufacturing jobs alone were made redundant. Total redundancies over the same period were well in excess of one million people. Every Friday evening, **Independent Television News** (ITN) broadcast a list of redundancies, with by far the worst of them in the manufacturing sector. In the first four years of the 1980s, some of the most famous names in British industry vanished, either being taken into liquidation or bought up by other companies: Dunlop, Thomas Tilling and Capper Neill, to name but three. The Coats Patons textile group shut down twenty-one plants in two years; ICI shed 40 per cent of its UK workforce – 41,000 people. Employment in manufacturing in 1979 was approximately eight million; in 1988 it had shrunk to five million.

Unemployment fell by one million from mid–1986 to the end of 1988, by when it was below the EC average and below the national rates in France, Italy, Belgium, the Netherlands, Spain and Ireland. Long-term unemployment decreased by some 450,000 in 1987 and 1988 to 900,000 at the beginning of 1989. Unemployment among workers under the age of twenty-five was then at its lowest level since 1983. Although tougher rules on eligibility to claim unemployment benefits and the expansion of the government's employment measures programmes (see pages 200–202) account for part of this fall, the rapid pace of GDP growth did have a significant impact on the jobs market.

Ethnic minorities

One of the sectors of the population which was disproportionately affected by unemployment from 1979 to 1989 was that of the ethnic minorities. In the depths of the recession, in the spring of 1981, the Labour Force Survey established that unemployment rates were much higher among non-whites than among whites. Though the high unemployment rates among minority groups were partly related to differences in age distributions, levels of qualifications and proportions of married women in the different ethnic groups, rates were in general significantly greater for non-whites than for whites with similar characteristics. For example, the rates among West Indian men and Asian women were especially high, at 20.6 per cent and 17.9 per cent respectively, with the corresponding rates among white men and women at 9.7 per cent and 8.7 per cent.

The Labour Force Surveys carried out between 1984 and 1986 found that some 4.6 per cent of the population of working age, or approximately 1.54 million people in the United Kingdom, were from ethnic groups. Each of the main ethnic groups had a distinctive pattern of involvement in the labour market, and particular ethnic groups tended to be clustered in certain regions, occupations and industries. Once again, in this later study, it was established that the unemployment rates for ethnic minorities were about double those for whites: 20 per cent, compared with 10 per cent, over the three-year period. It was also found that, from 1983 to 1986, as the economy emerged from the recession, unemployment rates reduced by about 0.5 per cent among whites and the rate for ethnic minorities in total was estimated to have reduced by approximately 1 per cent. In view of the higher unemployment rate among ethnic minorities, this fall represented a similar proportionate reduction for whites and ethnic minorities alike.

Job creation

Despite the high rates of unemployment which were present among certain sections of the United Kingdom's population during the 1980s, the country did enjoy outstanding success in creating new jobs. From 1983 to 1989 the number of people in employment rose by over two million, surpassing by far the achievements of any other European economy.

From 1979 to 1989, self-employed companies with five or fewer staff almost doubled to three million. Small businesses employing fewer than 200 persons increased by 60 per cent to 1.6 million. These firms employed a quarter of the workforce and produced a quarter of the nation's wealth. In 1988, new businesses were registering at a rate of over 100,000 per year (see also page 203).

But what sort of work was created? The trend was clearly towards greater employment in the services sector. From 1984 to 1988, employment increased in transport from 897,000 to 927,000; in hotels and catering from 995,000 to 1.6 million; and in banking, finance and insurance from 1.6 million to 2.5 million. Of the fifteen major employment categories, only four registered an employment loss between 1984 and 1988. These were agriculture, forestry and fishing; coal, oil and natural gas extraction; electricity, gas, other energy and water supply; and manufacturing.

Skills shortages

At the beginning of the 1980s, the recession in the United Kingdom was exacerbated because it coincided with the time when the number of young people reaching school-leaving age peaked at more than a million. At the end of the decade skills shortages which emerged during a period of rapid economic growth since the mid-1980s were aggravated by a decline in the number of young people coming into the job market. By 1995, the proportion of 16 to 24-year-olds will have fallen by 20 per cent compared with 1987.

According to a report published by Hay Management Consultants in 1989, a shortage of graduates had already existed for some time. Most employers from the mid-1980s onwards were finding it increasingly difficult to attract sufficient graduates, and the problems would get worse. For the year 2000, there was a predicted demand for 20 per cent more graduates than in 1986; the supply of graduates would, however, be only 5 per cent greater.

Hardest hit of all in the 1980s were the electrical and electronics industries. Here there had been a shortfall of graduates since 1979. During the 1980s large companies had shopping lists for graduates which always exceeded the numbers available. Control and instrument engineers were in particular short supply, and towards the end of the decade, competition for software engineers and computer scientists grew rapidly.

Sponsorship of students through their undergraduate, and sometimes postgraduate, courses was tried as a recruitment tool but produced mixed results. In 1989 one in three undergraduates studying electronics and mechanical engineering was sponsored by companies, but many of them did not join their sponsors once they had completed their studies. Some engineering companies attempted more devious techniques, offering to fund research projects and university chairs in return for introductions to students. Other firms located their research and development centres close to universities and polytechnics. Students were allowed to use company facilities, and the firms spotted the talent.

Faced with these problems, companies at the end of the decade were looking increasingly towards Continental Europe to recruit young staff. West Germany in particular was proving attractive to the United Kingdom's recruiters on account of the graduate surpluses to be found there (see page 32). But how these young West Germans would settle in a business culture where engineering is widely held to be a dirty profession is quite a different issue.

Business and trade unions

The business culture in the United Kingdom has changed radically in so far as it is affected by the relationship between business and the trade unions. The atmosphere of industrial relations in the 1970s was completely different from at the end of the 1980s. Then many employers walked in fear of militant trade union leaders and intransigent shop stewards; by 1989 management had regained the freedom to manage, and the will and incentive to do so.

After the 1978–79 'winter of discontent', newspapers and magazines throughout the world were far from complimentary about the state of relations between business and the trade unions. An Australian newspaper coined the phrase 'British disease' to depict industrial strife. *L'Espresso* even referred to the United Kingdom's trade unions as a 'sovereign power'. Concern about trade unions and their power was also widespread in the United Kingdom itself. In 1978, a **Market & Opinion Research International** (Mori) poll established that 82 per cent of Britons believed the trade unions were 'too powerful'. When asked the identical question in 1989, only 41 per cent of respondents were of the same opinion. At the turn of the decade 58 per cent of Mori respondents thought that bad management was more to blame than the unions for the country's economic problems, while only 19 per cent held the unions to be more culpable.

The transformation in industrial relations in the United Kingdom was brought about by a series of government reforms, aided no doubt by the massive rise in unemployment during the recession. This sea-change encompassed a reduction in trade union power, a decline in trade union membership, fewer days lost through industrial disputes, and a spirit of 'new realism' among certain trade unions. In addition, the **Trades Union Congress** (TUC) has at last embraced the concept of Europeanization, which could lead to far-reaching changes in its relationship with the Labour Party.

Trade union reform

'When Margaret Thatcher declared she would curb the power of the union bosses, we academics scoffed', observed Dr Gavin Mackenzie, senior tutor at Jesus College, Cambridge, and lecturer in industrial relations, in an interview with *The Times* on 11 April, 1989. 'If Churchill, at the height of his powers and popularity, could not curb the miners in 1942 . . . how could she?'

The Conservatives under Margaret Thatcher came into government in 1979 convinced that the balance of power between trade unions and employers and trade unions and their own members was weighted too heavily in favour of the unions. The restrictions subsequently introduced on the legal immunities of trade unions reflected a fundamental belief among the Conservatives that the long-established tradition of keeping the law out of industrial relations had actually been a contributory factor in the growth of disorder and confrontation.

The clue to the Conservatives' success in reforming the trade unions lies perhaps in the fact that they adopted a step-by-step approach to correcting these imbalances. One huge tranche of what would have been perceived as 'union-bashing legislation', such as was attempted in the early 1970s, might possibly have failed because the unions could have mustered all their opposition to a single piece of legislation. It might not even have been supported by the employers. The unions found it impossible to mobilise, demobilise and remobilise against a series of measures, especially in the midst of a severe recession.

The 1980 Employment Act addressed the most obvious manifestations of excessive union power by making secondary picketing illegal.

The 1982 Employment Act narrowed further the scope of the trade unions to take secondary action and defined even more tightly the term 'trade dispute' within which unions can take industrial action without being sued for damages. The Act also reformed the legal liabilities of trade unions so that not only union officials but also the unions themselves can now be held responsible for any unlawful actions undertaken by their officials. Finally, the Act required all existing membership agreements to be confirmed or not by periodic ballots, thus attacking the 'closed shop'.

The 1984 Trade Union Act switched the accent of reform to the internal decision-making processes of the unions themselves. It demanded that elections to the official bodies be conducted through secret ballots and direct election by every member of the union. The Act also requires a union, before pronouncing an official stoppage, to ballot all its members who may be involved, in order to establish whether they wish to take strike action. If a union either fails to ballot its members or ignores the outcome of the ballot, a stoppage which may otherwise be legal loses its immunity from legal action.

The 1988 Employment Act was in many ways a response to experiences of union resistance to earlier legal controls. In particular, the Act enlarged upon the concept of an individual member's rights as a control mechanism over errant union leadership. It gives the trade union member the specific right to prevent his or her union from calling for industrial action without first holding a secret ballot and affords protection against union discipline if he or she decides to work during a strike or return to work before the strike has ended.

Although the welter of legislation in the 1980s is often dismissed by committed left-wingers as typical Tory anti-unionism, it is unlikely that a future Labour government would seek to repeal these laws. In 1989 Michael Meacher, former Labour Party Employment Spokesman, was quoted as saying: 'We will never return to the era of beer and sandwiches', when trade union leaders trooped to 10 Downing Street to give the government the benefit of their opinions, not only on industrial relations but on policy in general.

Trade union membership

One yardstick of the changing influence of trade unions is represented by the level of union membership. Between 1969 and 1979, membership increased by almost 28 per cent to 13.2 million or approximately 53 per cent of the employed labour force. However, from 1979 to 1989, the unions lost over four million members. Although union membership in 1989, at some 9 million, still accounted for about 40 per cent of the workforce in employment, the trend since 1979 has been one of unbroken decline.

The reasons for the reduction in membership can be ascribed to: a rise in unemployment during the recession of the early 1980s, especially in the sectors of employment where trade union membership was traditionally concentrated, such as manufacturing and public-sector industries; more efficient use of labour by companies which survived the ravages of the recession; and increased use of microchip technology.

Almost all the trade unions lost members during the period from 1979 to 1989. The massive **Transport and General Workers Union** (TGWU), with membership in almost every industry, lost approximately one third. The membership of the **National Union of Mineworkers** (NUM) contracted sharply as a result of pit closures and the formation of the breakaway **Union of Democratic Mineworkers** (UDM) following the coal strike of 1984–5. Between 1979 and 1987 the NUM forfeited over 43 per cent of its membership. Even the white-collar unions, the **Association of Scientific, Technical and Managerial Staffs** (ASTMS) and the **Association of Professional and Executive Officers** (APEX), sustained heavy losses. By contrast, membership of the **Royal College of Nursing** rose by 96,000, an increase of 59 per cent, possibly as a result of its no-strike pledges.

The overall fall in trade union membership has, surprisingly, contributed little to any acceleration in the reduction of the total numbers of unions. Ever since the mid-1960s, when there were 622 different unions, numbers have been declining at the rate of approximately 20 per cent every ten years. In the 1980s, smaller unions appear to have been willing to merge with larger ones for reasons of survival, and larger unions with smaller ones for purposes of diversification. Thus, in 1988, ASTMS and the **Technical Administration Supervisory Section** (TASS) merged to form **Manufacturing, Science and Finance** (MSF) which, with 650,000 members, now forms the sixth biggest union in the United Kingdom and the largest white-collar union in Europe.

Many unions are still relatively small. In 1986, over half the unions numbered fewer than 1000 members, but these accounted for only 0.4 per cent of total union membership. By contrast, over 80 per cent of union membership was concentrated in just twenty-four unions with over 100,000 members each. In 1989, the number of trade unions totalled 343. The number affiliated to the TUC dropped from 112 in 1979 to 78 in 1989, mostly as a result of mergers. But this still leaves most large manufacturing plants organized in several, sometimes competing unions. While this situation remains, the danger of demarcation disputes will persist. In fact, the much-discussed model of one union per industry, along the lines of the system developed in West Germany (see page 34), often seems farther from realization than ever.

Industrial disputes

During the 1970s, an average 13 million working days per year were lost through industrial disputes. The picture was very different by the end of 1988 (Table 4.7). From 1986 to 1988, the number of stoppages was lower than at any other time since 1940.

Table 4.7 *Working days lost through disputes*

Year	Days lost
1979	29,474,000
1980	11,964,000
1981	4,266,000
1982	5,313,000
1983	3,574,000
1984	27,135,000
1985	6,402,000
1986	1,920,000
1987	3,546,000
1988	3,702,000
1989	4,068,000

Source: *Employment Gazette*

The number of days lost in a particular year is greatly influenced by a few large disputes. In the 1984 figures, for example, approximately 22.5 million days lost out of the grand total of 27.1 million are accounted for by the coal strike. However, the days lost due to smaller stoppages, which form the vast majority of all disputes, dropped dramatically from 7.1 million working days per annum in the 1970s to 2.8 million in the 1980s. Nonetheless, these figures are still higher than for West Germany, France, Japan or the United States. Moreover, there has been no perceptible improvement in absenteeism. On every working day in 1983, the most recent date on which absenteeism was monitored, 12 per cent of workers were not present at their place of work for one reason or another.

New realism

At the end of the 1980s, the trade union movement appeared to be divided between so-called traditionalist, left-of-centre unions and realist, right-of-centre unions, with the TUC caught in the middle trying to arbitrate between the two factions. Ironically enough, neither the effects of the recession nor the new legislation, nor even declining memberships, were directly responsible for the split. The movement parted company over the issue of single-union agreements.

These agreements were pioneered by the **Electrical Electronic Tele-communications and Plumbing Union** (EETPU) in the printing industry and at new Japanese electronics plants. The EETPU's example was followed by the **Amalgamated Engineering Union** (AEU) which, by 1989, had concluded approximately forty single-union deals of which half were with Japanese companies. The bulk of these agreements contain provisions which make strikes improbable, such as binding arbitration. Contrary to popular opinion, the agreements do not render strikes impossible: they merely incorporate substantial anti-strike measures. They cannot, therefore, be classified or dismissed as no-strike agreements.

It is not feasible for the TUC to countenance single-union agreements because, as the umbrella organization for seventy-eight different unions, it cannot give its blessing to a development which advantages one faction and directly disadvantages another. As a result, the EETPU and its 387,000 members were expelled from the TUC in 1988. If the same fate should befall the AEU, the second largest union in the TUC, with 815,000 members, there is the prospect of the formation of an alternative TUC, tentatively called the **Modern Union Confederation** (MUC). In addition to the EETPU and the AEU, the MUC might also comprise the UDM.

New realism, however, does not begin and end with the promotion of single-union agreements. Nor does it necessarily embrace those unions which have indulged in new-look logos, promotional videos, credit cards, cheap mortgages and cut-price insurance for their members. New realism implies a willingness to accept the new democratic processes which have been forced on the trade unions in the 1980s. But above all the term signifies an acceptance on the part of the union that it sees nothing wrong in being associated with a profitable company. This is where the AEU and the EETPU stand out from the rest because they actually run training courses for some of their companies. 'Engineers 2000', 'Skills Centres' and 'TAPS' are evidence of the AEU's commitment not only to raising the skill level of its members but also to contributing to firms' profitability.

The way ahead

Gavin H. Laird, General Secretary of the AEU, wrote in *The European Business Journal* in February 1989: 'One of the few positive outcomes of the 1988 Trades Union Congress at Bournemouth was the long overdue embrace of Europe. Trade unionists across a wide variety of unions saw in 1992 and the Presidency of Jacques Delors new opportunities opening up for a productive, cooperative and fair future.'

Shortly before the Bournemouth Congress, the TUC had published a document on the impact of 1992 and the EC's single market. Behind the report lay the conviction that the TUC has virtually no role to play as a lobbying force for legislative change under a right-of-centre Conservative government. Since, however, much of future employment law to affect the United Kingdom's trade unions will be formulated in Brussels, and not in Westminster, it follows that it is towards the EC that the unions must direct their lobbying powers if they are to achieve success.

The TUC commitment to European trade unionism was endorsed at the Blackpool Congress in 1989. The strategy adopted there was to undermine Margaret Thatcher by taking advantage of the increased Socialist Group presence in the European Parliament, in the wake of the 1989 European elections, to ensure that the EC's single market will resemble much closer the 'social dimension' format of Jacques Delors than the free-market model preferred by Margaret Thatcher. The outcome will be highly significant for the power and influence of the trade union movement in the United Kingdom. In marked contrast with much of the Conservative legislation under Margaret Thatcher, workers would have a right under the Community Charter of Fundamental Social Rights to: a minimum wage; vocational training throughout their working life; information, consultation and participation in their companies; cover from collective agreements; and protection under social legislation. In 1989, the TUC was taking Europe so seriously that it voted to establish an office in Brussels.

But where does such a switch in the focus of lobbying leave the relationship between the United Kingdom's trade unions and the Labour Party? The Labour Party was born out of the trade unions who, with their huge assets, an annual income of tens of millions, vast investments and very large pension funds, still act as paymasters and underwriters of the Labour Party. For this the unions exact a price which is paid annually at each Labour Party Conference, where the trade unions command over 89 per cent of the vote while the constituency representatives share less than 10 per cent. The TGWU alone, for whom Neil Kinnock, the Leader of the Labour Party, is a sponsored Member of Parliament, has one fifth of the total union block vote at its disposal.

The trade unions will continue their financial support for the Labour Party just as business supports the Conservative Party. Otherwise, the TUC no longer conducts itself like an alternative government and has concentrated on basic issues such as the modernization of the services it offers to members rather than party politics. Although the TUC may well move to a new arm's-length relationship with the Labour Party, there is little likelihood that the unions will revert to their former roles as 'friendly societies' – an idea which has been canvassed in certain quarters of the Labour Party and the press. The days of mass unionism may be numbered but the trade unions are still far too important a force in the land to be confined to running the social security system.

Business, education, training and development

The business culture in the United Kingdom has suffered, to judge from the reports, for over a century and a half from its lack of commitment to the training and development of the country's workforce. As early as 1835, Richard Cobden stressed the need to remodel the system to match the quality of the Americans. The Royal Commission on Technical Instruction of 1884 drew unfavourable comparisons between Britain and conditions in Germany, France, Italy, the Netherlands, Switzerland and Austria.

In more recent times business has played a vital role in alerting government to the shortcomings of the United Kingdom's education system. Moreover, complaints that school-leavers were arriving on the factory floor unable to read or write, perform simple arithmetic or express themselves clearly, have finally been heeded. The **1988 Education Reform Act**, fresh initiatives by the Department of Employment, and a heightened awareness among companies of the need to develop their managers mark the beginning of the end, it is hoped, of a long period of comparative neglect of education, training and development for business in the United Kingdom.

Education

Towards the end of the 1980s there emerged a broad consensus that the country's education system bore part of the responsibility for the relatively weak performance of the economy in the post-war period. This resulted in demands for both changes in its structure and an overhaul of its funding process.

The focus of most critical commentaries had been on the low level of numeracy of United Kingdom workers compared with those of competitor countries and the low percentage of sixteen to eighteen-year-olds continuing in full-time education. The *Financial Times* of 5 December, 1988, pointed out that the average Japanese thirteen-year-old is more adept at mathematics than a British fifteen-year-old. Moreover, in West Germany approximately 30 per cent of age group leave school at sixteen with a certificate for which they are examined in ten subjects embracing compulsory German, a foreign language and mathematics; a comparable level is reached by only 12 per cent of English youngsters leaving school. Over 95 per cent of young people in Japan are in full-time education to the age of eighteen, compared with 32 per cent in England. About 48 per cent of North American and 38 per cent of Japanese eighteen-year-olds enter higher education. A mere 15 per cent of British youngsters continue into tertiary studies.

As a consequence, the government targeted improved education as a main priority but relied on policy measures to achieve this end rather than major increases in levels of funding. In 1988 it presented the Education Reform Act, which contained radical reforms for state education. A new national curriculum was adopted throughout England and Wales, designed to provide all pupils with a thorough knowledge of the core subjects – English, science and mathematics. Children's progress through the core subjects is checked by means of tests at the ages of seven, eleven, fourteen and sixteen years. Moreover, the success rate of individual schools in these tests is published. This latter stipulation is aimed at providing parents with more information about the attainment levels of schools within their area so that they are able to choose the best school for their children. In addition, some of the control over schools was taken away from the local authorities which fund them, and given over to governors and head teachers. If a simple majority of parents voting in a secret ballot so wish, a school can opt out altogether of local authority control and take on the status of an independent charitable trust receiving a direct grant from the government. By the beginning of the 1989–90 academic year, eighteen schools in England and Wales had elected for independent, grant-maintained status.

None of the provisions of the Education Reform Act, however, addresses one of the central weaknesses of the system: high-quality education of the type which will be needed to meet the future demands of business is dependent on high-quality teachers. From 1983 to 1987 teachers in the United Kingdom were engaged in a dispute over pay and conditions. It was terminated by a settlement imposed by Act of Parliament which deprived teachers of their pay negotiating rights and laid down a detailed set of contractual terms. At the end of the 1980s teachers' pay was modest, their morale poor, and their motivation low. Small wonder there was a severe shortage of teachers in mathematics and science – both core subjects in the national curriculum!

Shortly after his appointment as the new Secretary of State for Education and Science, John MacGregor told *The Sunday Times* of 20 August 1989: 'If we are going to achieve continued economic performance and higher standards of living . . . and also enable more and more of our people to fully exploit what life can offer today, then we have got to ensure that our educational system delivers our capacity to be competitive, and to take full advantage of this fast-changing world.' If John MacGregor is to master his task of implementing the provisions of the Education Reform Act, he might be advised to exploit his Treasury background to secure improved pay and conditions for teachers. Otherwise, a disaffected profession, one which has even gone so far as to form 'escape committees' to assist colleagues to leave teaching, will fail to deliver the reforms on which so many hopes are pinned.

Training

The United Kingdom languishes close to the bottom of the international training league although it was estimated that in 1886–7 employers spent some £18 billion per annum on training. Approximately £13.5 billion went on trainees' wages and other labour costs; only £4.7 billion on training materials. Over the same period, the government spent an additional £3 billion, mostly on young people and the unemployed. Yet despite expenditure on this scale, in the period from 1986–7, half of all employees received no training and a third of employees claimed that they had never received any training. A third of companies had no training budget; a fifth of companies provided no training; a further fifth did not evaluate the training they had carried out.

As was pointed out earlier (see page 42), every year in West Germany approximately 650,000 youngsters start on apprentice training courses which lead to a commercial qualification. West Germany trains two to three times more qualified building craftsmen, fitters and electricians than the United Kingdom and about five times more clerical staff. Similarly, France produces two to three times as many qualified mechanics and electricians as the British, and this is done through vocational schools.

The United Kingdom, however, relies on the **Youth Training Scheme** (YTS). Introduced in 1983, over two million young people had been trained in YTS by the end of 1988, over one million since it became a two-year programme in April 1986. In September 1988 there were some 435,500 youngsters in training on YTS – the largest number that the country had ever seen. Of these trainees, it emerged in August 1989, 26 per cent had numeracy problems and 17 per cent literacy problems ranging from complete illiteracy to relatively minor shortcomings like a persistent inability to spell.

The education service contributes to YTS, with over 40 per cent of trainees attending college as part of their programmes, and the numbers of trainees securing recognized qualifications – some 55 per cent of those completing YTS in 1987–8 – have risen each year. However, the majority of the young people gaining a vocational qualification attain only the most basic available. 74 per cent of young people leaving YTS went into jobs at the end of 1988, or embarked on further education or training. With fewer young people coming into the labour market in the 1990s, the opportunity presents itself to raise standards. Some schemes should, ideally, run for three years or more, and the minimum off-the-job period should be made more flexible to fit the needs of different trainees and training programmes.

Since April 1988 every organization applying to participate in YTS has been obliged to secure Approved Training Organization status. Ten criteria have to be satisfied covering such matters as the training of supervisors, programme design, equal opportunities, health and safety standards. By 1989 over 3000 organizations had achieved the appropriate status, and there was sufficient youth training available for all sixteen and seventeen-year-old school-leavers seeking it.

Training for the adult unemployed no longer takes place under the **Job Training Scheme** (JTS). This was replaced in mid-1988 by **Employment Training** (ET), which succeeded in attracting over 200,000 participants within the first year of its existence. Claimed to be the largest and most ambitious training programme for unemployed people in the world, ET supplies up to twelve months' training. It offers training in the workplace and is available nationwide through over 1000 training managers, with 170 training agents advising potential participants.

Despite the welcome modifications to existing training programmes, the most far-reaching proposals for overcoming the country's skills deficit were published in *Employment for the 1990s*, a White Paper by the Department of Employment in December 1988. Here a new framework for training was foreseen at three different levels: the national level, the industry level and the local level. At national level, the main task was seen as developing policies for promoting training through the Training Agency within the Department of Employment. At industry level, the task identified was to set standards and monitor the quality of training provided by employers. At local level, the centrepiece of the new proposals, attention focused on operating the government's training programmes for unemployed people and ensuring that employers' own training endeavours are of the scale and quality required for the local labour market.

Employers have been given a leading role in setting local priorities and deciding how government finance for training should be spent. They will do this through the introduction of more than 100 employer-led **Training and Enterprise Councils** (TECS) in England alone. Employers in the private sector will be in the majority on the governing bodies of the TECS, occupying at least two-thirds of the seats there. Others on the TECs will include senior figures from local education and the trade unions which support the aims of the Councils. By no means all trade unions are, however, in favour of cooperation in the TECS.

The government believes that it has placed the ownership of the training and enterprise system where it belongs – with the employers. Improved training should be used, however, not merely to depress the unemployment figures in a locality or to provide workers to fill the vacancies on the job market. It should, ideally, help to move the economy away from the current low-skill level towards a high-skill equilibrium, with companies turning out higher-value-added products to which workers can contribute because they have been appropriately trained.

Development

Past neglect of a thorough educational, training and development ethos in the United Kingdom is evident at all levels in British companies, including management. In 1987, two major studies, the Handy report and the Constable/McCormick report, were published. The first investigated managers' education, training and development in West Germany, France, Japan and the United States, the second British managers'. The reports concluded that approximately 85 per cent of top managers in Japan and the United States, and 62 per cent in West Germany and France, have university degrees (see page 43). Approximately 25 per cent of British top managers were found in a 1975 survey to possess degrees. Similarly, more than 40 per cent of the largest American companies and most big firms in West Germany and Japan provide every manager with at least five days' training, or management development, off-the-job every year. In Britain, the average manager receives just one day's development per annum. However sharp or ambitious they may be, managers who are neither appropriately educated nor developed are unlikely to perform as effectively as their counterparts in competitor countries.

The Handy report recommended that a group of top companies should develop a Charter of good practice and that these companies should form a Charter Group which would set standards for management development and act as its advocate vis-à-vis government and other interested parties. It was suggested that the Charter might comprise such items as: a corporate development plan; a commitment to five days' minimum off-the-job development per annum for every manager; a personal development plan for every manager; reimbursement of tuition fees for approved self-education; foreign language instruction as a routine requirement; and much more.

The **Management Charter Initiative** (MCI) was duly established, and by the end of 1989 over 400 leading companies had pledged their support, in addition to twenty government departments. Unfortunately, some of the impetus from the Handy and Constable/McCormick reports was lost when a misguided attempt was made to introduce the concept of the Chartered Manager. Such had not been recommended in either of the reports because there was no desire to create a 'closed shop for managers' which might have discouraged the entrepreneur from entrepreneuring or the natural manager from managing.

Despite the increased willingness of more companies to train and develop their staff at all levels, one main difficulty remains. Company investment in training and development is risky because staff can change jobs and move to another firm which has perhaps not taken the trouble to train. In a job-hopping business culture such as that which obtains in the United Kingdom, this means that many companies are still reluctant to provide the right amount of training and development. Not until the vast majority of companies, large, medium-sized and small, subscribe fully to the training ethos will their employees, and with them the companies themselves, benefit from the enhanced levels of skills which will secure both employment and profits in the 1990s and beyond.

Business and enterprise

Ever since the publication of the Bolton report on small firms in 1971, various governments in the United Kingdom have attempted to promote the start-ups of new companies and to encourage the growth of small businesses. But not until the return to power of the Conservatives in 1979 did the term 'enterprise culture' enter popular parlance and begin to exert an influence on the wider business culture in the country. Yet 'enterprise culture' embraces much more than the promotion of small firms: it entails a diminution of the role of the state, which since 1979 has mainly taken the form of privatizations; it involves allowing managers to manage, through reform of the trade unions; it also implies giving greater economic responsibility to the individual through improving incentives to enterprise and efficient working.

Small firms

From 1979 to 1989, self-employed companies in the United Kingdom with five or fewer staff practically doubled in number to approximately three million. Some of these small companies were helped by government aid packages which, by 1988, had become so numerous and complex that a decision was taken to simplify the sixty-four existing schemes and to place them under the aegis of the Department of Trade and Industry (DTI).

As Professor Paul Burns et al. point out in a Cranfield School of Management working paper entitled *Small Business in the United Kingdom*, the schemes introduced since 1979 had addressed four main problem areas for small business. First, the financing of new and small firms was facilitated by the Loan Guarantee Scheme, while the Business Expansion Scheme increased the attraction for taxpayers to invest in small companies. Second, the activities of the Small Firms Service were expanded to provide a greater degree of inexpensive or even free business information. Third, small companies were exempted from certain constraints placed upon them by employment legislation. Fourth, corporate rates of taxation were cut substantially (see page 164).

The **Enterprise Initiative**, embracing much of the substance of the former schemes, was duly launched in January, 1988, by the DTI. The broad objective was to encourage companies to use their own initiative by spotting business opportunities and seizing them. To this end, it is planned to allocate some £250 million to the Enterprise Initiative by 1991. The money is available to independent businesses in most sectors of the economy employing fewer than 500 people. Grants are forthcoming to subsidize business development consultancy in the fields of design, marketing, quality assurance, manufacturing, export, business planning, financial information systems, research and technology.

By the end of 1988, response to the Enterprise Initiative had exceeded expectations. Moreover, 95 per cent of companies taking part in the scheme reported satisfaction with the aid and advice received. However, even with maximum take-up by 1991, the Enterprise Initiative will have reached only 45,000 of the estimated 1,250,000 companies eligible throughout the country.

In the meantime, enterprise in the form of the establishment of new companies has continued to flourish: it was calculated in 1989 that business start-ups were well in excess of 100,000 per annum. As Professor Sue Birley of Cranfield School of Management, and Liz Watson, comment in their report on *Successful British Entrepreneurs*: 'It is clear that enterprise has now firmly re-visited the United Kingdom, that starting your own business is a respected and accepted lifestyle more than ever in recent history.'

Nonetheless, many new businesses quickly fail. Analysis of Value Added Tax (VAT) registrations and deregistrations reveals that approximately one third of new businesses run into serious trouble in the first three years of their existence, and nearly half close by their fifth year. In a survey conducted in September 1989 by the Small Business Research Trust, it was established that certain facets of the country's business culture conspire against small companies. 27 per cent of the directors questioned in the survey had been involved in a business which failed. Half the directors identified management shortcomings as the reason for the close-down, while 37 per cent placed the blame on a shortage of capital. Banks were criticized for their high charges and for demanding excessive security before lending to small firms. 20 per cent of directors found fault with accountants for being too slow and costing too much. Solicitors were subjected to reprimands of a similar nature.

High interest rates are foremost among the worries of small companies. 75 per cent of the respondents in the same survey complained that such interest rates had also made some of their customers slower in paying their bills. Among the slowest payers were the United Kingdom's largest companies, while only 37 per cent of respondents criticized small firms and the public sector for delays in payment. However, 52 per cent confessed to having experienced trouble with the Post Office, and 33 per cent levelled accusations of poor customer service against British Telecom.

The identification of successful small businesses throughout the country is rendered difficult by a lack of comprehensive statistics. However, certain measures based on financial criteria can be used, with caution, to locate such businesses. One source of information is the Growth Companies Register, which contains the 1000 unquoted companies with the highest growth rates in pretax profits. The data include those companies with shares traded on the Unlisted Securities Market and the Over the Counter Market. According to the 1986 data, Greater London was responsible for 23 per cent of the fastest-growing small to medium-sized companies, and the rest of the South East accounted for a further 21 per cent. The North West and the West Midlands were also well represented at about 10 per cent, while the North East and Northern Ireland recorded disproportionately smaller numbers. These percentages tally with the regional growth rate patterns indicated earlier (see page 168).

Management buyouts

Enterprise does not exhaust itself in the establishment and running of new small firms. A willingness to seize opportunities and take risks is also evidenced by **management buyouts** (MBOs). Here a manager or team of managers purchase the company or the part of the company for which they are actually working in the conviction that they can run the operation more efficiently than existing management.

Although there is nothing intrinsically novel about MBOS, what is new is the large increase in the number and scale of MBOs in the United Kingdom in the 1980s. As Tom Nash, Assistant Editor of *Director*, pointed out in the February 1989, issue of the journal, the first evidence of increased MBO activity in the country emerged in the late 1970s when the leveraged buyout originally became a legal tool for purchasing a business. This activity gained further momentum in the recession at the start of the 1980s when subsidiaries of some of the United Kingdom's older companies not essential to the core business were bought out by their managements.

MBOs in the United Kingdom became a growing aspect of the business culture throughout the 1980s when the market for such developed into the second largest in the world after the United States. The number and size of transactions increased from 205 buyouts with a total value of £315 million in 1983 to 335 accounting for £3,250 million in 1987. Included in the 1987 totals is the largest European transaction of this nature to date, the Charterhouse-led buyout of MFI from ASDA MFI plc, which cost £718 million. The average value of individual buyouts also increased over the 1983–7 period from £1,540,000 to £9,700,000. Buyout activity continued to grow in 1988 when there were approximately 350 transactions with an estimated value of £3,800 million.

There is every sign that the United Kingdom buyout experience is following that in the United States, with the number and size of the transactions both on the increase. American trends are also being emulated in terms of the relationship between financial institutions and management. As Norman Murray observed in the December 1988, issue of *The Accountant's Magazine*, a variation on the buyout, namely the **management buyin** (MBI), is being practised. Here underperforming companies are identified by the institutions. External management teams are then put together and financially supported by the institutions in order to undertake a turnaround.

Buyouts in the United Kingdom have also provided an alternative to flotation on the stock exchange for the privatization of parts of the public sector. Two notable examples are the National Freight Consortium, where not only incumbent managers but also employees purchased the company for which they worked, and the break-up of the National Bus Company. The National Freight Consortium was subsequently floated on the stock exchange, with considerable financial gains accruing for managers and employees alike.

Further incentives to enterprise

The large salaries paid to the chief executives of the country's top companies could be regarded as incentives to enterprise, as indeed could the pay of most managers. Unfortunately, many of the salaries paid to company officials in either group are not performance-related, although bonuses as a percentage of salary are on the increase.

Financial rewards of this order of magnitude are guaranteed to arouse

Table 4.8   *The top ten earners (1988)*

	Name	Company	Pay (£)
1	P. Sykes	Paul Sykes Group	6,000,000
2	W. Brown	Walsham Brothers	2,015,083
3	C. Heath	Baring Securities	1,339,219
4	Lord Hanson	Hanson	1,239,000
5	M. Hatter	IMO Precision Con	1,232,700
6	P. S-Darling	Mercury Asset Man	1,051,000
7	R. Rowland	Lonrho	1,015,000
8	R. Halpern	Burton	996,000
9	M. Fromstein	Blue Arrow	935,463
10	J. Nott	Lazard Brothers	885,235

Source: Datastream

angry comment. Whenever such lists are published, trade union leaders question the need for their members to accept wage restraint since chief executives are rewarded so generously. Even Conservative politicians, who are not paid anything like so well, have gone on record as objecting to what look like inflated salaries. Nevertheless, the vast majority of the country's executives are still worse off than their counterparts in other European countries.

At the end of August 1989, the European Remuneration Network (ERN) issued its first report on the pay of some 30,000 managers in France, Switzerland, Italy, West Germany, the Netherlands, United Kingdom, Belgium and Ireland. The report compares the pay of three kinds of manager – managing directors, heads of finance and of production – in companies with no more than 100 employees, and in those with between 250 and 1000. It also takes into consideration such factors as personal taxation and cost-of-living indices.

Provided they are subject to broad interpretation, the results offer a rough guide to European differences in the going rates for various managers. After tax and cost of living considerations, the United Kingdom's managing directors, aged forty-five and employed by manufacturing companies turning over £75 million, were £15,000 worse off than if they had been working in Switzerland, and £9,000 down on their West German counterparts. Finance directors in the United Kingdom subject to the same conditions would have been £7,500 per annum better off working in Italy and almost £3,000 richer in France.

Such comparisons on a European scale are also useful because they provide an insight into the remuneration priorities of companies in different countries. Broadly speaking, Italy, France, Switzerland and West Germany all pay their heads of finance less than their heads of production, while in the United Kingdom this is not the case. Similarly, West Germany even pays its research and development directors more than its finance directors. In the United Kingdom, the emphasis is reversed. The differences in remuneration priorities act as valuable indicators of the business orientations of companies in the various business cultures.

U·K

The response of business to the EC's single market

Business in the United Kingdom, in response to the EC's single market, appears to have taken its cue from the politicians: reaction to date has been hesitant and lacking commitment. Although Europe was responsible for some 50 per cent of the country's exports and even 53 per cent of imports in 1988, a survey early in the same year by Ernst & Whinney, the accountancy firm, found that fewer than 40 per cent of company board directors were aware of plans to create a single market in the EC. In addition, only 30 per cent of British directors at board level stated that their companies had a strategic plan for 1992. Moreover, the vast majority of firms with a strategy were large companies which already had business interests in Continental Europe. The government's own publicity campaign for 1992 was subsequently launched on 18 March 1988, with the mailing of an information pack to 125,000 companies.

If business in the United Kingdom has been slow to take up the challenge of Europe, then much of the blame must attach to the attitude of the Conservatives since 1979, and that of Margaret Thatcher in particular. She set the tone at her first EC summit in Dublin by repeatedly demanding, 'I want my money back'; in her first speech on the EC as Prime Minister in 1979, she emphasized its tendency to 'dwindle into bureaucracy'; in her Bruges speech in 1988, she castigated the European Commission for its plans on economic and monetary union, and the Delors social charter; she also allowed the Conservative party to go into the 1989 elections to the European Parliament with such xenophobic slogans as 'Stay home on 15 June and you'll live on a diet of Brussels' (and paid the price with the Conservatives polling 6.7 per cent fewer votes than in the 1984 elections as well as forfeiting thirteen seats). Finally, she lost her Chancellor of the Exchequer in October, 1989, because Nigel Lawson favoured the United Kingdom's full membership of EMS, and she and her advisers did not.

Yet all this high-profile Euro-hostility disguises a deeper commitment to Europe at a different level. In Brussels, the United Kingdom has one of the best reputations of any country for implementing EC directives on time and to the letter. Similarly, the United Kingdom was one of the first in the EC to lift controls on capital entering or leaving the country. In addition, the United Kingdom's road haulage rules are more liberal than all but those in the Netherlands, while the openness of the country's insurance market to outside competitors is rivalled, once again, only by the Netherlands.

Strengths

(Indeed, one of the United Kingdom's major strengths lies in its tradition of open trading, which attracts investment from companies outside Europe anxious to gain a foot-hold within the EC) The United States and, more recently, Japan have both taken full advantage of the country's open markets and established considerable business interests. In 1988 the United Kingdom continued to be the target for the largest foreign investment in Europe by non-EC buyers.

(A second major strength can be adduced from the fact that the United Kingdom's companies have gradually become more competitive as a result of a decade of a free-enterprise climate and a growing economy) Moreover, in 1989 the United Kingdom featured, for first time in years, as many large companies in the non-financial sector in Europe as West Germany, when measured by turnover. Of the top 100 European companies, according to *Director* magazine, thirty were West German and an equal number British. If the top ten companies had been ranked by profits, British or part-British companies would have occupied six of the first seven places.

(A third area of strength has already been noted – that of financial services. London's reputation as an international banking centre is unchallenged anywhere in Europe, with 400 overseas banks operating there at the end of 1989. Moreover, the City's financial markets exceed in size any others in the EC by a long way) Yet British financial institutions have been reluctant to forge cross-border collaborations in the run-up to 1992, while Continental European banks have indulged in a veritable frenzy of alliances. By the end of 1989, NatWest had bid for the French Banque de l'Union Européenne; the Royal Bank of Scotland possessed a cross-shareholding with Banco Santander of Spain; Hambros had also joined several European alliances; but most British institutions had still to make any significant moves across the Channel.

(A fourth strength is to be located in the United Kingdom's retailing companies) The system which has been developed in the country is probably the most efficient in Europe, and British retailers featured in 1989 among the largest in Europe by any measure. Sainsbury, Marks and Spencer, Tesco and Gateway (pre-reconstruction) all ranked in the top six retailers by sales, although Carrefour of France was the largest in this sector.

Weaknesses

It is significant that many more British than West German companies would have appeared in the top ten companies in Europe if the rankings had been ordered according to profits rather than turnover. While the profit-making orientations of the United Kingdom's companies may be regarded as a strength in the short-term, they are responsible at the same time for harmful longer-term weaknesses.

Thus a major weakness of the United Kingdom's economy is to be located in the erosion of the manufacturing base since 1979, due in part to lack of long-term investment in capital equipment and R & D. Even working at near full capacity, manufacturing was incapable, by the end of 1989, of supplying domestic demand by the equivalent of 4 per cent of GDP. Although British Steel took position eighty-one in the league table of Europe's largest companies in the non-financial sector when measured by turnover and even third position for profit growth, the rest of the United Kingdom's engineering and electrical firms were sadly underrepresented.

Similarly, the lack of investment in human capital over the longer term has contributed to a further acknowledged British weakness in the approach to 1992. Public companies have been too preoccupied with the profit expectations of City analysts to devote enough of their capital and cash flow to the education of their workforces. As a result, the economy as a whole suffers from a low-level skill equilibrium, and certain future-oriented sectors such as electronics are virtually incapable of expansion on account of skills shortages.

Although the services sector of the country's economy as a whole must be regarded as one of its outstanding strengths, one area in this sector which was giving cause for concern towards the end of the 1980s was that of mail order. With the advent of 1992, home shopping has been highlighted as the retail area most easily translated across borders. A Verdict Research survey in 1989 reported: 'The ability for the customer to choose products from all over Europe and for a company to deliver them without cross-border documentation present a major opportunity.' But La Redoute of France held 26 per cent of the British company Empire Stores, and Gecos, the Italian group, had taken its stake in Empire to above 24 per cent. Otto Versand of West Germany, and the largest mail order group in the world, had a 5 per cent stake in Fine Art Development, a small British company.

Opportunities

(While the United Kingdom has constantly been the largest target for direct foreign investment in Europe by non-EC countries, British companies since 1980 invested substantially more abroad than foreign companies in the United Kingdom (£73.5 billion compared with £29.6 billion to the end of 1987.) However, the focus of much of direct British foreign investment during this time was not the EC but the United States, with 65 per cent of such investment in 1987 being placed on the other side of the Atlantic and only 12 per cent in the rest of the EC.

Investment in the United States is not necessarily mistaken, yet it has been interpreted as evidence of lack of British commitment in Europe. But towards the end of the decade things were changing. In 1989 British companies were set to make more acquisitions in mainland Europe than in the United States. In the first nine months of 1989, they invested a total of £2.1 billion, acquiring 278 businesses in Continental Europe. This compared with £1.6 billion spent on such acquisitions in the same period in 1988.(In the run-up to 1992, France, West Germany, the Netherlands and Spain proved to be the most popular areas for British companies seeking to expand.)

Threats

(Although the focus of British companies' direct foreign investments may be changing, there remain substantial grounds for disquiet about their general state of preparedness in anticipation of the completion of the single market.)In January 1989 the CBI surveyed a sample of its members and established that 90 per cent of companies with sales over £20 million were pursuing no market research at all in mainland Europe. 93 per cent were taking no initiatives to train employees in Continental languages. 95 per cent had no sales agents in the rest of the EC, and only one in 100 was opening any manufacturing plants on the Continent. Quoting the CBI survey, Michael Heseltine, the former Minister of Defence who resigned over the Westland scandal in 1986, comments in his book, *The Challenge of Europe*: 'If that is Britain's corporate response, we are in trouble. I hope that the overwhelming majority of British firms will rise above that attitude; and fear that the rest will not be around long enough to do more than temporary harm.'

(In common with most other countries in the EC, the United Kingdom was experiencing problems in interesting smaller companies to explore export opportunities. Although many competitive products from smaller, innovative British companies are incorporated in the goods produced by larger companies, these smaller firms still remained to be convinced that much of their future prosperity depends on servicing all their larger corporate customers throughout Europe, and not just those in the United Kingdom.

(The British response to the EC's single market may have been diffident and faltering, but companies still have time to take recourse to the outstanding feature of the business culture in the United Kingdom – its sheer adaptability.) Indeed, M Ernest-Antoine Seillère, Vice-President of the Conseil National du Patronat Français, confirmed in an interview with *The Times* on 13 October, 1989, that the British enjoyed many advantages in the approach to 1992.(Among them figured the fact that English was the language of business in most of Europe.)But above all he praised(British business people's facility to adapt rapidly to changed economic circumstances and to large international organizations such as those which could be anticipated upon completion of the internal market.

The adaptability which permeates the whole of the business culture in the United Kingdom must now be joined by a sense of greater urgency if the country's companies are to take full advantage of a single market of 320 million consumers by the end of 1992.)

References and suggestions for further reading

Accountant's Magazine, The, various issues between 1979 and 1989.
Acquisitions Monthly, various issues between 1987 and 1989.
Bassett, P. (1987), *Strike Free: New Industrial Relations in Britain,* London: Macmillan.
Bean, C. and Symmons, J. (1989), *Ten Years of Mrs T,* LSE Centre for Labour Economics, working paper no. 1119.
Burns, P. and Dewhurst, J. (1989), *Small Business and Entrepreneurship,* Basingstoke and London: Macmillan.
Channon, D. F. (1977), *British Banking Strategy and the International Challenge,* London: Macmillan.
Clutterbuck, D. and Devine, M. (1987), *Management Buyouts,* London: Hutchinson.
Constable, J. and McCormick, R. (1987), *The Making of British Managers,* London: BIM and CBI.
David, R. (1980), *English Law and French Law,* London: Stevens.
Director, various issues between 1979 and 1989.
Economist, The, various issues between 1979 and 1989.
Economist Intelligence Unit (1989), *United Kingdom Country Profile, 1989–90,* London: The Economist Intelligence Unit.

Economist Intelligence Unit (1989), *United Kingdom Country Report*, London: The Economist Intelligence Unit.

Employment Gazette, various issues between 1979 and 1989.

Financial Times, The, various editions between 1979 and 1989.

Fortune, various issues between 1979 and 1989.

Grady, J. and Weale, M. (1986), *British Banking, 1960–85*, Basingstoke: Macmillan.

Handy, C. et al., (1988), *Making Managers*, London: Pitman.

Heseltine, M. (1989) *The Challenge of Europe*, London: Weidenfeld and Nicolson.

Hindley, B., *Europe: Fortress or Freedom?*, London: The Bruges Group.

HMSO (1988), *Employment for the 1990s*, London: HMSO.

James, B. (1989), 'The dam bursts – and the old apathy is swept away', *The Times*, 11 April © Times Newspapers Ltd 1989.

Lewis, R. (1986), *Labour Law in Britain*, Oxford: Blackwell.

Liston, D. and Reeves, N. (1988), *Invisible Economy: A Profile of Britain's Invisible Exports*, London: Pitman.

Narbrough, C. (1989), 'French chief sees . . . after 1992', *The Times*, 13 October © Times Newspapers Ltd 1989.

OECD Economic Surveys, United Kingdom, various years between 1979 and 1989.

Parnaby, J. (1988), 'Creating a Competitive Manufacturing Strategy', in *Production Engineer*, July/August.

Perry, F. E. (1986), *The Elements of Banking*, London: Methuen.

Price Waterhouse (1986), *Doing Business in the United Kingdom*, London: Price Waterhouse.

St John-Brooks (1989), 'MacGregor means business', *The Sunday Times*, 20 August, © Times Newspapers Ltd 1989.

Sunday Times, The, various issues between 1979 and 1989.

Times, The, various editions between 1979 and 1989.

Wiener, M. J. (1981), *English Culture and the Decline of the Industrial Spirit, 1850–1980*, Cambridge: CUP.

5 The business culture in Spain
Kevin Bruton

Introduction

Spanish companies, at the end of the 1980s, became caught up in an infectious popular enthusiasm for more contact with Europe and the wider world. Optimism and the desire to compete successfully with companies in other countries which have not had to experience Spain's long recent period of political and economic repression coexist with apprehensiveness and anxiety about the consequences of free, unfettered trading.

It is, however, the dynamism and outward-looking philosophy of the business culture in Spain which most strikes the foreign observer. This is evident in a number of ways which include:

- The continuing boom in the Spanish economy, with GDP improving by 5 per cent in 1988 and 5 per cent also in 1989, considerably above the OECD average.
- Export success, with manufactured exports estimated to continue rising by a minimum of 8 per cent annually up to 1992, partly the result of government initiatives to raise Spain's export profile through the Chambers of Commerce at home and government offices abroad.
- Very high levels of investment in plant and machinery, often through imported technology, in order to modernize industry.
- An explosion of interest among the business and the wider community in the activities of Spanish and international companies, revealed by the plethora of publications emerging in the 1980s – *Comercio e industria* (circulation up from 34,000 in 1983 to 144,000 in 1987), *Actualidad Económica*, *Dinero*, *España Económica* (issued in 1989 as a supplement to the prestigious weekly news journal, *Cambio 16*) etc.

Spain's business culture also has a number of weaknesses which need to be addressed in the 1990s. The principal deficiencies are as follows:

- The very high proportion of small companies, often with a conservative mentality and prone to foreign takeover or collapse through free competition.

- Inadequate numbers of suitably-trained people, at all levels from shopfloor to management.
- Public services and infrastructure, especially roads, railways, health, education, post and telegraph, which are inferior to most of Spain's EC partners and, in some cases, deteriorating.
- The lack (at the end of 1989) of a social compact between government and trade unions, and the threat this causes to economic policy and company planning and profitability.
- Continuing ETA terrorism, which is crippling, economically, the Basque region, the traditional heartland of Spain's heavy industry.

The Spanish government is prioritizing some of these deficiencies by increasing investment in infrastructure and attempting to overcome the terrorism problem. The terms of Spain's EC accession in 1986 meant that Spanish business was preparing for 1992 and the completion of the single market before most other EC countries. The preparation has often been painful but it has also been painstaking so that Spain's business culture, despite its weaknesses, is in a better position than ever to play its part in the opportunities opened by a year, 1992, which has so much symbolic importance for Spaniards.

Business and government

The business world in Spain has had to come to terms with some of the most dramatic changes in the structures of government experienced by any Western European country in the last thirty years. Leaving behind the authoritarian and centralized dictatorship of Franco which for most of the period between 1939 and 1975 effectively isolated Spain from the rest of Europe, Spanish business has successfully confronted the challenge of transforming itself, over a decade of fragile democratic governments, into a significant competitor in the Western world. The impetus given by EC membership (1 January 1986) has propelled the Spanish economy – and much of business with it – into the forefront of world economies, with booming growth in the late 1980s, which outstripped that of most other countries. (Real GDP growth in Spain in 1988 at nearly 5 per cent was 1.5 percentage points above the EC average.) The problems and successes need to be set within the context of a new framework of democratic central and regional government.

Central government

Since October 1982 Felipe González's Socialist Party, with three general election victories, has pursued a tight monetarist policy based upon containing inflation, promoting greater freedom and flexibility in business, and carrying through a policy of industrial 'reconversion', i.e. a rationalization and modernization of Spain's heavy industry. EC accession in 1986 has assisted the government in its objective of opening Spanish business up to European competition. This 'cold shower' of competition for Spanish industry after years of protection from tariff barriers has met with mixed reaction from the business world. The González government policy in large part though was determined by a number of major economic deficiencies inherited from the Franco era, including:

- The multiplicity of small firms (i.e. employing less than fifty people) in Spain, estimated to constitute some 90 per cent of all companies.
- Technological backwardness vis-à-vis established Western democracies.
- The survival of an inefficient agricultural system, also backward.
- A relatively low level of education and training in the population, with the loss of many skilled workers abroad during the Franco era.
- The Francoist legacy of corporatism, i.e. the large role within the overall economy occupied by a massive infrastructure of State-owned industries, characterized by bureaucratic overmanning and heavy financial losses.

González's incoming 1982 government also faced a decade of rapidly deteriorating macroeconomic indicators, following the first oil price shock. Spain's performance in this period was substantially worse than other European economies, especially in employment. Spain's unemployment rate in 1982 was 16.2 per cent compared with an EC average of 9.3 per cent while inflation at 13.8 per cent was also higher than the EC 9.3 per cent.

Following 1982, the government's implementation of a stabilization programme featuring monetary and budgetary policies which converged on the policies of EC member states, as well as action to moderate wage rises, allowed progress towards reducing inflation, which was moving into single digits by the end of 1986, and towards improving the balance of payments which, after a decade in the red, finally went into the black in 1984.

Despite a manifesto promise in 1982 to create 800,000 new jobs in Spain, González's first period in office actually saw unemployment increase by almost a million to reach 21 per cent in 1986, the highest in the OECD. The increase was in large part the result of the government's industrial 'reconversion' policy, a major restructuring of Spain's overmanned steel mills and shipyards, which awakened trade union militancy at the massive job losses entailed.

González won his second general election in June 1986, a victory founded largely upon his success in achieving EC membership for Spain on 1 January that year and upon the absence of a viable opposition party. The government's economic policies continued much as before, but with Spanish industrialists now trying hard to come to terms with the fierce competition from other EC member states.

In the first two years of EC membership an estimated 150,000 small firms went to the wall as a result of foreign competition, as Spanish business paid the price for moving from a protected economy to a competitive one. Customs barriers and taxes which made it difficult for foreign firms to compete previously have gradually been removed since 1986, allowing a flood of imports into Spain. In fact in the first year of membership, imports to Spain from the EC went up by 32 per cent while trade between Spain and the EC moved from a surplus position of 268,000 million pesetas in 1985 to a deficit for Spain of 139,000 million pesetas in 1986. In other words, the reduction of tariff barriers in 1986 which gave Spanish products an average 25 per cent price advantage over competitors to half that level at 12.5 per cent saw a 400,000 million peseta boom for EC competitors in 1986. The impact of the complete removal of tariffs by 1992 can be imagined, especially on industries which are considered the most vulnerable in Spain, such as light engineering (including manufacturers of bicycles, motorcycles, electrical appliances and machinery), clothing and some food industries.

The initial reaction of some Spanish business people was to affirm that increased imports from Europe merely provided jobs elsewhere in the EC and that the loss of competitiveness of Spanish firms would be disastrous in the long term for Spanish industry.

More enlightened employers, along with the government, reject this view and claim that a significant proportion of the increase in imports has been due to plant and machinery urgently needed to modernize and revitalize industry into more dynamic competitive attitudes. Additionally, the government point to a 10 per cent increase in Spanish exports to the EC over the period 1986–8 as proof of the fact that there are Spanish industries competing successfully in Europe.

While companies like the Valencia-based Tycesa group, which manu-factures Western Europe's best selling Lois jeans, demonstrate that Spanish business can be as efficient as any in the world, there is evidence that many Spanish industries still fear competition. The main employers' confederation, the **Confederación Española de Organizaciones Empresariales** (CEOE), has carried out studies which reveal the extent to which the legacy of corporatism persists and claims that at no point in the government's negotiations for EC entry was there any discussion of the private sector's role in the economy. Instead the question was debated in terms of what the government was or was not doing to help business.

1987 and 1988 witnessed a major turnaround in the Spanish economy with unemployment starting to move downwards on a month by month basis from a high point of over 21 per cent, to stand at 17.9 per cent in the first quarter of 1989. The improvement reflected the government's promotion of special employment programmes and tax incentives to industry to create new jobs as well as a growth in real domestic demand, which saw a 30 per cent rise between 1983 and 1989 (compared with an EC average of 18 per cent), and a general moderation in wage settlements.

Fixed investment grew by 15 per cent in both 1987 and 1988 while investment in plant and machinery rose by 15 per cent in 1988. The volume of exports also increased by 9 per cent in 1988, almost twice as fast as 1987. Net long-term capital inflows at $10 billion in 1988 were up from $9 billion in 1987, revealing direct investment in Spanish business and real estate by foreign companies and increased foreign participation in Spanish firms.

Government fiscal policy generated rises in government tax revenues, especially from higher income taxes, and a major campaign was launched to stamp out the widespread tax evasion which has been endemic in Spanish society for decades. Extra tax receipts were used in part to finance additional government expenditure.

Inflation, which had been a major success story for González's government over a six-year period from 1982, which saw a reduction from 13.8 per cent to 5.2 per cent, started to upturn, however, in 1989 and an estimated year-end figure of 6.9 per cent threatens the government's tight monetary policy.

Another problem for the González government, as it faced a General Election on 29 October 1989, lay in increasing opposition from the trade union giants, the socialist **Unión General de Trabajadores** (UGT) and the communist Workers' Commissions, to which further reference will be made (see page 245), which culminated in a general strike on 14 December 1988. The government policy of limiting wages and trying to force through Parliament a Youth Employment Programme to create 800,000 temporary jobs on minimum wage levels was resisted by trade unions who demanded for their members a share of Spain's increasing prosperity, pointing for example to the escalating pretax profits of private Spanish companies (an increase of 65 per cent in 1988!).

With a budget deficit of some $2.5 billion in current account terms predicted for year-end 1989, following a four-year period in surplus, the government, surprisingly, in 1989, produced its first expansionist budget, an 18 per cent rise in expenditure vis-à-vis 1988, with the primary aim of improving Spain's infrastructure and public services. As a leading government spokesman stated in early 1989: 'At present, with 1992 on the horizon, Spain needs more roads rather than more cars.' Hence, the government's unprecedented 40 per cent increase in public works' investment in 1989.

The Bank of Spain, however, in the early months of 1989, was concerned that GDP growth in Spain was almost too strong and that the boom might bust.

Table 5.1 *Spain's growth rates (1977–89)*

Year	(%)
1977	3.0
1978	1.4
1979	− 0.1
1980	1.2
1981	− 0.2
1982	1.2
1983	1.8
1984	1.8
1985	2.3
1986	3.3
1987	5.5
1988	5.0
1989	5.0

Source: OECD

As González's third term of office began in November 1989, his government faced the still unresolved problem of a total breakdown in communication with the trade unions. With consumer demand still buoyant and inflation still rising slowly, an agreement with the trade unions would seem to be the *sine qua non* of future wage moderation and control of inflation. Since the tripartite agreement, between government, employers and trade unions, the Economic and Social Accord, came to an end in 1986, a new consensus has seemed increasingly remote yet still appears crucial if the government is to press ahead with plans to spend more on the infrastructure essential for Spain's businesses to compete successfully. An ambitious programme to raise the share of infrastructure expenditure within GDP to 1.9 per cent by 1992 from 0.9 per cent in 1987 (mainly on roads and railways) is accompanied by plans to give priority to education and training in order to overcome hard evidence of a growing mismatch between employer demand and labour supply. Both aims will need to be realized if Spain's economic boom of the late 1980s is to be translated into long-term stable growth and a healthy business culture within which individual Spanish businesses can flourish.

Regional government

The regional government system ratified by Spain's Democratic Constitution of 1978, which establishes seventeen regional governments, with elected parliaments, represents a totally new framework in Spanish history within which business must operate.

While central government decides overall policy for taxation and income, social security contributions, defence, foreign affairs, internal security and justice, the seventeen autonomous regions have considerable independent powers. Three types of transfer of central government monies are made to the regions:

- Automatic transfers, decided by size of population, *per capita* income, area size, degree of isolation, relative poverty etc. These types of transfer are not subject to negotiations.
- Transfers via an **Inter-territorial Compensation Fund** (FCI), usually for new investments aimed at correcting regional disparities and therefore distributed according to the infrastructural needs of each region.
- Transfers of central government funds for earmarked purposes.

Regions have the right to levy certain taxes, e.g. wealth taxes, and also to add surcharges on government income tax. At present regions are operating within the guidelines of a five-year plan, 1987–91, which allocates them wide discretionary powers over expenditure, although the degree of spending autonomy varies across regions with only a few, for example having *full* responsibility for education and health.

Local authorities, i.e. town and provincial councils, also exist with considerable freedom over expenditure but not over raising of revenue. The regions' and local authorities' expenditure has grown since 1978 and accounts, for instance, for half of spending on state education, a fifth on health care, and two-thirds of total fixed investment. The trend throughout the 1980s was toward greater regional expenditure rather than local decentralization, as some regions press for greater responsibilities at the end of the present five-year period in 1991.

The two arguably most famous regions, the Basque Country and Catalonia (which includes Barcelona) have each had their major problems in recent years. The Basque Country, historically one of the leading industrial areas of Spain, especially for shipbuilding and iron and steel, has been crippled economically by the long ETA terrorist campaign which has driven many firms to move to safer parts of the country and inhibited foreign investment there. Catalonia, a prosperous area with a powerful regional government, will, of course, host the 1992 Olympic Games in Barcelona but has witnessed a series of complex and bitter disagreements between central government, regional government and the Town Council over the infrastructural and service arrangements for the Games.

Business and the economy

It is difficult to overstate the tremendous structural changes in the economy with which Spanish business has had to contend in the past thirty years. An industrial revolution which in other European countries happened over a hundred years before, in Spain only really arrived in the 1960s, a decade which witnessed an acceleration of the exodus from countryside to town, the phenomenal growth of mass tourism, and the first stages of an opening-up of the economy to the Western world that was to culminate in Spain's EC accession in 1986. Throughout this entire period, the massive state-owned industries have continued to dominate the Spanish economic scene, even arguably, at the beginning of the 1990s, where the principal challenge for much of Spanish business is to throw off the shackles of recent decades by major capital investment in plant and machinery in order to be able to compete successfully in the modern era against established Western rivals. Thus the advent of a marketing-orientated philosophy has come later to Spanish companies, but the performance of many of these companies, for instance in the new sectors of electronics and telecommunications, shows that the new lessons are being applied.

With consumer demand growing at 7 per cent in 1989, Spanish firms are enjoying fuller order books and company profits are mounting. These profits, helped by a fall in oil prices, led to unprecedented levels of investment in Spain and the creation of new jobs. With the economy growing at 5 per cent though, albeit high, the difference between what Spain produces and consumes is imported and, as a result, foreign firms in the late 1980s benefited enormously. However, the response of Spanish firms is dynamic, with government estimating that in 1987 and 1988 at least 40 per cent of industrial capacity has been updated. The current growth levels in the Spanish economy may then be superseded in the 1990s once all of the results of new capital investment are seen.

Heavy industry and INI

Long dominated by the state-owned industries of the public holding company, the **National Institute for Industry** (INI), the sheer economic power of heavy industry has set the business agenda in prominent regions of Spain such as the Basque Country.

The government's 'industrial reconversion' policy, launched in 1984, aimed to enhance competitiveness by adjustments to capacity and cuts in the workforce, financial restructuring and technological modernization, supported by public subsidies and credits. By the end of 1987, 85 per cent of envisaged job cuts (approximately 71,000) in shipbuilding, carbon-based steel, specialist steels, etc. had been achieved.

The restructuring has been successful. INI in 1988 registered its first profits since 1975 after record losses in 1983. Thirty firms have gone and of the fifty-eight firms still left in INI, forty-nine improved their financial position in 1988, with the largest profits being made by Endesa, the Electricity Giant, Inespal, aluminium manufacturers, and Iberia, the Spanish airline. The Spanish shipyards, Astilleros Españoles, was the worst performer. Government aid bolstered INI's success in the late 1980s but this will no longer be possible, according to EC directives, after 1992.

INI is one of the fifty biggest trading groups in the world and in Spain accounts for more than 30 per cent of all production, in a wide range of industries – coal, iron and steel, shipyards, electricity, aluminium, air and rail transport, etc. INI's industrial production is 10 per cent of industrial GDP and its internationalization process has gone further than most Spanish firms, with 30 per cent of its sales in 1988 coming via exports as against the average for all Spain of 14 per cent. Its R & D budget is again 23 per cent of the national total.

Tourist industry

It is estimated that one million Spanish families work directly or indirectly in the tourist trade which thus constitutes the largest employer in Spain, providing work for roughly 10 per cent of the active population. Spectacular growth since the 1960s shows little sign of plateauing out, as new tourist resorts continue to spring up and diversification of supply attracts more tourists to the cultural hinterland or away from high season.

Table 5.2   *Spanish tourism*

Year	Numbers of foreign tourists (millions)	Income (millions $)
1975	30.1	3.404
1980	38.0	6.967
1985	43.2	8.151
1986	47.4	12.058
1987	50.5	14.760
1988	54.2	16.780

Source: *Anuario El País*

What is astonishing about Spain's revenue from tourism (Table 5.2) is that it is generated by very low levels of expenditure, as revealed by comparative figures for 1986 which show that Spain's income of 12.058 million dollars was matched by only 1.512 million dollars expenditure, an income/expenditure ratio of 8 to 1. France, the UK, the United States, and countries such as Switzerland and Austria had virtual parity of income/expenditure in the same year while West Germany's ratio was 1 to 3.

Construction

The construction industry in Spain, after experiencing sector crises between 1975 and 1985, is now more powerful than ever, with a one million workforce and some of the top companies in Spain, notably Cubiertos and Dragados, which are benefiting from a property boom in Madrid and Barcelona, and from increased government spending on infrastructure, especially roads.

Electronics and telecommunications

The electronics industry in Spain is booming, with a 60,000 workforce in 1989 (from a virtually zero base five years previously) and 24 per cent growth over 1987. Its 70 billion pesetas worldwide sales in 1988 are expected to double by 1992. The industry is beginning to make its presence felt internationally with 0.6 per cent of global electronics production and 2.5 per cent of European production. A recent overhaul of the electronics and information technology (IT) industry in Spain has made this possible and government strategy to build up Spain's IT base has been crucial in wooing foreign investors to Spain. The 1986 agreement between ATT and the Spanish telecommunications company, Teléfonica, led to the construction outside Madrid of Western Europe's biggest microchip factory.

The telecommunications industry grew rapidly in 1988, with a 57 per cent rise in consumption and 37 per cent in production. Again, a National Telecommunications Plan for 1989–92 envisages continuing government investment in the industry of the level of 500,000 million pesetas annually, equivalent to between 1.1 per cent and 1.5 per cent of GDP. Spain's first Communications Satellite, *Hispasat*, is to be placed in orbit in December 1991 and will be used to support transmission of the 1992 Olympic Games in Barcelona.

In 1988 this sector saw major involvement by Scandinavian firms for the first time, with Electrolux buying two firms in Catalonia and Ericson moving into telecommunications in Spain.

Car industry

Spain is the fourth largest car manufacturer in the EC (after West Germany, France and Italy) but with perhaps the greatest potential for continued growth. In 1987, the car market in Spain grew by 33.7 per cent (compared with 8.2 per cent for France for instance) and, in 1988, the 1,090,000 cars sold in Spain represented a 16 per cent increase on 1987. Of these, approximately 30 per cent were imported. In terms of exports, Spain leads the field in Europe with 800,000 of the 1.5 million cars manufactured in 1988 destined for the export market. Of the six multi-national automobile

Table 5.3   *Spanish car market*

	1977 share (%)		1987 share (%)
Renault	28	Renault	23
Seat	38	VW Audi-Seat	17
Citroën	12	PSA Group	18
Chrysler	12	G. Motors	14
Ford	10	Ford	16
		Fiat	8
		Others	4

Source: Cambio 16

giants, five have factories in Spain, the exception being Fiat which has the major share of imports.

Francis Stahl, Chief Executive of Renault, stated in late 1988 that Spain had future potential in the automobile industry because of low labour costs, a workforce surplus and the possibility of further modernization to reduce costs. Thus, Ford and General Motors locate their small models in Spain while Renault divides production between Spain and France.

Car ownership in Spain is low at 296 cars per 1000 inhabitants, the equivalent of the EC twenty years ago and 20 per cent lower than the EC average. Estimates suggest a minimum of 5 per cent yearly growth up to 1992. Production figures for 1989 are likely to be 5 per cent higher than 1988, and exports also 6 per cent higher.

The proliferation of small and medium-sized firms in Spain, known as the PYMES, – **Pequeñas y Medianas Empresas** – has determined major shifts in business planning in the last few years. Coinciding with Spain's Presidency of the EC in the first half of 1989, the Industry and Energy Ministry launched a new programme geared to 1992 specifically for PYMES with a triple aim: the promotion of R & D; the strengthening of greater communication at European level with the involvement of PYMES in such schemes as Sprint, BC-NET, Europartenariat, etc; and the stream-lining and simplification of often bureaucratic management structures.

Also in the late 1980s, a movement towards new (for Spain) types of financial corporations, holding companies and consortia was becoming evident, as the PYMES, supported by the government, seek wider markets in Europe. Thus Spanish firms, both large and small, have begun to diversify horizontally, i.e. into areas unconnected with the business of the original firms, and vertically, i.e. in the same sector. Cement and real estate firms are the leaders in this diversification drive which has attracted private and state-owned concerns. Indeed, the state tobacco company Tabacalera, has pioneered the trend, since it now owns twenty-six firms unconnected with tobacco, which account for 25 per cent of all sales, a figure projected to rise to 50 per cent by 1992.

In terms of exports, Spain's performance over the period 1960–87, an annual improvement of 8.5 per cent, is the highest in the OECD with the exception of Japan, Greece and Turkey and comfortably outstrips the EC average at 5.8 per cent, West Germany at 5.7 per cent, the United Kingdom at 4.2 per cent and France at 6.4 per cent. Imports, however, in the same 1960–87 period, were the highest in the OECD at 10.4 per cent, which compares with the EC at 5.8 per cent, West Germany at 5.9 per cent, the United Kingdom at 4 per cent and France at 6.5 per cent.

The major trend in exports has seen trade with the EC commanding a larger share over the past ten years, while exports to North and South

Table 5.4   *Spain's exports*

	1977 (%)	1987 (%)
France	16	19
West Germany	11	12
United Kingdom	6	10
Italy	5	9
Other EC	11	14
Other West Europe	5	4
Eastern Europe*	3	2
North America	11	9
South America	10	4
Other	22	17

* includes Soviet Union
Source: OECD

America, perhaps surprisingly, have fallen from 21 per cent of overall exports in 1977 to 13 per cent in 1987 (Table 5.4). Within the EC, Spanish companies were most successful in the 1980s in increasing exports to the United Kingdom, Italy and France.

Despite the fact that government economic policy since 1982 has actively welcomed increased foreign investment in Spanish companies, at the end of the 1980s there was widespread fear in Spain that the process of foreign takeover was going too far. With Spain's rapid growth, opportunities mushroomed for foreign investors and multinationals, especially in the private sector, where long isolation had left few Spanish firms in a position to withstand competition. State-owned industry and the banks have, to date, been most successful in defending Spanish interests.

Spain's chemical, cement and insurance industries have been the most popular sectors for foreign investors with for, instance the Kuwaiti group, KIO, buying Enfersa, a chemical group, previously part of INI. In a sector where foreign competition accounted for 26 per cent of total consumption in 1988, and where Spain's biggest company, Ecros, is only in twentieth place in Europe, it is difficult to resist foreign intervention.

Arab and British companies have been at the forefront of recent wholesale acquisitions of Spanish firms. While the Arabs have bought into food companies, stationery, finance and real estate, British companies in 1989 led the field with, for example, the acquisition of Alhambra publishing by the Pearson Group, the olive oil giant José Guiu by Unilever, and the Petromed refinery by BP.

Most purchases though have been worth less than 50 million pesetas, perhaps suggesting that foreign companies are buying into Spain gradually with one eye on 1992. The Spanish government has not been immune from selling off state-owned firms to foreigners. Additionally, foreigners spent approximately 300,000 million pesetas a year in the late 1980s, purchasing property in Spain.

Regional inequalities, which have always existed, have become exacerbated in recent years as Spain's growth has generally benefited already prosperous areas, notably the area around the two major cities of Madrid and Barcelona, the Valencia region and the Balearics and Canaries, at the cost of the traditionally poorer agricultural areas of Extremadura, Castile, Andalusia and Galicia. The Basque provinces, the heartland of Spain's heavy industry throughout this century, is in crisis due to the industrial reconversion programme which has decimated its steel mills and shipyards. Despite specific employment programmes and the establishment of **Zones for Urgent Reindustrialization** (ZURs) in areas hit particularly hard by job losses, there seems little evidence as yet that the nettle of unequal regional development has been grasped by government or the business community.

The Socialist government also inherited sudden wage rises which followed Franco's death in 1975 and which saw real labour costs rise more rapidly in Spain until 1983, admittedly from a very low level, than in any other Western European economy. The rise occurred when real labour costs were actually falling in countries like Denmark and the Netherlands.

While Spanish wage levels are generally lower today than in her EC partners, this advantage is to some extent offset by lower productivity levels and, as a result, with wage costs still continuing to rise faster than production, the maintenance of high levels of employment constitutes an everpresent challenge.

Although, as was indicated previously, global foreign investment in Spain is growing yearly, there is a major question mark as to whether it is growing quickly enough in a country where indigenous sources of capital are limited and the banks, historically, (though the trend is changing), have preferred to invest in real estate rather than in industry.

One drawback of the multinational presence is that it does little to stimulate local research. And it is in this area that the structural weakness of Spanish industry is glaringly apparent. According to the OECD, the only member countries to spend less on R & D than Spain are Portugal, Greece and Turkey. Without basic research it may be that Spain's commercial future will remain mostly in intermediate industries such as car manufacturing.

Table 5.5   *Spain – the regional picture*

Region	% all GDP (1987)	% total population (1987)	Index of level of development (1986) (National average = 100)
Catalonia	19.5	15.4	108.7
Madrid	16.5	12.5	115.5
Andalusia	12.5	18.1	95.6
Valencia	10.4	9.8	105.8
Basque Country	6.0	5.5	103.9
Castile and León	5.9	6.6	92.0
Galicia	5.8	7.4	80.8
Canaries	3.7	3.9	100.3
Aragón	3.5	3.0	97.9
Castile and La Mancha	3.3	4.3	89.2
Balearics	2.7	2.8	110.3
Asturias	2.7	2.8	90.9
Murcia	2.2	2.7	98.7
Extremadura	1.8	2.8	79.0
Navarre	1.5	1.3	101.1
Cantabria	1.3	1.4	92.5
La Rioja	0.7	0.7	99.4

Source: Banesto and Economist

Services

A major complaint of the trade unions and opposition parties in 1989 was that public services had deteriorated since 1982. Government critics point to the transport system, especially roads, education and health, the postal and telegraph services.

The criticism is not all justifiable. After the first oil shock, investment on the transport infrastructure declined in real terms but the trend has been to a considerable extent reversed since 1982, although there is no doubt that the infrastructure has not been able to cope with the strong demand from an economy in growth.

Between 1975 and 1984 cumulative fixed investment in road transport per tonne-kilometre and passenger kilometre was more than two-thirds below the OECD average for Europe. In 1984 the ratio of road network per

1000 inhabitants was only 4 km in Spain as against an 11 km Europe average.

In terms of the rail network Spain was one of the very few countries in Europe where passengers and freight by rail actually declined in the decade up to the 1980s.

The González government's plan to improve the transport infrastructure involves a major programme to build 1700 extra motorway kilometres and a further 1200 km of trunk roads by 1992. Similarly, railway investment is scheduled to be equivalent to a yearly rise of 1 per cent of GDP (at 1988 prices) up to 1992 and beyond. The major part of this expenditure will involve the introduction of high-speed trains, purchased from West Germany, on the Seville–Madrid and Madrid–Barcelona routes as well as the commencement of an operation which will go well into the next century, to narrow the gauge to that of her EC partners. The wider gauge of 1.668 m compares with 1.435 m in France. The problem of mountainous terrain, however, remains to inhibit the aim of laying more double track in many areas.

One major transport success in the 1980s was the development of domestic air travel, in line with the recommendations of a 1980 Plan to strengthen regional airports and facilitate commercial travel. Thus an initial 57,000 million pesetas investment for the period 1981–6 helped to improve facilities at the airports of Madrid, Barcelona, Valencia, Seville, Málaga, Tenerife, Palma de Mallorca and Santiago. Five other airports important to the tourist trade – Alicante, Ibiza, Lanzarote, La Palma and Menorca – also received infrastructural subsidies. The resulting improvements and a consequent increase in domestic air travel have been of enormous benefit to the Spanish business community, faced with lengthy alternative journeys by road or rail.

Business and the law

Although operating openly in a democratic environment, business enterprises in Spain are still largely bound by a legalistic framework established during a Franco era in which the business community was 'given its head'. Most existing legislation governing business practice goes back to before 1975 and in the case of the legal status of limited liability companies, dates from the early 1950s. The most glaring anomaly is the failure under Franco to compel firms to carry out independent audits and the consequence has been wide popular mistrust of published accounts. Only in recent years have the majority of firms been persuaded that external auditing is in their own interests, as they learn to take seriously the views of shareholders and employees.

Spain's Democratic Constitution of 1978 recognizes the rights of private enterprise and states that these should be exercised in accordance with the overall requirements of the economy and within the general framework of government economic policy. All types of business, except sole trader, are obliged to register their existence in the Mercantile Register of the provincial capital in which the company's head office is located, a requirement which also extends to foreign companies setting up in Spain. The details are open to public inspection.

The principal types of company permitted by law are briefly summarized below. A more comprehensive account can be found in Donaghy and Newton's *Spain: A guide to political and economic institutions.*

1 Sociedad anónima – SA (company)

This is the most prestigious type of company in Spain. It can be in the public as well as the private sector and may be a large company quoted on the stock exchange or a smaller family business. No minimum size is stipulated but, hitherto, in accordance with 1951 legislation, any company with capital in excess of 50 million pesetas must register as an SA company. New legislation, however, reduces the minimum capital requirement to 3 million pesetas.

2 Sociedad de responsabilidad limitada – SRL/SL (company)

This type of company has no minimum capital requirement and therefore offers more flexibility. Often found in the retail and service sector, where an SRL company is quoted on the stock exchange, there are legal restrictions on the transfer of shares. There are, however, few other formal legal requirements on this type of company, for example, to provide audits or reliable financial information.

3 Sociedades colectivas (partnerships)

Partnerships are not widely found in Spain although two types exist in law: the **sociedad colectiva**, or general partnership, with unlimited liability; and the **sociedad en comandita/sociedad comanditaria**, or limited partnership, with a minimum of one general unlimited partner and one limited partner.

4 Cooperativas (co-operatives)

The most famous Spanish cooperative, Mondragón, in the Basque region, has attracted worldwide attention since its foundation in 1956 and still welcomes foreign delegations of interested politicians, economists and business people anxious to discover the secret of (arguably) the world's most successful cooperative. Over 100 enterprises, employing almost 20,000 people (and spanning consumer goods, capital goods, agriculture and construction) constitute a cooperative whose international fame undoubtedly derives from its unique supporting organizations: its own bank, with 100 branches in the Basque region; social security system; medical and hospital care; and a technical college.

The Spanish Constitution encourages the development of cooperatives and a separate Cooperative Register exists. The Ministry of Agriculture has pioneered the establishment of cooperatives in recent years, in an attempt to overcome the **minifundio** problem of tiny plots of farming land. Both small cooperatives, involving six or seven plots of land, and very large cooperatives, comprising up to 200 plots, have enjoyed considerable success.

5 **Comerciante (sole trader)**
Extremely numerous in Spain, comerciantes are found in many sectors especially food and drink, retail, crafts and services and are automatically members of the local **cámara de comercio** (chamber of commerce).

6 **Joint ventures**
The multiplicity of small firms in Spain has encouraged the government to provide financial incentives to firms to establish joint ventures. Such ventures the government sees as crucial to improving Spain's export performance. 1982 legislation allows two kinds of collaboration: temporary consortia of companies for a maximum ten-year period; and permanent contractual arrangements among groups of companies.

7 **Foreign investment**
Usually up to 50 per cent of the share capital of a Spanish company can be purchased by foreign investors without prior authorization. Any shareholding in excess of 50 per cent can only be approved by the **Dirección General de Transacciones Exteriores** (Directorate General of Foreign Transactions) where the share capital does not exceed 25 million pesetas. In some sectors, however, the investment percentage requiring authorization is lower, e.g. in shipping, mining, and banking.

Foreign companies therefore have considerable freedom to buy into Spanish companies, with the only exceptions being the defence industry and the mass media, where no foreign investment is allowed. Restrictions operate with regard to banks, but foreign companies are able to set up **sucursales** (branches) in Spain.

Business and finance

The banking system enjoyed a large role under Franco in a country where industry was able to find few alternative sources of finance, although for most of the period up until the early 1970s, the banks found themselves hidebound by a bureaucratic system of rules and regulations, which prevented new initiatives and rapprochement with Western Europe. Legislation in the 1970s though finally relaxed the restrictions to allow new Spanish banks to emerge and also, in 1978, to permit foreign banks to set up in Spain.

The Banco de España

Spain's Central Bank, the Banco de España, was nominally in private hands until 1962 when it was nationalized. In the 1970s, the Banco de España was accorded an important role in managing monetary policy and is now responsible for the monetary system and for supervising the banking system to the government Ministry of Economy and Finance. In this role it performs similar functions to central banks in other countries.

The Banco de España played a crucial interventionist part in the banking crisis which hit the country between 1978 and 1983 and which affected fifty-one of the then 110 banks operating in Spain. The reasons for the crisis were multifarious, including: the oil shocks; the rise in inflation caused by post-Francoist wage settlements; and the tight monetary policy pursued by the first governments of the democratic transition.

The Banco de España was instrumental in establishing a Deposit Guarantee Fund in 1977 to alleviate the crisis for troubled banks or depositors, and itself guaranteed half of the fund, to be matched by compulsory deposits from the Spanish banks. The Fund, run by its own Board of Management, was in fact used to provide help for twenty-six banks in financial crisis between 1978 and 1983 as well as to give some protection and/or compensation to depositors.

As the Banco de España's role has moved closer to that of its EC financial counterparts, so inevitably its role has been crucial in supporting real growth in Spain and in determining interest rates. Above all, the Banco de España has endeavoured to carry through the González government's objective of bringing the rate of inflation into line with that of major trading partners, notably countries participating in the European Monetary System, which Spain itself joined on 19 June 1989, with the peseta located, like the Italian lira, within a 6 per cent margin of fluctuation. The Banco de España's success in assisting the downward trend of inflation from the very high levels experienced up to the mid–1980s can be gauged from Table 5.6.

International comparisons reveal that inflation in Spain has been high through much of this period. As pointed out by the *1988/9 OECD Economic Survey*: 'Starting with a small positive inflation differential at the

Table 5.6　*Spanish inflation (1977–89)*

Year	(%)
1977	24.5
1978	19.8
1979	15.7
1980	15.5
1981	14.6
1982	14.4
1983	12.2
1984	11.3
1985	8.8
1986	8.8
1987	5.3
1988	4.8
1989	6.9

Source: OECD

beginning of the 1970s, the margin relative to the OECD average widened dramatically between the two oil shocks, peaking at almost 16 per cent in 1977. It then diminished equally fast to reach a low of 2.6 per cent in 1980 before attaining a new high of close to 7 per cent in 1983. Since then there has been a rather steady narrowing of the gap to no more than 1 per cent in 1988, only temporarily interrupted in 1986 by the introduction of the VAT which pushed the level of consumer prices up by an estimated two percentage points.'

The inflationary trend in 1989 was however upwards, with the December 1988 level at 5.8 per cent and with a level of 6.9 per cent for 1989. With unit labour costs in manufacturing also predicted to rise by 4 per cent in 1989, there are obvious worries in Spain that inflation may disrupt the strength and confidence generated by recent growth. However, further deregulation and trade liberalization may well assist the Banco de España in keeping inflation to manageable proportions.

An interesting footnote is that, according to IMF figures, Spain is fifth in the world league table of countries in terms of foreign currency reserves. The Banco de España's reserves are higher than the United Kingdom, France, Canada or Switzerland. Clearly, this is a reflection of international prestige and confidence of foreign investors and another indication of how Spain has become fashionable in international business.

Private banks

According to a 1985 study, there were eighty-five banks in Spain, thirty-seven of national scale, thirteen at regional level, and forty-eight at local level. This classification into national, regional or local banks, is preserved by the **Consejo Superior Bancario** (National Banking Council), which operates as a clearing house for information and statistics on the banks and provides a forum for meetings between representatives of the private and public sector banks.

Since 1985 the number of banks in Spain has increased to 140, in 1988, of which twelve showed losses. The increase is due to the high profitability of banks since the mid-1980s (Table 5.7).

Table 5.7   *Spanish Banks – profits in thousands of millions pesetas*

Year	Profits
1980	84
1981	104
1982	97
1983	125
1984	139
1985	192
1986	229
1987	305
1988	382

Source: Cambio 16

The trade unions have complained to the government about the excessive profits generated by the banks under a Socialist government and the government itself is unhappy. In fact, in 1988, the government stepped in to demand that the banks allocate a proportion of their profits to the modernization and restructuring of their operations. The banks themselves were not too preoccupied, since they have been sensitive to the charges of excessive profiteering.

Banks' profits must be seen though in the context of profit generated by companies. A survey undertaken by the Banco de España in 1987 of 4000 firms revealed a doubling of profits over 1986 and hence the view of a leading banker in Spain is hardly surprising when he asserts: 'When companies do well, we do well. If firms are doubling profits, then no one should be amazed if we increase ours by 40 per cent!'.

Spanish banks in 1989 had (with the approval of the government) the highest interest rates, along with the United Kingdom, in Europe. In 1988 they were also the most profitable in the EC, in a year when EC banks generally performed well. Spanish banks though are wary of the increased competition with EC banks which the single market will bring, especially where interest rates are seven or eight percentage points below Spain's.

The biggest three banks in Spain are the Banco Bilbao-Vizcaya (BBV), Banesto, and the Banco Central. The BBV is the product of a merger between the Banco de Bilbao and the Banco de Vizcaya which was actively supported by government. It is perhaps no coincidence that the present Minister for Finance, Carlos Solchaga, as well as the Industry Minister, Claudio Aranzadi, both began their careers with the Banco de Vizcaya or that important links between the BBV and the Town Council of Madrid provide the BBV with direct access to the Socialist Party power base.

The BBV has important stakes in three of Spain's principal electrical companies, Ibuerduero (11 per cent), Sevillana (5 per cent) and Hidrola (4 per cent). It owns a variety of firms in the food industry, for instance Kas, the Savin wine group and Garavilla conserves. It is the biggest client of INI, the state-holding company, and in recent years has been buying firms in strategically vital areas of industry as well as in information technology, electronics and communications.

Spain's second and third banks, Banesto and Banco Central respectively, have, during 1988 and 1989, been engaged in on-off merger discussions which have catapulted the 'two Albertos', Alberto Cortina, and his cousin, Alberto Alcocer, two directors of Banco Central with a 12.5 per cent equity holding, into the popular press and the public limelight. The flamboyant cousins, having built a huge economic empire in the 1980s, pushed for merger with Banesto but, defeated by Banco Central's President, Alfonso Escámez, resigned from the board in June 1989 to pursue a series of law-suits against Central's directors.

Foreign banks

Forty-four foreign banks in Spain have, until 1988, been restricted to the wholesale sector, with a maximum of three offices, and not been allowed to compete with Spanish banks at high street level. In fact, the only foreign banks hitherto permitted to operate freely at retail level are either those that acquired Spanish banks during the banking crisis from 1978 to 1983, such as Barclays and Citibank, or alternately those few banks already with a historical base in the market, such as Lloyds.

The top six Spanish banks control approximately 75 per cent of the market and have managed to convince the Banco de España to protect them from foreign competition. The Spring of 1989, however, signalled a distinct change of attitude when Mariano Rubio, President of the Banco de España, gave permission to the Deutsche Bank to take complete control of the ailing Banco Comercial Transatlántico. At the same time, the National Westminster Bank was negotiating to acquire control of another bank, the Grupo March.

Foreign banks account for 16 per cent of total loans in Spain but crucially account for 84 per cent of loans to firms who invoice more than 5,000 million pesetas a year. Unsurprisingly, the foreign banks have complained of being unfairly discriminated against, in a context where their highest share of the banking market was 10.6 per cent in 1984, stabilizing since then at 9 per cent.

It appears that foreign banks have not benefited as much from the consumer boom as domestic banks, although 1988 was a particularly good year for them, following a relatively poor one in 1987. Pretax profits rose by 54 per cent in 1988 compared with 23 per cent in 1987.

The Banco de España still, though, operates restrictions on foreign banks which resulted in two banks pulling out of Spain in 1988 – the Bank of Nova Scotia and the Chemical Bank. Mariano Rubio stated in mid-1989 that foreign banks will not be allowed to buy into or buy out the major Spanish banks but may, under certain circumstances, be allowed to purchase branches and offices in the big cities from thirty-three small and medium-sized banks.

The foreign banks have been working up new strategies to counter continuing restrictions, none with greater success than Barclays which saw its pretax profits rise 34 per cent in 1988. Barclays took advantage of the Spanish banking crisis to purchase thirty-three outlets from the Banco de Valladolid in 1981. It now has 135 branches in Spain, with an amazing total of fifty, i.e. virtually one per week, opened in 1988. Barclays' strategy is to open small branches, with a maximum of five staff, on the basis that more Spaniards are preferring a 'boutique' approach to the traditional Spanish 'department store' approach in banking. Barclays' success and the events of 1989 are certain to presage greater competition from foreign banks in the 1990s and greater liberalization of the regulations to allow freer and fairer competition.

Cajas de ahorros (savings banks)

The Cajas are an important banking institution and may be compared to the building societies in the UK, i.e. with no shareholders and designated

Table 5.8   *Banking institutions in Spain (1983)*

	No. of institutions	No. of offices	% total deposits	% total loans
Banco de España	1	53	0.2	15.1
Banks	135	16,062	61.0	51.8
Cajas	80	11,787	34.7	23.0
Others (e.g. cooperative credit agencies)	155	3,221	4.1	10.1
Total	371	31,123	100.0	100.0

Source: Banco de España

as non-profit making. Their importance can be gauged from a 1983 Banco de España comparison of the different banking institutions (Table 5.8).

The big two Cajas, La Caixa (from Barcelona), and CajaMadrid are as large as the second and third banks in Spain, Banesto and Banco Central, and have also been engaged in merger talks which so far have produced only informal agreement to cooperate and plan together in certain areas.

Until recently, the Cajas, almost all of which are regional or local in origin, have been limited by law to a certain geographical area. Although legislation now allows them to operate freely across the country, a new 1989 Law, the LORCA (**Ley de Organos Rectores de Cajas de Ahorro**), is designed by the Socialist government to have the eventual effect of handing over control of the Cajas to the seventeen autonomous regional governments. The ultimate consequence of this would seem to be to reduce the seventy-seven Cajas existing in 1989 to just seventeen, or one per region.

Pension funds

An area in which the Cajas are competing openly with the banks is the pension funds market. In 1989 it is estimated that 60 per cent of pension funds business is in the hands of the banks, 22 per cent with the Cajas and 10 per cent with insurance companies.

The dual appeal of pension funds is that operations involving them do not attract VAT and profits from investments do not attract company tax. The largest holdings are with the main banks especially BBV, Banco Central, Banco de Santander and Grupo March.

The trade unions have also become involved, with the Socialist UGT

establishing an insurance company and the Communist Workers'
Commissions also setting up a pension fund company.

Stock markets

In the past few years, Spain's stock exchanges have laboured under an
antiquated structure which goes a long way towards explaining why
Spanish stock markets have been among the least active and least
important in the Western world. Spain has three long-established
exchanges in Madrid (1831), Bilbao (1915) and Barcelona (1915), and a
newly-opened exchange in Valencia (1980). Madrid accounts for about 80
per cent of all stock market transactions, Barcelona about 15 per cent while
Bilbao and Valencia between them represent a paltry 5 per cent.

The traditional recourse of Spanish companies to the banking system for
finance to expand meant relatively few transactions on the exchanges until
the mid-1980s when a series of reforms transformed the exchanges into
modern entities with the latest technology. The process was initiated with
a 1978 Commission to examine ways in which to stimulate activity on the
exchanges. Reforms followed in the early 1980s, which were successful in
persuading more companies to issue new shares as a means of generating
more capital for expansion.

The reforms have involved greater decentralization, the establishment
of a new body to oversee stock market transactions, and finally in 1989, a
Law (the **Ley de Reforma del Mercado de Valores**) to streamline practises
and bring them more into line with other Western exchanges. Early signs
are that large investors have benefited most from the changes, amid
greatly increased stock market activity which has also attracted foreign
investors to the Spanish exchanges. Foreign investors are free to invest but
are only allowed to acquire up to 50 per cent of a company's stock. Larger
stakes need special authorization.

Despite comparatively low levels of exchange activity, more Spaniards
appear to be viewing the stock market as a good investment. In 1989, for
instance, the average profit increase of firms quoted on the stock market
was estimated to be 21 per cent, while a minimum annual rise of 12 per
cent is predicted until 1993. Banks and electrical firms comprise 60 per cent
of all firms on the exchanges. A proliferation of real estate companies in
the late 1980s reflected the property boom in Spain.

Also in the past two years, six Spanish firms (three state-owned, three
private) have taken the revolutionary step of entering Wall Street, with
flotation on the US stock exchange. The three state-owned companies –
Telefónica, Endesa and Repsol – have met with considerable success to date
but the three private banking concerns, – Banco Bilbao-Vizcaya, Banco

Central and Banco de Santander – have encountered serious problems in appealing to US investors, apparently with long memories of the Latin American Foreign Debt crisis earlier in the 1980s which ruined a number of US banks and which has left investors wary of 'Hispanic' banks ever since. However, the very fact of just 'being on Wall Street' is seen as prestige enough in Spanish quarters and further evidence of Spain's desire to be part of the Western financial scene.

According to the *1988/9 OECD Economic Survey*, the recent Spanish overhaul of the stock exchange including the abolition of the monopoly position of brokers has already had a favourable impact on the international community.

Business and the labour market

The principal factors providing the background to the labour market are located in Spain's rapid industrialization since the 1960s, set against the authoritarian isolationism of the Franco dictatorship. Thus a massive exodus of workers from Franco's Spain which began with the close of the Civil War in 1939 when an estimated half a million left the country as political refugees was to be supplemented in the decades that followed by a continuing haemorrhage of manpower seeking employment in the more developed countries of Europe, as well as in the USA and Latin America. In 1989 2,800,000 Spaniards still worked in these countries and provide much-needed revenue for their home country.

Alongside emigration, the 1950s, 1960s and 1970s also witnessed wholescale domestic migration from the countryside to the towns and from the agricultural, poorer areas, such as Extremadura and Andalusia, to the more prosperous urban environments of Barcelona, Madrid and Bilbao.

As in other countries, Spanish women began to enter the workforce for the first time in the 1960s and unemployment, in the early post-Franco years of the democratic transition, began to soar, illustrating the human cost of Franco's failure to modernize Spain's economic infrastructure. Spain's business culture is still struggling to come to terms with the impact on the labour market which the sea-changes of the past three decades have generated on a population which at year-end 1987 stood at 38,914,000.

Demographic trends – general

The single biggest concern for Spain is a fall in the birth rate more dramatic than that in virtually any other European country. In 1975 live births per 1000 inhabitants stood at nineteen but, by 1986, this had fallen to eleven. Also in 1986, the average number of children per woman in Spain was 1.5 compared with 2.8 in 1975. The figures demonstrate that women in Spain are having fewer children, later, and that more are joining the workforce. In fact, four out of every five new job-seekers are women, although only a third of Spanish women constitute part of the workforce, again one of the lowest levels in Europe.

Social factors are obviously an important contributory factor with fewer marriages in Spain in the 1980s and with the legalization of divorce in 1981, and abortion (under certain legally-defined circumstances) in 1985. While every survey conducted indicates that cohabitation and sex before marriage are now widely accepted, despite being religiously taboo in traditional Spain, it is nonetheless the case that a mere 20,000 marriages a year end in divorce and that illegitimate births constitute only 7 per cent of the total.

Demographic trends – Madrid

The drop in the number of young people in the 15–19 age group in Madrid since 1981 almost certainly is paralleled in other principal urban areas of Spain (for which, however, no information is available) and represents a nationwide problem which threatens business recruitment in the labour market as well as the vitality of Spain's main business centres (Table 5.9).

Table 5.9   *Madrid – fall in numbers of young people*

	15–29 age (000s)	15–19 age (000s)
1981	741	293
1986	778	269
1991 (projected)	787	241
1996 (projected)	696	189
2001 (projected)	568	141

Source: Boletín Estadístico de Madrid

From 1981 to 1986 Madrid lost 100,000 inhabitants in total, while the average age increased from 31.6 years to 36.8 years. By the year 2000, Madrid is expected to have half of the total 15–19 year age group that it had in 1986, with a predominance of over-65s. Madrid's birth rate, symptomatic of urban Spain as a whole, has fallen by a third in the last ten years to 1.4 children per couple, the lowest of any capital city in Western Europe.

Madrid's problem has prompted central and local government initiatives to counter the drift away from the major conurbations. The Mayor of Madrid, Juan Barranco, fears the trend could destroy the essential fabric of town centres in Spain and states: 'It could leave us with a centre of offices and shops, heavily depopulated, with only an ageing wealthy residential class.'

One of the main reasons for the population exodus is the spectacular rise in housing prices which has driven young people in particular to live in dormitory towns hours away from the centre or to abandon urban living altogether. The boom in house prices has meant an increase in new-build upmarket housing, inaccessible to most of the labour market, but the virtual disappearance of municipal housebuilding. For those entering the job market or those on low incomes in the first years of employment, the only alternative for the majority of young people is to remain in the family home. 20 per cent of married couples, at the end of 1986, were living with parents. The housing crisis has resulted in severe overcrowding with Madrid's 3.5 persons per dwelling one of the highest levels of any European capital.

A vicious circle has now emerged, with 62 per cent of males in Madrid between the ages of twenty-five and twenty-nine unmarried in 1986 (compared with 48 per cent in 1981). A similar trend for women further accentuates the decline in birth rate.

Labour market trends

In 1960 38.7 per cent of the Spanish working population in civilian employment were employed in agriculture. By 1987 this figure had fallen to 15.1 per cent, a level equivalent to Spain's Mediterranean EC partners but still significantly higher than France, with 7.1 per cent employed in agriculture in 1987, West Germany with 5.2 per cent and the United Kingdom with 2.4 per cent.

Spain's manufacturing workforce changed very little in this period, from a much lower base, with 23 per cent employed in manufacturing in 1960 and 22.8 per cent in 1987. The 1987 figure can be compared with France (22.1 per cent), West Germany (31.9 per cent) and the United Kingdom (23.6 per cent).

Spain, like all of its EC partners, saw a continuing rapid expansion of employment in services between 1960 and 1987, although the scale of growth in Spain was even higher than in other countries. Thus, in Spain between 1960 and 1987 the percentage employed in services increased from 31 per cent to 52.8 per cent. (In France employment in this sector rose from 39.9 per cent to 62.1 per cent, in West Germany from 39.1 per cent to 54.3 per cent and in the United Kingdom from 47.6 per cent to 67.8 per cent).

Table 5.10   *Spanish civilian employment (1987)*

By sector	(%)	GDP at factor cost by origin (%)
Agriculture	14.4	5
Industry	23.8	30
Construction	8.7	8
Services	53.1	57

Source: OECD

Unemployment

Spain's dramatic transition from dictatorship to democracy has been accompanied by the highest rates of unemployment seen in OECD countries as Spain's economy has undergone the severest adjustments (Table 5.11).

The very acute employment crisis of the 1980s was caused by many factors including:

- A slowdown in economic growth through the 1970s exacerbated by the oil shocks and the uncertain political climate.
- A vigorous surge in wage costs following Franco's death in 1975.
- A marked deterioration in fixed investment in the 1970s.
- Delays in adjusting production structures.

From 1974, when employment stood at a record level, to 1982, employment fell by over two million, and a further fall of 1,900,000 was registered between 1983 and 1986. By 1985 also the participation rate (i.e. the ratio of employment to population of working age) had fallen to 43.7 per cent, the lowest level of any industrialized country. As early as 1978, Spain's unemployment rate topped the EC average and in 1985 climbed above 21 per cent, i.e. twice as high as EC member states. In addition, the length of time for which people remained unemployed and the composition of unemployment by age and sex were both unfavourable to Spain. Thus, the proportion of long-term unemployed (i.e. for twelve months or more)

Table 5.11   *Spanish unemployment rates (1977–89)*

Year	(%)
1977	5.2
1978	6.9
1979	8.5
1980	11.2
1981	13.9
1982	15.8
1983	17.2
1984	20.0
1985	21.4
1986	21.0
1987	20.1
1988	19.1
1989	16.9

Source: OECD

at 54.2 per cent in 1986 was higher than all other EC partners, with the exception of the Benelux countries. Youth unemployment (16–24 age group) at 47.5 per cent was also the highest in the OECD in 1987, and can be compared with the United Kingdom at 33.6 per cent, France at 33 per cent and West Germany at 22.7 per cent.

A breakdown of the unemployment rate in 1987, compared with an already poor 1981, (Table 5.12) illustrates the severity of the problem.

Table 5.12   *Unemployment breakdown*

	1981 (%)	1987 (%)
Male	13.0	16.8
Female	17.5	28.0
Under 25 years	34.3	43.0
25–54 years	9.3	15.0
Over 55 years	5.7	9.4

Source: OECD

Due to the economic policies pursued by the government (and outlined earlier), however, the unemployment problem began to turn around in 1987 and especially 1988.

While the agricultural labour force continued to decline, 400,000 new jobs were created in other sectors in 1988, a net increase in the number of employed of 300,000 or 3 per cent. Employment growth in the construction sector in 1988 was running at three times previous levels. In the service sector, female employment grew twice as fast as male employment while overall female participation rate increased from an average of 29.3 per cent in the 1983–85 period, to 32.5 per cent in 1988. Next to Ireland, though, female participation rates in 1988 were still the lowest in the OECD.

Also in 1987 and 1988, greater flexibility in the labour market resulted from a number of Employment Promotion Programmes in firms, sponsored by the government, which initially created many thousands of temporary and part-time jobs. About half of these jobs have, however, since been converted to permanent contracts, with the assistance of tax changes introduced in 1988 designed to encourage firms to create new permanent forms of employment.

Male unemployment fell by 1.6 percentage points between 1987 and 1988. Youth unemployment, significantly, had the sharpest reduction, mainly due to the special Employment Programmes, although at 40 per cent in 1988, the 16–24 age group still compared poorly with the 25–54 age group, at 13.5 per cent. Also in 1988, further evidence of economic growth in Spain finally influencing the job market, was provided by a reversal in the earlier steep upward trend in long-term unemployment. Thus, in 1989, each succeeding month brought a further improvement in the unemployment situation, with unemployment in the second half of 1989 dipping below 17 per cent.

Unemployment training schemes

Additional to government Employment Programmes outlined earlier, the **National Institute for Employment** (INEM) has been devoting increasing resources (70,000 million pesetas in 1989) to training for the unemployed. Centres have been established throughout Spain but especially in areas affected by industrial 'reconversion'. Emphasis has been upon training in the new technologies and on collaborative ventures with the trade unions. INEM has worked also in close conjunction with regional governments and with the European Commission since it derives half of its budget from the European Social Fund.

Business and trade unions

A crucial element in Spanish business culture has been the development in the last decade of a free trade union structure, from the ruins of an undemocratic system of 'vertical syndicates' under Franco in which everyone who worked was obliged to be a member of one of twenty-eight vertical syndicates, arranged by industry, and constructed hierarchically to include all employees from top management to shop-floor worker. There was central control of the system, with the Minister for Syndical Relations a member of Franco's nominated government. The essentially undemocratic nature of the system can be gauged by the fact that as late as 1971 only 391 people were eligible to vote directly for the President of the Metal workers' syndicate, although the union had 1,300,000 members.

The collapse of vertical syndicalism, undermined from within by the Communist trade union, the Workers' Commissions (**Comisiones Obreras**) and from without by the unassailable march towards political pluralism, paved the way for a free trade union structure which since the late 1970s has had an increasing influence on the business culture. Led by the Workers' Commissions and the Socialist UGT (General Union of Workers), the trade unions initially, in a period where many companies had to learn how to negotiate with genuine worker representatives, adopted in the early 1980s a policy of conciliation and consensus, exemplified by the signing of a number of social and economic pacts with government and/or employers' confederations.

In the late 1980s, increasing disillusionment with government monetary and fiscal policies, which accepted very high levels of unemployment and appeared to strike at workers' purchasing power, saw the unions turn towards open conflict with government and employers, a process culminating in Spain's first general strike for fifty years on 14 December 1988. Continuing trade union malaise underlay the general election of 29 October 1989 which, with only the narrowest overall majority for Felipe González's Socialist government, left the necessity for early government/employers/trade unions conciliation high on the new government's agenda.

Industrial democracy

Evolution of free trade unions from the vertical syndicates took place in the 1960s and 1970s, with Franco still in power, as employers increasingly began to negotiate with genuine though illegal, workers' representatives rather than through the official vertical organization. Although present-day trade unions have had only a brief modern history, the four decades of Francoism were unable to erase completely from collective memory an earlier period at the start of the last century and up to the 1930s in which Spanish trade unions were among the largest and the most powerful in the Western world. Industrial democracy's recent history has a number of important benchmarks:

Late 1950s/ early 1960s	The birth of the Communist trade union, Workers' Commissions, as an illegal and clandestine movement, to infiltrate the official vertical syndicates. Quickly spread throughout Spain to assume national importance.
1962	The first big demonstration of nascent free trade unionism with a Miners' Strike in the North of Spain leading to Franco declaring a state of emergency.
1968	A report of the International Labour Organization acknowledges the primacy of the illegal free trade union movement.
1960s/ 1970s	Internal rebirth of the Socialist trade union, the UGT, helped by the rise of González's Socialist party.
1975	The last Franco government tinkers with vertical syndicalism to allow for emergent trade unions but the attempt fails.
1975–7	Increasing industrial unrest as free trade unions demand full recognition.
1977	Legalization of free trade unions and abolition of vertical syndicates.
1978	First trade union elections to choose workers' delegates in firms.
1980	Workers' Statute becomes law. The Statute lays down workers' rights, representation and collective bargaining procedures. A minimum wage level is to be fixed annually by the government in consultation with unions and employers. The works' committees are established as the effective voice of the workforce in companies, able to negotiate with employers over working conditions and over wages, although local, regional or national wage negotiations will usually determine the parameters.

The tremendous pressure exerted by the workforce on the fragile democracy that was emerging in Spain in the mid-1970s is obvious when one examines the strike record and the number of man-hours lost as a result in the period from 1966 up to 1980. The ten-fold increase in man-hours lost between 1975 and 1976 is the most telling indicator of the Spanish people's reaction to Franco's death, although, as can be seen from Table 5.13, the figure continued to mount to a peak of 171,067,049 hours lost in 1979.

Table 5.13   *Spanish industrial disputes (1966–80)*

Year	No. strikes	Man-hours lost
1966	205	1,785,462
1970	817	6,750,900
1975	855	10,355,120
1976	1,568	110,016,240
1977	994	92,572,050
1978	1,356	128,738,478
1979	1,789	171,067,049
1980	1,669	108,625,662

Source: Spanish Employers' Confederation (Confederación Española de Organizaciones Empresariales)

Social and economic pacts

The fact that strikes in 1980 were still at a high level despite a reduction from 1979 was probably caused by two main factors: works' committees, initially, had insufficient power to represent workers' interests, being restricted to negotiating over health and safety issues; and, also, many Spanish firms were incredibly slow to recognize the reality of the changing situation and instead of engaging in direct dialogue with the workforce, asked government for greater protectionism for their industries. Such dilatoriness merely encouraged workers to join unions and formulate demands.

A developing battle between the Communist Workers' Commissions and the Socialist UGT was exacerbated by a bilateral agreement in 1980 signed between the UGT and the Spanish Employers' Confederation, the **CEOE**, a historic pact (the **AMI**), the first ever in Spain between employers and a national union. The main points of the pact were that wage rises of between 13 per cent and 16 per cent in profit-making companies would be paid and works' committees in each firm were to have access to company balance sheets and to be consulted in any management decision on employment policy, productivity, working methods or conditions.

During 1980, the AMI pact was on the whole a success, with widespread adherence to the wage rise guidelines, and the UGT negotiating successfully to halt potentially major strikes in the car industry and the dockyards. The pact also paved the way for a new agreement, known as the **ANE**, in which the Workers' Commissions joined the UGT, the Employers' Confederation and the government as co-signatories. This pact, which was to last until the end of 1982, kept wage rises to 10.5 per cent maximum (with inflation running at a rate of about 15 per cent), modernized collective bargaining procedures and secured promises from the government to improve employment and social security provision. A further agreement, (the **AI**), this time between the unions and employers alone, extended cooperation into 1984 when the most far-reaching of the agreements to date was signed, the Economic and Social Accord (**AES**), a tripartite agreement between the UGT, management and the first Socialist government of Felipe González.

The Accord, covering 1985 and 1986, importantly, was the first of the agreements in which the government negotiated public spending plans with both sides of industry. Divided into two parts, the first part of the Accord detailed government commitments, and the second part was a legally-binding agreement between the signatories. The main components of the first part were:

- A government promise to create 190,000 jobs in 1985, via increased public sector funding and extra stimulus for private industry.
- A 'solidarity fund' of £284 million, raised by equal contributions from workers, employers and government, to support training and retraining schemes and innovatory job creation projects, along the same lines as the EC's European Social Fund.
- An increase in personal allowances, the removal of more low income earners from the tax net, and an extension of unemployment benefit from the 25 per cent eligible in 1984 to 48 per cent by the end of 1986.
- A government allocation of £237 million for investment in labour intensive sectors to modernize plant and machinery.

The second part of the Accord applied to around 5 million workers covered by collective agreements in the public and private sectors and comprised:

- A pay increase band of between 5.5 per cent and 7.5 per cent.
- An agreement to increase productivity, lower absenteeism and reduce systematic overtime by eradicating the common practice in Spain of multiple employment or double-jobbing.
- A rationalization programme to reduce the number of collective agreements signed at individual company level (3500 running in 1984) by introducing more national and regional bargaining.
- A new system for resolving disputes through voluntary mediation and arbitration.

Since 31 December 1986 when the Accord terminated, no new pact has been signed in Spain, and there is evidence of growing trade union disenchantment with government economic policies. Whereas the Workers' Commissions refused to sign the Accord, the UGT later came to condemn its sister Socialist party in government for increasing job losses and eroding purchasing power. The Accord can be said, though, to have been successful in maintaining wage moderation, and a symptom of its success, paradoxically, is the mounting social disruption and political uncertainty which followed in the three years from 1987–9 when no pact was in place.

Trade unions' power battle in firms

The battle between the Communist Workers' Commissions and the Socialist UGT has centred around trade union elections in which the workforce select delegates on works' committees to negotiate with management. The balance of power between the unions is shown in Table 5.14.

Table 5.14 *Spanish trade union elections*

Trade union	Percentage of delegates elected to works' committees		
	1978 (%)	1981 (%)	1986 (%)
Workers' Commissions	34.5	30.7	34.9
UGT	21.6	29.7	41.0
USO (Workers' Syndical Union)	3.7	9.5	4.0
Regional unions	1.0	3.9	4.0
Others/Independents	39.2	26.2	16.1

Source: *Cambio 16*

The election results show the rise of the UGT through the 1980s, although the overall picture after 1986 tends to mask a switch in allegiance in large firms of 1000 employees upwards from the UGT to Workers' Commissions. The Communist union also won twice as many votes as the UGT in the telephone and telecommunications industry and scored major successes in other crucial industries, including gas and energy, the railways and the banks. The UGT performed well in small and medium-sized firms and in the tobacco industry, its only stronghold among large firms. This was surprising, given the fact that in September 1986 the Socialist government had provided its UGT ally with a £21 million subsidy (and over 100 buildings) for its election campaign, representing the return of union assets seized by the Franco régime after the Civil War. The Workers' Commissions, having emerged only in the late 1950s, received practically nothing.

Trade union/government conflict

Increasing industrial unrest in 1987 and 1988, following the breakdown of the AES, the last social compact, reflected growing union anger at the effects of government policy and culminated in a general strike on 14 December 1988.

In the years preceding the strike, the Socialist government, in the view of the unions, had been accommodating the demands of employers, to achieve greater flexibility of labour. For instance, the government introduced six-month, fixed-term contracts in firms as a means of creating new jobs and proposed to abolish the statutory minimum wage for workers aged 18–24, to reduce redundancy payments and to extend part-time labour. At the same time, Spain's low labour costs were being advertised as a national asset as the government attempted to attract multinational enterprises and foreign investment. According to the US business magazine, *Fortune*, in 1987: '. . . labour costs in Spain are mouth-watering.' Some firms expect to pay Spanish workers up to 30 per cent less than workers elsewhere in Western Europe. Ford's Valencia plant – in which the UGT enjoys a major presence – has the lowest costs of any of the company's eight European factories.

In the absence of a new social pact the UGT has been in bitter conflict with the government since 1987. The UGT opposed González's decision to keep Spain within NATO, UGT MPs voted against the government over pensions legislation and, finally, the UGT leader, Nicolás Redondo, resigned his parliamentary seat in protest at the 1988 Budget.

A 1988 UGT report on Spain's economy from 1977 to 1987 spends 300 pages condemning the government for a 'monetarist and fiscal policy more conservative than Helmut Kohl or Margaret Thatcher'. In contrast to the UGT report, the Spanish Employers' Confederation (CEOE) has been enthusiastic in its support for government policies with José María Cuevas, the Confederation's President, declaring in 1988: '. . . the government should continue to fight inflation, improve firms' competitiveness and bring more flexibility into the labour market.'

1988 general strike

The general strike of 14 December 1988 was monumentally successful, with about six million strikers – two-thirds of the working population – paralysing the country. The trigger for the strike was the government's Youth Employment Plan, which sought to allocate £15,000 million to firms to engage unemployed workers below the age of twenty-five on short-term contracts at the minimum wage level. The UGT condemned the plan as 'the worst attack on workers since the Franco era', arguing that it would not solve the long-term unemployment problem. Redondo complained that 'only 18 per cent of jobs in Spain's expanding textile industry are permanent and over 30 per cent of production is in the hidden economy'. The labour market, he argued, has become 'the law of the jungle'.

Young workers in Spain form a reserve army for a huge black economy which some estimates put as high as 15 per cent or 20 per cent of legal GDP. Of every two people unemployed in Spain, one is between the ages of sixteen and twenty-five. There were over 1,400,000 in this category at the start of 1989 and over 800,000 who have never had a job.

Following the success of the general strike, the UGT and Workers' Commissions agreed to meet Felipe González only if five prior conditions were met: scrapping the Youth Employment plan; compensating employees in state-owned industries and pensioners for their 2 per cent drop in real earnings in 1988; increasing to 18 per cent the number of jobless entitled to unemployment pay; recognizing civil servants' right to collective bargaining; and bringing the minimum pension into line with the minimum wage. These demands are only some of a whole battery of social and economic measures the unions are pressing on government to redistribute wealth, protect employees and expand trade union rights and participation in the management of industry. The unions contend that when Spanish companies made low profits in the early 1980s the workforce tightened their belts to boost profitability. Now that profits are higher, they argue, the workforce deserve their share.

Throughout 1989 there was an impasse between the unions and government, with the Socialist party even threatening to set up its own trade union in competition with its long-time ally, the UGT. Most importantly the general strike saw the greatest cooperation yet between Spain's two main trade unions, determined to increase the union movement's power to the level of some of her neighbouring countries. The task is a difficult one in an economy based mainly on hundreds of thousands of small firms and where trade union membership is between 20 per cent and 25 per cent of the working population (see below). As one UGT leader commented in early 1989: 'With such low membership the unions are left out of the major economic decisions made in Spain. Most of the government's plans for the economy we learn about through the newspapers!'

Trade union membership

The unreliable figures provided by the unions themselves make membership levels difficult to estimate, although independent observers believe that membership in recent years has fallen away from the late 1970s when it may have reached a maximum of 30 per cent of the working population. The current level is unlikely to be much higher than 20 per cent, the level attained in 1981, and the lowest in Western Europe.

Table 5.15   *Spanish trade union membership (20 per cent) (1981)*

Trade union	No. of members	% total membership
Workers' Commissions	730,000	42.0
UGT	692,000	39.9
Workers' Syndical Union (USO)	205,000	11.8
Basque TU (ELA/STV)	58,000	3.4
Others/Regional TUs	53,000	2.9

Source: Cambio 16

A May 1989 article in the Spanish magazine *Cambio 16* estimates current membership at 17 per cent, but what is certain is that existing trade unions are poorly organized and inefficient. Poor collection procedures mean that between 50 per cent and 70 per cent of total membership dues are probably not collected. Strike funds are minimal so that extended strikes are only possible in small companies or those areas where the local population identify closely with the demands of the workforce.

New initiatives

The UGT estimates that within a few years half of their funds will derive from the profits of a new holding company it is establishing, **UGT SA**. The holding company will be led by a new Trade Union Bank; by a house-building corporation, **PSV**, which will promote cooperative ventures; and by an insurance company, **UNIAL**.

These three companies will form the basis of a holding company, as UGT attempts to achieve financial autonomy and distancing from the Socialist party, and sets out to become a huge service trade union like its counterparts elsewhere in Western Europe. UNIAL, with forty-six offices projected throughout Spain, and with the use of UGT offices, has ambitions to attract business beyond the UGT membership itself. UGT points out that in Sweden, for instance, one person in two invests in a trade union insurance company, while in Austria a union company is market leader in the sector.

Employers' organizations

The main Employers' Confederation, CEOE, formed in 1977 from 165 employers' organizations, claims to represent 1.3 million companies controlling 75 per cent of all jobs in Spain in the private sector. 90 per cent of firms employ fewer than fifty workers. An organization for small and medium-sized firms, **CEPYME**, was integrated into CEOE in 1980 but still preserves special autonomous status and has appeared as a separate signatory in the social and economic pacts made with government and the unions. CEOE, increasingly combative and assertive since 1980, has assumed an important public profile in the 1980s, taking advantage of the unions' weakness through lack of funds, lack of unity (until recently) and the employment situation.

Business, education, training and development

In evaluating the contribution made to the Spanish business culture by education, training and development, it must be realized that Spain is starting in this area from a very low base. The decades of Francoism held back educational reforms and it was only in 1970 that an Education Reform Act introduced the present-day educational structure. The Act however, in revolutionizing schooling, did not solve many of its attendant problems. Hence, a major plank of the first Socialist government's legislative programme in the 1980s was further educational reform, to be effected by two new Laws, the 1983 **University Reform Law** (LRU) and the **1985 Organic Law on the Right to Education** (LODE), designed to democratize and modernize the school and university system. As the leading Spanish magazine *Cambio 16* commented at the time, it will be at least ten years before the success or failure of these Laws can be assessed.

The democratic transition inherited from Franco one of the least-educated or trained workforces in the Western world. The impact of 1970 education legislation was felt however as the percentage of unskilled workers fell from 46 per cent in 1963 to 33 per cent in 1976. The increase in skilled workers was particularly noticeable in administrative jobs which constituted 12 per cent of wage earners in 1963 but increased to 19 per cent by 1976. The overall standard of education changed also so that in the 1970s education among workers to secondary school level became common for the first time, whereas previously the majority of workers had only reached primary level, if that. In 1964, only 5 per cent of the active population had secondary education. By 1980 it was almost 25 per cent.

Primary and secondary education

Divided between state and private schools, all pupils between the ages of six and fourteen study the compulsory **Basic General Education** course (the EGB). At the age of fourteen, the more academically able go on to study for a two-year **Bachillerato** while for others a course of vocational training known as **Formación Profesional** (FP) is available. The separation at fourteen has caused innumerable problems since parents have tended to keep their children in the academic lane by having them repeat years rather than allowing them to proceed along the less prestigious FP route. FP diplomas have also been slow to gain acceptance from Spanish employers.

Access to the universities is generally via the **University Orientation Course** (COU), a one-year pre-university course which involves compulsory subjects (Spanish language and literature, a foreign language and mathematics) and three optional subjects. In recent years other 'selectivity' exams have provided a route to higher education, which saw a rapid expansion in the 1970s and 1980s to the present level of 960,000 university students in the academic year 1988–9 (compared with 383,000 in 1975).

Universities

The spectacular rise in student numbers has caused chaos in a university system originally designed to accommodate only a tenth of the current student population. It has added to the problem of 'massification', i.e. the anonymous, impersonal, distant and bureaucratic treatment of students by institutions living, until recently, in the last century. The González government has, in the University Reform Law, attempted to update the universities, by placing tighter limits on the numbers admitted, in order to improve academic standards, by reorganizing university departments along Anglo-Saxon lines, and by reducing the bureaucracy which was strangling the system. (For instance, the Law reduced the forty-five categories of university teachers to four!) Naturally, the restrictions on numbers generated the most vociferous public protests and demonstrations.

Currently, there are thirty-four universities in Spain, thirty state-run and four private church-owned universities, the consequence of the 1953 Concordat between the state and the Catholic Church. These four universities suffer the least from 'massification'. The biggest universities in Spain are the Complutense in Madrid, Barcelona Central, Santiago de Compostela and Valencia. In all of them there is a space crisis, with Salamanca's half a square metre per student not untypical. The top universities, in terms of research expertise, are Complutense and Barcelona Central but, overall, the universities suffer from a lack of teaching staff with expertise in business and management studies, and in technology.

Spain also has its **National University for Distance learning** (UNED) – the equivalent of the United Kingdom's Open University – which was inaugurated in 1972 but has been consistently underfunded ever since so that numbers have scarcely increased beyond the 60,000 students registered in 1980–1.

Government plans for universities

In 1989 the Spanish government, looking beyond 1992, was planning a further overhaul of the university system. The main components of the new plan are as follows:

- The criteria of productivity is to be applied in determining the salaries of university lecturers, with top rates for academic high-fliers,
- Students, for the first time in Spain, will be able to study at any university, rather than at the nearest,
- A ranking list of universities is to be drawn up to encourage more competition in the sector,
- New, more relevant, and shorter degree courses are to be phased in, e.g. eighty new (mostly three-year) degrees were introduced in 1989–90.
- Spain's first non-religious private university is to be established, specializing in Law and Economics (the **Escuela Libre de Derecho y Economía**),
- New university campuses are to be founded in Madrid and Barcelona,
- The Ministry of Education is to create a new system of university grants. Until now grants have been few and difficult to obtain.

Opposition from staff trade unions to some of these measures is not expected to prevent full implementation from a government recently awarded a third term.

New private universities

A Bill presented in the Spanish parliament in the spring of 1990, has facilitated the creation of new private universities in Spain and will decide who runs them, with the intention that they should commence operations in 1991. Four projects are currently being examined, with two in Madrid, and one each in Barcelona and Valencia. The Catholic Church, owners of private schools, and a number of major companies are all expressing interest in the idea.

While the Private University of Madrid, run by private school proprietors, is expected to be first to commence operations, with 12,000 students on two campuses, the most innovative aspect of the venture is the interest being shown by Spanish companies. The banks BNP and Hispanoamericano, Repsol (the petrol giant), and El Aguila (brewers) all want to be involved, but perhaps the most unusual application is that of the oil company Petromed which is pursuing its interest in a private university jointly with Mercedes-Benz under the aegis of the EC ERASMUS initiative.

While university student numbers have grown in recent years, so also have pupils studying vocational training under the FP banner. Numbers have doubled between 1975 and 1985. In the same decade, the enrolment rate in education overall increased by two-thirds while the number of students in higher education as a share of the total population rose by 50 per cent.

A growing mismatch between employer demand and supply of labour at all levels has been increasingly noticeable in the 1980s. Industry has

Table 5.16   *Spanish education: input and output indicators*

	1975	1985
Pre-university education		
Number of pupils (thousands)	7,517	8,696
State schools	4,340	5,593
Pre-primary	920	1,127
Compulsory	5,473	5,594
Post-Compulsory (FP)	305	737
Post-Compulsory (General)	818	1,238
Numbers of teachers in state schools (thousands)	156	271
Higher education		
Students (thousands)	557	822

Source: OECD

experienced longer delays in filling vacancies. A recent survey by the Ministry of Labour demonstrated that **Formación Profesional** is not providing the skills and qualifications which firms need. Hence, with government support, new Professional Training Programmes have been initiated in order to improve the quality of labour supply, especially in sectors with a skilled labour shortage.

Management training

The Ministry of Labour estimates that Spanish firms require a minimum of 30,000 executives per year trained in business and management studies. Spanish business schools in fact are only producing 11,000 per year and not all of these are trained to a sufficiently high level.

The first MBAs appeared in Spanish business schools in the mid-1960s and the schools themselves are flourishing, but the failure to apply strict criteria on the qualifications awarded has meant that any educational institution can appropriate the title 'Masters' and apply it to virtually any course of any standard or duration. Thus, many business schools and even the in-house training agencies of the Cajas de ahorros have been attaching the 'Masters' label to courses on an indiscriminate and arbitrary basis. Another problem is that in Spain, unlike the USA for example, no ranking list of business schools is produced.

Despite the problems, demand in the marketplace is very high indeed, with Spain's top business school **IESI**, in Navarra (**Instituto de Estudios Superiores de Empresa**), attracting 2000 applications for its 200 MBA places in 1988–9, and with even the less prestigious schools receiving at least four or five applications per place. One of Spain's leading business magazines, *España Económica*, suggested in November 1989 that the market could probably absorb ten times the number of places currently available.

By general consent, the top business schools in Spain, of a standard comparable with other EC countries are IESI, **ESADE** in Barcelona (**Escuela Superior de Administración y Dirección de Empresas**), and the **Instituto de Empresas** in Madrid. New schools are opening up though to supply market demand, e.g. the new Madrid Business School. IESI estimates that each student graduating with a qualification receives an average of three job offers, while other schools claim this can rise to eight per student. The business schools of Madrid and Barcelona account for about 80 per cent of student intake amid ferocious competition for the best students.

An indication of rising standards and the growing esteem in which the top Spanish business schools are held is the increase in US, Canadian and

European students on MBA courses in Spain. The US magazine, *Fortune*, in its recent ranking of the top five business schools in Europe put IESI (which incidentally introduced the oldest MBA in Europe, in 1964, in conjunction with Harvard) in fifth place behind INSEAD (Fontainebleau), London Business School, IMEDE (Lausanne) and IMI (Geneva). IESI's ranking is undoubtedly due to its rigorous training programme for would-be lecturers who spend three or four years in a top US school such as Harvard before returning to lecture in Spain.

Research and development

In February 1988, the government approved a National Plan for Scientific Research and Technological Development. The Plan, which came into operation in the Autumn of 1988, aims to raise the scientific and technological base, especially in terms of research, in higher education and in companies. The base, historically, has been very low, with research grants, which were first awarded in 1968, having little or no relevance to the world of business.

For many years R & D has constituted only about 0.4 per cent of GDP, although this level has doubled in the second half of the 1980s, increasing from 0.48 per cent GDP in 1984 to 0.85 per cent GDP in 1989 (equivalent to 300,000 million pesetas). The Plan aims to raise the level further to 1.2 per cent GDP by 1992, a substantial increase, although this must be set against the 3 per cent GDP devoted to R & D in West Germany (see page 14).

A prime aim of the Plan is to train greater numbers of personnel up to Masters' and Doctorate level in order better to face the challenge of 1992. A massive investment in training in priority areas includes the provision of sending more Spaniards abroad for training. Over 20 per cent of the National Plan's budget is allocated to the training of researchers in a bid to elevate the total of 25,000 trained researchers estimated to be working currently in Spain.

Considerable progress has already been made under the auspices of the Plan. Thus, the number of research grants awarded has gone up from 3002 in 1986 to 5210 in 1988, an annual increase of 32 per cent. In 1988 7000 scientists were receiving training and this figure rose to 9000 in 1989, as the government improved its funding by 60 per cent over the previous year. In addition, a number of regional governments are now begining to budget for research grants. This has helped to raise the international profile of Spanish researchers, as evidenced by the *Science Citation Index* which recorded a 13 per cent growth in Spanish publications in the world's top scientific journals between 1987 and 1988. Initial results are therefore encouraging, but the 1988 experience also indicated that demand for research grants to study abroad in certain vital areas is woefully inferior to the country's requirements. Less than twenty applications apiece were received in the areas of agrarian research, marine research, and information technology, while some areas such as robotics attracted no applicants at all.

The National Plan also aspires to establishing some kind of research base in industry, which has hitherto virtually ignored R & D. The Plan envisages the establishment of structures to improve the integration of scientific research with technological knowhow and industrial experience, i.e. the Plan proposes to link the universities, government research councils and Spanish companies. A crucial element in this is the creation of a national network, the **Office for Relay of Research Results** (OTRI), which will coordinate research projects and findings in all of Spain's universities and will eventually access these to Spanish industry. The Plan also seeks to boost the participation of Spanish firms and universities in the various EC programmes such as EUREKA.

Javier Solana, the Education Minister, also announced in November 1989 that an additional 11,000 million pesetas is to be spent on scholarships and funding for training research students. This is an enormous boost to the Ministry's recent campaign to increase the number and quality of researchers and scientists. In 1982, the Ministry was spending just 1,000 million pesetas on funding research training; in 1987 the figure had only risen to 3,150 million pesetas.

Business and the environment

The business culture in Spain is only just beginning to be aware of environmental issues, which are relatively new on the political and business agenda and which occupy the nation's attention far less than in most other EC countries. Thus, while ecology groups and 'green' parties have emerged in Spain in the 1980s, they have not hitherto achieved the public profile or the electoral support seen elsewhere. In the general election of October 1989, the environment was one of the lesser campaign issues and only one party, the opposition Popular Party, advocated the creation of a government Ministry of the Environment to bring Spain in line with her European partners.

The rapid changes of the past thirty years, however, have created in Spain a massive environmental problem, the scale of which Spaniards are finally appreciating when, for instance, the air pollution in towns like Madrid makes it virtually impossible to breathe on occasions or when the polluted nature of Spain's Mediterranean beaches and coastal towns attracts the unwelcome attention of the foreign media (as happened in the summer of 1989 when the resort of Salou, south of Barcelona, was condemned by the British popular press). The results of an industrialization process which brought a massive exodus from the countryside to the towns in the 1960s, and the uncontrolled development of manufacturing industry, were accompanied by all the depredations which mass tourism and its service industries brought to Spain's coastlines. The 1980s perceived the problem; the 1990s must address it.

Responsibility for the environment

Central government promulgates environmental legislation while the regions may pass supplementary regulations. Only in 1972 did Spain approve its first legislation on the environment and establish a public body to coordinate environmental policy, known as the **Comisión Interministerial del Medio Ambiente** (Inter-ministerial Committee for the Environment), responsible to the **Ministerio de Obras Públicas y Urbanismo** (Ministry for Public Works and Town-planning). CIMA's decisions, however, are not legally binding and its limited scope prevents it from achieving many objectives. Environmental issues emerge under different government ministries – Industry, Agriculture, Health, Transport, etc. – but the lack of a single government department responsible for environmental affairs is an obvious impediment to rapid address of the problem. At regional level, notably in Andalusia and Asturias, some attempts have been made to establish **Agencias de Medio Ambiente** (Environmental Agencies) but these have not so far met with conspicuous success.

Since the scale of Spain's environmental problem far outweighs the remedial measures taken hitherto, the major environmental issues which the political and the business community must face in the 1990s are summarized below. Where appropriate, the response to date of government and business is outlined.

Air pollution

1972 legislation governs the prevention, monitoring and correction of air pollution, and establishes acceptable emission levels. Special provisions were made for the worst-affected areas, mainly the areas with the highest concentration of heavy industry – Bilbao, Madrid, Avilés, Huelva, Cartagona – and the first anti-air pollution campaigns were launched with government grants. The worst offenders in terms of industrial air pollution are power stations, oil refineries, iron and steel works and cement works.

Table 5.17 *Spanish emissions of atmospheric pollutants by industry (1980)*

Sector	Particulates (1000 tonnes)	Sulphur dioxide (1000 tonnes)	Nitrogen oxides (1000 tonnes)
Power stations	341	1,610	186
Oil refineries	–	130	17
Iron and steel works	214	178	–
Cement works	268	50	11
Sulphuric acid plants	–	38	6
Paper mills	21	44	8

Source: European Commission

In the late 1980s, government and industry began to work together to counter air pollution. As well as grants and tax concessions to firms, government has also made available to firms in high pollution areas special subsidies for up to 30 per cent of the total cost of installing anti-pollution equipment. Also in 1985 the first legislation was passed to improve vehicular air pollution, when the lead content of petrol was reduced from 0.6 g/l to 0.4 g/l, in line with EC regulations.

Waste pollution

In 1985 Spain's 39 million population generated 10.6 million tons, or 265 kg per person per year, of urban solid waste. A high proportion of urban waste disposal is accounted for by uncontrolled dumping, an estimated 46.5 per cent of the total in 1985. Spain's forty composting plants make 700,000 tons of compost each year from 1.5 million tons of waste. Although it is government policy to support schemes for the recovery of raw materials from urban waste, the high cost and energy consumption of reclamation plants are becoming prohibitive. Few towns, and few industries, have equipment for selective material recovery. Despite this, government has drafted guidelines to encourage local authorities to rationalize urban waste management. More and more recycling – of glass, paper, board, etc. – is taking place yearly. In 1982 for instance only five towns in Spain had bottle banks, which recovered 837 tons of glass but, by 1986, 179 towns recovered 13,318 tons of glass.

Over 10 million tons of industrial waste are generated yearly of which 1.5 million tons is considered hazardous. Several centres for the treatment of hazardous waste have been established, notably the acid neutralization plant in the Basque region and three oil regeneration plants run by the oil company, CAMPSA. Even though 1986 legislation makes contraventions punishable by fines and banning, there are insufficient waste treatment centres to deal with industrial waste.

Water and sea pollution

A new Water Law was passed in 1986 which established a single body to manage surface and ground waters. Serious river pollution increased in the 1980s and the government responded by allocating grants to the regions to install water purification plants. Firms have also been awarded subsidies to introduce recycling plants. The proportion of the population served by water treatment plants went up from 18 per cent in 1980 to 40 per cent in 1986.

Mass tourism and its attendant industries have helped to create a major threat to Spain's 6121 km of coastline, 63 per cent of which is rocky terrain, 23 per cent sand, 8 per cent man-made and 4 per cent mud flats. 20 per cent of Spain's 3090 beaches are estimated to be in danger of disappearing from a combination of all factors including increasing urbanization along coastal areas which now accommodate 12 million of Spain's population and 65 per cent of industry. Government has sponsored schemes to clean up the coastline and monitor sea pollution. Thus, of the 190 towns on the Mediterranean coast, approximately two-thirds had sewage treatment plants by the end of 1989, with more under construction.

Forestry

Spain has more natural forest land than any other EC country (the ratio is twice as great as France and four times as great as West Germany and Italy). Concern now focuses on the gradual depletion of natural forests as farmers clear and cultivate woodland sites and on the poor condition of trees that remain. With 73.8 per cent of the territory in private hands, the government's 1984 legislation to replant land has affected only a small proportion of the total area and even this has met with criticism from ecology groups unhappy with the methods or species used.

The greatest threat to Spain's natural environment comes from forest fires and their contribution to soil erosion. The 1980s has seen a sharp increase in the incidence of forest fires which in 1985 damaged an area four times greater than the reforestation of 1984. Soil erosion now is a bigger problem in Spain than any other EC country. In 1986 alone, 64.2 per cent of Spanish land surface was affected by high or moderate levels of soil erosion.

Parks and nature reserves

Although Spain was the first EC country to introduce the concept of National Parks in 1916, little was done until 1975 to protect the huge areas of countryside which 10 million people now visit each year. In recent years the creation of 250 special nature recreation areas for picnicking, camping, bathing, etc. has been accompanied by a national campaign to elevate the status of nature studies.

Flora and fauna

1980 legislation created protected areas and game reserves for 300 threatened species and, yet, forty-three species are currently in danger of extinction due to uncontrolled hunting, urbanization, new agricultural methods, etc. These include the Spanish imperial eagle, the black vulture, osprey, brown bear and ibex. Similarly, national legislation (1984) and supplementary regional regulations have done little to protect an estimated 1277 endangered species of endemic plants.

A 1988 directive from the EC to Spain to spend 300,000 million pesetas in industry and technology to improve the environment is only one indication of the tremendous strides Spain needs to make in order to catch up with EC partners. Failure to prioritize the environment on the part of government and a virtually non-existent environmental industry does not suggest that this task is likely to be undertaken in the near future. It is to be hoped that increasing public concern and EC pressure will cause government and business to devote more attention and resources to Spain's environmental problems.

The response of business to the EC's single market

The Spanish business community looks forward to the EC's single market with guarded apprehension alongside keen anticipation. The apprehension is based upon the painful adjustments already made since the demise of Franco and entry into the EC in 1986. Accompanying the apprehension, however, is a realistic acceptance of the price Spanish industry must pay if it is to be a serious major international competitor. Investment in modern plant and machinery has been rapid, as the business community reflects the near-unanimous enthusiasm for Spain's full participation in the EC among the general population. Such enthusiasm has meant that, within the institutions of the EC, Spaniards have quickly acquired a reputation as wholehearted Europeans.

The Spanish media have appeared to be obsessed with the implications of 1992, not least because the completion of the single market coincides happily with the Barcelona Olympics, Expo 92 in Seville and the fifth centenary of Columbus' discovery of America. While there is little evidence to suggest that Spanish industry as a whole is examining its own response to 1992 with the same thoroughness, nonetheless a new breed of younger, business-school trained, European-minded executives is emerging in enough Spanish companies to encourage longer-term optimism. Symbols are potent in Spain and the new captains of industry look to the successful example of Spain's 'Lois' jeans in the 1980s where, against the odds, a Spanish product took on French and Italian fashions in one case and the jeans market in the other. In both cases, hard-and-fast rules of reinvesting were observed by a single shareholder company that put a high premium on advertising and kept growing.

Strengths

The fact that Spanish manufacturing labour costs in 1987 were just 54 per cent of West Germany's (see page 13) and that Spain's wage levels are still (after Greece and Portugal) the lowest in the EC gives Spanish business a head-start over competitors. Even though inflation rose by almost 7 per cent in 1989, unit labour costs in manufacturing were expected to rise by 4 per cent. Even with continuing trade union militancy, as long as real wage rises do not exceed productivity growth, Spanish business can hope to continue expanding in an endeavour to boost foreign trade, only 38 per cent of Spain's GDP in 1988. New planned legislation on restrictive business practices will further enhance competition, already galvanized by the lifting of import quotas and the halving of tariffs since EC accession. Spain's historical links with Latin America and her friendly relations with the Arab world are other factors which give Spanish business a distinct trading advantage over EC partners, a fact acknowledged by some foreign companies which have bought into Spain precisely to gain a foothold in markets notoriously difficult to penetrate.

No one should underestimate the positive motivational influences on the business community which the worldwide fashionableness of Spain in the past few years has generated. Spanish fashion (**diseño**) and the complex sociocultural phenomenon of the **movida** – an explosion of the plastic and fine arts combined with a youth-pop cult – have been exported successfully to other EC countries. A proliferation of fashion shows and exhibitions in the major cities of Europe (e.g. Harrod's one-month 'made in Spain' exhibition in 1988) has been accompanied by renewed enthusiasm for Spanish artists. In 1988, for instance, plays by Lorca were staged to great acclaim in Paris and London; Italy feted some of Spain's best-known writers; and the film director, Pedro Almodóvar, became a cult figure. *Newsweek's* issue of 23 May 1988, a special devoted to Spain, captured the mood succinctly with its front cover picture of Felipe González and a caption which read: 'Spain. Racing into the Future. Europe's Tortoise turns into a Hare.'

Some commentators believe that the conglomeration of events in 1992 – the Olympics, Expo 92, Madrid's stint as cultural centre of Europe etc. – has already helped to forge a unity of national purpose in Spain as the country fights to meet a deadline of the kind which Spaniards, well-known for their improvisation rather than their planning, excel at fulfilling. Sponsorship on a massive scale has been secured from Spanish and foreign companies for the events of 1992. The Olympic Games have attracted Coca-Cola as their biggest sponsor, and the US Company is also sponsoring the Spanish team. Expo 92's main sponsors have been the Spanish banks – Banco de Bilbao y Vizcaya, Español Central de Créditos, Banco Hispanoamericano and the Banco Exterior de España. Even before 1992, Spain was the second most successful country in the world – behind the US – in terms of sponsorship income. Clearly, the entrepreneurial spirit is thriving and looking forward eagerly to all of the various opportunities afforded by 1992.

Weaknesses

The legacy of underinvestment, overmanning, and poor training has been outlined in previous sections as have the tremendous efforts made by the business community and by government to overcome these deficiencies. Infrastructural weakness – the roads, railways, etc. – is, as we saw, also being addressed. Spanish industry will have to wait well beyond 1992 to reap the full rewards of such labours, despite individual company successes. It remains to be seen, though, how the essential framework of a business culture founded upon a proliferation of small and medium-sized firms will withstand the growing intensity of competition from Europe (and the world's) multinationals.

The traditional weakness however of Spain's agricultural system, based upon the equally inefficient **latifundios** or large tracts of land in the South and the **minifundios** or tiny plots in the North West, continues to underlie Spanish economic growth and to undermine the efforts of the business community. Spanish agricultural products are moving gradually towards parity of price with other EC countries and although they enjoyed a competitive price advantage in 1989, this will have disappeared by 1992. Under the terms of Spain's EC accession, restrictions will continue until the end of 1995 on the export of certain products, including oils, fruit and vegetables, which the Spaniards produce too cheaply for the comfort of the French and Italians. Spain would like to see these restrictions removed at the end of 1992.

In November 1988, the European Commission sanctioned a new system of aid to small farmers in Spain which parallels existent schemes in other countries and will benefit half a million Spanish farmers to the tune of 20,000 million pesetas yearly up to 1992. The aid, half funded by the EC and half by central government, is intended to put Spanish agriculture on a more competitive basis with its Northern neighbours. New machinery and modernization to reduce the costs of harvesting will mostly go to farmers under the age of thirty-five in an endeavour to rejuvenate the agrarian workforce. The new subsidies, strictly awarded on the investment potential of small farmholdings, supplement youth programmes previously initiated by the government to assist 30,000 young farmers. If the reforms are successful, Spain will become more efficient in its agriculture and the subsidizing of surplus produce by the EC – which in 1988 allocated 200,000 million pesetas for Spain's unproductive surpluses – will gradually be phased out.

Opportunities

Many Spanish businesses are opting for joint ventures with counterparts in other EC countries as a means of seizing the opportunities afforded by the single market. Spain's fourth biggest bank, the Banco de Santander, is a pioneer in this field by linking in 1989 with the Royal Bank of Scotland. The Banco de Santander's youthful chief executive, Juan Inciarte, typifies the new entrepreneurial breed of Spanish executive who dismisses any suggestion of Spanish inferiority, by asserting in July 1989 that: 'In Spain, we have a combination of people and products second to none. That gives us a competitive advantage that foreigners cannot provide easily.'

The tie-up between the two banks justifies the Spanish bank's belief that there are other ways of growing apart from takeovers and that flexibility is needed to cope with the wide variations between what *pace* 1992 are still separate and hugely different markets. The link between Banco de Santander and the Royal Bank of Scotland will elbow them into each other's home markets at a fraction of the cost of building up a branch network from scratch. Juan Inciarte insists that the move towards a single financial services market is not going to happen overnight adding that: 'Many corporate institutions are looking at Europe as a single country, but if a bank does not have the ability to differentiate Scotland from Italy, it will lose in the battle for the future.' The most profitable area for collaboration looks like being between Banco de Santander's merchant bank and the Royal Bank's subsidiary, Charterhouse. The Spanish bank is keen to import expertise in financial engineering into a country where techniques such as leveraged buyouts are still in their infancy.

Other Spanish companies are looking at networking arrangements such as the Banco Bilbao-Vizcaya which is joining a fee-sharing network of banks across Europe that includes Bayerische Vereinsbank in West Germany, Instituto Bancario San Paolo di Torino in Italy and the Hambros group in the UK.

Spain's textile industry is another example of an industry which is now starting to look at joint ventures with foreign firms to gain access into new markets. With 315,000 legal workers and tens of thousands of undeclared ones, the textile industry is a major employer and the pillar of the economy of Catalonia. Better equipped and capitalized than ever before after a state-aided investment blitz from 1982–6, productivity has increased by 40 per cent since 1982. The recent slump in European textiles and clothing generally, plus undercutting by cheap imports, however, put the industry into deficit in 1987 and 1988. Spain's textile industry, with low wages and high levels of skill and design but, with poor marketing abroad hitherto, exemplifies the kind of business which ought to excel in the single market context. An appreciation of the problems and the application of new marketing techniques should place this industry in an excellent position to expand in the 1990s.

The Spanish IT industry is the fastest-growing in the world, at 1.5 per cent GDP in 1988, and 23 per cent growth in 1989. Predictions are that the industry will grow at four times the rate of the economy overall up to 1992 but of the 1988 sales of 758,439 million pesetas only 11 per cent is accounted for by exports, suggesting again that potential for growth overseas is enormous. The single market represents an outstanding opportunity for IT, textiles, the banks and many other business sectors to implant themselves firmly in foreign markets. Early indications are that the Spanish business community is gearing itself up to do exactly that.

Threats

In an important sense, 1992 merely means 'more of the same' to Spanish industry. In other words, more imports from abroad at increasingly competitive prices and more interest from foreign firms in buying into or buying out Spanish firms.

The market for electrical household goods best exemplifies the problem. Already in the years since EC entry, Spain has experienced an invasion of imported goods – Italian washing machines, West German televisions,

French refrigerators and Dutch hi-fi equipment. The gradual reduction of tariff barriers and import taxes since 1986 is set to continue with a further 12.5 per cent reduction on 1 January 1990, followed by 12.5 per cent in 1991, 12.5 per cent in 1992 and a final 10 per cent in 1993. Any product carrying a 100 pesetas tariff before 1986 paid only 35 pesetas in 1989 and will pay nothing in 1993.

Imported cars now represent Spain's biggest consumer goods import and, in the first six months of 1989, imported car sales amounted to 233,800 million pesetas, while Spanish sales abroad, still ahead but with the gap narrowing, totalled 399,400 million pesetas. One in three vehicles now on Spanish roads is of foreign manufacture.

The retail chain-store giant El Corte Inglés, in 1989, signed an agreement with an Italian producer of electrical goods to supply its stores. Previously El Corte Inglés had always used Spanish manufacturers. The majority of Spain's supermarkets have foreign capital behind them, with French interests predominant, and with the gradual removal of tariff barriers, are retailing more imported goods.

Spain's traditionally strong electrical sector illustrates the threat to Spanish ownership of companies. 1000 companies make up the sector, with 70 per cent privately-owned and 30 per cent in state hands. Twenty-one firms, however, produce 98 per cent of the total, in which 1.5 million small shareholders have a stake. The market is vulnerable to rationalization and foreign intervention. The West German company RWE was negotiating in 1989 with Spain's leading company in the sector, Unión Fenosa, to acquire 5 per cent of the home firm's shareholding, with the right to buy another 5 per cent on the stock market. The intention is to move up to a 20 per cent shareholding by 1990. Although the two companies have a history of collaboration which goes back eighteen years, the Ministry of Industry has so far vetoed RWE's plans, demonstrating government fears of the foreign threat to its industrial base. Since foreign capital apparently believes that Spanish firms in the electrical sector are quoted on the stock market at only half their real value, the question arises as to how long the government can hold off foreign interest in vulnerable sectors of the economy. Foreign investment in Spain has increased 600 per cent since 1982 and 1992 will only see an acceleration of the trend.

Strategies

The Spanish business community is understandably wary about the implications of the single market and yet has been prepared to undertake the necessary readjustments, often painful, of capital modernization and manpower training which full European integration involves.

A new breed of business executives genuinely aspires to establish Spanish business in European markets, while defending domestic interests against foreign incursions. A 1989 study published by the business consultants SRU gives hope that the aspiration can become a reality. According to the study, the ideal executive to lead companies into the 1992 single European market will be from a small country, multilingual, of flexible mind and social brilliance, will come from a multicultural family, will be a male graduate of a business school, and will almost certainly not be British.

This identikit picture could describe the new executive breed in Spain, usually from the wealthy classes, often with an MBA from a US university. José Barroso, twenty-eight-year-old head of the multimillion peseta enterprise, Don Algodón, with over 100 fashion shops in Spain, fits the picture exactly. Barroso, from a comfortable upper middle class Madrid family, borrowed £350 from a bank when he was seventeen years old, started selling T-shirts to schoolfriends, and, at twenty, travelled to Italy to bid successfully for the Benetton franchise in Spain. In 1989, with plans to extend the Don Algodón operation across Europe, Barroso's company – with the successful example of Lois jeans to follow – seems certain to be one of the first of a whole succession of Spanish companies to take full advantage of the opportunities afforded by the single market.

References and suggestions for further reading

Anuario El País, published yearly, Madrid: Altamira.
Cambio 16, published weekly, Madrid.
Donaghy, P. J. and Newton, M. T. (1987), *Spain: A Guide to Political and Economic Institutions*, Cambridge: CUP.
Economist Surveys on Spain.
European Commission Statistics.
European Information Development (1983), *Problems of Enlargement – Taking stock and proposals*, London.
Gillespie, R. (1989), *The Spanish Socialist Party*, Oxford: Clarendon Press.
Gilmour, D. (1985), *The Transformation of Spain*, London: Quartet.
Graham, R. (1984), *Spain. Change of a Nation*, London: Michael Joseph.
Harrison, J. (1978), *An Economic History of Modern Spain*, Manchester: Manchester University Press.
Hooper, J. (1986), *The Spaniards*, London: Penguin.
OECD Economic Surveys, Spain, Paris, 1989.
OECD Statistics, OECD Publications, Paris.
Preston, P. (1986), *The Triumph of Democracy in Spain*, London: Methuen.
Preston, P. and Smith, D. (1984), *Spain, the EEC and NATO*, London: RKP.

Sagardoy Bengoechea, J. A. and León Blanco, D. (1982), *El Poder Sindical en España*, Barcelona: Planeta.

Sampedro, J. L. and Payno, J. A. (1983), *The Enlargement of the European Comunity – Case Studies of Greece, Portugal and Spain*, London: Macmillan.

Shlaim, A. and Yannopoulous, G. N. (eds) (1976), *The EEC and the Mediterranean Countries*, Cambridge: CUP.

6 The business culture in the Netherlands

Peter King

Introduction

Business culture in the Netherlands, more even than in Scandinavia, has pre-eminently the advantage of a basic education in three or more foreign languages. The business personnel's ready access to other European languages not only facilitates communication, but also means that technical literature in other languages is immediately available to them in their training and research. The Dutch, it is often said, are always thinking across frontiers. Dutch business culture is very definitely export-minded, and in their market resourcefulness they are willing to go abroad, work abroad and engage in novel forms of trade and technical experimentation.

Moreover, enforced inactivity during the Occupation in the Second World War provided an opportunity for visionary planning for peacetime, and the loss of 30 per cent of its capital assets and 96 per cent of its stocks meant that, like West Germany, it could replace with modern equipment and introduce automation rather earlier than the United Kingdom.

Since the 1960s rationalization has advanced rapidly, and a consequent rise in wage costs led to an intensification in capitalization at a rate comparable with West Germany's and the United Kingdom's, but ten years ahead of West Germany and fifteen years ahead of the United Kingdom in 1960. It is the success of the resultant growth in productivity that is a major factor in the present high-unemployment situation in the Netherlands.

Another common post-industrial development is cartel formation. This is almost unrestricted in the Netherlands, so that there are about 600 registered cartels, the majority of which are price cartels.

Although it was American models that were followed in the rationalization of industry and commerce, the Dutch still regard the West Germans as their trading partners and (like it or not, for there is still a marked love–hate relationship with that country) they admire their business efficiency. They respect knowledgeable authority, they like the idea that someone 'really knows' or 'is an expert', and they are certainly not flamboyant speculators. On the other hand, their trading and colonial traditions show through in their explicit commercial instincts, and there is in their business culture a recognition of the importance of a mix of social graces and general aptitudes in higher posts.

Despite its impressive history of trading and agriculture, the Netherlands has, since the war, become an important industrial producer. It is internationalist and anti-protectionist in outlook, which accounts for its early promotion of the Benelux Union; it is politically stable, has a well-educated workforce and a high standard of living.

Business and government

The post-war cabinets from 1945 to 1958 were dominated by the Socialist principles of Willem Drees, who had earlier been a co-author of the radical **Plan van de Arbeid** (Labour Scheme). So it was consistent with this that the first cabinet in 1945 announced that the reconstruction of the country's economy could only succeed on the basis of a social as well as an economic and financial programme. One outcome of this was the introduction in 1950 of the **Publiekrechtelijke Bedrijfsorganisatie** (PBO), (the Statutory Industrial Organization), and the **Centraal Planbureau** (CPB), (Central Planning Office), both of which still exist. The PBO ensures that every trading organization has an elected council of equal numbers of employers and employees, with a central advisory board, the **Sociaal-economische Raad** (SER) (Social and Economic Council) representing on equal terms management, shop floor and **kroonleden**, (crown appointees) i.e. independent advisers to the government. The SER took over many of the functions of an earlier **Stichting van de Arbeid** (Labour Council), at one time providing a three-cornered board to maintain a balance between wages and prices, agreed by an equal representation of kroonleden, management and labour.

The government, with its free-market policy in recent years, has withdrawn from its intervention in private business, though the SER has remained to advise the government on particular matters. The CPB provides economic forecasts, in cooperation with the **CBS** (Central Bureau of Statistics).

With the help of some Dfls 80,000 million of Marshall Aid and a remarkable discipline in wage and price restraints, the economy in the 1950s expanded very rapidly, assisted by the establishment in 1948 of the Benelux Union. It was largely to Drees's personal credit that his policies achieved a reasonable distribution of income. His own frugality was widely known by the fact that he frequently preferred the tram to his car to take him to his office!

The mainly centre-right cabinets of the 1960s and 1970s introduced budgets that increased public spending (including national insurance) from 38.7 per cent of GNP in 1960 to 70.2 per cent in 1983. This was largely due to considerable revenues from the gas (and more recently oil) discovered in 1959 at Slochteren, which in 1985 were still worth Dfls 23,100 million. But the 1973 oil crisis that increased the value of this revenue had a far greater adverse effect, raising import prices by 35 per cent and consumer prices by 10 per cent. Moreover the gas revenues had overheated the economy by boosting the GNP and allowing wage increases that compounded the recession in 1973 by making the Netherlands less competitive and hence introducing an alarming increase in unemployment.

In the 1960s growth in GNP had been sustained at about 5 per cent per annum and, because of investment in technology and concentration into larger concerns, productivity continued to rise. But the unionized workforce, no longer content with full employment alone as it had been in the 1950s, began to demand higher and higher wages in a market where labour was in such demand that foreign workers were being brought in by the thousand. The subsequent rise in nominal wage rates set up a spiral of cost inflation. At the same time, with inflation running up to 10 per cent before the oil crisis, successive centre-right cabinets (and one centre-left) launched welfare programmes introducing widows' and orphans' pensions, child allowances, supplementary benefits and disability pensions, as well as an increase in the minimum wage.

To counter this, the government under Den Uyl's premiership (1973–7) adopted a Keynsian policy of allowing a budget deficit to rise to 3.5 per cent of GNP in 1977. This, with the subsequent increase to 8 per cent of GNP under Van Agt's administration (1977–82), accounts for the serious balance of payments crisis which Lubbers as prime minister inherited in 1982. As Den Uyl's finance minister Lubbers had already introduced the **Wet op de Investeringsregeling** (WIR), (Investment Act), a truly labyrinthine piece of legislation intended to replace existing subsidies by selective incentives for particular (regional, energy-saving, milieu-friendly, etc.) investments. It was abandoned in 1988 and replaced by reductions in employers' insurance contributions and in corporation tax.

This was in keeping with the policies of Lubbers' first (centre-right) cabinet, 1982–6, soon popularly recognized as the 'no-nonsense-cabinet', with a VVD (Volkspartij voor Vrijheid en Democratie – free-market, conservative) minister of economic affairs and CDA (Christian Democratic Appeal, a fusion of the Protestant and Catholic parties) in the posts of Finance and Social Services. His three-point programme of deregulation and privatization was aimed at restoring investment and economic growth, reducing unemployment, redistributing labour, and maintaining price levels. To achieve this, drastic steps were needed to cut back on government spending and lower the budget deficit by reducing the wage base and employment in the public services sector. A reduction of 4.4 per cent in the former and cutbacks of some 75,000 jobs in the latter achieved a decrease in the deficit of almost Dfl 29,000 million by 1986.

The election in 1986 showed the general approval of Lubbers' deflationary policy by giving his CDA party nine additional seats (to a total of fifty-four out of 150 members). The new government's policy statement began: 'The situation facing the new cabinet differs considerably from the crisis situation confronting the previous cabinet in 1982. Then there was an almost hopeless unemployment situation rising by over 10,000 per month. . . The financial deficit was approaching 11 per cent of the national income: the purchasing power of workers and recipients of social benefits plunged as a result of constantly rising taxes and national insurance contributions.'

However, an unemployment rate of 14 per cent gave no grounds for relaxation. The new programme envisaged a reduction to half a million unemployed by 1990, a further cut in the financial deficit to 5.25 per cent of GNP by 1990 with a stabilization of public expenditure. Further measures aimed at reducing the gap between gross wage costs and net income and continued promotion of (re)training, the redistribution of labour, and part-time working. The similarities with Thatcherism are obvious.

The new cabinet had scarcely held its first meeting when disaster struck. Oil prices slumped. As a consequence Ruding, the finance minister, announced that natural gas revenues would drop by at least Dfls 12,000 million, i.e. 3 per cent of GNP. To meet a shortfall in total income of about 8 per cent, Ruding budgeted to save a further Dfl 5,500 million on public expenditure and to raise an additional Dfl 7,000 million from income and corporation taxes, withdrawing depreciation and wealth tax relief, and raising VAT and the duty on oil products.

The stock market crash in 1987 proved less serious than expected. 1988 indeed showed an encouraging improvement in production (3.5 per cent) and exports rose by 8 per cent (both excluding gas and oil). Unemployment, however, remained persistently indifferent to all the reforms. In 1987 and 1988 unemployment stagnated at around 685,000. A further complication was the shortage in 1988 of highly-qualified personnel in, for instance, financial management and information technology. The Social and Economic Council and the Central Planning Office advised a reduction of 15 per cent in the minimum wage, estimated to reduce the unemployment of unskilled workers by 150,000 and produce savings of Dfl 2,000 million in unemployment benefit. The Socialist and CDA parties in Parliament and the trade unions successfully resisted repeated efforts of the government to act on this advice.

Otherwise Ruding's measures were entirely successful. The budget deficit responded as planned, and in 1988 income tax was reduced, followed in 1989 by a reduction in VAT. The **Investment Act** (WIR) was also modified to cut employers' national insurance contributions and corporation tax. A more important change is envisaged in a radical reform of the taxation system. If the policy of the last government is followed after the September 1989 elections – Lubbers' second government fell in June 1989 when the VVD refused to support his proposal to cut tax relief on travelling to and from work – the present nine taxation rates will be reduced to three, at 35, 50 and 60 per cent, with a uniform base-line for direct taxation and national insurance contributions.

Nevertheless, the outward signs of prosperity in the Netherlands conceal the fact that the austerity measures of the Lubbers government's terms of office have, despite their successes, failed to master the two major problems: a huge budget deficit and high unemployment. The national debt is running at 80 per cent of GNP, unemployment has been at 14 per cent or more throughout the 1980s, and in spite of Dfl 900 million allocated to job-training schemes in the public sector, the original goal of reducing unemployment by 200,000 has been put back from 1990 to 1992. The CPB forecasts 585,000 jobless in 1989, though this was probably optimistic, and their forecast of wage increases of 2.25 per cent was threatened by union warnings of demands for 5 per cent. This must be set against the CPB's assumption of a 2 per cent growth in GNP, and a central government financing deficit of Dfl 23.5 billion, 5 per cent of GNP. The CBS predicted a growth of 2 per cent in 1989 (3 per cent in 1988), though the OECD was less sanguine about Dutch recovery, assuming a growth of 1.75 per cent.

Taxation (at 72 per cent in the top range) and national insurance premiums are among the highest in the world and will remain so even if and when taxation is restructured. Government receipts take a higher percentage of GDP than any country outside Scandinavia.

The largest opposition party, the **Partij van de Arbeid** (PvdA) (Socialist) accuses the government of underinvesting in the country's infrastructure, (and it was a related issue that brought Lubbers' second cabinet down). Despite the vast budget deficit, the (recent) government earmarked Dfls 400 million for infrastructural improvements from 1990. The PvdA also contests the cut in VAT from 20 per cent to 18.5 per cent and the reduction in corporation tax from 42 per cent to 35 per cent. It also deplores the widening gap in income distribution (echoes of Westminster!) and calls for an end to the government's eight-year freeze on minimum wage and unemployment benefit levels. The IMF will doubtlessly be following the results of the recent elections in Holland with interest!

The considerable fluctuations in the economy can be seen from the figures in Table 6.1.

Table 6.1   *Percentage changes, volume (1980 prices)*

	1983	1984	1985	1986	1987	1988
Private consumption	0.4	− 0.6	2.0	3.0	1.25	1.5
Government consumption	1.4	− 1.6	0.7	0.5	− 2.75	0.25
Gross fixed capital formation	0.5	4.4	2.5	3.75	2.25	5.25
Final domestic demand	0.6	0.2	1.8	2.75	2.25	2.0
Change in stockbuilding*	0.1	0.7	0.7	− 0.25	0.0	0.25
Total domestic demand	0.6	0.9	2.5	2.5	1.0	2.25
Exports of goods and services	3.6	7.2	4.9	1.25	2.0	7.0
Imports of goods and services	3.3	5.9	6.0	2.75	2.5	6.5
Change in foreign balance*	0.2	0.9	− 0.4	− 0.75	− 0.25	0.5
GDP at market prices	0.9	1.8	2.0	1.5	0.75	1.0
GDP implicit price deflator	1.7	2.7	2.2	1.25	− 0.25	2.75
Memorandum items						
Consumer prices	2.9	2.6	2.3	− 0.25	0.5	0.75
Industrial production	0.5	6.2	2.0	2.75	2.25	2.75
Unemployment rate	15.0	15.4	14.4	14.0	14.25	12.5
Current balance ($ billion)	3.7	4.8	5.9	8.5	7.5	4.25

* As a percentage of GDP in the previous period.
Source: OECD

Business and the economy

Government departments rely heavily on medium and long-term planning forecasts. This means that econometrics is a serious business in financial planning, and the primary function of the CPB is to provide the government with a macroeconomic forecast in September each year, at the time of the budget.

The economy of the Netherlands has many similarities with that of the United Kingdom. Both countries depend largely on their trade – with their colonies before the war and with Europe since, and both have industries that process raw materials into finished and semi-finished goods. Like the United Kingdom, the Netherlands is an important producer of gas and oil, though revenue from these sources is now declining because earlier revenues were boosted by substantial exports which have seriously depleted the supply.

In the 1960s and up to the middle of the 1970s the economy expanded more rapidly than the other major industrialized countries. In general, however, the economic performance in the Netherlands since 1965 bears most similarity with West Germany's. The annual shifts in GDP are not dissimilar in both countries, the value of the Dfl (since 1971) has risen at about the same rate as the DM, and inflation rates settled down from their higher level in 1980 to the same as West Germany's in 1985 (2.6 per cent) achieving some deflation (−0.7) in 1987 against West Germany's 0.3 per cent (see also page 21). The economies of the two countries are closely related by more than their membership of the EMS since they are traditionally trading partners exchanging some 30 per cent of their output.

Real GDP growth increased from 1.5 per cent in 1987 to 2.75 per cent in 1988. With moderate wage increases and lower import prices, inflation 'was virtually the lowest in the OECD area'. There was an external trade surplus increase from Dfl 6 billion in 1987 to Dfl 10.5 billion (2.25 per cent of GDP) in 1988. Factory wages, which increased in the United Kingdom by 8.4 per cent in 1988, increased in the Netherlands by 1.3 per cent. Wholesale price increases of 5.2 per cent in the six months to March 1989 in the United Kingdom compare with an increase of 1.8 per cent in the Netherlands, with consumer price increases of 3.6 per cent in the same period comparing with a decrease in the Netherlands of 0.2 per cent. Unit labour costs were 7.75 per cent up in the United Kingdom in 1988 and down 0.75 per cent in the Netherlands. On the other hand, at the end of 1988 the index of West German industrial production stood at 109.2 (1985 = 100) and United Kingdom production at 111.7, whereas the Dutch achievement was only 102.8 (seasonally adjusted).

The striking differences between the Netherlands and West Germany, as we should expect from previous comments, are in government spending, with the Dutch state spending some 14 per cent more of its GNP than the West Germans in the peak year, 1983, and in 1986 still spending 59.1 per cent as against 46.6 per cent of GNP in West Germany. This inevitably results in higher taxation and social security payments in the Netherlands, and it may also account for the far higher rate of unemployment – in 1986 12.5 per cent as against 9 per cent in West Germany, and now (1990) running at 14 per cent with only a modest reduction to 13.8 per cent forecast (see also page 29).

With its unparalleled advantages of port facilities and an extensive rail, road, pipeline and waterway infrastructure over a flat terrain (not to mention a highly-integrated and efficient airport at Schiphol) transport makes a relatively important contribution to the tertiary sector, which is a major factor in the Dutch economy, accounting for about 46 per cent of net domestic product at factor cost. Industry, including manufacturing, construction and the energy industries accounts for 35 per cent. Agriculture, forestry and fishing account for just 4.5 per cent and the government sector claims the remainder. About the same number are employed in trade, catering, hotels and transport as are employed in industry and construction.

Services

With the vast increase in population mobility and the fact that Holland offers a modern hotel network and an attractive coastline to tourists (who know that they will hear their own (West-European) language spoken almost universally), the hotel, catering and transport sectors maintain a high employment rate. Rotterdam, handling twice as much cargo as New York and more than Antwerp, Hamburg, Le Havre and London combined, has over 300 shipping lines offering scheduled freight services to well over 1000 ports.

Schiphol, Amsterdam's airport, has sixty airlines with scheduled services to 180 cities in seventy-five countries and a freight centre handling half a million tons of goods each year. The Rhine has an inland fleet of 6000 vessels with a carrying capacity of 5 million tons. A highly-developed road network carries over 40 per cent of the goods crossing European frontiers.

An extremely reliable public transport network brings most towns to within 1½ hour's travelling time of each other, but the ubiquitous **snelweg** (motorway) entices the motorist away from the railways, producing notorious congestions at major intersections even far outside the conurbations. Without the relief provided by 4350 miles of waterways and efficient freight distribution by rail, the density of 1126 people to the square mile would throw up almost insuperable problems.

Industry

Manufacturing industry (excluding construction and public works), with some 27,000 companies. accounts for 27 per cent of net domestic product, and employs 29 per cent of the total labour in the economy. Business output rose by 2.75 per cent in 1986, although gas and oil actually declined. Its rate of growth fell to 1.5 per cent in 1986 due to shorter working hours, but recovered to 4.25 per cent in 1988, with wage levels rising by 2.5 per cent and production prices by only 0.5 per cent, so that the labour share of business income was down to 81 per cent. The league table of turnover is headed by the food, beverage and tobacco sector (dominated by Heineken's brewery and a tobacco consortium controlling 90 per cent of the market), followed by the petroleum and chemical industries, centred in the extensive refinery and storage complexes at Europoort, (with a turnover of more than Dfl 10 billion) and electrical and mechanical engineering, printing, publishing and allied industries, metal products, basic metal industries, transport equipment, building materials (including earthenware, glass and glass products), and paper and paper products in descending order in the Dfl 2–10 billion range. Textiles, leather goods, rubber and plastics and wood products continue to be minor contributors, despite government attempts to stimulate growth in regional development areas (the North and East).

In 1982, however, the government transferred its programme of subsidies from the weaker sectors (notably shipbuilding) to high-technology and innovative ventures, though this new **WIR** (Investment Act) has since been abandoned. It remains to be seen whether the proposed tax reforms will do more to revitalize industry than the complex system of allowances and subsidies ever did in the past, and the reduction in 1986 of the corporation tax from 48 per cent to 43 per cent, together with the lower cost of energy, will certainly compensate for the loss of Dfl 1.8 billion in subsidies.

Dutch industry is dominated by the four multinationals – Philips, Unilever, Royal Dutch Shell and Akzo, of which Unilever is 50 per cent British owned and Shell 40 per cent. In 1980 about half of the industrial labour force was employed by these and other multinationals, 30 per cent of them in Dutch-owned concerns and 20 per cent in foreign-based firms. While the considerable growth in exports (from 32 per cent of GNP in 1950 to 51 per cent in 1986) is largely attributable to the activities of the largest companies, they must also be held responsible for the dramatic decline in internal investment. The 1970s and 1980s saw a steady increase in the flow of capital abroad: an increase of Dfl 16,500 million in investment abroad between 1974 and 1984 and in the same period a decrease of Dfl 9,000 million in direct investment in the home industry – a net capital outflow of Dfl 25,000 million. So that whereas up to 1973 investments in the Netherlands from abroad roughly equalled Dutch investments abroad, the adverse ratio since then has been at least two to one. A university economist's report on this export of capital concludes: 'If we then compare domestic and foreign investment in the expansion of Dutch firms over an extended period, we discover a sorry development for domestic employment. Whereas expansion investment abroad between 1969 and 1971 only represented 16 per cent of expansion investment at home, in the period 1980 to 1983 that increased to 57 per cent. In other words there has been a landslide affecting the geographical location where Dutch concerns decided to expand.'

More than half of these investments were in EC countries, and there was also a strong flow of capital to the USA. Indeed, for some years the Netherlands was a leading foreign investor in the United States. Apart from the environmental attraction of such investment (labour supply and cost, available markets, raw materials, infrastructure etc.), tax havens are particularly seductive for businesses paying high corporation taxes. It is estimated that of the 114 largest Dutch concerns, no less than seventy-six have a finance company in one or more tax havens. The Dutch Antilles alone list fifty such offices belonging to Dutch multinationals.

The business culture of the Netherlands also has a good track record in attracting foreign investment. The USA, for instance, has invested in the Netherlands twice the average investment in Europe as a whole. This is in no small measure due to the activities of the **Commissariaat voor de Buitenlandse Investeringen** (CBIN), (Commissariat for Foreign Investment), a department of the Ministry of Economic Affairs. It was this commissariat that took immediate advantage of the relaxation in the Taiwan law on foreign investment, attracting three Taiwan firms to the Netherlands in 1987.

Between 1979 and 1984 the turnover of foreign businesses in the Netherlands increased from Dfl 80,410 million to Dfl 125,170 million. The leading sectors for this investment are foodstuffs, chemicals and electrical engineering. More recently mergers and share-swopping deals have increased with 1992 in mind. Instances of this are the Leyland-DAF merger in 1987 and the share swop in 1988 between the Pearson publishing, banking and industrial group and the Elsevier publishing house.

Since the 1960s some 2 per cent of GNP has been spent annually on research, most of it generated by industry, and in particular by the largest concerns, the four leaders and DSM (Dutch State Mines) accounting for two thirds of R & D expenditure. The rationalization of the last three decades has often followed Taylor's theory of scientific management. As a result the organizational structure has tended more and more towards a production bureaucracy in which:

● The production line is 'scientifically' analysed by outside experts.
● The work is rationalized and more tightly structured, leaving less room for decision-making margins and flexibility on the factory floor.
● There is increased centralization of the control of the timing and sequence of operations.
● Routines and work units are the order of the day.
● The increased standardization and adherence to routines tend to accrue manpower which in turn increases labour costs.

Mining and energy

With the discovery in 1959 of a natural gas field in the northern province of Groningen (the largest proven reserves in Western Europe), the anthracite mines in Limburg (in the south east) were phased out, with consequent problems of re-employment of a large workforce. There is also some oil, providing about 23 million barrels a year, but this is dwarfed by the 75 million cubic metres of natural gas annually produced from a source confidently estimated at 1,900,000 million cubic metres in 1987, and expected to last for some thirty years.

In the 1960s and 1970s the industrialization of the country was greatly helped by this windfall, half of which could be exported as excessive to the country's needs. In the early 1980s gas production accounted for about 7 per cent of GDP and contributed about 15 per cent to government tax revenue. The resultant bonanza in the development of energy-intensive production lines, and heavy government investment in welfare provision and education, resulted in what has subsequently been recognized as the **Dutch disease**. The symptoms were seen in the rising value of the guilder, forced up by an increasing surplus in the balance of trade, and hence loss of competitiveness in the international market on which the Netherlands with its small home market has to depend.

Second, as a result of higher labour productivity in the high-energy industries, a spiral in demands for wage increases followed, labour-intensive industries saw their labour costs outstripping the economics of cheap energy, and redundancies ensued. Since the public services were simultaneously expanding, a resultant rise in unemployment was delayed until the more recent cutbacks in government expenditure were needed to reduce the financial deficit.

Dutch disease was further exacerbated by the decline, and sometimes slump, in oil and hence gas prices since the 1970s, and too late the economists realized that the gas revenues had been spent in private and public consumption rather than on modernizing the manufacturing base of the country. As *The Economist* recently stated, vast quantities of cheap energy 'became a mixed blessing for a trading nation'.

A policy of energy conservation now means that new industrial plants may use gas only as feedstock, not as a fuel for firing purposes. Spare storage capacity in Europoort (the area south of the Maas estuary) is being used to build up large stocks of imported coal, and there are plans for the extraction of coal gas. Two nuclear plants currently operate in the Netherlands, and nuclear capacity will only be increased if safety and environmental safeguards can be guaranteed. Energy research is directed towards providing new industrial development in specialized equipment, measurement and control systems, transport and storage and all forms of insulation, and energy investment as a percentage of total investment is expected to increase considerably.

Agriculture

The agricultural sector (with fishing) employs 268,000 person years, that is 5.7 per cent of the total workforce. The value added to the domestic product is 4.5 per cent of the total, and this indicates that Dutch farming is very intensive, highly capitalized, and employs a high degree of modern technology.

More than half of the agricultural product is exported. Dutch horticulture is internationally recognized for its marketing techniques and auctions, and the Dutch dominate the world export markets in cut flowers and potted plants. They are also the world's largest exporter of dairy products, yielding annually 12.5 million tonnes of milk, 270,000 tonnes of butter and 560 tonnes of cheese. It is the glasshouse growers' boast that orchids cut in the morning will regularly grace the tables of the New York Waldorf Astoria the same evening. The chitted seeds of new strains raised in their highly-developed research programmes are constantly improving the standards of greenhouse products in other countries.

Such intensive farming, sustained with the help of huge imports of feedstuffs and fertilizers, is not without its costs. A country partly below sea-level cannot afford water pollution, and the overproduction of manure and high levels of fertilizer application are testing the ingenuity of the biochemists in their efforts to deal with this. The problem is compounded by the contamination of so-called sweet-water rivers by industrial effluent produced outside the country, and by the constant struggle against salination, seepage under the dunes into the coastal lands below sea level.

Distribution of labour

With almost half of the total population of nearly 15 million living in the **Randstad**, the urban arc consisting of Amsterdam, Utrecht, Rotterdam, The Hague and the intermediate towns in the west of the country, it is obvious that serious congestion has to be remedied by government attempts to disperse industry to the less-populated regions in the north, east and southeast. This has been little more successful than similar initiatives in the United Kingdom, though there is not the same employment and cost-of-living differential in the Netherlands as there is between North and South in the United Kingdom (see page 168).

Where there is a marked difference is in the distribution of males and females in the labour market. The proportion of employed women in the Netherlands is smaller than in the surrounding countries, and is similar to that in Greece, Italy and Ireland. This suggests that religious tradition imposes some restraint, and this may have an influence. But it is also true that although the trend is now towards house purchase, the large majority of dwellings are still rented. This, even in a country with mortgage rates a fraction of those in the United Kingdom, means that there is less economic necessity for married women to contribute to the household budget.

In 1987, 36 per cent of women and 64 per cent of men were in employment, respectively 53 per cent and 9 per cent of whom were in part-time work. Women are also concentrated in a small range of occupations, almost entirely within the service sector. The divide between men and women in occupations is referred to as **beroepssegregatie** (job segregation), and this appeared to be lessening in the 1970s. But this did not in fact mean much of an improvement in the status of women, since it was brought about by the increased number of men in traditionally female occupations.

Women are paid less than men. The average wage of women was 24 per cent less than of men in 1984. This is not so much due to a lower rate for the same job as to the fact that many more women than men are doing work below the levels justified by their training and experience. A survey conducted in 1985 concluded: '. . . although the Act introducing equal pay for men and women has been in force for a decade, there is no mention of a reduction in the inequality between the pay of men and women in the labour market.'

Business and the law

Foreign investment is welcomed in the Netherlands, which is proud of its principle of non-discrimination. The status of a foreign-owned company is normally the same as that of a purely Dutch enterprise, apart from a few exchange control formalities. Moreover, some of the rules restricting the powers of shareholders in large enterprises have been specifically relaxed for foreign-owned firms.

Every new business entity must register with the local offices of direct taxation, indirect taxation and social security, and must be entered in the **Handelsregister** (Trade Register) of the district in which its registered address or legal domicile is located. This rule also applies to the appointment of trade agents who are authorized to conclude agreements on behalf of foreign principals. The Trade Register is kept at the municipal or regional office of the **Kamer van Koophandel** (Chamber of Commerce), of which all companies must be members and to which they pay a mandatory annual fee.

The **Hinderwet**, or Public Nuisance Act, requires that any enterprise that is likely to cause danger, damage or nuisance to its surroundings must apply for a licence from the municipal authorities. Other provisions concerning water or air pollution, as set out in the **Wet Verontreiniging Oppervlaktewateren** (Pollution of Surface Waters Act) and the **Wet Inzake de Luchtverontreiniging** (Air Pollution Act), must also be complied with if applicable.

Until 1971 the Netherlands did not have a special form of enterprise available to a small group of associates wishing to operate with limited liability, such as the GmbH in West Germany or the Sarl in France (see pages 18 and 81). The plc form had to be used by enterprises with only two or three shareholders. As a result of company law harmonization throughout the EC, the Netherlands introduced a private corporate form, the **Besloten Vennootschap met beperkte aansprakelijkheid** or BV, a private company with limited liability. Now, most small or closely held businesses, including subsidiaries of many foreign parents that do not need to raise funds from the public, are formed as BVs. The liability of shareholders (**aandeelhouders**) is limited to their capital subscriptions; the company is an independent legal entity that can enter into contracts and sue and be sued; shares can be transferred (subject to certain restrictions) without affecting the continued existence of the company, although they may not be offered for public subscription or trading.

A BV must be organized by at least two individuals, who sign the **Akte van oprichting**, (articles of association, usually referred to as **statuten**) before a public notary. A **notaris** is a public official appointed by royal decree, whose legally prescribed functions include drawing up articles of incorporation. A founder need not be a Dutch resident or citizen. As a group, the founders must pay in a minimum capital of Dfl 40,000 in cash or other assets. The public notary must submit a draft of the articles to the Minister of Justice to obtain a 'declaration of no objection' (**geen bezwaar**). Since the formalities take some time, a company is allowed to start trading on a provisional basis before the declaration geen bezwaar is obtained, but it must signify this by adding IO (**In Oprichting** – in formation) to the initials BV. Until completion of the formalities and the company's registration in the Trade Register, its directors are personally liable for its acts and obligations.

The articles, which must be in the Dutch language, set out not only the aims and objects of the company but also its internal regulations. No separate document containing bye-laws is required.

The shareholders in a BV may be either corporate bodies or individuals, and in general all shares may be held by foreigners. Types of share issued are mostly similar to their counterparts in other countries. **Gewone aandelen**, ordinary shares are usual, but **preferente aandelen**, preference shares, which may or may not have cumulative rights, may also be issued. Shares may be divided into fractional or subshares (**onderaandelen**).

A small company need only have one **directeur** or director and no **commissaris** or supervisory director. The **raad van bestuur**, or board of directors of a larger company, is advised by the **commissaris** who is not an executive, and his appointment is only compulsory for larger companies. The **Wet op de Naamloze Vennootschappen**, the 1971 Structure of Corporations Act, requires companies with consolidated assets of at least Dfl 12 million and 100 or more employees to establish a **raad van commissarissen**, a supervisory board, consisting of at least three supervisory directors. Its members are elected by the general meeting of shareholders to oversee the management and allow employees to have some influence in the company's affairs. Unlike smaller BVs, these large BVs must file their annual accounts and audit report in the Trade Register.

The **Naamloze Vennootschap** or NV, the public company, is the form adopted by entities that wish to raise capital publicly, whether listed on the stock exchange or not. It corresponds to the public company or corporation form in most other countries. There is normally no restriction on the issue or transfer of an NV's shares. The regulations applicable to NVs are mostly identical to those applicable to BVs. Such difference as there is between the two was widened by the EC's second directive on company law which became effective in the Netherlands in 1981. This meant that the minimum for paid-up capital was raised from Dfl 35,000 to Dfl 100,000, that shares issued for cash must be at least 25 per cent paid up on subscription, and those issued for other consideration must be 100 per cent paid up, and the company may not purchase more than 10 per cent of its own shares.

An NV may issue both **aandelen op naam**, registered shares and **aandelen aan toonder**, bearer shares, except that shares cannot be in bearer form until fully paid up. A 1947 decree, **Beschikking Beursverkeer** (stock exchange trading order), stipulated that shares may be bought and sold only through certain banks or stockbrokers. A proposal by the board to apply for a stock exchange listing for any of its company's securities must be approved by the supervisory board, and the company's share capital must be at least Dfl 2.5 million for a listing on the stock exchange itself, or Dfl 250,000 for the over-the-counter market.

In 1971 some 35,000 NVs became BVs. Since then more than 100,000 new BVs have been established. In 1988 there were about 140,000 BVs and 1815 NVs in the Netherlands.

A **Vennootschap onder firma** (FOV, normally referred to simply as 'firma') is the usual form of commercial partnership, in which all partners are jointly and severally liable for all its debts and obligations. Partnerships are not legal entities separate from the individuals who compose them. The word **maatschappij**, literally meaning a partnership, is often adopted by professional firms, but it denotes a civil and not a commercial law entity.

A **Commanditaire Vennootschap** (CV) is a limited partnership in which the general partners are fully liable for the debts of the partnership, but there are also one or more limited partners liable only to the extent of the contributions they have made to the partnership capital. The limited partners (**commanditaire** or **stille vennoten**) can take no part in the management of the business.

All partnerships must be registered in the Trade Register. For a general partnership, a **firma-akte**, a written partnership agreement is required, but not a notorial deed. Partnership accounts do not have to be published, but partnerships with thirty-five or more employees must set up a works' council (see below).

Bijkantoren or **filialen** are branches or establishments of a parent body, in whatever form that body carries on its business, and as such, like the partnerships, have no separate legal entity.

The **coöperatieve vereniging** or cooperative is a popular institution in the Netherlands. It is legally defined as an association to promote the material interests of its members. It is a legal entity and the liability for its exploitation is borne corporately by its members. Its function falls into one of the following categories:

- Production cooperatives, e.g. building firms.
- Credit cooperatives, accumulating a reserve fund for capital expenditure as required, e.g. farmers and horticulturists.
- Purchasing cooperatives, buying in bulk for distribution to members, e.g. farming and horticulture, retail traders, consumers.
- Processing cooperatives, processing and marketing raw materials provided by their members, e.g. dairies, sugar factories.
- Marketing cooperatives, e.g. auctioneers, dairy, potato and corn farmers.
- Service cooperatives, supplying goods and services for specific needs, e.g. machinery for farmers, staff for offices.
- Housing cooperatives, e.g. housing associations.
- Mutual insurance cooperatives, large general offices and smaller specialized insurers.

Every cooperative must give some indication of its objectives, and its name must include certain initials to indicate the liability of its members: WA (unlimited liability), BA (limited liability) or UJA (no liability).

Eenmanszaak (sole trader) although a business carried out by a single individual whose liability for the settlement of debts is unlimited, may employ a large number of people (for example Ford in the United States and previously Verolme in the Netherlands).

Overheidsbedrijven (state-controlled enterprises) are increasingly acquiring the legal form of NV, in which the government is the sole shareholder, as in the Staatsdrukkerij (cf. HM Stationery Office) and PTT (Post Office), the Dutch Railways, the Nederlandsche Bank and DSM (Dutch State Mines). There are also a number of companies in which the state is a principal shareholder, such as KLM, and the Royal Dutch Foundries and Steel Mills.

Similarly, provincial and city councils own their own enterprises (e.g. Amsterdam has its own insurance office, gas and elecricity boards, port industry and giro bank). The national and regional industries seem to avoid criticism by operating efficiently and cost-effectively.

Cartels and monopolies have in principle been allowed if not actually encouraged. Only abuses are controlled by the **Wet Economische Mededingen** (Economic Competition Act), resulting in hundreds of cartels in the Netherlands, and this despite the EC treaty of 1956, whose article 85 specifically forbids formations that limit competition.

Business and finance

The Nederlandsche Bank

Monetary policy is controlled by the Nederlandsche Bank, whose head office is in Amsterdam, and the Minister of Finance. The **1948 Bank Act** entrusted three tasks to the Nederlandsche Bank: 'The Bank shall regulate the value of the Dutch currency so as to further the country's prosperity and at the same time to stabilize that value as far as possible.' Second, the Bank controls the cashflow between the trading banks as well as issuing banknotes and releasing foreign currencies. Third, the bank controls credit facilities by its instructions to the trading banks.

Though since 1948 the Bank has been entirely state-owned, it still retains a considerable measure of autonomy. Its policy is to maintain as closely as possible the link between the values of the guilder and the Deutschmark. In this it has been largely successful, although the Dutch rate of inflation has been fairly consistently rather higher than the West German rate. The **Wet Toezicht Kredietwezen** (Credit Control Act) empowers the Bank to exercise considerable control over almost all the banks in the country by setting levels for their capital reserves and liquidity. It can also introduce any of three measures to control the economy: by fixing the bank rate, by purchasing or selling treasury bills or bonds, and by regulating the reserves to be held by banks against credit, or limiting the credit facilities of the banks.

In 1977 the Bank introduced credit controls, lasting until 1981, as a result of a surge in liquidity in the previous year. In the 1980s, however, the Bank recommended the minister to moderate the monetary policy, which was not controlling public spending and was indirectly adversely affecting unemployment, and this policy has since been abandoned.

The Bank is the licensing authority for foreign exchange transactions, but authorizes the commercial banks and other institutions to act as intermediaries in handling international payments. It also supervises the issue of securities on the international market through a gentleman's agreement with the other banks. In accordance with this agreement, each domestic public issue of securities of Dfl 16 million and over requires a 'declaration of no objection' from the Bank. The Bank itself does not engage in commercial business.

General banks

Banks in the Netherlands have an excellent reputation for the range and quality of their services. The four general banks, the Rabobank, ABN (Algemene Bank Nederland), Amrobank and NMB (Nederlandsche Middenstandsbank) are 'universal' in their scope, like the West German banks (trading in stocks and new issues). Many have joined consortia operating from London or elsewhere. Exceptionally, the ABN has established its own branches – 249 in 44 countries throughout Europe and the world. Future trends may be marked by present negotiations between the AMRO (Amsterdam-Rotterdam) Bank and the Belgian bank Société Générale for a fusion with a 10 per cent participation in each other's capital. This would make the new institution the largest Benelux bank and the sixth largest in Western Europe, even without the proposed further extension to include the French Banque de Suez.

The four leading Dutch banks rank seventh among the world's 100 largest banks, according to their assets, capital reserves and profits. They have gained from the very high level of foreign investment in the Netherlands, particularly from the USA, due to a higher rate of return on capital than in other Western European countries, with no restrictions on the repatriation of capital, profits, royalties or loan interest. Most of the $8 million of US direct investment in the Netherlands in 1984 was in the petroleum and chemicals sector, and foreign investment in the Netherlands has continued to strengthen. Investment abroad has also been high – Dfl 10,000 million in 1985 and Dfl 8,000 million in 1986, much of it in the form of direct investment by the Dutch multinationals in the USA and Third World.

Forty foreign banks have established offices in the Netherlands, among them the leading institutions from North America, Europe and Japan.

Although the commercial banks have broadened their range in recent years, there is still a certain amount of specialization in that they tend to concentrate on short-term lending. However, several of them have set up their own medium-term credit subsidiaries, and have diversified into such areas as merchant banking, housing finance, leasing and factoring. Moreover, deregulation measures introduced by the government in the late 1980s will encourage penetration of the Dutch security markets from abroad. Indeed, there is already some foreign ownership of Dutch banks, such as the former Slavenburg's Bank, taken over by the French Crédit Lyonnais in 1983 as the Crédit Lyonnais Bank Nederland, which later also took over the Nederlandsche Credietbank in 1988. Short-term bank finance is usually provided through overdraft facilities rather than by setting up bank loans or discounting bills.

Interest at very low rates is usually allowed on current accounts, although small charges are made for any special services provided. Cheques are, however, seldom used in settlement of debts because of the efficient giro system in the Netherlands.

For personal accounts, the **Postbank** (national giro) is undoubtedly the most important banking institution in the Netherlands. It has seven million account holders (almost half the population!), served by over 3000 post offices and 724 cash points. Originally a state-owned subsidiary of the postal and telegraph service, the post office savings bank, as it then was, handled 45 per cent of all transactions after the Second World War. The commercial banks, complaining of unfair competition, succeeded in pressing for legislation to cede a large part of its business accounts to them. In 1977 a fusion of the savings bank and giro service resulted in the establishment of the independent Postbank. The high street banks again objected, this time to the state control of the bank. They were supported in this by the right-wing parties, so that in 1984 legislation was passed to privatize the bank, which started operations in 1986 as a limited company, with the state as sole shareholder. The Postbank, with assets of Dfl 48 billion, is now strictly limited to the retail trade with only marginal credit facilities, at least until 1990.

In the postal giro transfer system, or PCGD, each depositor has a numbered account and receives a book of preprinted transfer forms. Since a transfer form is not a negotiable instrument, security risks are reduced as the only consequence of loss is the non-execution of the transfer. Whenever the balance in a giro account changes, the depositor receives a new statement. No postage is required for any transaction and no charges are imposed. Accounts may be overdrawn by no more than Dfl 500. Since the depositor is also issued with non-negotiable orders, **betaalkaarten**, which can be used universally for payment or withdrawals, the flexibility and efficiency of the system has reduced the need for personal cheques and credit cards. The advantages of economies, achieved by minimizing its overheads in using post office staff at its outlets, outweigh the disadvantages of a relatively impersonal service offered by staff who are not trained bankers and cannot handle complex transactions.

Hypotheekbanken are banks dealing in long-term mortgage loans, for the construction of industrial or commercial buildings and private houses. The slide in property prices in the mid–1980s has left these banks in a weaker state, with truncated assets.

Spaarbanken are savings banks whose funds are normally invested in government or similar bonds, and can provide finance for private house purchase.

The **Nationale Investeringsbank** in The Hague, is an investment bank jointly owned by the state and a number of large banks, granting long-term interest-bearing loans. The **Nederlandse Participatie Maatschappij** is an offshoot of the National Investment Bank, and it provides equity capital. Long-term loans granted by the Investment Bank are generally of Dfl 100,000 or more, for terms of about ten years. Government guarantees may be available, and regional institutions have also been set up to provide finance in special cases. Where investment in promising enterprises is stimulated by loans of Dfl 250,000 to Dfl 50 million, these may offer conversion rights into share capital.

The **Maatschappij Industriele Projecten**, (the Company for Industrial Projects) is a venture capital fund with Dfl 500,000 million paid-up capital supplied by the government, major banks and institutional investors. It works independently (only two of its nine members are representatives of the government), and it can be compared to similar funds in other countries. Its principal aim is to set up high-technology companies in the Netherlands, employing the talents of local as well as foreign entrepreneurs. Its participation, which may not exceed 49 per cent of the total investment, usually amounts to more than Dfl 4 million.

There are also some twenty Private Participation Companies with a minimum capital of Dfl 1 million licensed by the Netherlands Bank to invest in small businesses.

Onderhandse leningen (debt contracts) are provided by institutions (e.g. insurance companies and pension funds) and private investors, offering loans for ten to twenty-five years. They are far more widely used than bonds or notes through the stock exchange, and the market for them **(onderhandse markt)** is used by institutional investors. They are a major source of finance in the Netherlands, and have several advantages for the borrower: quick access to funds, low issue costs and tailormade terms.

Share capital, as distinct from retained reserves, does not form as high a proportion of capital employed in the Netherlands as it does in some other countries. Loan capital is much more important. Banks rarely take up share capital as principals.

The **Wet op de Investeringsregeling**, the Investment Act of 1978, popularly known as the WIR, used to provide tax-free bonuses to encourage investment in fixed or capital assets. The bonuses are offset against tax assessments. Since 1984 the bonus rate has been set at 12.5 per cent.

Grants under the **Investment Premium Regulations** (IPR), or investment subsidies, are given to encourage investment in 'assisted areas', in addition to WIR bonuses. The assisted areas comprise the north-eastern provinces of Groningen, Friesland and Drenthe, the northern part of Overijsel, the south of the south-eastern province of Limburg and some towns and cities in the province of North Brabant.

There are also regional development corporations offering up to 49 per cent of equity holdings with one seat on the supervisory board. They are generally also able to offer a subordinate loan, guaranteed by the government at the interest rate of the capital market.

Stock markets

The official stock exchange is in Amsterdam. As the world's oldest stock exchange, it can trace its history back to the beginning of the seventeenth century. It lists about 230 Dutch companies' stocks and 320 foreign ones as well as government and other bonds. Private investors are estimated to hold nearly one half of all listed equities, and institutional investors are less influential than in some other countries. The new-issue functions of the stock exchange are at present relatively small. Amsterdam is also the home of the first European options exchange, which began operations in 1978.

The exchange is governed by the Association of the Stock Exchange, a group of banks and other share brokers who, by law, must have their headquarters in Amsterdam. They are the only persons who may buy or sell securities in the exchange. The Association is supervised by the Ministry of Finance.

Business and the labour market

The population of the Netherlands steadily increased during the 1980s from nearly 14 million to nearly 15 million. This increase was due to net immigration and longer life expectancy, rather than to a rise in the birth rate. Between 1980 and 1990 the age group 20–64 years will have increased by 1.1 million, while the 0–19 year age group will have decreased by 800,000 and the 65+ group will have grown by 200,000.

Immigration rose throughout the 1980s from about 8000 per annum to about 40,000 per annum. About one third of this number came from European countries outside the EC and about one half came from the Third World.

Although the proportion of employed women is increasing relative to males, the traditional belief that a woman's place is in the home (and there was no war industry to bring women into the factories) still affects a situation in which only just over one third of the workforce is female. The gradual increase in the percentage of women seeking employment, together with the half million increase in the employable population in the past decade, accounts for a substantial part of the present (1990) figure of 670,000 unemployed, so that the reduction in the labour demand is in real terms about 150,000. In other words, without these demographic increases, the present unemployment rate would be only 2.8 per cent. It is ironic, therefore, that the population growth – a classic indicator of economic prosperity – dictates a need not just to combat the decline in the labour demand, but to create a higher level of labour intensity in order to increase the labour market. The alternative is, of course, to increase the labour market by job-sharing or by curtailing the working life/hours of those in employment. This problem is by no means confined to the Netherlands where, as we have seen, it is compounded by government overspending.

The unemployment curve (see Table 6.2) broadly follows that of most OECD countries, and is attributable to the same factors, but the high rate of immigration, and the very favourable unemployment benefits available until very recently, may have aggravated the situation. While there was no obligation on people seeking employment to accept a wage lower than that for which they were professionally qualified, with a guaranteed unemployment benefit initially of 80 per cent (now 70 per cent) of the last wage, there was no great incentive to find work, particularly when income could be supplemented by 'black' labour.

Unemployment in the Netherlands, as in other countries, hits the migrant 'guest workers' the hardest, as Table 6.3 shows.

The explanation for the discrepancies between autochthonous and immigrant unemployment lies largely in educational levels. Whereas 73

Table 6.2 *Dutch unemployment rates (1978–89)*

Year	(%)
1978	4.0
1979	4.0
1980	4.6
1981	6.9
1982	9.7
1983	11.7
1984	12.0
1985	13.2
1986	15.7
1987	14.0
1988	12.5
1989	9.5

Source: OECD

Table 6.3 *Unemployment of ethnic minorities in absolute numbers and as percentages of the labour force as at 1 January 1987*

	Absolute	As percentage
Indigenous Dutch people	605,940	14
Surinamese	18,960	ca. 45
Antilleans	4,430	ca. 43
Moluccans	6,100	ca. 45
Turks	24,970	ca. 40
Moroccans	16,400	ca. 40
Others (refugees etc.)	12,510	ca. 50

Source: Ministry of Employment and Social Security

per cent of the Dutch unemployed had only some secondary education, the same applied to 87–99 per cent of the ethnic minority groups (with the exception of 'others', at 69 per cent).

The high labour costs in the 1970s had a knock-on effect in the rising unemployment in the 1980s. With wage costs per unit at twice the level of net earnings, labour costs in the Netherlands were higher than all its competitors in Japan, the USA and Europe apart from West Germany. This was exacerbated by the appreciation of the guilder, and it was only by reducing the levels of social security contributions and, until 1983, imposing wage controls, that the situation could be rectified in the 1980s, when, in 1984, Dutch labour costs were for the first time lower than its competitors.

Trends in employment

With the exception of the primary sector (agriculture and fisheries), which has declined steadily since 1950, increasing its productivity with a reducing labour force, there was a steady growth in employment in the 1950s and 1960s, levelling off in the 1970s and thereafter declining, except in the government sector. In the first of three phases in the secondary sector (manufacturing), expansion (horizontal investment) was encouraged by low wages under a policy of wage control. In the 1960s a labour shortage and resultant wage demands together with growing competition, necessitated modernization of the production process and consequent vertical investment. Investment, however, was concentrated mainly in chemicals and mining, and where output failed to match productivity, manufacturing (as for instance in textiles) ran into serious problems. In the 1970s growth in output slackened off further, investment dropped, productivity grew – more slowly – and employment levels dropped rapidly.

The service sector fared rather better. Commercial services (advertising, transport) benefited from the increase in industrial output and increasing prosperity raised the demand for recreational provision and insurance. But the retail trade was doubly hit in the 1980s, by the reduced domestic demand as a result of government economy measures and the knock-on effect of price-cutting and discount trading. In 1970 chain stores with eighty or more branches had a 35 per cent share of the market and the 'corner shop' retailer 65 per cent. Fifteen years later the situation was reversed, with multiples taking 60 per cent of the market. In the six years prior to 1984 some 170,000 jobs were lost in retailing – an annual decline of about 2.8 per cent in employment as compared with about 1 per cent in manufacturing.

The social services obviously benefited from the new social security legislation, until in the 1980s the government cut back on public spending.

The increase in the labour force from 3.9 million in 1947 to about 6 million in 1985 was mainly due to the natural increase in the population. As mentioned earlier, the relative increase in the employment of women shows in the rise in the percentage of women in employment from 27 per cent in 1947 to 34 per cent in 1985 as against a drop in male employment from 85 per cent in 1947 to 66 per cent in 1985. The particular decline since 1975 in the male employment of under-24-year-olds and over-50s is due to prolonged education in the former and early retirement in the latter (under a state scheme with compensation as part of its work-sharing legislation).

The external factors contributing to the decline in employment are well known: the oil crises, the expansion of production from the developing countries (undercutting, for instance, the clothing trade) and the massive rise in Japanese exports. But variations in the exchange value of the guilder have also affected the problem. Between 1970 and 1983 the guilder appreciated by about 40 per cent. It has been estimated that a $0.1 rise in the value of the guilder costs the Dutch economy Dfl 2 billion a year, and the appreciation of the guilder in the 1970s cost the Netherlands 10 per cent of its export total.

By 1983 the Dutch economy was clearly in crisis. There was no longer any question of economic growth and real national output was declining. Between 1979 and 1983 more than 300,000 jobs were lost. Within five years unemployment rose to more than 800,000. Production began to recover in 1983 and in 1985 employment again showed a modest expansion.

In one respect, the Netherlands may be moving in a direction shared in the EC only by the United Kingdom. In 1980 the **Wetenschappelijke Raad voor het Regeringsbeleid** (WRR), a prestigious government advisory body or 'think tank', published a report stating that the Netherlands was in a process of 'deindustrialization'. Their reasons for this were:

- The Netherlands since the war has specialized in intermediate products (e.g. petrochemicals and steel), electrotechnical apparatus, foodstuffs and luxury goods. Capital goods scarcely figure in Dutch output.
- Dutch industry is very energy-intensive and its export is mainly EC-oriented.
- World trade is now growing in those sectors in which the Netherlands is weak.
- The output of intermediary products in the Netherlands has now levelled off.
- The 'sensitive' sectors (textiles, leather, clothing, wood, furniture) have suffered a far greater decline in the Netherlands than elsewhere.

In the event, this report has proved too pessimistic. Nevertheless, the huge foreign investments of the multinationals have probably cost the Dutch labour market some 16,000 to 30,000 jobs in the decade up to 1984.

Business and trade unions

Labour relations in the Netherlands have a reasonably good record (Table 6.4).

Table 6.4 *Working days in the Netherlands lost through disputes (1975–87)*

Year	Days lost
1975	732
1980	56,832
1980	89,390
1986	38,858
1987	58,276

Source: Statistical Yearbook of the Netherlands, 1988.

A number of factors favour stability. Coalition governments resulting from an electoral system with proportional representation reduce the polarity between right and left-wing interests, and the trades union movement broke its association with the Dutch Labour Party after the Second World War. The unions themselves are organized according to branches of industry and commerce and not by individual craft, so that there are far fewer unions than in some other countries and few demarcation disputes. Moreover, the unions historically owe their origins to confessional or ideological loyalties arising out of a vertical pluralism across social boundaries. Although this typically Dutch phenomenon of **verzuiling** (literally, pillarization) is now rapidly dissipating, its effects, as we shall see, still provide an enviable stability in legislation and hence in labour relations and social reform.

It has been said that the fragmentation of political and social organization because of the triple structures of Catholic, Calvinist and non-confessional partisanship in all aspects of Dutch life must result in frustration or ineffectual compromise. Arend Lijphart has, however, demonstrated in his *The Politics of Accommodation* that the necessity to legislate within clearly defined pluralist parameters has produced a remarkably consistent and stable form of democracy. The shift in the balance of power between one coalition government and the next will always be minimal and transitional, and there will thus be no economic or social U-turns. If this minimizes confrontation in politics, it also reduces the risk of confrontation in labour relations.

As a result of the 'ontzuiling' ('depillarization') in recent years, the basically socialist NVV joined with the **Nederlandse Katholieke Vakvereniging** (NKV) in 1976 to form the **Federatie Nederlandsche Vakbeweging** (Federation of Dutch Trade Unions) with almost 900,000 members in 1985 (58 per cent of organized labour). Since its inauguration the FNV has provided an effective bargaining power for the shop floor. Labour is, however, far less organized in the Netherlands than in other countries. Since the closed shop is virtually unknown in the Netherlands, only 30 per cent of the labour force are in fact union members.

It is interesting to note that whereas a recent political alignment brought the two Christian parties together in the CDU, the trade union movement brought the Socialists and Catholics together, leaving the Protestant **Christelijk Nationaal Vakverbond** (CNV) on its own. In 1970 it reaffirmed its specifically confessional approach to social reforms, retaining the independence of its twelve trade unions in a federation with 300,000 members in 1985. On the other hand, the Protestant Public Servants Union did merge with the Catholic Civil Servants Union to form the **Algemeen Christelijke Federatie van Overheidspersoneel** (CFO) which has joined the CNV.

Finally two Official and Management unions merged to form the **Vakcentrale voor Middelbaar en Hoger Personeel** (MHP).

An Association of Employers, the **Verbond van Nederlandse Ondernemingen** (VNO), was formed from the fusion of two associations, one emphasizing the social and the other the economic aspects of management–worker cooperation. It has about ninety branch associations with 10,000 members or firms. A smaller association was created by the fusion of the Protestant and Catholic Employers Associations into the **Nederlands Christelijk Werkgeversverbond** (NCW) with under eighty branches, of which some 70 per cent are also members of the VNO.

Medium and small firms are represented in two federations, the **Koninklijk Nederlands Ondernemers Verbond** (KNOV) and the small splinter-group, **Nederlands Christelijk Ondenemersverbond** (NCOV), an evangelical Protestant association.

The farmers and market gardeners have (predictably) retained their separate Protestant and Catholic unions, and have a high membership of 75 per cent. Though they are thus well organized, much of their power has now fallen to the EC, whose restructuring policy is largely responsible for reducing the number of businesses by 49 per cent, with a consequent loss of 48,600 jobs.

In the last sixty years the system of negotiating wages has turned full circle. In the 1930s wage agreements made by individual firms were replaced by **Collectieve Arbeidsovereenkomsten**, (CAO) (collective labour agreements) applied to the whole branch of an industry. After the Second World War, wage control became a matter of national policy in order to level upwards the wages of depressed industries and to strengthen the country's economic position by controlling labour costs. In recent years, when it was believed that wage-fixing stifled incentives in expanding employment, CAO have been replaced by local wage negotiations.

The **Stichting van de Arbeid** (Labour Council), and the **Sociaal-economische Raad**, (SER, Social and Economic Council) that took over many of its functions, at one time provided a three-cornered council to maintain a balance between wages and prices, agreed by an equal representation of *kroonleden*, management and labour. Deregulation has reduced the powers of the Labour Council and the Social and Economic Council to negotiate wage agreements but they are still retained as advisory boards to the Minister of Social Affairs. They take part in the preparation of the budget, discussing such matters as unemployment, retraining and supplementary pension schemes. Since 1982 industry and government have concurred in the decentralization of wage negotiations, and the Labour Council's central plan of 1983 agreed to strive towards wage restraint, shorter working hours and increased productivity.

Ondernemingsraden (works' councils), which are a legal requirement for all firms employing thirty-five or more employees, have the right to advise on decisions that must be reported to them. In enterprises with 100 or more employees, the works' councils must be consulted on all important matters such as mergers, closures, changes of location and major reorganizations, and they have a right of veto in decisions regarding personnel.

The maximum working week is forty-eight hours, though forty hours is now normal, decreasing from an average of 40.6 in 1980 to 40.3 in 1986. Firms are now encouraged to introduce work-sharing by government subsidies offered to employers with at least 10 per cent of their workforce working part time.

Since the SER has to be consulted by the government on all important matters affecting social or economic policy, and since the central organizations of management and labour are represented on the SER, those engaged in producing the nation's income still have, despite deregulation, some influence in its management. In much of the social and labour legislation, the advice of the SER has been taken by the government.

The employers' associations stimulate scientific research in business management, provide specialist information, and run courses through their **Nederlands Instituut voor Efficiency**.

Wages, benefits and pensions

There is a statutory minimum wage for employees between twenty-three and sixty-five years, with a stepped decrease for those under twenty-three. Recent legislation (1987) provides for disability pensions, child allowances (paid to men or women) for all children under the age of eighteen (and thereafter if they are in full-time education), old-age and widow(er)'s pensions. Health insurance is provided for those below the **welstandsgrens** (income limit), and contributions are levied equally from the employer and employee. There is a mandatory holiday allowance of 8 per cent in addition to normal pay (for a minimum of twenty working days, normally extended), and a 'thirteenth month's pay' is often paid to clerical and managerial staff as a bonus at Christmas. These provisions claimed 10.8 per cent of net national income in 1963 and 22.2 per cent in 1986. The seriousness of this financial burden can be gauged from a comparison with the lower increase in taxation: from 24.8 per cent of net national income in 1963 to 29.0 per cent in 1986. It was for this reason that the severe cutbacks were introduced in 1985 to reduce the state's contribution to social security to just over 3 per cent.

The combination of social security contributions and taxation creates a 'wedge' between labour costs for the employer and net income for the employee. This means that on average a worker costs his employer twice to two-and-a-half times the take-home pay of the worker, which is a far higher ratio than among almost all foreign competitors.

Business, education, training and development

Dutch management is very well educated. The majority of managers are qualified with university or higher technical degrees and relatively few of them have 'worked their way up' on native ability. Managers are also vocationally educated, with qualifications (as in most Continental countries) in engineering, law, economics, or applied technical and business specialisms,

The orientation towards technical grounding is less marked than in West Germany, but in the words of the Finniston report (1980), '. . . the engineering dimension is stronger and more readily definable in management in the Netherlands than in Britain.' Their qualifications are more substantial and technical functions (as elsewhere abroad) have a higher standing than in the United Kingdom. The technical universities; in the Netherlands are more securely established and their role vis-à-vis industry is more universally recognized than are the polytechnics in the

United Kingdom. Engineers may well spill over into non-technical functions in general management.

Dutch attitudes to management fall somewhere between the American or British preference for the 'good all-rounder' eschewing tight professional labels, and the West German emphasis on specialization in qualifications, recruitment and promotion.

An enquiry among Dutch managers of the qualities they sought in applicants indicated their ideal of the well-rounded man/woman. They tended to strike a balance between knowledge and analytical grasp on the one hand and social and personality factors on the other. As one manager put it: 'There is a well-trained explicit behaviour in attaining your own targets. One is always in a bargaining situation. The successful manager is always a good bargainer. A sound integrator. We say, **hij is handig**, he makes good manoeuvres, not Machiavellian, not just social integration, and certainly not just task-oriented, but handig.' So the qualities of bargaining and reconciling implicit in this word handig, suggest that management work involves judgemental rather than dogmatic qualities.

A survey carried out by the Nederlands Centrum van Directeuren and Hay Management Consultants in 1985 shows a significant rise in the number of respondents attaching importance to product innovation compared with responses in the 1982 survey. But the stolidness often attributed to the Dutch does often consist in an overconcern with details, and the business person attempting to innovate may be confronted with proceduralism and factual nit-picking. Their **degelijkheid** (solidity and reliability) also makes them very security-minded, and hence concerned with tenure and pension provisions. The Dutch have a reputation for being absolutely honourable in business. (There is no more truth in the adage 'the fault with the Dutch is giving too little and asking too much' than there is in the saying that the Scots are mean.) And if their business culture is honest, this is certainly reflected in the generosity of Dutch politics where international agencies and Third World development are supported with very substantial aid, little of which is tied.

Dutch business people are even less careerist than the West Germans, and career planning or management development are almost dirty words. A top personnel executive of a Dutch multinational considers that consensus strategies for the graduate trainee are more important than leadership qualities. The danger is, of course, that the promising graduates are not moved out of a post that they are content to do well in, because they do not themselves take the necessary initiative.

Despite their pride in their egalitarianism, the Dutch do tend to recruit from the top echelons, so that the Netherlands is really not much less meritocratic than the United Kingdom is believed to be. On the other hand, Dutch business people are still surprised at the unpredictability of some of their English colleagues, and they retain an apocryphal belief that all British business deals are settled at the lunch table or on the golf course. It is, however, striking how the older generation also clings to the conviction that Churchill's spirit must survive in the British at large.

There is an unusually low mobility between companies in the Netherlands. Regionalism and confessional differences tend to discourage geographical relocation, and it is 'not done' since it implies disloyalty to the firm. In any case, the specialist nature of management qualifications makes sideways movement difficult. Finally, pension rights are not transferable and recent attempts to remedy this have so far failed. With the importance placed on pension rights, this is certainly a disincentive. Clearly this does not affect multinationals, which move personnel at will and also attract personnel from smaller companies. This means that all but the largest companies promote internally, with senior executives normally ending up on the board.

Legislation traditionally aimed at limiting the disparity in wage and salary levels has resulted in a situation in which net salaries in the Netherlands are lower than in all West-European countries, and directors are particularly hard hit by taxation and insurance premiums, though this will be ameliorated by the tax changes soon to be introduced. As a result (or cause?) there appears to be little material motivation, i.e. crudely put, it is very un-Dutch to ask for a rise. On the other hand, companies are very reluctant to fire poor performers, and who can blame them when it costs about Dfl 700,000 in severance pay to fire a manager earning Dfl 100–120,000?

Because of the resistance to inter-company mobility, the 'brain drain' has not been conspicuous in the Netherlands (except at certain times among academics), and yet there was in 1989 a shortage of professionally qualified people, particularly of engineers and marketing and computer specialists. This is entirely due to the lack of enrolment in the relevant courses in the 1970s, just before the recent upturn in the economy.

In the recruitment of personnel, the Dutch often use psychological and aptitude tests, not just for government posts and industry, but also for educational streaming.

Lifelong learning

The state educational and training structure is extremely diverse and comprehensive and there is practically no private education – or rather, education at the primary and secondary level is all private in the sense that it is independent, but entirely financed by the state.

There are seven universities in the Netherlands, two more in formation (at Tilburg and Maastricht) and three technical universities. They admit all students qualifying by passing the grammar school final examination, they have longer courses, larger taught lecture classes and higher drop-out rates than in the United Kingdom. The oldest technical university is at Delft and specializes in engineering and architecture. Electrical engineering and electronics are the specialisms in the foundation (1948) at Eindhoven (the home and world headquarters of Philips), and more recently a third technical university has been established at Twente. There is no 'Oxbridge' or Ivy League discrimination in Holland, though Leiden likes to remember that it is the oldest university, founded in 1574 by William the Silent as a reward for the town's heroic resistance in the Spanish Revolt. There are two further institutions with university status and awarding their own degrees: the Landbouwhogeschool at Wageningen, a university specializing in agriculture, and Nijenrode, exclusively offering management education.

Hoger Beroepsonderwijs (HBO, higher vocational training) provides an education at a slightly lower level than the universities to some 10–15 per cent of school-leavers, They can be compared with technical colleges in the United Kingdom, awarding diplomas similar to HNCs and HNDs. They specialize in one of a large number of branches, such as engineering (**Hogere Technische Scholen**, HTS), teacher training, social work and personnel management (**Sociale Akademies**), economics and commerce (**Hoger Economisch en Administratief Onderwijs**), police training, administration for civil servants (**Bestuurs Akademie**) and so on.

With the need for retraining and for 'topping up' courses for those in employment, part-time vocational courses are on the increase alongside the full-time courses, but entry qualification is a six-subject examination taken at school at seventeen. The present trend towards high unemployment rates among university graduates is causing a growing number of school-leavers qualified for university entrance to opt for vocational courses, where life is more structured and disciplined than at the universities, and where the choice is more varied; (there are thirty-four HTSs but only three technical universities, and the HTSs are sometimes more progressive than the universities).

HBO lecturers normally have practical experience as well as formal qualifications (university or HBO), though this is not a legal requirement. Practical training is included in the HBO course, with placements of about six months in the third year.

The HBO Act of 1986 put the financing of HBOs on a par with the universities, and encouraged them to engage in research. This, together with the amalgamation of colleges in the same geographical area, will enable them to compete better with the universities in their contacts with the business world.

The structure of research in the Netherlands has changed considerably since the mid-1970s. This reflects government policy, but at the same time changes in government policy reflect developments that have taken place in the world of research. Recent developments have had six policy objectives:

- Research should be geared towards the wishes of the market.
- 'Horizontal' technologies should be stimulated and developed. Examples are biotechnology and microelectronics, which can influence virtually every branch of science and many sectors of society.
- The link between fundamental and applied research should be strengthened through 'strategic' research and in other ways.
- The quality of research should be improved, and it should be given new stimulation.
- Science and technology should be better integrated into society.
- International cooperation should be increased.

The 1979 White Paper on innovation, published by the Ministry for Science Policy, played a major role in achieving this for industrial users.

Progress in this direction has also been made in the fields of energy, space, health research and the social sciences. This marked the start of an era of specifically-directed stimulation of science and technology. A research programme in biotechnology was launched in 1981 in response to the White Paper. Dutch research is now in a relatively strong international position in terms of its quality, organization, concentration on promising topics and broad industrial applicability.

In 1984 Dfl 1,700 million was allocated by the government to stimulate information technology in education, research and the market sector, and to inform the public on the subject. The activities proposed in a five-year plan under this scheme are extensive, and include a project to stimulate IT research in the Netherlands, known as SPIN, which is one of several activities that will help to bridge the gap between fundamental and applied research. Allocations will be made to publicity, education, research, the private sector and the public sector in roughly the following percentages respectively: 1 per cent, 21 per cent, 13 per cent, 59 per cent, 4 per cent, so that education and the private sector will benefit most. Much of the educational allocation is being used on hardware and course programmes throughout secondary and tertiary educational establishments.

In the private sector small and medium-sized firms are the major target, where information, advice and education are particularly necessary. The further promotion of telecommunication is working towards an integrated network of a broadband system of glass fibres for the transfer of speech, data and pictures. In the country having the world's third largest output of integrated circuits (at Philips), microelectronic development is obviously also important, and part of the government's R & D budget will support research into the development of a new generation of megabit chips, now being developed jointly by Philips and Siemens.

In energy research, a joint project with France has been running since 1982. Lievense, a hydraulic engineer, has published a scheme using wind turbines and energy storage in high water reservoirs which could provide 20 per cent of Dutch electricity requirements. Feasibility studies have shown that the scheme is viable. Future programmes envisage further research in the deep-sea production of oil and gas, further development of durable energy resources (sun and wind) and new conversion techniques, such as fuel cells.

Business and the environment

No one could be more aware of their environment than the Dutch. They know that many of the windmills romantically associated with the flat countryside were built to keep the water out – with good reason, since 48 per cent of the country lies below sea level, much of this in the most highly populated areas. It is, after all, a delta country, of aluvial deposits, polder clay and sand. This accounts for the intensive dairy production on the high-yielding grasslands, but it also explains the high costs of civil engineering in the building and maintenance of opening bridges and dykes, and in pile-driving, not only for buildings but for roads and railways in the west of the country.

This also raises environmental problems of its own, since new building in the areas where it is most needed involves transporting (often by pipeline) vast quantities of sand from the Veluwe regions in the east, to provide a blanket overlay before piling and building. This affects the landscape of the rare wooded areas in the centre of the country. More spectacular, and hence better known, are the reclamation schemes and sea-defence works in the IJsselemeer or Zuiderzee and the delta of the great rivers (Scheldt, Maas and Rhine) which have produced substantial increases in agricultural land, urban development areas, and recreational facilities.

But though these works have now been completed, relieving the huge public finances needed for them, the 'overheads' of sustaining an economy in such a geographical location will always remain high.

Problems of environmental pollution have been with the Dutch since long before green became a political colour. A perennial and age-long problem in the coastal areas below sea level has been the salination of farmlands due to seepage from the sea under the dunes. The universal problems of irrigation and drainage in a low-lying country whose fresh-water supply comes largely from other countries, are not alleviated by the massive industrial pollution of the major rivers, specifically the Rhine and Maas. And as, for instance, in such matters as the debatable use of nuclear power stations, international claims can lead to acrimonious counterclaims and procrastination.

As far back as the early 1960s, a movement among Amsterdam students, the **provos**, conducted a jocular campaign against air pollution (by painting the tops of factory chimneys white) and against traffic congestion (by leaving unlocked white bicycles all over the city for anyone's use). Unfortunately the burgomaster's sense of humour did not rise to the occasion and the police were deployed in force. Later, when there was some pressure on the movement to enter politics, it voluntarily disbanded itself. But it certainly laid the foundation for the established political lobbying of the greens and ecologists.

The origins of the problem

Of the 41,160 square km of land mass, 7300 square km are waterways, lakes and inland seas, so that nearly 15 million Dutch people live within an area of 33,860 square km – a population density of 440 persons per square km. About 6.5 million people live in the conurbation known as the **Randstad**, a horseshoe-shaped crescent in the west of the country including Amsterdam, The Hague, Rotterdam and Utrecht. The concentration of petrochemical refineries to the west of Rotterdam has, of course, provided particularly serious problems in a highly-populated region, and the planners' well-meaning intention of placing people in high-rise flats near to their place of work proved to be a disastrous mistake when they could not open their windows in hot weather because of the fumes. But more generally the overpopulation of the western area causes, as we have seen, serious infrastructural and social congestion, resulting in a widespread claustrophobia. This is relieved by those that can afford it by the purchase of second homes in the rural provinces of the north or in the French Dordogne, and by the less affluent in the phenomenon of **bermtoerisme**, the week-end exodus of families picnicking on the grass verges of the roads leading out of the towns.

The numerous canals make traffic dispersal more difficult, and the high water table makes tunnelling for underground railway systems very costly, though Amsterdam and Rotterdam now have metro networks. Probably the most efficient and relatively extensive motorway network in Europe has offered an apparently irresistible alternative to the equally efficient electric train service and the slower, but also environmentally preferable waterway freight service. In 1987, 234 million tons of freight were carried by road, 195.5 million tons by barge and only 5 million tons by rail.

The political response

In 1971, for the first time, political action was taken in the establishment of environmental protection within the new Ministry of Public Health and the Environment, and in 1973 the Minister of Science Policy initiated a National Research Programme. Various studies were carried out which proved valuable later on: for instance, risk-perception, industrial safety and the environment, and carbon dioxide discharge. When the national programme drew to a close in 1980, the group's activities were taken over by a newly created **Council for Environmental Research and the Physical Sciences**. Although this new group received no funding, a number of projects were set up with a systems approach. In the last few years, projects have been replaced by programmes. In all this, the example of West Germany has undoubtedly provided a model for the Dutch, and if the West German experience can be relied on, there will be an increase in employment in the environmental projects of some 70,000 to 78,000 person-years in the next decade.

The first legislation was the passing of the **1979 Waste Substances Act** to deal with the 28 million tons of waste generated annually in the Netherlands. An amendment to this bill was passed, establishing an Indicative Multiyear Programme for Waste Substances which forms a basis for ministerial directives under the Act. This was followed in the same year by the **Chemical Waste Act**, and both were designed to replace dumping as far as possible by recycling. A comparison with other countries throughout the world shows that the Netherlands is relatively successful in the separation and reuse of waste, taking one of the two top places in the charts. No one familiar with Amsterdam would take comfort from this. In the capital of a country once renowned for its cleanliness, the canals can look like open drains.

In 1985 the three Ministries of Physical Planning and Environment, Agriculture and Fisheries and Transport and Water Management published an integrated *Environmental Programme of the Netherlands, 1986–90*. It incorporates the programmes on waste disposal referred to above, together with subsequent policy statements on air, noise, radiation and water. This report inaugurates an 'environmental renovation' plan involving the government, firms and households over a five-year period, implemented by proposed legislation. The plan envisages three phases. In the first of these the government will target specific areas for attention, and the source causes of the polution there. The second phase will involve the

Finance Ministry in determining the financial support necessary to carry through the programme and in the third phase the target groups responsible for harming the environment will be made responsible for carrying out the renovation required in the legislation.

The total costs to be borne by central and local government, the water boards (**waterschappen**), firms and households are expected to rise from Dfl 4.3 billion in 1985 to Dfl 5.3 billion in 1990. The government's share of this cost will reduce from 30 per cent to 21 per cent, households' will remain constant at 20 per cent, traffic's contribution will increase from 3 per cent to 6 per cent, industry's will increase from 44 per cent to 45 per cent and agriculture's from 3 per cent to 6 per cent. The costs of controlling acid deposits, for instance, will rise from Dfl 210 million to Dfl 680 million, and of fertilizer discharge from Dfl 170 million to Dfl 325 million. A proposed reduction in fertilizer deposits by 75 per cent within ten years will necessitate a revolution in the means of production. Attempts are being made to develop a completely closed production for horticulture under glass, from which there would be no more emissions whatsoever. The agricultural sector is paying at least half the financial cost of staff and equipment for research. The capital cost per individual undertaking will be in the order of Dfl 100,000–200,000.

High on the list of priorities in the environmental programme are water-shortage, underwater soil pollution, carbon dioxide emissions, environmental conditions in the Third World and the quality of the indoor environment.

The problem of water shortage is in fact rather one of dehydration due to heavy demands on groundwater for agriculture and domestic use in the conurbations. This is causing an extensive reduction in the native flora and fauna in certain areas.

Pollution of the soil under the rivers means that sludge brought up during dredging operations has to be treated to avoid spreading the pollution. The surface water of the Rhine and Maas contains heavy metals, chromium, copper, cadmium, lead, arsenic and mercury, and organic compounds such as polychlorinated biphenyls, polycyclic aromatics and pesticides, and these collect in high concentrations in the bottom where the current is sluggish. It is hoped that the **Surface Waters Pollution Act** will be supported by the International Rhine Commission.

Carbon dioxide emissions and Third World environmental problems are on the Dutch agenda for government cooperation in the EC, OECD and international agencies concerned with these issues.

Air pollution in the Netherlands is attributable mainly to refineries, power stations and traffic. Oil refineries are responsible for 30 per cent of the sulphur dioxide emission (101,000 tonnes), and electricity generation for a further 29 per cent, and these will be reduced to 13 per cent and 5.3 per cent by the year 2000.

The 5,300,000 private cars travel some 140 billion passenger kilometres per annum, emitting 1000 tonnes of lead, 175,000 tonnes of hydrocarbons and 250,000 tonnes of nitric oxide into the atmosphere every year. It is assumed that lead emissions will be eradicated by the year 2000 and that hydrocarbon and nitric oxide discharges will be reduced to 50,000 and 185,000 tonnes respectively. This is on the assumption that automobility will increase at the rate of 1 per cent per annum. EC standards of controls in new car engines came into force in 1988, but will only have a cumulative effect.

It is in conclusion worth noting that the cabinet crisis in the summer of 1989 arose over the government's policy on road usage, and even before the government fell, the Minister for Transport and Waterways resigned on the principle of environmental protection.

The response of business to the EC's single market

It is perhaps not surprising that the Dutch appear to be 'taking the single market in their stride', since it is only an extension of what has been the practice in the Benelux Union since 1948, and their export policies have been Europe-oriented since the Second World War.

The strong support for the Lubbers administration in the 1989 European elections was confirmed in the national election in September, when Lubbers' CDA party was returned with an increased majority. The other major parties lost some ground, but the two progressive parties D66 (Democracy 1966) and Groen links (an amalgamation of radicals) made some gains. The present coalition cabinet of CDA and the Socialists led by Lubbers contains many experienced ministers, and this means that the Netherlands may be expected to cope well initially with the coming challenges.

Strengths

The Netherlands Institute for Banking and Stock-trading has issued a report forecasting that since the Netherlands, the United Kingdom and Luxembourg have the most competitive tariff rates, they will be least affected by the anticipated drop in prices in the financial sector of the 1992 internal market. The exception here is the stock market, where the powerful competition and efficiency of the Dutch financial sector is believed to be able to withstand foreign competition, as it does at the moment, and even to expand its share of the market.

Although some smaller insurance companies and banks are combining operations, (notably in the recent agreement between AMEV – the General Society for the Exploitation of Insurance Companies – and the Verenigde Spaarbank – the United Savings Bank), the indications are that the larger insurance companies will remain independent of the commercial banks.

Regulations preventing mergers between banks and insurance companies are indeed being reviewed, and although such a merger between a large bank and a large insurance office would command a powerful strategic position in a small country, short-term gains might be offset by losses since at present the larger banks and insurance houses do a great deal of business with each other.

One of the conclusions of this report states: '. . . the relatively advanced international activity of the Dutch banks stands them in good stead for further expansion in the EC. Their size is also relatively favourable in terms of the size of the Dutch economy. They are, however, somewhat vulnerable in their market value which is lower than their visible intrinsic value. As national fiscal authorities have to yield their controls over bank mergers to a European fiscal authority in the future, a new situation will arise involving the possible statutory protection of banks. An answer to this problem may lie in cross-holdings, such as the recent arrangement between the AMRO bank and the Belgian Société Générale.'

The CBS (Central Bureau of Statistics in the Netherlands) has produced two sets of forecasts, one based on the assumption that the US federal government deficit will almost disappear by 1993 and that other industrial countries will carry out a neutral monetary policy, and a 'bad weather' forecast anticipating a further depreciation of the dollar to Dfl 1.40, with a recovery to Dfl 1.65 in 1992, and assuming that the negative consequences of falls in share prices will be worse than expected and affect confidence in financing.

The more optimistic of the two forecasts shows an upward trend vis-à-vis 1988 in the percentage terms shown in Table 6.5.

The current account balance will increase from Dfl 7 billion to Dfl 13 billion; unemployment will drop from 665,000 to 535,000 and the total government financing deficit will fall from 7.25 per cent to 4.75 per cent of GNP.

Even allowing for the lower expectations in the 'bad weather' forecast, these figures must be read with some caution, for it is the dip in the economy 1978–88 that makes the gains towards 1992 look stronger than they are relative to 1987. Two factors do, however, represent a steady improvement in an otherwise flat picture of the economy: the decrease in total unemployment and the significant reduction in government expenditure. The austerity measures for 1989–90, if carried through, will cut some Dfl 3.4 billion from the social security budget, and a simplification of the tax system will introduce lower taxation rates, a reduction in the

Table 6.5 *Economic forecast 1991–2*

	(%)
Wage per employee in the company sector	2.25
Private consumption (volume)	2.0
Corporate investment	4.5
Merchandise exports (volume)	5.0
Merchandise exports excluding energy	5.5
Merchandise imports (volume)	4.75
GNP (volume)	2.25
Prices private consumption	0.75
Export prices	1
Export prices excluding energy	0.5
Real disposable income	1.75

Source: Central Planning Office

number of tax brackets and the withdrawal of some tax deductions, involving in all some Dfl 4.3 billion. These are actions recommended by the OECD, and they may well affect the growth rate in the early 1990s. On the other hand, if this optimism is not justified, it will be because of stagnation in world trade, and in that case the Netherlands' trading position *relative* to the rest of the EC in 1992 will remain roughly the same.

Weaknesses

The assumption written into the forecasts that oil prices will remain stable is challenged by the OECD which expects a drop in oil (and hence North Sea gas) prices. A loss of revenue in this area will have serious repercussions on the administration which will have to slash public expenditure further in order to reduce the budget deficit while maintaining tax cuts. The further measures promised to combat the 'black economy', due to what is taken to be widespread tax fraud, may not be simple to implement, and the further (re)training programmes that are needed will certainly require a substantial revenue.

Threats

It seems highly likely that the **1956 Economic Competition Act** will have to be reviewed in the light of the EC's own ruling, unless the Dutch can satisfy the European Court that their numerous cartels do not limit competition, at any rate outside the Netherlands.

Opportunities

Against the threat to small and middle-sized firms of takeovers can be set the growing awareness in the Netherlands that 'work is the best means of self-fulfilment' should replace the old dictum 'work is a duty'. This means that individual enterprise and self-employment are on the increase (an increase of 45 per cent is forecast in the decade up to 1992), and the leisure and hotel industries will certainly benefit from increased tourism without necessarily being exposed to takeovers. Where large concerns in surrounding countries will certainly continue to establish themselves on Dutch soil, this will bring with it welcome investment, and will presumably continue to be part of economic planning in the Netherlands, in which Dutch companies will also themselves continue to reach out abroad. Moreover, such a high foreign investment in the Netherlands (slightly above even that in the United Kingdom and five times that in France) will shield it from additional excessive foreign competition.

The 1989 OECD report certainly gives grounds for reasonable optimism if, as it suggests, real GDP continues to expand at 3–3.5 per cent, and business fixed investment grows at an average of 5 per cent per annum. With a growth in imports in 1989, due to the purchase of aircraft by KLM, export surplus will fall back that year, but will pick up again after that.

The Dutch may give the impression of self-effacement in their internationalism and lack of respect for their own language and culture, but let no one be deceived by this. They secretly believe the saying, 'God made the world, but the Dutch made Holland', and if they can tame the elements, they are survivors!

References and suggestions for further reading

Blume, S. S. (1985), *The Development of Dutch Science Policy in International Perspective 1965–85*, (Raad van Advies voor het Wetenschapsbeleid), The Hague: Distributiecentrum Overheidspublicaties.

Buunk, H. (1986), *De Economie in Nederland*, Groningen: Wolters-Noordhoff.

Cock Buning, A. de and Verheijen, L. (1987), *The Netherlands in Brief*, The Hague: Ministry of Foreign Affairs.

Commission of the EC (1988), *Panorama of EC Industry*, Luxembourg: Commission of the EC.

Department of Trade and Industry (1986), *Country Profile, Netherlands: Export Europe*, London: Department of Trade and Industry.

Dunnen, E. den (1985), *Instruments of Money Market and Foreign Exchange Market Policy in the Netherlands*, Dordrecht: Nijhoff.

Hartog, F. (ed) (1988). *De Sociaal-economische Besturing van Nederland*, Groningen: Wolters-Noordhoff.

Knoester, A. (1989), *Economische Politiek in Nederland*, Leiden: Stenfert Kroese.

Lawrence, P. (1986), *Management in the Netherlands: A Study in Internationalism?* Loughborough: University of Technology, Department of Management Studies.

Lijphart, A. (1975), *The Politics of Accommodation: Pluralism and Democracy in the Netherlands*, 2nd edn, London: University of California Press.

Ministerie van Economische Zaken (1986), *Nederlandse Industrie 1985: Plaats en Ontwikkeling*, The Hague: Ministerie van Economische Zaken.

Ministry of Economic Affairs (1984), *An Investment Guide to the Netherlands*, The Hague: Ministry of Economic Affairs.

Ministry of Housing, Physical Planning and Environment/Ministry of Agriculture and Fisheries/Ministry of Transport and Water Management (1985), *Environmental Program of the Netherlands 1986–90*, The Hague: Ministry of Housing, Physical Planning and Environment/Ministry of Agriculture and Fisheries/Ministry of Transport and Water Management.

Penninx, M. J. A. (1988), *Minderheidsvorming en Emancipatie: Balans van Kennisverwerving ten Aanzien van Immigranten en Woonwagenbewoners*, Alphen a. d. Rijn: Samson.

Tempel, W. J. and Dam, J. E. van (1986), *Trends in Research and Development in the Netherlands – the Influence of National Science Policy between 1973 and 1986*, The Hague: Distributiecentrum Overheidspublicaties.

Vries, J. de (1983), *De Nederlandse Economie Tijdens de Twintigste Eeuw: Een Verkenning van het meest Kenmerkende*, Bussum: Fibula van Dishoeck.

Wensveen, B. M. N. van (1989), *Het Europese Bankwezen op weg Naar 1992*, Amsterdam: Nederlands Instituut voor het Bank-Effectenbedrijf.

Wintle, M. J. (1988), 'The Netherlands Economy', in *Western Europe 1989*, pp. 356–65.

Index